Reading Dido

D1593222

MEDIEVAL CULTURES

SERIES EDITORS
Rita Copeland
Barbara A. Hanawalt
David Wallace

Sponsored by the Center for Medieval Studies
at the University of Minnesota

Volumes in the series study the diversity of medieval cultural histories and practices including such interrelated issues as gender, class, and social hierarchies; race and ethnicity; geographical relations; definitions of political space; discourses of authority and dissent; educational institutions; canonical and noncanonical literatures; and technologies of textual and visual literacies.

Reading Dido

GENDER, TEXTUALITY, AND THE MEDIEVAL *AENEID*

Marilynn Desmond

Medieval Cultures
Volume 8

University of Minnesota Press
Minneapolis
London

Parts of this book have been previously published, in slightly different form, as "When Dido Reads Vergil: Gender and Intertextuality in Ovid's *Heroides 7*," *Helios* (1993), reprinted with permission of *Helios*; and "Bernard Silvestris and the Corpus of the Aeneid," in *The Classics in the Middle Ages*, Medieval & Renaissance Texts & Studies 69 (Binghamton, N.Y., 1990), 129–39, copyright Center for Medieval & Early Renaissance Studies, State University of New York at Binghamton, reprinted with permission.

Published by the University of Minnesota Press
111 Third Avenue South, Suite 290, Minneapolis, MN 55401-2520
Printed in the United States of America on acid-free paper

Library of Congress Cataloging-in-Publication Data

Desmond, Marilynn, 1952–
    Reading Dido : gender, textuality, and the medieval Aeneid / Marilynn Desmond.
        p.   cm. — (Medieval cultures : v. 8)
    Includes bibliographical references (p.) and index.
    ISBN 0-8166-2246-9.— ISBN 0-8166-2247-7 (pbk.)
    1. English literature—Roman influences.   2. English literature—Middle English, 1100–1600—History and criticism.   3. French literature—To 1500—History and criticism.   4. Literature, Medieval—History and criticism.
5. Dido (Legendary character) in literature.   6. Carthage (Extinct city)—In literature.   7. Literature, Medieval—Roman influences.   8. Sex role in literature.
9. Queens in literature.   10. Virgil. Aeneis.
I. Title.   II. Series.
PR127.D47   1994
809'.93351—dc20   94-6447

To G. J. K.
—for the age of miracles hadn't passed—

Eneidos liber quartus incipit :

At regina graui iamdudum saucia cura
Vulnus alit venis · et ceco carpitur igni
Multa viri virtus animo · multusq̃ recursat
Gentis honos ; herent infixi pectore vultus
Ex bais : nec placidam membris dat cura quietem ;
Postera phebea lustrabat lampade terras
Mentemq̃ auroram polo dimouerat vmbram
Cum sic vnanimem alloquitur male sana sororem :
Anna soror · que me suspensam insomnia terrent
Quis nouus hic nostris successit sedibus hospes
Quem sese ore ferens : quam forti pectore et armis ;
Credo equidem · nec vana fides genus esse deorum
Degeneres animos timor arguit ; heu quibus ille
Iactatus fatis que bella exhausta canebat

Frontispiece: Aeneid 4 *incipit*: top left, Mercury; bottom left, Dido pleads with Aeneas; upper right, Aeneas departs; bottom right, Dido's suicide. Lyons, Bibliothèque municipale, Palais des Arts 27, *Aeneid* fol. 108r. Fifteenth century. By permission.

But I would have dared to be Dido. This is where I begin to suffer in a woman's place. Reading Virgil again, in the Aeneid (Books 3 and 4); one sees how the venerable Aeneas, who is destined to found a city, is kept from the feminine danger by the gods.

Less of a bastard than Jason, less "pure" in plain, brute jouissance than Theseus, more moral; there is always a god or a cause to excuse or explain Aeneas' skill at seeding and shaking off his women, dropping them. . . .

Mercury who is sent by Jupiter intervenes in the name of the league of empire builders: so you are building a beautiful city for a woman and forgetting your kingdom and your own destiny? Thus pious Aeneas will be saved from shame. The next scenes would have been unbearable for him; grief, love, and Dido's beauty are mingled in heartrending songs, and Aeneas doubtless would have weakened. But "the fates are against it, and a god closes the hero's serene ears." He hurts, but he has his law, and that is what he espouses: and his law is clear, because, by dying, Creuse is giving him a sublime strength. The good love for man is his country, the fatherland. A masculine land to hand down from father to son. For Ascanius then. . . .

In Dido's place. But I am not Dido. I cannot inhabit a victim, no matter how noble. I resist: detest a certain passivity, it promises death for me. So, who shall I be? I have gone back and forth in vain through the ages and through the stories within my reach, yet find no woman into whom I can slip. My sympathy, my tenderness, my sorrow, however, are all hers. But not me, not my life. I can never lay down my arms.

Hélène Cixous, The Newly Born Woman

Contents

✣

Preface

❖

Reading Dido is a study of the reception and revision of the figure of Dido as she emerges from ancient texts and circulates in medieval textual cultures. This study also records my reception of cultural theory and my revision of my earlier work. Most notably, *Reading Dido* marks a revisionary departure from my dissertation on Virgil's *Aeneid* in medieval French and English literature (Berkeley, 1985). In the course of writing my dissertation, my research on the vernacular reception of the *Aeneid* brought me back again and again to Dido and to *Aeneid* 4. However, it was not until I had begun to teach women's studies courses in medieval literature at Binghamton that I began to work closely with feminist theory in such a way that I could formulate the critical categories for my scholarly awareness of Dido's centrality to medieval vernacular reworkings of Virgil. From that point on, I have been engaged in the sort of critical *inventio* necessary to present a coherent (but by no means exhaustive) study of the medieval Dido. Starting with my paper at the Modern Language Association in December 1987 on "Caxton's *Eneydos* and the Problem of Dido," I have presented papers on the medieval Dido at a series of conferences over the intervening years—Medieval Institute at Kalamazoo, 1988, 1991, 1992; and the Medieval Academy in 1992.

In the collegial and intertextual world of academic subcultures and the conferences that support these subcultures, I have found a number of learned and generous colleagues who have assisted this project in numerous ways. I am particularly grateful to Kathleen Ashley, Jane Chance, Rita Copeland, Sheila Delany, Earl Jeffrey Richards, and several anonymous readers, all of whom read a complete draft of this project and offered critical suggestions. I am especially indebted to Louise Fradenburg, whose careful reading of this manuscript was exceptionally generous and helpful. Several people read portions of this book in progress and offered support of various kinds; among them I would especially like to thank Janet Abshire, Leslie Cahoon, Leslie Abend Callahan, Rebecca Coogan, Elizabeth Crachiolo, Margaret Driver, Tamara Jetton, Johanna X. K. Garvey, Ruth Ann Lawn Johnson, Diane Marks, Francis X. K. Newman,

Jerome Singerman, and Alvin Vos. I am also grateful to the members of my 1990 writing group—Deborah Britzman, Elsa Barkley Brown, Carole Boyce Davies, and Susan Sterret—none of whom is a medievalist, which makes their willingness to work through a project such as this quite heroic. Jean Wilson and Pamela Sheingorn gave me invaluable advice on working with visual material. Conversations with Kathleen Biddick, who shared her work in progress with me as well, helped keep several theoretical issues in focus. It is a pleasure to thank Phillip Damon and Anne Middleton, whose direction and support during my doctoral work and the early years in which I worked on this project helped launch this study. I also owe an enormous debt to Mary Louise Lord—whom I have never met—since her work on Dido literally paved the way for this study. My frequent citation of her work in the notes does not do justice to my reliance on her magisterial 1969 article on Dido. In addition, several people have given me notice of Dido sightings/citings over the years, which has enriched the scope of this study; among these, Barbara Adams, Jeanne Krochalis, and Nicholas Havely deserve special mention.

Sidonie Smith and William Spanos provided the sort of collegial support at a critical moment in this project—and in my career—that deserves a special thanks. Likewise, special thanks are due to a group of graduate students at Binghamton that includes Laura Barefield, Lynn Blanchfield, Ellen Brand, Rebecca Coogan, Helene Scheck, Mary Sokolowski, Christine Owens, and Ginny Whetsall, in addition to people I have already mentioned, who provided an ongoing dialogue about feminist theory and medieval studies during the years this book was taking shape. The women's studies community at Binghamton helped me survive the writing of this book and much else.

A book such as this depends heavily on libraries and library staff; I am particularly grateful to the Department of Manuscripts at the British Library in London, the Bodleian Library in Oxford, the Cabinet des manuscrits of the Bibliothèque Nationale in Paris, the Bibliothèque municipale in Lyons, the Rosenwald Collection at the Library of Congress, the Spencer Collection at the New York Public Library, the Morgan Library, and the rare book room at Cornell University for access to manuscripts and early printed books, and for permission to reproduce photographs. I also spent countless hours in the Reading Room at the British Library and the Wertheim Room at the New York Public Library; I found both environments conducive to research and writing, and I am grateful for the privilege of working in both places. Likewise, Carol Clemente and the members of the interlibrary loan staff at Binghamton deserve special note for their prompt response to my endless requests; I am also grateful to the many other libraries that provided photographs and permission to reproduce them. During the time that I worked on this project, I received financial support from the National Endowment for the Humanities, from a Nuala Drescher award at Binghamton University, and from a Dean's research semester. The Vice-Provost at Binghamton University provided funds for the purchase of photographs. Portions of this book appeared in earlier versions as articles: "Bernard Silvestris and the *corpus* of the *Aeneid*," in *Classics in the Middle Ages* (Binghamton, 1990), pp. 129–39, and "When Dido Reads Vergil: Gender and Intertextuality in Ovid's *Heroides* 7," in *Helios* 20 (1993), pp. 56–68. Both are incorporated here by permission.

In the course of preparing this manuscript, I relied at times on Phyllis Kuhlman and Lisa Fegley-Schmidt, whose cheerful assistance and friendship make it a pleasure to record my thanks. Stacey Wahrman earned my eternal gratitude for her assistance with the index. Also, I am pleased to thank Biodun Iginla, David Thorstad, and the staff at the University of Minnesota Press—Meg Aerol, Kerry Sarnoski, and Elizabeth Stomberg—who saw the promise of this project even at an early stage, and who saw it—and me—through the final process.

Abbreviations

❖

EETS, e.s.	Early English Text Society, extra series
EETS, o.s.	Early English Text Society, original series
PL	*Patrologia latina*, ed. J.-P. Migne (Paris, 1844–64)

Introduction

Gender and the Politics of Reading Virgil

A golden bough. The torch is passed on. His son clutches his hand, his crippled father clings to his back, three male generations leave the burning city. The wife, lost. Got lost in burning. No one knows what happened to her, when they became the Romans.

Rachel Blau DuPlessis[1]

The monopoly which Latin exercised in formal education combined with the structure of society in the West up until the past few generations to give the language its strangest characteristic. It was a sexually specialized language, used almost exclusively for communication between male and male.

Walter J. Ong, S.J.[2]

Virgil's *Aeneid* has historically been read in circumstances that support social and cultural hierarchies, a fact characterized by Thomas Greene: "Virgil's earlier poetry was taught in Roman schools even before his death, and from then on, from the first century to the nineteenth, he was generally at the core of European education. . . . If he [Virgil] teaches the school*boy* style, to the *man* he imparts nobility"[3] (emphasis added). Given such a Eurocentric reading context, one would expect the reception of the *Aeneid* to epitomize the patriarchal concerns of Western culture. And to a large extent, it does. As a narrative of cultural origins, the *Aeneid* delineates a Roman foundation myth based on patrilineal Trojan survival that necessitates the loss of Creusa in book 2, the death of Dido in book 4, and the final achievement of a political alliance between the Trojans and the Italians through the marriage of Aeneas and Lavinia—the justification for the wars in Italy that constitute the last half of the epic.[4] The history of Virgil readership has frequently emphasized the imperial mythic program of the *Aeneid*, as we shall see. Nevertheless, to many readers, the Dido story eclipses the plot of the *Aeneid* as a whole, and the reception of the *Aeneid* story has at times foregrounded the character of Dido, often at the expense of Aeneas.[5]

Although Dido is one of the most memorable characters in the *Aeneid*, her story actually occupies a small part of the narrative: when the Trojan refugees are shipwrecked off the coast of Carthage in *Aeneid* 1, Dido receives them into her city. Through the help of the gods, who bring on a thunderstorm during a hunt, Dido and Aeneas eventually enter a cave and there succumb to their incipient desire. The cave scene is perhaps the most indeterminate moment in the *Aeneid*: the characters themselves never agree on the social significance of the events in the cave. Dido interprets their partnership as a marriage, not without reason, but incorrectly (at least according to Aeneas). When Iarbas—a neighboring African king—becomes angered at Aeneas's comfortable presence in Carthage, he begs Jupiter to intervene. Aeneas is consequently reminded of his divine mission to found Rome, and he thereupon makes it clear to Dido that he is not bound by any legal or official marriage vows. His plans for departure precipitate Dido's final disintegration, and by the end of *Aeneid* 4 she commits suicide. Virgil's narrative continues for another eight books, which include Aeneas's journey to the underworld and his eventual conquest of Italy.

As Dido's story, *Aeneid* 4 has had a separate itinerary all its own in Western literary traditions; perhaps only *Aeneid* 6—the journey to the underworld—has been so frequently "cited" and rewritten over the centuries.[6] Medieval and Renaissance vernacular literatures, in particular, focus attention on Dido, even to the exclusion of Aeneas. Indeed, a discernible tradition in the medieval vernacular adaptation of the *Aeneid* is characterized by the intense interest among vernacular poets in the character of Dido. For vernacular readers from the twelfth through the fifteenth centuries, reading Dido—that is, thematizing Dido's story (sometimes only momentarily) as the central plot of the Virgilian text—constitutes a visible response to the *Aeneid* story. By displacing the epic hero Aeneas, the tradition of reading Dido disrupts the patrilineal focus of the *Aeneid* as an imperial foundation narrative.

Readers of the *Aeneid* may focus on Dido and thereby call into question Aeneas, his destiny, the empire he founds, as well as the reiteration of imperial ideologies in the repetition of empires throughout the West.[7] In the passage quoted earlier, Hélène Cixous evokes Dido as a possible mythic ancestor and thus calls into question the place of Virgil's *Aeneid* in the history of Western culture. Once posed, Cixous's question about Dido may take us even beyond the *Aeneid*. Cixous's position—writing as a French-Algerian Jewish woman reading Dido—might evoke a series of other stories that Cixous does not specifically allude to in *La jeune née*. Readers such as Cixous might also recognize in the texture of Virgil's *Aeneid* a palimpsest that allows a glimpse of other versions of Dido's story, versions that also circulate in other texts, before and after the production of the *Aeneid*. Dido's other story emphasizes her heroic exploits as a Phoenician exile—a Semitic woman who founds a major settlement in North Africa and who never meets Aeneas and thus avoids inclusion in the narrative of the Roman empire.[8] This other story, which we will trace in the course of this study, allows us to see Cixous's evocation of Virgil's Dido as an enactment of Trinh Minh-ha's scene of writing for the "native"/colonized woman: "Words empty out with age. Die and rise again, accordingly invested with new meanings, and always equipped with a secondhand memory. In trying to tell something, a woman is told, shredding herself into opaque words while her voice dissolves on the walls of silence."[9] Behind the canonicity of the *Aeneid* is the secondhand memory of Dido's other story, which Cixous does not know or cannot tell. That secondhand memory—recently revisioned in a postcolonial novel about the historical Dido by the Tunisian-born novelist, Fawzi Mellah[10]—can tell us much about the structures of literary history and textual traditions.

Cixous's privileging of the Virgilian Dido in her search for textual examples of mythic female ancestors illustrates the cultural relationship between the canon and colonialism. The city Dido founds as Carthage not only became a Roman colony but becomes identified centuries later as the French colonial city of Tunis. As a Jewish schoolgirl in a North African French colony, Cixous is introduced to a canonical version of Dido's story that works to erase the status and agency of Dido as the founder of Carthage, since Virgil emphasizes her role as consort to Aeneas, which actually leads to the destruction of her city. The other identities of Dido, the other versions of her story, might assist readers of Virgil and readers of Cixous in the sort of postcolonial feminist project Gayatri Spivak has referred to as "un-learning our privilege as our loss."[11]

The medieval interest in Dido provides the modern reader with a set of texts that chart the cultural appropriation of a classical pagan figure by later readers. Given the alterity of classical Latin texts in medieval cultures, the medieval Dido repeatedly signals her status as a classical literary figure recuperated by the later medieval reader who rewrites the past. Dido and her shadow—her existence in earlier pagan texts, her other stories—constitute a set of textual traditions that the modern reader might juxtapose to the traditions of reading Virgil's *Aeneid*.

The *Aeneid* and the Modern Reader

The significance of Dido's status in Western literary traditions must be understood in relation to the social implications of reading Virgil. As a school text, the *Aeneid* has generally been read by one segment of the population—the male elite, destined by education and/or birth to occupy powerful positions in a hierarchically arranged social structure, a structure in which Latin literacy played a significant role in the formation of a "persecuting society," in R. I. Moore's term.[12] The centrality of the

Aeneid in the Roman curriculum guaranteed Virgil a prominent place in late antique education, an institution that survived in various forms long after the collapse of imperial military and political institutions.[13] By the twelfth century, educational structures had been modified to meet the needs of clerical cultures and the bureaucratic requirements of medieval government and religious institutions.[14] Although medieval educational practices vary considerably according to century, institution, and region, it is clear that Virgil's *Aeneid* was a canonical text read in institutional settings throughout the medieval West, often, though perhaps not exclusively, as a Latin primer.[15]

The Latin hexameter of Virgil's text has been an acquired, even artificial, language for more than a millennium,[16] and since the Middle Ages, the reading of the *Aeneid* has been associated with the study of Latin, thereby placing Virgil at the heart of institutionalized education; consequently, the history of education in the West has—until very recently—paralleled the history of Virgil readership.[17] And groups historically excluded from institutional education have also been excluded from Virgil readership: women of any class, including Virginia Woolf's "daughters of educated men," men and women of the working classes, and much of the bourgeoisie. Such readers, if they read Virgil's *Aeneid* at all, read it in translation.[18] Although there are always exceptions to such large categorical statements, such a description holds, especially for *groups* of readers.

The exclusion of women from the study of classical languages has historically kept women marginalized and socially subordinated within the elite formations of culture—a fact intensely resented by women writers well into the twentieth century.[19] Perhaps Virginia Woolf provides the most eloquent commentary on the status of classical texts in relation to gender, class, and readership. In the third essay of *Three Guineas*, for instance, she bitterly mocks the reading of classical texts as an elite male prerogative when she purports to answer a letter requesting a monetary contribution to help protect "culture and intellectual liberty":

> Suppose that the Duke of Devonshire, in his star and garter, stepped down into the kitchen and said to the maid who was peeling potatoes with a smudge on her cheek: "Stop your potato peeling, Mary, and help me to construe this rather difficult passage in Pindar," would not Mary be surprised and run screaming to Louisa the cook, "Lauks, Louie, Master must be mad!" That, or something like it, is the cry that rises to our lips when the sons of educated men ask us, their sisters, to protect intellectual liberty and culture.[20]

Similar sentiments are found throughout Woolf's essays and fiction; as readers of Woolf know, almost every page of her nonfiction writing chronicles her own reading, from the book reviews she wrote for publications such as the *Times Literary Supplement* and the *Guardian* to a text such as *A Room of One's Own*, where she locates herself as a reader, removing books from a shelf and meditating on women's relationship to texts, books, and reading. One of the most powerful scenes in *A Room of One's Own* is the narration of her (fictional) self being turned away from the entrance to the Bodleian library and her comment "that a famous library has been cursed by a woman is a matter of complete indifference to a famous library. Venerable and calm, with all its treasures safe locked within its breast, it sleeps complacently and will, so far as I am concerned, so sleep for ever. Never will I wake those echoes, never will I ask for that hospitality again, I vowed as I descended the steps in anger."[21]

Throughout Woolf's novels, readership is an important clue to character, particularly in relation to the classics. In *Jacob's Room*, for instance, Fanny Elmer—under the influence of an infatuation for Jacob—resolves: "She would learn Latin and read Virgil."[22] And in *To the Lighthouse*, Mr. Carmichael is characterized by the fact that he "liked to lie awake a little reading Virgil, [he] kept his candle burning rather longer than the rest."[23] As Woolf repeatedly emphasizes, the ability to read Virgil's Latin epic represents a specific privilege, one that men like Jacob and Mr. Carmichael might take for granted but that nonetheless marks them as elite participants in their culture.

In contrast to Woolf's angry commentary on gender and reading in relation to classical texts, the Eurocentric politics of World War II led other readers of her generation to embrace the imperial potentials of Virgil's text. T. S. Eliot, in his presidential address to the Virgil Society in 1944, finds in the *Aeneid* not only the most definitive example of the "classic," but

[Aeneas is] the symbol of Rome; and, as Aeneas is to Rome, so is ancient Rome to Europe. Thus Virgil acquires the centrality of the unique classic; he is the centre of European civilization, in a position which no other poet can share or usurp. The Roman Empire and the Latin language were not any empire and any language, but an empire and a language with a unique destiny in relation to ourselves; and the poet in whom that Empire and that language came to consciousness and expression is a poet of unique destiny.[24]

Eliot's faith in the centrality of Europe and his vision of European history as a civilized, Christian destiny is echoed in the classical scholarship of his day. W. F. Jackson Knight's influential study, *Roman Vergil* (1944), for instance, gives Virgil partial credit for the "good order" and the "human principles" of the Roman Empire.[25]

If Eliot's Virgil—a mature poet of good manners and delicate sensibility—is not wholly attested to among modern readers, Eliot's emphasis on imperial themes has survived its wartime context.[26] Greene refers to the *Aeneid* as a "handbook for political domesticating" and states: "*Empire* is the key idea—empire over the world, over nature and peoples, over language, and over the heart."[27] Eliot's "doctrine of imperial reading" has more recently found a proponent in Frank Kermode, who attempts to recuperate Eliot's concept of "Virgil as the very type of classic" by way of modern semiotics and the inherent plurality of texts that require the "co-operation of the reader's imagination."[28] Kermode appeals to empire as a metaphor for the "classic": "The implication remains that the classic is an essence available to us under our dispositions, in the aspect of time. So the image of the imperial classic, beyond time, beyond vernacular corruption and change, had perhaps, after all, a measure of authenticity; all we need to do is to bring it down to earth."[29] Kermode's attempt to retain a canonical version of Eliot's Virgil in the face of contemporary theory actually invites us to consider the connections between "classics," the "canon," and cultural imperialism.[30]

Such readings of Virgil's *Aeneid* thematize the imperial program of the text and thereby produce a totalizing discourse for a Eurocentric, colonializing view of history. As David Quint aptly characterizes the imperial focus of the *Aeneid*: "Virgil's epic depicts imperial victory as the victory of the *principle of history*—a principle lodged in the West, where identity and power are transmitted across time in patrilineal succession."[31] Readers such as Eliot and Kermode embrace an imperial reading of Virgil's *Aeneid* as a historical paradigm that legitimates and defines modern European identities; that is, the imperial Virgil justifies and is justified by the history of the West. But, as Homi Bhabha notes, the modern national identity depends on specific constructions of narrative as memory: "Being obliged to forget becomes the basis for remembering the nation."[32] Like national identities, the celebration of Eurocentric values and European history authorized by the imperial Virgil depends upon historical amnesia. The *Aeneid* has been especially available for a European colonial vision because its canonicity has guaranteed its presence in educational institutions and pedagogical discourses.

The imperial Virgil is still with us, especially since the *Aeneid* continues to occupy a privileged space in the literary canon, obscuring Virgil's *Eclogues* and *Georgics*. But the late twentieth-century reader—in academic circles at least—is just as likely to assume that the West has essentially exhausted the potential of empire and depleted its reserve of faith and confidence in the centrality and destiny of European civilization.

Since much contemporary literary theory exploits the possibility of reading literary texts for their potential to represent a postcolonial distrust of hierarchies in all social forms, particularly in relation to race, class, or gender, the *Aeneid* must obviously be detached from the "doctrine of the imperial classic."

Classical studies has perhaps paved the way for a postcolonial reading of Virgil. Recent scholarship has recontextualized the *Aeneid* by emphasizing Virgil's other poems and by reexamining the historical context of Augustan Rome.[33] In addition, one school of Virgil criticism—dubbed the pessimistic Harvard school by W. R. Johnson—has produced a series of studies of the *Aeneid* that, in Johnson's words, "calls into question not only the heroism of Homer's poems but also Augustan heroisms and indeed any heroism."[34] Johnson himself characterizes the text as a "heartbreaking, disconsolate poem that is too big for poetry, that cannot be constrained by the limits of art and explodes its frame."[35] This strain of Virgil criticism, with its emphasis on the "second voice" or the "doubleness of vision" in the text, complements the focus of a critical attempt to dismantle imperial or colonial discourses of the sort exemplified by the "imperial Virgil."[36] Although most versions of the "imperial Virgil" encourage the reader to focus on the mythic program the *Aeneid* ostensibly represents and to ignore the play of differences in the text, the context of postcolonial cultural theory encourages us to consider the implications of difference that course through Virgil's text. And Virgil's Dido—in her colonized and gendered identity—figures difference writ large. It is this difference, this quality of otherness in relation to the imperial, masculine identity of Rome, that medieval vernacular poets implicitly delineate in their textual homage to the character of Dido. The traces of reading Dido in medieval vernacular culture might direct us in our efforts to read differently and to read difference.

Reading Practices/Gender Performances

Contemporary theories of reading emphasize that all readers "read" from particular subject positions; as Diana Fuss expresses it, "readers, like texts, are constructed; they inhabit reading practices rather than create them *ex nihilo.*"[37] The range of possible positions available to any given reader at any time results, at least in part, from specific material conditions, such as access to texts, acquisition of literacy and languages, and so forth. The construction of readers is a historical process that often becomes self-perpetuating, so that a text might *appear* to restrict the reader to a narrow set of possible subject positions.

Not only have readers of Virgil historically been men, but the reading of the *Aeneid*—as part of Latin training—has been associated with a class-specific performance of masculinity. As a school text used to instruct male students in the Latin language, Virgil's *Aeneid* was, until the last century, an important part of the initiation rite schoolboys underwent in their acquisition of a public language basic to their acquisition of a mature masculine identity.[38] In Walter Ong's description of Renaissance educational practices, he stresses the connection between the study of Latin and corporal punishment that resulted in a "relatively violent puberty rite setting, a sense of existence on a threshold, within a marginal environment (associated with forced seclusion from the company of women and to a certain extent from one's own family), in an atmosphere of continuous excitement."[39] Not surprisingly, twentieth-century interpretive approaches to Virgil's *Aeneid* tend to reflect this aspect of its historical readership. In modern literary studies, this gender-specific readership has resulted in reading Virgil as a man—that is, even readers who otherwise identify as female are culturally constructed as male readers, or "immasculated readers" in Judith Fetterley's terms. Fetterley elaborates on the condition of female readers: "As readers and teachers and scholars, women are taught to think as men, to identify with a male point of view, and to accept as normal and legitimate a male system of values, one of whose central principles is misogyny."[40]

Critical attitudes toward the *Aeneid* frequently reflect the conditions (and the larger cultural practices they support) of Virgil readership. In the modern American university, a coeducational institution that provides a large share of the marketplace for the products of the literary studies industry, Virgil's *Aeneid* appears routinely in two distinct segments of the curriculum. While Virgil's texts obviously have a central place in classics departments in the advanced study of Latin literature—especially at the level of doctoral study—the *Aeneid* still holds a distinctive place early in the study of Latin, in beginning Latin literature courses. But the *Aeneid* is also taught in translation in a range of introductory "great books" courses under the rubric of "Western literature," "Literary Masterworks," "Western Civilization," or even (as in my own department) "Foundations of English Literature"; such courses also appear in universities and colleges that have no classics department.[41] In such courses, the *Aeneid* is read in the context of a lineage of "great books" (Homer—Virgil—Dante—Milton) rather than in the context of the Roman culture and literary traditions that produced it.

This "great books" context for Virgil readership in contemporary American education clearly accounts for a critical text such as Harold Bloom's collection of essays entitled *Virgil*. Although obviously intended for an undergraduate or lay audience rather than the specialist, Bloom's collection is nonetheless drawn from the works of recognized Virgil scholars. The collection exhibits a discernible sort of readerly "male bonding" that is one feature of Virgil studies: the essays in this collection, all of which are authored by men, focus the reader's attention on the male characters of the *Aeneid*, especially on Aeneas, Lausus, Augustus, and Pallas. None of the essays concern Dido or Camilla.[42] Bloom's tendency to emphasize the role of male characters—evident in statements such as "I suspect that, if he [Virgil] *was* in love with any of his own characters in the poem, it was with Turnus, rather than Dido, let alone Aeneas"[43]—is reflected throughout the collection, which includes the essay by Greene cited earlier, as well as an essay by E. R. Curtius that sets out to define the modern audience for Virgil's *Aeneid*:

> Engraved in the heart of every reader of the *Aeneid* are the flower-like youths—*"purpereus veluti flos"*— Nisus and Euryalus, Lausus and Pallas, and, above all the rest, Ascanius. The very word *puer* acquires, in Virgil's usage, a tender, almost sacred tinge. . . . Virgil's young male figures . . . undoubtedly vibrate with the recollection of his own youth and that of Octavian. . . . They cast upon the grave dignity of the *Aeneid* a luminous shimmer of youthful beauty that is still capable of mysteriously touching receptive young people today.[44]

In its emphasis on the *pueri*—to the exclusion of women warriors such as Camilla and Juturna—and its implicit exclusion of women from the group of "receptive young people today," this essay enacts the reading of Virgil's *Aeneid* as a performance of masculinity.

Such performance of masculinity is highly regulated. The reader responses marked by male bonding in that performance constitute, in Eve Kosofsky Sedgwick's term, "homosocial" behavior—the formation of "social bonds between persons of the same sex," a pattern of behavior in modern culture notable for "male friendship, mentorship, entitlement, rivalry."[45] And as Sedgwick points out: "At least since the eighteenth century in England and America, the continuum of male homosocial bonds has been brutally structured by a secularized and psychological homophobia."[46] That is, modern institutions that encourage male bonding and homosocial desire just as forcefully prohibit and prosecute homosexual desire, granting adult male entitlement to those who successfully negotiate what Sedgwick terms a "coercive erotic double-binding."[47]

The homosocial traditions of Virgil criticism have been additionally complicated by the tradition of Virgil's "homosexuality," a trait mentioned in the ancient biographies that is consistent with the sexual politics of ancient culture.[48] John Boswell characterizes Roman attitudes toward sexuality as follows: "Neither the Roman religion nor Roman law recognized homosexual eroticism as distinct from—much less inferior to—heterosexual eroticism. . . . Roman society almost unanimously assumed that adult males would be capable of, if not interested in, sexual relations with both sexes."[49] Latin erotic literature demonstrates, according to Boswell, "the absolute indifference of most Latin authors to the question of gender."[50] "Nor," he adds, "were any exaggerated claims made for homosexual passion: it was not imagined to be the only noble form of love, and its adherents were not thought to possess any special genius."[51] Thus the biographical tradition concerning Virgil's sexuality is not at all inconsistent in the historical context of Roman culture, but in the context of modern academic cultures, structured by the "hegemonic, homoerotic/homophobic male canon of cultural mastery,"[52] it provokes a range of responses that tell us much more about contemporary constructions of sexuality than about ancient literature.[53]

Many twentieth-century responses to Virgil's *Aeneid* express homophobic stereotypes, as does Robert Graves's attempt to attribute what he sees as Virgil's misogyny (represented by Juno) to a homosexual fear of women.[54] Likewise, W. F. Jackson Knight, while alluding to the ancient biographies for support, sees in Virgil a "femininity of mind" that makes his authorial performance female: "If less were known of him, it might be argued that the poet of the *Aeneid* . . . was a woman."[55] Discussions of Virgil's sexuality frequently avoid the term "homosexual"; Curtius, for instance, echoes a comment from the ancient biographies that Virgil was called "Parthenias" (maidenly);[56] another critic simply dismisses the relevance of "biographical hearsay."[57] Some scholars have felt called upon to construct a defense of Virgil,[58] or to evoke the biographical data to apply authorial intention to the homoerotic themes perceived in the text.[59] The "homosocial" subject positions available to readers of the *Aeneid* appear to solicit homoerotic responses that circulate in a homophobic regime.

The intensely regulated homosocial masculinity of Virgil readership directs critical attention away from the female characters and their social context in the epic. Although Virgil criticism tends to be sophisticated and sensitive to the complexities of the text of the *Aeneid*, the texture of such criticism all too often emphasizes the male concerns in the text, or reads the female characters exclusively from a male point of view, while it simultaneously demonstrates a misunderstanding of homosexual practices, a misunderstanding derived from contemporary homophobic stereotypes. Brooks Otis's discussion of *Aeneid* 4 perhaps illustrates the extent to which the masculine norms of the modern critical context can restrict a reader as sensitive and sophisticated as he is, and whose concept of the "empathetic-subjective" style contributed enormously to Virgil studies in the past quarter century. Otis's awareness of the complexity of Virgil's manipulations of point of view leads him to distinguish the shifting focus between Dido and Aeneas in *Aeneid* 4. Nonetheless, Otis comes to empathize fully with Aeneas and to view Aeneas's discarding of Dido as normative and necessary in terms of the plot.[60] Otis ultimately has eyes only for Aeneas:

> We now (via Jupiter-Mercury) see Aeneas and his guilty submission to Dido in the perspective of fate itself, just as Mercury sees him in Tyrian costume building the new Carthage. But his contrition and his recovery of *pietas* are *also* human and psychological: he sees he has been false to his father, his mission, his men, Ascanius, etc. Dido's *amor* becomes, when thwarted, the *furor* of hatred and reckless malevolence. . . . Aeneas (once more *pius*) puts to sea in an atmosphere which repeats—on so much deeper level—the *furor* of his arrival and yet measures the tremendous significance of his departure.[61]

Despite his formulation of the empathetic-subjective style, Otis clearly does not empathize with Dido, though he carefully analyzes the subjectivity with which Virgil represents her.

When modern readers acknowledge the sense of loss created and dwelt on in the poem, they frequently betray their ultimate sympathy for Turnus and the cast of male victims—Pallas, Nisus, Euryalus, Lausus—and they implicitly accept the loss of Dido or Creusa as given by fate. R. D. Williams goes so far as to indulge in a form of "blaming the victim." He concludes: "Dido is brought to disaster by her own desire for Aeneas, which she might have resisted more strongly than she did. Under this pressure to yield to a love which—as we shall see—she knows is both wrong and impossible, she gives in."[62] Such readings of Virgil's *Aeneid* implicitly endorse and vigorously emphasize patriarchal biases that *appear* (to their readers) to be inherent in the text.

This consideration of the masculine cultural context that remains normative for contemporary readings of Virgil's *Aeneid* is not meant to be an exhaustive survey of Virgil scholarship but to tease out of modern scholarly traditions the most egregious effects of the masculine subject positions of modern Virgil readership. Such a metacritical gesture is a necessary first step in projects of feminist literary history precisely because the patriarchal perspectives of the critical establishment—often more purposefully patriarchal than the patriarchal discourses evident in the texts we read—deprive us of the ability to situate ourselves as women readers. This is, of course, especially true of a text such as Virgil's *Aeneid*, to which women have historically been denied access, since until recently they were excluded from formal and institutionalized education where Virgil's Latin was taught and Virgil's text was read. And the mas-

culine subject positions of Virgil readership work to privilege the patriarchal discourses evident in the *Aeneid*. The patrilineal Trojan survival
that forms the basis of Roman cultural origins requires the loss of Creusa,
the death of Dido, and the final substitution of Lavinia as Aeneas's consort. Even the Trojan women are left behind in Sicily and thereby left out
of Roman history.[63] Imperial Roman power takes on a masculine identity, so that Mihoko Suzuki sees Creusa and Dido as "female victims who
are sacrificed on the altar of Rome."[64] To overlook or to ignore this cultural paradigm of imperial power in relation to gender, or to fail to appreciate the significance of the pattern of substitution (Creusa—Dido—
Lavinia), is to participate in a cultural silencing best characterized by
Christine Froula: "Metaphysically, the woman reader of a literary tradition that inscribes violence against women is an abused daughter. Like
physical abuse, literary violence against women works to privilege the
cultural father's voice and story over those of women, the cultural daughters, and indeed to silence women's voices."[65]

The degree to which the narrative of the *Aeneid* inscribes violence or
abuse toward women is seldom acknowledged in Virgil studies. The issue
of Aeneas's treatment of women, for instance, is often avoided or bypassed, or even at times straightforwardly dismissed. As one critic comments on the end of *Aeneid* 4: "In some respects, Aeneas comes off badly
in his departure. But that is beside the point."[66] Nonetheless, as Christine
Perkell has shown, a consideration of Aeneas's behavior toward his
wives/consorts has implications for our understanding of the entire text.
In looking at the events of the plot from a feminist perspective, she
observes: "The women's deaths are at least partially attributable to the
manner of Aeneas' departure although Aeneas does not acknowledge this.
To Creusa Aeneas is fatally inattentive. To Dido he is also irresponsible,
even treacherous."[67] And she concludes:

My hypothesis is that this collocation of departure, female casualty,
denied responsibility, and *pietas* is intended to reflect an incomplete humanity in Aeneas and in the *pietas* which he exemplifies. If
Aeneas epitomizes *pietas*, as his repeated epithet would indicate,
then perhaps Virgil is suggesting that *pietas* so conceived is a flawed
ideal since it seems not to require humane virtues or any personal
loyalty or affection which does not ultimately subserve what we
might term political or military goals. Love for Anchises and Iulus,
as expressed in *pietas* towards them, is consistent with Roman
political goals; love for Creusa and Dido is not. . . . The significance
for the *Aeneid* as a whole of Aeneas' behavior towards Dido and
Creusa is that it reveals his otherwise astonishing brutality in books
10 and 12 to be not entirely anomalous.[68]

Although Perkell's conclusions are certainly consistent with the more pessimistic strain of Virgil criticism, her emphasis on the displacement of women in the development of the Roman mythic program exposes the critical silence around issues of gender in the text. The foundational narratives of imperialism and epic—and the modern critical apparatus that supports the privileged canonicity of epic as a genre—seem to oblige us to overlook the repeated sacrifice of women.[69] The Dido episode offers the reader an opportunity to intervene in the gendered discourses of colonialism and the canon.

Reading Gender and Power

In order to explore the implications of the medieval Dido for the modern reader, especially for the modern reader interested in creating or occupying subject positions compatible with feminist or postcolonial theory, one must first consider the social and cultural construction of gender in Virgil's text. The modern performance of gender often appears to derive from a cultural construction of male/female opposition, an elaboration of discrete categories of identity that are produced and maintained (even policed) by social practices. Nonetheless, much recent work in gender studies, such as Judith Butler's *Gender Trouble*, not only demonstrates the constructed nature of the categories of masculinity and femininity, but it explores as well the degree to which such categories fail to account for the full spectrum of performances and identities that are produced, in spite (or perhaps as a result) of the vigilant nature of gender maintenance efforts. We must theorize gender in relation to (but not limited by) sexual practices, sexual orientation, and sexual identities in addition to the reproductive functions and roles. Gender is simultaneously produced by and reproduces power; as Joan Wallach Scott emphasizes, "gender is a primary way of signifying relationships of power . . . gender is a primary field within which or by means of which power is articulated."[70] If gender is central to the colonial hierarchies through which regimes of power are articulated, attention to the gendered nature of power has the potential to disrupt those regimes and hierarchies. In Trinh Minh-ha's words, "the notion of gender is pertinent to feminism as far as it denounces certain fundamental attitudes of imperialism and as long as it remains unsettled and unsettling."[71]

Such theoretical assumptions make it possible to consider the variability of gender in relation to the diffuse operations of power. Virgil's epic world represents gendered identities in specific relation to power, since the world of mortals constitutes a horizontal axis of power, which is juxtaposed to the vertical relationships between mortals and immortals. This arrangement creates a grid that clusters the possibilities of gender around four quadrants: male immortals, female immortals, male mortals, and female mortals. However, the boundaries between mortal and immortal are extremely fluid, since some mortals, such as Aeneas, are destined eventually to receive immortality, and some immortals, especially female figures such as Allecto and Juturna, are ranked quite low in the immortal hierarchy and cannot, in terms of their status—measured by their agency and value—be placed above the highest-ranking mortals, especially the males.[72] The narrative of the *Aeneid* involves a shifting set of power relations that challenges any binary assumptions about gender and power in the epic world.

In addition, the relationship between gender and power is embedded in a set of cultural constructions of sexuality that must be distinguished from our modern, normatively heterosexist perspective. The ancient world allowed elite males great latitude in terms of sexual preference; in classical Rome, both boys and women could be seen as sex objects, reified by the male gaze as objects of desire. Female sexualities are thereby not positioned solely in opposition to or as a supplement to male desire, and ancient constructions of sexuality did not depend on a dichotomy between heterosexuality/homosexuality, as John Boswell has demonstrated.[73] Boswell suggests instead that sexuality was categorized around a concept of a "penetration code" that was "clearly not related to a dichotomy of sexual preference, but to uses of power, dominance and submission."[74] Although women are not exclusive inhabitants of the submissive role, they cannot occupy the dominant role, according to this particular model.

The mortal women in the epic occupy shifting, uncertain categories of gender, particularly in relation to power. As women who perform masculine, heroic roles, Dido and Camilla both appear to transgress the boundaries of normative categories for women in the epic world. Both women are leaders with constructive energy that is openly acknowledged and praised in the text. Both represent the potential of power to be autonomously wielded by female leaders. Although both undergo extreme reversals, their characters nonetheless provide a representation of power as a female prerogative, if only momentarily, in the epic. The luminous quality of the description of Dido's city in book 1 is not wholly obliterated by the concluding events of book 4:

instant ardentes Tyrii: pars ducere muros
molirique arcem et manibus subuoluere saxa,
pars optare locum tecto et concludere sulco;
iura magistratusque legunt sanctumque senatum.
hic portus alii effodiunt; hic alta theatris

14

fundamenta locant alii, immanisque columnas
rupibus excidunt, scaenis decora apta futuris.[75] (1.423–29)

The eager Tyrians work hard: part constructing the walls and building the fortress and rolling rocks in their hands; part selecting a
place for a house and enclosing it with a ditch; they choose laws
and the magistrates and the sacred senate. Here some excavate a
port; here others establish the deep foundations of a theater, and
cut enormous columns from rock, a suitable ornament for a future
stage.

Nonetheless, Roman history requires that we—like Virgil's audience—
recognize this city as Carthage, a city to be both subjugated and destroyed
by Roman imperial power.

Gender and the Dynamics of Reading

The gendered identities traceable in a literary text might be read as performances that help to gender the subjects who enact them; that is, if we
go beyond an analysis of literary characters as figures of a given sex ("the
image of the woman" approach), or as figures who exemplify the social
expectations of gendered subjects ("the role of the woman" approach), we
might explore the cultural assumptions that govern gender as a category.
We might also investigate the textual gendering of author-functions,
readers' responses, as well as the textual conventions that ascribe genders
to the characters in a literary text. This approach depends on the assumption that gender is never a universal category but a historically situated,
social construction achieved—at least partially—through language.[76]
Such an analysis must be open to a range of interpretive possibilities. As
Judith Butler asserts: "When the constructed status of gender is theorized
as radically independent of sex, gender itself becomes a free-floating
artifice, with the consequence that *man* and *masculine* might just as easily signify a female body as a male one, and *woman* and *feminine* a male
body as easily as a female one."[77] As language, literary texts participate in
such constructions and may be analyzed as sites where gendered textual
identities may produce, contest, or confirm the social and cultural categories of gender. Texts both produce and are produced by the "technologies of gender" that structure gendered and sexual identities in any given
culture.[78] Medieval readers of Virgil's text repeatedly categorize Dido as a
virago—a woman who performs as a man. As part of the complex alterity
of the *Aeneid* as an authoritative Latin text from a pagan Roman culture,
the contested nature of Dido's identity as a masculine woman—and her
consequent resistance to cultural appropriation—frequently exposes the

gendered dynamic behind the medieval vernacular appropriation of classical texts.

As I have already noted, Roman culture did not gender its male subjects around a model of compulsory heterosexuality. Indeed, the development of a doctrinal, legally codified social structure that elaborates a normative, "reproductive heterosexuality"[79]—along with an alternate model of voluntary and highly valued chastity—belongs to the Christian Middle Ages.[80] The direction of Dido's itinerary in medieval textual traditions owes much to the cultural elaboration of heterosexual desire, in its multiple effects in medieval cultures, as we shall see. As modern readers of ancient or medieval texts, we must diligently interrogate categories, particularly categories of genders or sexualities, that might seem so universal and immutable, perhaps even "natural," to us, situated as we are in a gendered worldview that can be seen as the product of various historical processes.[81] We need especially to remain aware of the extent to which our reading practices implicate us in what Kaja Silverman terms the "dominant fiction" of our culture, the cultural mechanisms that "bring the subject into conformity with the symbolic order by fostering normative desire and identifications."[82]

For the medieval poet, reading Dido implicitly acknowledges his/her belated position in relation to the pedagogical and poetic authority of the classical textual past. Yet as the act of reading becomes an act of textual and cultural appropriation—as the reader becomes the writer who translates, paraphrases, cites, or even briefly evokes the *Aeneid* story as a pretext—the rhetorical dynamic of reading structures the later text, often leaving visible traces. And the rhetoric of reading is often understood in sexual terms whereby the act of interpretation becomes an aggressively seductive gesture enacted on a model of heterosexual textual play.[83] Within the material worlds of medieval culture, the text as artifact might easily be figured as a body laboriously inscribed—even etched deeply—with traces of past writers. As Michael Clanchy notes, the medieval terms for the page of parchment insistently note its status as the skin of an animal.[84] Although medieval books were not all made from parchment, this corporeal status of the text appears pervasive in medieval textual cultures. In confronting the body of the text, the medieval reader entered into an interpretive contract that potentially situated the reader in the subject position of a male heterosexual confronting the alluringly feminine textuality of poetry and narrative. Furthermore, as Mary Carruthers has demonstrated, the process of readerly engagement with a text produced a highly visual image for the reader.[85] The medieval Dido is—with few exceptions—the object of the male gaze within a highly specular, heterosexual economy of readerly desire, though within Latin textual cultures, that desire is ultimately implicated in a paradigm of homoerotics as well. Faced with the authority of the classical Latin text, the vernacular poet in particular attempts to regain a position of interpretive mastery through the specular gestures of interpretation.

Dido and Intertextuality

The reception of the *Aeneid* in medieval culture provides the modern reader with a vast set of interlaced "Virgilian" texts. As a text of enormous cultural authority, Virgil's *Aeneid* engendered a multitude of other texts, particularly commentaries and allegorical adaptations in Latin that implicitly defer to the textual authority of the Latin "original." In addition, texts such as Augustine's *De civitate Dei* rewrite the theme of Roman destiny in the *Aeneid* to suit the imperial vision of the late antique Christian. For Latin readers, such dynamic textual dialogue authorized the medieval adaptation of classical authority.

The presence of vernacular literatures, however, suggests an alternate paradigm for the cultural reception of Virgil's *Aeneid*. Vernacular poets read and imitated, adapted or even "translated" Virgil's text, yet vernacular texts could never fully participate in the textual authority represented by the Latin *Aeneid*. The difficulties of this intertextual drama are explicitly foregrounded in Dante's *Commedia* as a vernacular reworking of the Christian imperial thematics central to Augustine's authoritative Latin revision of Virgilian empire in *De civitate Dei*. Dante, of course, strove to claim traditional authority for vernacular poetry; that is, he would have vernacular poetry participate in Latin authority. Unlike Dante, most vernacular poets show less direct investment in the textual authority of Virgil's *Aeneid*. In addition, in the vernacular context for the *Aeneid* story, Dido is frequently the thematic center of the narrative. One might read the medieval vernacular Dido as a countertradition to the Latin commentary and allegory traditions, traditions colonized by the textual authority of elite, Latin literary culture.

The medieval Dido may take many forms; the design of this study is intended to keep such multiplicity in view as much as possible and yet simultaneously work closely with a range of texts. Consequently, the first chapter provides an overview of several possible categories for Dido—the historical Dido, the Virgilian Dido, the Ovidian Dido, the medieval Dido—both historical and Virgilian, and so forth. These categories are hopelessly intertwined, and the survey of chapter 1 is intended to demonstrate the extent to which these various versions of Dido's story implicitly or explicitly overlap. In this context, the most important category to keep in mind is the version drawn from historical texts (henceforth labeled the historical Dido), a pre-Virgilian version of Dido's story in which she never meets Aeneas, but commits suicide in order to preserve her chastity and her oath of fidelity to her deceased husband Sychaeus. The historical Dido is a significant presence in late medieval Latin texts, specifically Boccaccio's humanist treatises, which provide the conduit by which the historical figure enters vernacular texts such as Caxton's *Eneydos* or Christine de Pizan's *Cité des dames*. But the late medieval figure of the historical Dido is, as a rule, evoked against the Virgilian tradition; thus, in chapter 1 I have tried to explore these various categories for Dido in terms of their embedded connections in a variety of texts in order to articulate a sense of the ground against which we may read the Dido figure in a series of specific, literary texts.

The rest of the chapters are organized around clusters of texts that constitute—by virtue of their own explicit references—some sort of textual dialogue that participates in the reading of Dido. Chapter 2 considers texts from the medieval commentary and allegory tradition on Virgil's *Aeneid*, texts that articulate the medieval curricular and pedagogic purposes of reading Dido, which produce a homosocial paradigm similar to the modern critical traditions of reading Virgil that I have just explored. The remaining chapters examine the presence of Dido in a series of medieval French and English texts. Although the arrangement of these chapters suggests a chronological approach—chapter 3 focuses on the twelfth century, chapter 4 the fourteenth, and chapters 5 and 6 the fifteenth and early sixteenth centuries—the sequence of textual analysis does not follow a strict chronological framework. In chapter 3, for instance, I consider Chrétien de Troyes's brief evocation of Dido in *Erec et Enide* (ca. 1170) before treating at length the earlier *Roman d'Eneas* (ca. 1156), and I place the chapter on Caxton's *Eneydos* (1490) and Gavin Douglas's *Eneados* (1513) before the chapter on the early fifteenth-century texts of Christine de Pizan. In privileging Christine as the end point of this study—an arrangement that refuses a framework of linear temporality—I hope to challenge what Kristeva terms "a certain conception of time: time as project, teleology, linear and prospective unfolding; time as departure, progression, and arrival—in other words, the time of history."[86] This sequence of chapters, in reorganizing the paradigm of "time of history," offers an alternative model of inquiry. Christine explores a range of possibilities for reading Dido in a set of interpretive models that finally produce the city as monumental interruption of linear temporality in the *Cité des dames*, as we shall see. By contrast to the openness of Christine's interpretive methods, Gavin Douglas's approach to Dido a full century later not only demonstrates the narrow possibilities that result from his particular "manly" concern with "translation," but the explicit misogyny of Douglas's texts—the product of a "vernacular humanism" in the early sixteenth century—adds forceful resonance to Joan Kelly's rhetorical question, "Did women have a Renaissance?"[87] By placing the Christine chapter last I hope to challenge our conventional assumptions about literary studies and perhaps suggest alternate paradigms that might free us from some of the tyrannies of historical chronologies that provide the standard framework for literary study and often appear to thwart feminist projects.

This study is also meant to exploit the potentials and possibilities of intertextuality as a feminist methodology. If by intertextuality we wish to invoke not just the *intertexte* but the wider set of cultural paradigms with which a text might engage,[88] the presence of Dido in medieval texts invites the consideration of gender as a significant set of cultural discourses performed by textual agents—authors, characters, readers. Thus, texts enact various readings of Dido—Ovid attempts to read *Aeneid* 4 as Dido might; Augustine, for instance, reads Dido as a boy; Chaucer reads Dido as a loveless male narrator of classical stories; Caxton reads Dido as a compiler and a printer as much as a translator; Douglas reads Dido as a humanist translator; Christine reads Dido first as a man and then as a woman, and even as Dido reading Dido. Throughout this study I have attempted to explore the historically contingent structures of gender that construct the reading positions behind all these author-functions. For that reason, I consider the feudal ideology that is evident in the *Roman d'Eneas*, the curricular practices that are perhaps responsible for the attitudes expressed in Bernard Silvestris's commentary on the *Aeneid*, the practices of silent reading that structure the narrator's masculine subject positions in Chaucerian texts, Boccaccio's humanist anxiety about women readers, and the siege mentality of the Hundred Years War that is evident in the allegorical structures of Christine de Pizan. Since each text requires a different set of historical negotiations from the modern scholar, the issues explored in each chapter are quite differently contextualized.

The texts selected for study in this exploration of Dido demonstrate the vernacular autonomy of Dido—the extent to which the medieval Dido drifts away from the medieval Latin tradition that authorized and disciplined the study of the *Aeneid*. Although Dido sometimes appears in texts that function as a retelling of Virgil's *Aeneid* 4, such as the twelfth-century *Roman d'Eneas* or Chaucer's *House of Fame* or Gavin Douglas's *Eneados*, Dido also appears in texts that do not explicitly refer to Virgil's Latin text but rather acknowledge the circulation of the vernacular Dido (whether historical or Virgilian), such as Christine de Pizan's *Mutacion de Fortune* and *Cité des dames*, or Caxton's *Eneydos*. In order to effectively study the vernacular Dido, we must envision a network of intertexts that in no way privileges Virgil's *Aeneid*—or even Dante's *Commedia*—as the "primary" text by which we measure the medieval Dido.[89]

In addition, vernacular texts, particularly the *Roman de la Rose*, the

Histoire ancienne jusqu'à César,[90] the French translations of *De claris mulieribus* or *De casibus,* often contain manuscript illuminations that depict various moments in the Dido story. Since Latin texts of Virgil's *Aeneid* seldom include illustrations before the second half of the fifteenth century,[91] these images of Dido in vernacular texts are not specifically indebted to a visual tradition based on Virgil's Latin text. One might consider the pictorial Dido as a vernacular creation that has become almost completely detached from the authority of Virgil's *Aeneid.* These images bear a complex relationship to the texts they are intended to illustrate; these manuscript illuminations allow for a consideration of the iconographic intertextuality central to the medieval efforts toward reading Dido. Such an arrangement illustrates an alternate vision of literary history, consistent with feminist critiques of literary practice: a history based on noncanonical prose texts such as the anonymous *Eneydes,* Caxton's *Eneydos* or Christine's *Cité des dames,* or relatively unknown poetic texts such as Christine's *Mutacion,* or "minor" texts by canonical authors, such as Chaucer's *House of Fame* or *Legend of Dido.* The vernacular reception of *Aeneid* 4 and the textual and visual representations of the medieval Dido challenge the conventional assumptions of "source" or "original" basic to studies of influence as studies of cultural patrimony.

Likewise, a consideration of gender and intertextuality makes possible an intervention in the patrilineal model of literary traditions based on concepts of source and influence or reflected in the paternal literary paradigm of Virgil and Dante. As Gayatri Spivak depicts the axis of literary history as cultural patrimony, "from Homer to Virgil to Dante to Milton to Yeats. Fill in the interstices and you have the Great Traditions of European Poetry."[92] The vernacular Dido allows us to trace the repeated disruptions of such master texts and by extension, the master discourse of standard literary history, which often constructs the medieval period as one of monolithic literary authority.

Readerly interest in Dido extends well beyond the Middle Ages—and well beyond the scope of this study—into Renaissance and early modern cultures throughout Europe. Marlowe's *Dido, Queen of Carthage,* or *Didon se sacrifiant* by Étienne Jodelle (two of approximately forty Renaissance dramas about Dido),[93] and Purcell's *Dido and Aeneas* illustrate the theatrical interest in the story of Dido in the early modern period. The Aeneas-Dido story has left traces throughout Shakespeare's plays.[94] In addition, *Aeneid* 4 was translated separately by Surrey in 1554, and the medieval interest in the Virgilian Dido perhaps culminates in the Renaissance interest in her character and her drama.

The Medieval Dido and the Modern Reader

Although this study is only concerned with the reception of *Aeneid* 4 in medieval cultures, that reception has much to tell us about our own reading practices in relation to gender and power. Whereas the Latin *Aeneid* was a highly canonical text embedded in elite social structures, the vernacular Dido allowed for disruptive reading practices, evident especially in the case of Christine de Pizan, that implicitly, perhaps indirectly, challenge the cultural value assigned to such an authoritative text. The medieval Dido offers a corrective to our conventional assumptions about the centrality of Virgil to medieval textual traditions. In the various categories of Dido's story—whether as the historical Dido who exposes the fictionality of Virgil's *Aeneid* 4 or as the Ovidian figure who labels Aeneas a traitor—the medieval Dido is frequently evoked to displace Virgil. In addition, a postcolonial reading of Virgil's *Aeneid* would emphasize the politics of identity at work in the loss of Dido. As chapter 1 demonstrates, Dido's geographic identity as an African queen—especially given her conflation with Cleopatra and her historical association with Carthage to an Augustan audience—illustrates the Roman formation of an orientalism that has been central to the ideologies of Western imperialism, as articulated by Edward Said.[95]

Reading Dido reminds the modern reader of the textual possibilities of a pervasive countermemory in the face of imperial ideologies and the canonical reading practices that support them. For the modern American reader, the imperial cultures we inhabit depend heavily on "the knowledge industry, on the production and dissemination of texts and textuality," as Said points out.[96] The secondhand memory of Dido's other stories, as well as the literary history of Dido's itinerary in medieval vernacular cultures, mark a disruption of the standard pedagogical focus of great books or Western civilization courses. Reading Dido offers an opportunity to explore what we have been, as Homi Bhabha puts it, "obliged to forget."

Critiques of the canon have rightly emphasized that we are what we read, but we are also constructed as cultural subjects by our reading practices—by how we read. The decade of the 1980s, which marked the second millennium of Virgil's death, saw the publication of numerous books and articles on Virgil's poetry,[97] many of which demonstrate a sensitivity to late twentieth-century concerns about reading and the social order, but only a few show much concern with Dido, or with other female characters of the *Aeneid*.[98] While the medieval interest in reading Dido does not provide late twentieth-century readers with a neat interpretive model, it helps expose a critical blind spot that supports the historical myopia of cultural imperialisms.

> The Aeneid, *I have tried to suggest, is polycentric, and every reader will find the center that suits him or her.*
>
> W. R. Johnson

> *We intend to find ourselves. In the burning city.*
> Rachel Blau DuPlessis

CHAPTER 1

Dux Femina Facti
Virgil's Dido in the Historical Context

*Et sane cur poeta doctissimus omnium atque optimus nam finxisse con-
stat haec finxerit cur cum vel aliam quamlibet heroidum ex numero
eligere, vel personam formare novam suo iure licuisset, unam hanc
elegerit . . . ut quam studio castitatis ac servandae viduitatis extinctam
sciret hanc lascivo amore parentem faciat.[1]*

Petrarch, *Seniles 4.5*

*And why indeed did the most learned and excellent poet of all invent
this—for it is well known that he invented it—when it had been permitted by his own rule to choose any other out of a number of heroines or to
form a new one; why did he choose one . . . whom he knew died out of
zeal for chastity and the preservation of widowhood and make her yield
to a wanton love?*

In this passage taken from his allegorical commentary on Virgil's
Aeneid, Petrarch questions Virgil's choice of Dido as the female counterpart to the exemplary hero, Aeneas (*vir fortis ac perfectus*). As
Petrarch carefully documents in his letter, Virgil's Dido is recognizably a
poetic invention, a fact all too well known to be ignored, since Petrarch
cites a number of historians and philosophers who testify to the "other"
Dido.[2] Given Petrarch's program of intensive reading, he is aware of two
conflicting textual traditions of Dido's story. For Petrarch, such awareness complements his allegorical approach to the *Aeneid* as a narrative
about the hero Aeneas who figures the brave and perfect man:[3] if Virgil
invented the story of Dido's affair with Aeneas, he did so in support of his
allegorical program.

Petrarch thus solves the interpretive difficulties posed by Dido's textual past by reading Virgil's Dido as a poetic adaptation of the historical
figure. For Petrarch, Virgil's Dido is a singularly authoritative revision of
a preexisting historical account of Dido. But Virgil is not the only poet or
reader who revises Dido: Ovid's Dido and, much later, Boccaccio's Dido
mark two influential interpretations of Virgil's Dido that function as
landmarks for medieval traditions of reading Dido. And, as we shall see,

23

Jean de Meun's highly visual citation of Dido fixes the image of Dido for several later vernacular poets.

This chapter traces the outlines of the significant traditions that shape the possibilities for interpreting the figure of Dido in medieval vernacular texts. Rather than an inclusive survey, this initial attempt to identify categories for the medieval Dido will, by necessity, look briefly at a series of texts that represent influential rewritings of Dido. In the first part of this chapter, I trace the transformation of Dido from a historical figure into an elegiac lover in classical Latin texts. The second half of this chapter, with its emphasis on medieval representations of Dido and especially on Boccaccio's interest in the historical Dido, provides the framework for the more thorough analysis of texts that follows in the later chapters. Vernacular poets and readers, especially Chaucer, Gavin Douglas, and Christine de Pizan, depend heavily on an awareness not only of the status of Dido's story in classical texts but also on the readings—both text and image—of Dido evident in Jean de Meun and Boccaccio. This chapter traces the readings of Dido that constitute the working paradigms addressed in later chapters.

The Historical Dido and Virgil's *Infelix Dido*

The extant historical texts present a portrait of Dido as a Phoenician exile and a founder of Carthage; this version of Dido's story does not include any mention of Aeneas.[4] The earliest account of the "historical" Dido is preserved among the fragments attributed to the Greek historian Timaeus of Tauromenium (ca. 356–260 B.C.E.).[5] Timaeus's version exists in a brief one-hundred-word summary that survives in two separate catalogs of women in later texts.[6] According to this account, Dido fled to Libya with a group of followers after her brother, Pygmalion, had killed her husband. When a Libyan king wished to marry her, she refused him; when she was compelled by her people to accept him, she pretended to stage a ceremony in order to release herself from a sacred promise to her husband. She built and lit a large funeral pyre next to her dwelling, and she threw herself into it from her house.[7] Even in this synopsis, Dido is a heroic figure; her suicide is an act of defiance that testifies to the nobility of her nature.

This brief account of Dido's exile and death testifies to a pre-Virgilian tradition for Dido, a tradition that represents her only as a leader. In addition to Timaeus's account in Greek, the Augustan historian Pompeius Trogus included an account of the historical Dido, drawn perhaps from the same source as Timaeus's version, in his universal history. Trogus's version survives in Justin's epitome, which dates from the second or third century C.E. but attests to the probable currency of the "historical" Dido during the early empire and the decades immediately following the publication of the *Aeneid*.[8] Although Trogus's account itself cannot be considered a "source" for Virgil's *Aeneid*, the similarities between Dido's story in Justin and in Virgil demonstrate the extent to which the Aeneas-Dido story in the *Aeneid* may be read as a revision of an existing tradition regarding the queen of Carthage. Justin's three-paragraph summary (18.4–6)[9]—the fullest treatment of the "historical" Dido in ancient texts—differs in a few details from Timaeus's version, and it provides much more anecdotal information beyond the outline of Timaeus's plot.

Justin narrates that Dido, a woman noted for her beauty, married her uncle Acerbas. Acerbas, though wealthy, hid his gold in the ground out of fear of Pygmalion, who had become king upon his father's death even though he was still a boy. Pygmalion hears about Acerbas's wealth through rumor (*fama*), and without respect for the *pietas* due to a brother-in-law, he kills him. For a while Dido shuns her brother, and then, as she prepares with a group of disaffected citizens to go into exile, she pretends to her brother that she wishes to move from her husband's house and into his. Pygmalion agrees to this plan, since he thinks that Acerbas's gold will be moving in with Dido. However, Dido leads Pygmalion's servants (sent by Pygmalion to her to assist in her move) into a ship with all her wealth, and once at sea, orders them to throw overboard packages of sand, pretending that they are casting her wealth into the sea as a funeral offering to Acerbas. She then conscripts the servants to attend her in exile since they cannot return to Pygmalion without the wealth.

The wanderers first land in Cyprus, where, at Dido's command, they abduct eighty virgins upon their departure ("virgines raptas navibus imponi Elissa iubet") in order to provide marriages for the youths and offspring for their new city. Pygmalion initially sets out to pursue her, but he is persuaded to let her flee; Dido and her followers arrive in Africa, where the local inhabitants welcome them as settlers. Having negotiated to purchase the amount of land that could be covered by the hide of an ox, she has her followers cut the hide into thin strips and thereby acquires enough land to establish Carthage. Iarbas, the king of the Maxetani, demands that Dido marry him under threat of war. Dido eventually appears to agree, though she takes three months to invoke her husband Acerbas with tears and lamentation. She has a pyre built on the outskirts of the city; as if to placate the spirit of her husband, she kills many hostages to be sent to the underworld prior to her marriage. Then she climbs the pyre, tells the people that she is going to her husband, and kills herself with a sword ("dixit vitamque gladio finivit"). Justin's summary ends with the comment that as long as Carthage stood, Dido was honored as a goddess.

Justin's text emphasizes Dido's agency; her story is a narrative of political maneuvers that exemplify her resourcefulness and cunning. In order to establish a new city, she confiscates servants and wealth, and she acquires land. As leader, she abducts a group of virgins (a motif reminiscent of the rape of the Sabine women that forms part of the Roman foundation myth) in order to distribute maidens to her followers in recognition that marriages and offspring will help establish and stabilize a new city.[10] Such "traffic in women," though a standard feature of Homeric epic, is unusual for a woman, even a woman warrior.[11] The abduction of virgins suggests the degree to which Dido's political behavior as leader situates her in masculine roles.

Dido's cunning allows her to deceive Pygmalion, and her suicide allows her to thwart Iarbas. But perhaps the most significant aspects of Justin's account are the heroic qualities of Dido's suicide. Timaeus's Dido had thrown herself from her house into a burning funeral pyre. Justin's version emphasizes the theatricality of Dido's suicide: she ascends the pyre and addresses the populace before taking her life with a sword. In substituting suicide by the sword—a warrior's death—for suicide by fire, the later historian emphasizes the nobility of this death, a death worthy of a male hero.[12] Such a suicide, however, is a political rather than personal gesture. Justin's Dido is a noble figure—the account of her activities from the time of Pygmalion's death until her suicide presents her as a heroic, competent, perhaps even ruthless leader, whose death exemplifies a tragic dignity and who is later venerated by her people as a deity. *Dux femina facti.*

Justin punctuates the story of Dido with a reference to Carthage's place in historical chronology: "Condita est haec urbs LXXII annis ante quam Roma" (18.6.9) (This city was founded seventy-two years before Rome). This is one of several dates given in historical accounts for the foundation of Carthage. Jerome's translation of Eusebius's *Chronica* gives another set of possible dates that place the founding of Carthage after the fall of Troy and the founding of Rome; these dates likewise make the meeting of Aeneas and Dido a historical impossibility.[13] Jerome's version of Eusebius became the standard authority for the Christian West, and this problem of chronology that makes *Aeneid* 4 a fiction is repeatedly acknowledged by historians and commentators. For instance, John Ridevall, one of the "classicizing friars" (ca. 1333), states the problem:

Si enim eamus ad veritatem historie, Eneas nunquam vidit Didonem, que fundavit Cartaginem et fuit regina illius civitatis, quia Eneas fuit mortuus antequam Cartago fuit condita per trecentos annos et amplius.[14]

If, moreover, we go to the truth of history, Eneas never saw Dido, who established Carthage and was queen of that city, because

Eneas was dead for three hundred years and more before Carthage was founded.

Although Ridevall does not go on to tell Dido's story, this concern with the dates of the founding of Carthage, the fall of Troy, and the founding of Rome betrays a faith in historical texts that frequently lends support to the historical Dido as the "true" Dido, as Petrarch implies. Justin's Dido is not thereby just one account among others but a truer account because his version of the Dido story does not contradict the received traditions regarding Mediterranean history.

Whether or not Virgil invented the affair between Aeneas and Dido is one of the more provocative questions that haunt classical studies.[15] Scholars have long debated whether some outline of the Aeneas-Dido story appeared in Naevius's *Bellum Poenicum;* however, so little evidence regarding Naevius's text survives that its potential as a source for *Aeneid* 4 is difficult to assess.[16] In any case, *Aeneid* 4 can essentially be read as Virgil's revision of the historical Dido; as Gian Biagio Conte asserts: "Virgil probably found Dido in Naevius, but the *Bellum Poenicum* certainly did not contain the substance of the fourth book of the *Aeneid.* In Naevius Dido can hardly have been more than a device for taking the date of the historical conflict between the two peoples [Carthaginians and Romans] back to a mythical age."[17] It appears to be Virgil's *Aeneid* that essentially transforms the Dido figure from a heroic exile into an abandoned woman undone by desire.[18]

The historical version of Dido's story functions as part of the "poetic memory," in Conte's phrase, that constitutes the raw materials of a text and thus directs, in some measure, its reception.[19] As a "poetic memory," the outline of the historical account still frames the *Aeneid* 4. Dido's loss of Sychaeus—narrated to Aeneas by Venus in Book 1—essentially rehearses the first part of the historical tradition as it appears in Justin. The spurned African king, Iarbas, remains a significant actor in Virgil's narrative, since his prayers to Jupiter cause Mercury to be dispatched to Aeneas. The funeral pyre retains an important dramatic purpose in the *Aeneid,* since its construction provides the setting for Dido's final speeches and her suicide—by the sword—in *Aeneid* 4. The resemblance of Virgil's Dido to her historical counterpart not only invites a comparison of the two characters, but the historical Dido provides a tradition against which Virgil's Dido could be measured by a knowledgeable reader such as Petrarch.

Virgil's Dido is a formidable character.[20] Her royal bearing, her wealth and generosity, the civilized city she establishes, and the building campaign she directs all contribute to her significance and power, at least initially, in Virgil's *Aeneid.* In this respect, Virgil's Dido is consistent with

the historical figure. However, in the course of *Aeneid* 4, Dido's regal status is compromised by her desire for Aeneas. *Aeneid* 4 departs from the
historical tradition in its treatment of Dido as a sexualized figure, a
woman tempted by *amor* to forsake both her oath to Sychaeus (which the
historical Dido died to preserve) and her role as leader.

Virgil's debt to the historical version of Dido's story is evident in his
depiction of Dido as a political figure. As Francis Cairns has shown, the
ideology of kingship provides a normative discourse for the *Aeneid*:
"Both Aeneas and . . . Dido are represented in Book 1 as good monarchs.
In Book 4, Dido deteriorates into a bad monarch, while Aeneas emerges at
its end as an improved good king."[21] Cairns's study demonstrates that a
"good king" is identified by a set of virtues necessary in a ruler; self-control and abstinence from pleasure are predominant among these kingly
virtues. The historical Dido, even within the brief outlines of Timaeus's
version, satisfies the requirements for a "good king" in ancient culture,
especially in her display of wisdom and courage, in addition to her self-
control.[22] Virgil transforms this antecedent Dido from a "good king"
("imperium Dido Tyria regit urbe profecta" [1.340]) into an erotic figure
("amans Dido" [4.101]), who suffers the consequences of her desire ("mis-
errima Dido" [4.117]); finally, out of her mind, she rages like a bacchante
("saeuit inops animi totamque incensa per urbem / bacchatur" [4.300–
301]). This reversal of fortune, made complete by Dido's suicide, invites a
comparison with tragedy, as scholars have frequently noted.[23]

The narrative texture of *Aeneid* 4 derives from the confrontation
between Dido—a royal figure of responsibility and power upon her entrance into the narrative—and Aeneas, who initially appears as a destitute, shipwrecked wanderer when he enters Carthage in a mist.[24] The
sweep of Virgil's narrative quickly reverses the position of both protago-
nists. The turning point for Dido, and the crux of the narrative for the
Aeneas-Dido story, is the cave scene. The entrance of the two characters
into the cave is motivated by the divinely orchestrated storm. Juno,
Earth, and the nymphs all participate in staging the wedding:

> Speluncam Dido dux et Troianus eandem
> deueniunt. prima et Tellus et pronuba Iuno
> dant signum; fulsere ignes et conscius aether
> conubiis summoque ulularunt uertice Nymphae.
> ille dies primus leti primusque malorum
> causa fuit.[25] (165–70)

Dido and the Trojan leader arrive at the same cave. Primal earth
and pronubial Juno give the signal; fires flashed and heaven was

witness to the marriage, from summit tops the nymphs shouted.
That day was first the cause of death and of evils.

This elliptical scene is first interpreted by an unusually authoritative comment by the narrator that the incident in the cave initiated death and sorrow. Nonetheless, the scene is highly indeterminate, and Dido and Aeneas each offer different interpretations of the events in the cave. The narrator summarizes Dido's understanding of her experience in the assertion that she called their union a marriage and thereby hid her guilt ("coniugium uocat, hoc praetexit nomine culpam" [172]). In preparing to depart, Aeneas, however, asserts in legalistic language that he never held torches as a bridegroom or took marriage vows (338–47).

The indeterminacy of the cave scene emblematically enacts the larger narrative uncertainties of the text. Dido's conviction that she has experienced a wedding receives support from the deities' outspoken intentions to delude her into such a belief; indeed, Juno straightforwardly states her intention to produce a real wedding (126). Dido's misinterpretation of the scene is perhaps willful, but not without corroborating evidence, especially given Aeneas's behavior. As Richard Monti notes: "It becomes clear that Aeneas has gone beyond merely living with Dido—or even acquiescing in Dido's interpretation of their relationship as marriage. He has actively assumed the role of consort and king."[26] Aeneas's legal formulation regarding the limits of his responsibility to Dido provides an adequate justification for his abandonment of her, yet it fails to fully exculpate him for his complicity in Dido's misunderstanding of his behavior. The narrative of *Aeneid* 4 plays on the indeterminacy of the cave scene and the audience's uncertainty, not so much about the events themselves (as one critic crudely put it, "Dido and Aeneas copulate as wild beasts")[27] but about the social significance of the events in the cave. Such indeterminacy is largely exploited and never resolved in the text.

The ambiguity of the cave scene is especially suggestive in the context of Roman marriage practices in the early days of the empire. As Gordon Williams has shown, at the time the *Aeneid* was composed "marriage could exist without ceremony and formality, simply by consent of both parties."[28] The ritual enactment of weddings was very informal—as were divorces[29]—which suggests that the openness of this scene might reflect cultural practices familiar to a Roman audience. In such a context, Dido's version of the events in the cave has a certain amount of legitimacy, especially when juxtaposed to the defensive position taken by Aeneas when he asserts that he was not technically married. Such interpretive uncertainty is reproduced in modern readings of Virgil, since no critical consensus exists regarding the cave scene. Although many scholars assume that Dido is deluded—perhaps understandably deluded—in her belief that a wedding has occurred, some assert that a wedding did in fact occur.[30] This disagreement over the meaning of the cave scene is paradigmatic of the larger ambiguities of Virgil's text. As we shall see, the cave scene is often embellished in medieval versions of the Aeneas-Dido story, both in Latin and vernacular texts; its elliptical quality seems to invite commentators such as Bernard Silvestris or poets such as the *Eneas* poet or Chaucer to fill in the gaps and silences and close off some of its ambiguities.

Dido's activities as a lover explicitly compromise her status as a "good king." Her sexual desire and her amorous enslavement to Aeneas are depicted in pathological terms throughout book 4; desire manifests itself in wounds (4.2, 67) and inflames her to madness (4.300–301). This view of love as disease and insanity reflects Roman attitudes toward *amor* as a dangerous emotion, one to be controlled and managed.[31] In Dido's case, the intensity of her passion—her erotic infection—undermines her self-control and destroys her ability to govern her city. Her abilities as a ruler decline, even before she has consummated her desire for Aeneas and well before he has signaled his intentions to leave her. Her city suffers even as a consequence of her infatuation; as soon as she acknowledges to Anna that she has an erotic interest in Aeneas, Carthage feels the effects:

> non coeptae adsurgunt turres, non arma iuuentus
> exercet portusue aut propugnacula bello
> tuta parant: pendent opera interrupta minaeque
> murorum ingentes aequataque machina caelo. (4.86–89)

> Towers, commenced, no longer rise; the youth no longer practice arms, or make ports and ramparts secure from battle. The works hang, interrupted, great threatening walls and a crane equal to the sky.

This connection between Dido's "health" and the prosperity of Carthage is significant; as a leader, Dido is defined by her city, and her identity is established by her political roles.[32] Although she succumbs to desire, she remains a political figure, and her amorous activities have political consequences. This passage demonstrates the extent to which the Virgilian Dido, transformed into a lover, nonetheless retains the political identity of the historical Dido.

Aeneid 4 juxtaposes erotic and political discourse in the narrative of Dido's disintegration and downfall; indeed, as Monti observes: "The emotional aspect of the Dido-Aeneas relationship does not obliterate its initial political character, but rather is an intensification and extension of it."[33] Monti also notes that the speeches between Aeneas and Dido have a political quality. In the end, however, Dido's political role is compromised by her sexual behavior, and the destructive quality of her sexuality culminates in the phallic overtones of her death.[34] Yet this suicide by sword is simultaneously a masculine death particularly appropriate to a tragic hero, so that Dido's death seems to cite Ajax's suicide in Sophocles' play.[35]

Both Aeneas and Dido engage in the sexual activity that brings on disaster in *Aeneid* 4, but only Dido becomes tainted by *amor* and suffers a reversal of fortune. As Cairns's "kingship" paradigm suggests, Aeneas is tempered by his brush with sexual danger and leaves Carthage a better king while Dido and her city are destroyed.[36] In her analysis of the politics of desire in Virgil's *Aeneid*, Mihoko Suzuki sees Dido as a character who embodies the "threat of the female Other."[37] However, Dido's status as "Other" derives from the destabilizing effects of her erotic desires; in her public, political performance as "king" or leader, Dido—like her historical counterpart—does not figure difference. Virgil's bifurcated delineation of Dido's behavior as king and lover reflects Roman constructions of gender during the period of the consolidation of Roman colonial power under the structure of empire so that the female might become identified with the colonized other. As Judith Hallett has shown, the "elite Roman male conceptualization of the female sex is a bipartite one. One part appears to reflect an assumption of *sex polarity* and female alterity, a concept of woman as *Other* . . . the other part of this conceptualization, categorizing women as *Same*, reflects an assumption of *sex unity*, a view that unifies male and female by ascribing to the latter qualities and talents culturally valued in the former."[38]

As a political leader, Dido exhibits the qualities that are valued in a heroic, male figure. As a woman who succumbs to erotic desire, Dido resembles another masculine stereotype, the "elegiac lover" in Cairns's analysis of the cultural allusions at work in *Aeneid* 4; the descriptions of Dido's role as a lover and her erotic symptoms of disease and sleeplessness conform closely to the elegiac stereotype of lovers.[39] Virgil has transformed the historical Dido—a "good king" who is venerated as a deity after her death—into a literary figure explicitly defined by his or her difference from cultural norms; as Cairns comments, "the elegiac lover was weak, foolish, worthless and morally culpable."[40] Virgil has eroticized the historical figure of Dido, and in the process he has feminized erotic desire as it is conventionally expressed in elegy.

It is a commonplace of Virgil criticism that Dido represents two critical moments in the history of Roman colonization in her prediction of the Punic Wars and her figural identification with Cleopatra. Both Hannibal and Cleopatra had acquired mythic proportions as enemies who mounted a North African challenge to Roman dominance. Although described as one "fati nescia" (ignorant of fate), Dido has a prophetic moment in *Aeneid* 4 when her final curse on the departing Aeneas predicts Rome's wars with Carthage. Not only does she foretell the rise of Hannibal (4.625) when she prophesies an avenger in her name, she also provides an ideological interpretation for the geographical placement of Carthage and Rome in her assertion that the two peoples be forever "litora litoribus contraria" (4.628). Virgil's audience would recognize in this curse a proleptic view of Roman history: the fulfillment of the Roman ideal, prophesied in books 1, 6, and 8, would involve a long and bitter struggle with North Africa and the "brutal destruction of Carthage by Rome," as Steven Farron puts it.[41]

In spite of the narrator's focus on her ignorance of fate, Dido's prophetic curse implicates her more directly in the telescopic sweep of Roman history than any of her other actions in *Aeneid* 4. Dido's identification with Carthage makes her a purposeful reminder that the narrative of Roman dominance in the Mediterranean was not a seamless myth of uncontested development and expansion: the centralization of colonial power depended on Roman ability to control and subjugate—if necessary—the territories at the periphery of the empire. Dido's status in the *Aeneid* allows us to consider the intersection of the discourses of gender and colonization at work in Augustan Rome and Virgil's text: Dido's colonial identity is emphasized by the fact that Virgil, in a departure from the historical tradition, connects Dido's death to the fall of Carthage, the rise of Hannibal, and eventually the subjugation of the city by the Romans. In Justin's account, by contrast, the city of Carthage survives the noble suicide of its queen.

Beyond her identification with Carthage, Dido also functions as a figure for Cleopatra;[42] indeed, Roman perception of Cleopatra's role in the events culminating in the battle of Actium and the establishment of empire resonated powerfully with Dido's use of the phrase "litora litoribus contraria." Within the geopolitics of empire, Cleopatra's challenge was seen as a feminine, sexualized, oriental threat to centralized Roman power.[43] As Ronald Syme has shown, Augustus worked to focus Italian attention not on his rival for supreme power—Anthony—but on fears that Anthony intended to "subjugate Italy and the West under the rule of an Oriental queen."[44] This particular vision of Actium is engraved on Aeneas's shield in *Aeneid* 8:

> hinc ope barbarica uariisque Antonius armis,
> uictor ab Aurorae populis et litore rubro,
> Aegyptum uirisque Orientis et ultima secum
> Bactra uehit, sequiturque (nefas) Aegyptia coniunx. (8.685–88)

On this side, with foreign wealth and diverse arms, Anthony, con-
queror from the Red Sea and peoples of the East; he carries Egypt
and the strength of the East and remote Bactra with him, and (hor-
ror!) an Egyptian consort follows.

The foundational discourse of Roman imperial power, particularly evident in the Augustan version of Actium visible here on Aeneas's shield,
relies heavily on a depiction of the colonial enemy as a sexualized, racialized female other.[45] In Dido, Hannibal and Cleopatra are eerily conflated
to evoke an imperial vision of the enemy from the periphery who
threatens centralized Roman power. In a discussion of Cleopatra, Lillian
Robinson comments on the sexual politics of such gestures: "[Cleo-
patra's] oriental nature, always emphasized in Roman propaganda despite
her Greek origin, implied unbridled sexuality."[46] *Aeneid* 4 emphasizes
Dido's sexuality, especially by contrast to Aeneas's dutiful behavior in
his departure from Carthage in obedience to the gods.

Virgil's Dido represents a transformation of the "poetic memory" of
the historical Dido in an orientalist gesture that displaces the erotic onto
Dido as an African queen of Asian origin. *Aeneid* 4 specifically delineates
the aspects of Dido's character that constitute a threat to Roman culture:
it is Dido-as-lover (a Virgilian interpretation of the figure), not Dido-as-
leader (the historical outlines of the figure), that embodies otherness and
danger. Dido and Aeneas both have their origin in the East; yet Aeneas's
story is that of a Trojan who becomes Italianized, while Dido's story suggests that she is, in the final analysis, incapable of suppressing her "oriental" nature. The Dido of *Aeneid* 1, whose "moenia surgunt" (437) is
less a threat than the eroticized figure of *Aeneid* 4 whose "non coeptae
adsurgunt turres" (86). It is not the female as sexual or female sexuality
that occupies the position of otherness in the imperial politics of the
Aeneid; rather, it is unconstrained sexuality itself that bears the mark of
gender. Dido's role in the narrative of *Aeneid* 4 works to render sexuality
in feminine terms. In the Roman ethnographic vision of the "oriental,"
the East is the locus of the dangerously sexual, and the dangerously
sexual, when figured by Dido or Cleopatra, becomes feminized.

When Dido Reads Virgil: Ovid's *Heroides* 7

Ovid's Dido in *Heroides* 7 is a literary creation intended specifically to
evoke Virgil's Dido rather than any feature of the pre-Virgilian, historical
Dido who quite possibly remained part of the "poetic memory" for
Augustan poets.[47] Composed within the generic demands of the love
elegy, *Heroides* 7 emphasizes Dido's role as lover in *Aeneid* 4; her attributes as *amans* thereby eclipse her role as *dux*. In the rhetorical display of

pathos that constitutes *Heroides* 7, Ovid presents a decontextualized Dido who revises her understanding of the events narrated in the *Aeneid*. In this regard, he initiates a long tradition of reading Dido; that is, a tradition of detaching Dido and her story from the *Aeneid* as a whole, thereby displacing Aeneas as the thematic focus of the text and implicitly disrupting the imperial context within which Aeneas acts. In *Heroides* 7, as in many later versions of the *Aeneid* in medieval and Renaissance literature—many of which derive specifically from Ovid's *Heroides* 7—the figure of Aeneas becomes a marginal character.

In *Heroides* 7, Ovid dramatizes the thematics of reading as interpretation in order to locate his Dido in direct relation to Virgil's Dido. *Heroides* 7 evokes Virgil's *Aeneid* in a series of scattered allusions and paraphrases that allow Ovid's Dido to reconsider Virgil's representation of her actions and understanding in *Aeneid* 4. Consequently, Dido's epistle, ostensibly addressed to Aeneas, requires its audience to read double: the reader who follows the quotations and echoes of Virgil's *Aeneid* in *Heroides* 7 not only recognizes the Virgilian discourse in the Ovidian text but simultaneously reads *Heroides* 7 against the *Aeneid*. In Dido, Ovid mimics the responses of a female reader of Virgil's *Aeneid*; in the process, he not only dramatizes his own relationship to Virgil, but he also presents a gender-based model of reading Virgil's text and Virgil's Dido.

As female-voiced poetry, the *Heroides* occupy a relatively unique position in Latin elegy, and they provide Ovid with the opportunity to construct a female point of view.[48] Throughout his poetry, Ovid demonstrates an interest in shifting identities and subject positions, a poetic perspective that receives its fullest treatment in the *Metamorphoses*, where he employs gender as a grammatical feature of language in order to depict identities as the product of linguistic performance. Warren Ginsberg has shown that "Ovid considers gender within the context of the power of language to create new definitions for newly formed objects."[49] The *Heroides* provided an early opportunity to explore the female point of view as a rhetorical performance that results from the construction of a feminine identity in language. Ovid's Dido, however, also represents an impersonation—an identifiably male poet ventriloquizing the reactions of a female reader of Virgil's epic, a male poet exploring the feminine subject position as the linguistic result of the "cultural meanings that the sexed body assumes."[50] For Ovid's public identity as a poet in Augustan Rome, the gendered performance of *Heroides* 7 made possible commentary on the role of poet as reader of authoritative pre-texts.

The Dido of *Heroides* 7 responds directly to many of the textual invitations of Virgil's narrative: she carefully and thoroughly reads between the lines and in the margins of the first four books of Virgil's *Aeneid*. Like his Dido, Ovid himself is a perceptive and skeptical reader; his poetry often demands that we see Ovid-the-poet as a reader of earlier texts. Of all precursor poets, Virgil would have required a particularly careful reading strategy on Ovid's part, since the canonical status of Virgil's poetry— even in the first decades of the empire—was likely to produce a certain amount of "anxiety of influence" in a later poet such as Ovid. Ovid's relationship to Virgil has occasionally been represented in such Bloomian terms, most notably in Brooks Otis's characterization of the *Metamorphoses* as a literary assault on Virgil.[51] Certainly, much of the *Metamorphoses* rehearses Ovid's dialogue with Virgil; at moments, such as in the five-line summary of *Aeneid* 4 that appears in *Metamorphoses* 14, Ovid appears to engage in a contest with Virgil:

> Libycas vento referuntur ad oras.
> excipit Aenean illic animoque domoque
> non bene discidium Phrygii latura mariti
> Sidonis inque pyra sacri sub imagine facta
> incubuit ferro deceptaque decipit omnes.[52] (77–81)

> They are carried by the wind to the Libyan shores. There Dido welcomes Aeneas into her heart and home; unable to endure the departure of her Trojan husband, she fell upon the sword, on a pyre fashioned in the semblance of sacred rites. Deceived, she deceives everybody.

The simplicity of this summary of *Aeneid* 4 effectively reduces and unravels the complexity of Virgil's text. This skeletal outline presupposes the reader's knowledge of the scenes and details that constitute *Aeneid* 4.[53] The bareness of its statement of plot ("excipit Aenean illic animoque domoque") omits both the divine explanation and the human motivation so carefully articulated in *Aeneid* 4 to represent the conditions under which Aeneas and Dido come together. The brief, concluding remark regarding Dido and her deceptions/delusions—"deceptaque decipit omnes" —conflates several incidents into a sort of epigrammatic summary,[54] a summary that nonetheless fully exploits the phallic quality of Dido's suicide and emphasizes an erotic perspective in the phrase "incubuit ferro."

In contrast to the reductive brevity of such summaries of the *Aeneid* in the *Metamorphoses*, Dido's lament in *Heroides* 7 rhetorically amplifies Virgil's text. Like the passage from *Metamorphoses* 14, however, *Heroides* 7 depends on the reader's prior experience of the *Aeneid* in order to activate the layers of reference and intertextual meaning. That the *Heroides* specifically refer to earlier texts and thereby depend on the audience's knowledge of a pre-text is a commonplace of Ovid criticism.[55] But more than any other epistle in the collection, *Heroides* 7 engages in a dialogue with a contemporary "master text." By taking Dido's point of view, Ovid directly addresses the most popular, most frequently read portion of Virgil's *Aeneid*, as he himself notes in the *Tristia*:

> et tamen ille tuae felix Aeneidos auctor
>   contulit in Tyrios arma virumque toros,
> nec legitur pars ulla magis de corpore toto,
>   quam non legitimo foedere iunctus amor. (2.533–36)

And yet that fortunate author of your Aeneid brought arms and the man into Tyrian beds, nor is any part of the whole work more read than the love not joined by a lawful covenant.

Dramatized as the writer of the epistle and simultaneously represented as the reader of Virgil's *Aeneid*, Dido brings an informed point of view to the interpretive tasks of her suicide letter. Virgil's Dido, to whom the narrator assigns the label "fati nescia" (ignorant of fate) (1.299) upon her entrance into the narrative, has a much more limited point of view. Explicitly characterized by her ignorance, Virgil's Dido is fatally affected by the blind spots in her understanding of fate as it is represented in Aeneas's narrative in books 2 and 3. In this respect, Virgil's narrative emphasizes Dido's limits as a reader: her responses to the narrative of *Aeneid* 2 (the fall of Troy) and *Aeneid* 3 (the wanderings of the Trojans until they reach Carthage)—the stories to which she listens with such rapt attention—are neither penetrating nor astute. In fact, as *Aeneid* 4 opens, Dido is doomed in part due to her inadequate interpretation of the long tale that has occupied Aeneas for the two previous books. At the end of *Aeneid* 3, Aeneas brings to a finish his narration—his rehearsal of divine fate ("fata renarrabat diuum" [717])—an effort that has given voice, shape, and arrangement to his experience. He has concluded a narrative, one that invites interpretation and one that has a powerful effect on his audience—especially Dido, who desires to hear the story repeated over and over (4.78–79).

Characterized as "fati nescia," Virgil's Dido cannot apprehend the large historical significance of the narrative she has heard; indeed, as he narrates his adventures in books 3 and 4, Aeneas himself does not fully understand the thematic importance of the divine destiny he rehearses in his narrative. The opening lines of *Aeneid* 4 represent Dido's responses to Aeneas's story. Aeneas's looks and words are impressed on her heart: "haerent infixi pectore uultus / uerbaque" (4-5) (his looks and words remain impressed in her heart). His words indeed have a powerful effect, leading Dido to a straightforward acceptance of the heroic themes of his text: "heu, quibus ille / iactatus fatis! quae bella exhausta canebat!" (13–14) (Alas, by what fates was he tossed! Of what wars endured, he told!). As narrator of books 2 and 3, Aeneas is the subject of the same verb (*canere*) used to authorize the inception of the *Aeneid* by the poet-narrator ("arma uirumque cano"). Dido validates Aeneas's authorial stance by her assessment of his heroic qualities as a character in his own narrative: "quem sese ore ferens, quam forti pectore et armis!" (11) (How noble in appearance, of what strong heart and arms!).

In books 2 and 3, Aeneas's narrative of his escape from Troy and his wanderings at sea have been punctuated throughout with revelations of his destiny—*fata*—in quite specific detail. These two books represent Aeneas's ever-growing awareness that he must seek a kingdom in Italy on the shores of Hesperia. Although the exact location of this land poses some problems for Aeneas, Dido's kingdom clearly is not this Italy, and neither she nor Aeneas ever thinks it is. Thus the cumulative effect of *Aeneid* 2 and 3 for the reader of the epic—the thematic emphasis on destiny and fate—is lost on Dido. Infatuated, deluded, and misled, she ignores the significance of *Aeneid* 2 and 3 and nourishes the destructive love that has already begun to undo her. Dido's ignorance of fate is thus compounded by her compassion for Aeneas and her uncritical acceptance of his character. Her responses to Aeneas's story are fatally inadequate.

Ovid's Dido enjoys a much more privileged point of view. Purportedly the text of a letter written immediately before Dido falls on Aeneas's sword, *Heroides* 7 pretends to insert itself into Virgil's narrative just before the close of *Aeneid* 4 and to thereby amplify Dido's final speeches in that text. The fictionality of this pretense is transparent, since Ovid's text explicitly presents itself as an epistle composed later in time and in a different meter. For Ovid's Dido, this retrospective position allows her to read *Aeneid* 4 with extreme skepticism. The ignorance of Virgil's Dido, represented in terms of her ignorance of fate, is cynically characterized by Ovid's Dido as her inability to recognize the gender bias of Aeneas's narrative. To Ovid's Dido, Aeneas's narrative in books 2 and 3 thematically asserts his priorities and politics in terms of gender. In focusing on this aspect of Aeneas's narrative, Ovid's Dido implicitly mocks Virgil's Dido for her inadequacies as a reader and explicitly presents her tragedy as the result of her limited interpretations of Aeneas's story and behavior rather than her ignorance of fate.[56]

Dido's point of view in *Heroides* 7 distorts the point of view constructed for Dido in *Aeneid* 4, but this distortion is partially the result of the rhetoric and structure of elegy. As a 198-line declamation, *Heroides* 7 allows Dido to indulge her passion to a much greater extent than is allowed Virgil's Dido by either the narrative framework of *Aeneid* 4 or the centrality of the character of Aeneas throughout Virgil's text. Although most of *Aeneid* 4 allows Dido to express her point of view, sometimes quite eloquently and powerfully, her version of the events in the narrative is not reinforced by the normative values of the poem as a whole. By comparison to the *Metamorphoses* and the *Aeneid*, the *Heroides* are rhetorical rather than narrative poetry, since the *Heroides* represent not the plots and scenes of narrative but rhetorical commentary on past events already recorded and represented in texts.[57] The rhetorical structure of the *Heroides* insures that we see only Dido's side of the story, and Ovid's Dido strikes an entirely different tone than Virgil's Dido. The anger expressed in the extreme and sometimes desperate rhetoric of Virgil's Dido (4.600–602) is erased from the lament of Ovid's Dido, who says that she does not hate Aeneas (29). Ovid's Dido blames herself for her foolishness (*stulta* 28), which tempers her discourse.

The rhetorical structure and purpose of *Heroides* 7 thus emphasize issues of causality and seek to produce closure—to explain and interpret the events narrated in Virgil's text and under reconsideration in Ovid's.[58] *Heroides* 7 ends as an explicit attempt at closure. Dido requests that her story be inscribed (*inscribar*) in a verse (*carmen*) as her epitaph:

> Praebuit Aeneas et causam mortis et ensem.
> Ipsa sua Dido concidit usa manu. (197–98)

> Aeneas supplied both the cause of death and the sword. Dido killed herself by her own hand.

As a final statement that purports to explain the events of *Aeneid* 4, this epitaph expresses only Dido's conviction that she has been betrayed by Aeneas. In the comparable passage in *Aeneid* 4, Virgil's Dido asserts her accomplishments as leader:

> uixi et quem dederat cursum Fortuna peregi,
> et nunc magna mei sub terras ibit imago.
> urbem praeclaram statui, mea moenia uidi,
> ulta uirum poenas inimico a fratre rcccpi. (653–56)

> I have lived and I have finished the course that Fortuna had given me, and now a noble image of me will go beneath the earth. I founded a renowned city. I saw my walls, in avenging a husband I punished a hostile brother.

Commentators frequently note the monumentalizing quality of lines 655–56. By contrast, the epitaph in *Heroides* 7 addresses only the immediate causes for Dido's suicide.[59] The single point of view articulated in *Heroides* 7 and the resulting attempts to produce closure illustrate the status of Ovid's text as a reading of Virgil's *Aeneid*. Given the interpretive authority that readers achieve in their attempts at closure, Dido's reading allows her to comment on the politics of gender and empire in Virgil's *Aeneid*.

Aeneas's description of his escape from Troy and the events leading to the death of Creusa illustrates the ambiguous status of women in Virgil's heroic world. In his narration of his family's departure from Troy, Aeneas reviews his decision to have Creusa follow along behind him ("et longe seruet uestigia coniunx" [2.711]), while he takes his father on his back and his son by the hand to lead them out of the burning city. Creusa slips his mind until it is too late: "nec prius amissam respexi animumue reflexi / quam tumulum antiquae Cereris sedemque sacratam / uenimus" (2.741–43) (I did not look back or turn back my thoughts to her, lost as she was, until we came to the mound of ancient Ceres and the hallowed site); and although Aeneas indulges in a long rhetorical expression of his loss (2.745–70), he does not blame himself for the decisions that led to Creusa's death. Indeed, he blames everyone but himself: "quem non incusaui amens hominumque deorumque" (745) (Distracted, whom did I not blame; what man or god?). Nevertheless, to the reader of Virgil's *Aeneid*, Creusa's loss clearly results from Aeneas's decision that his father and son deserve protection before his wife. Even within the context of a patriarchal culture, Creusa's death—as Aeneas tells it—presents disturbing contradictions. As Christine Perkell has shown, as Aeneas narrates this story to Dido, he unself-consciously represents the father and son as the only significant members of his family even as he mourns the death of his wife.[60]

In *Heroides* 7, Dido reacts to the implications in Aeneas's account of the loss of his wife. In the context of Aeneas's impending departure from Carthage, Dido reconsiders the whole narrative of his escape from Troy and his dutiful attention to the Penates and to his father:

Sed neque fers tecum nec quae mihi, perfide, iactas
   presserunt umeros sacra paterque tuos.
Omnia mentiris; neque enim tua fallere lingua
   incipit a nobis primaque plector ego:
Si quaeras ubi sit formosi mater Iuli—
   occidit a duro sola relicta viro.
Haec mihi narraras. . . . (79–85)

But you do not carry them with you, nor did your Penates or your father press your shoulders, as you, perfidious one, declare to me. You lie about everything. Nor does your deception start with me, nor am I the first to suffer: If you ask what has become of the mother of beautiful Iulus—she perished, abandoned alone by her harsh husband. This you had narrated to me. . . .

Ovid's Dido interprets Aeneas's role in this episode to his disadvantage. For instance, Ovid's Dido appears to echo and question Dido's assertion in *Aeneid* 4 about her understanding of Aeneas's character: "quem secum patrios aiunt portare penatis, / quem subiisse umeris confectum aetate parentem!" (4.598–99) (They say of him that he carried the paternal penates! That he supported with his shoulders his father, worn out with age). She not only challenges Aeneas's representation of his dutiful attention to his father and his household gods, but she also blames him specifically for Creusa's loss, since by not extending protection to Creusa, Aeneas abandoned his wife to her fate at the hands of the Greeks. In addition, Dido notes one further irony of *Aeneid* 2. Virgil's Dido listens to the account of Creusa's death without reacting. Ovid's Dido implies that Aeneas's account of this scene might have proved a warning for Virgil's Dido, had she heeded its implications. In this passage, Ovid's Dido adumbrates the unstated implications of *Aeneid* 2: that Aeneas himself tells Dido ("haec mihi narraras") of his behavior to his wife, behavior that Dido might have read more cynically, behavior that would have told her what Aeneas's actions in the *Aeneid* confirm— the queen of Carthage could expect no better treatment than Creusa had received.

In *Heroides* 7, Dido also reconsiders her understanding of the events in the cave (4.165–68). Ovid's Dido represents the scene in language that evokes and all but quotes the passage from Virgil:

Illa dies nocuit, qua nos declive sub antrum
    caeruleus subitis compulit imber aquis.
Audieram voces, nymphas ululasse putavi:
    Eumenides fatis signa dedere meis. (93–96)

That day destroyed me, when a dark storm cloud with sudden rain forced us under the steep cave. I had heard voices; I thought the nymphs had shrieked: the Eumenides gave the signal for my fate.

Having acquired the retrospective knowledge and understanding of a reader, Ovid's Dido shares the privileged point of view to which only the authoritative narrator had access in Virgil's text. In her comment "Illa dies nocuit," she echoes the interpretive authority of Virgil's narrator, whose own assertion emphasizes the implications of the cave scene for the unknowing Dido ("Ille dies primus leti primusque malorum / causa fuit"). In her allusion to the earlier, omniscient statement, and in her newly acquired omniscient point of view as speaker of *Heroides* 7, she exposes the limited understanding of Virgil's Dido as a participant in the cave scene. Likewise, she revises her understanding of the mock ritual in the cave and assigns the Eumenides the role ("Eumenides fatis signa dedere meis") that *Tellus* and Juno had played in Virgil's representation of the cave scene ("prima et Tellus et pronuba Iuno / dant signum"). By inserting the Eumenides into the cave scene, Ovid's Dido cites the Eumenides' appearance in a simile (469–73) used by the Virgilian narrator to describe Dido's later disintegration; Ovid's Dido thereby conflates the textual details of *Aeneid* 4 and exhibits the point of view of a reader of Virgil's text rather than a character in it. In this interpretation of Virgil's text, Dido implicitly questions whether Aeneas's presentation of himself as *pius Aeneas* (1.378) provides a valid category for understanding his character and motivations in the text as a whole, particularly in relation to his treatment of Creusa and Dido.

Heroides 7 echoes the language of *Aeneid* 4 throughout.[61] Most significant, however, are the passages that transform the implications of the passage alluded to in the earlier text. In Aeneas's final interview with Dido in Virgil's text, he sets forth a series of justifications for his departure, none of which satisfy Dido. He appeals, of course, to the divine plan that he found a new city in Italy, summarizing his commitment to this plan to the exclusion of all else: "hic amor, haec patria est" (4.347). As part of his explanation for his devotion to duty, he states that a messenger from the gods ("interpres diuum" [356]), as well as his father's ghost, have stressed the urgency of his mission. By this point in *Aeneid* 4, Virgil's Dido is already beyond hearing Aeneas's explanations with any degree of understanding and she rages wildly rather than responding directly to his speech (4.365–87).

In the *Aeneid*, Dido's response includes a brief comment about this divine messenger: "nunc et Ioue missus ab ipso / interpres diuum fert horrida iussa per auras" (377–78) (Now sent by Jove himself, the agent of the gods carries horrible orders through the air). Ovid's Dido mimics this response and characteristically engages more directly in the significance of Aeneas's assertions in the context of his own narrative. She challenges the adequacy of the divine plan as an explanation for human action by reference to Aeneas's own relationship to the gods:

"Sed iubet ire deus!" Vellem, vetuisset adire
Punica nec Teucris pressa fuisset humus.

> Hoc duce nempe deo ventis agitaris iniquis
> et teris in rapido tempora longa freto. (141–44)

"But a god orders you to go!" I wish he had forbidden you to come,
or that the Punic ground had not been trodden by Teucrians.
Certainly, led by this god you are blown on adverse winds and you
waste a long time in swift rapids.

Dido comments on the irony inherent in Aeneas's story—that Aeneas's
journey is certainly slow and difficult for a hero under divine protection.
In this passage she not only demystifies the relationship between mortals
and the divine, she likewise attempts to demythologize the sense of destiny and fate that the *Aeneid* so problematically represents. Ovid's Dido
punctuates her commentary on Aeneas's sense of duty when she offers
Carthage to Aeneas, not in abstract terms of *amor* and *patria*, but in terms
slightly devalued and more representative of Aeneas's needs as a fugitive:
"hic pacis leges, hic locus arma capit" (158) (Here holds a place for the
laws of peace, here a place for arms). In questioning the abstract values to
which Aeneas appeals and in mocking his excuses that the gods have
ordered his departure from Carthage, Ovid's Dido ultimately exposes the
imperial values to which Aeneas refers in his justification for his departure and his treatment of her.

Ovid's Dido also subverts the predominantly tragic, epic tone of
Aeneid 4 by emphasizing elements of pathos. In a moment of rhetorical
embellishment, she amplifies Virgil's Dido's wish that she were pregnant
(4.328–29) by carefully entertaining the possibility and referring to this
hypothetical, unborn child as Julus's brother (139). In the *Aeneid*, Dido's
desire to be pregnant is an expression of her desire to compel Aeneas to
honor his obligations to her; as Monti comments about this speech:
"Dido speaks like a Roman dynast."[62] Ovid's Dido, however, speaks as a
woman; she pointedly explores the possibility of this hypothetical pregnancy from a maternal, not a political, point of view—a gender-specific
interpretation of *Aeneid* 4. Compared to Virgil's Dido, whose concern for
the future of Carthage and the fate of the Carthaginians as a consequence
of Aeneas's departure makes possible the tragic scope of *Aeneid* 4, Ovid's
Dido emphatically foregrounds her personal concerns and her responses
as a particular woman overcome by desire, not a queen.

The pathos of *Heroides* 7 often depends on Ovid's literal interpretation
of the language of *Aeneid* 4. For instance, Dido reifies Aeneas's sword and
invites Aeneas and the reader to visualize her with Aeneas's sword on
her lap, wet with her tears and soon to be bathed in her blood (186–90).[63]
One fifteenth-century illumination of a French translation of *Heroides* 7
clearly accepts this invitation, an image that points to the sword as a fetish

in Ovid's text, a text that implicitly emphasizes the phallic value of the sword and the erotized quality of Dido's suicide in *Aeneid* 4. (See *figure 1.*) Such an attempt to visually evoke the poetic details of Virgil's narrative, however, works to expose the textuality of the *Aeneid*—its manipulation of metaphor and symbol in its depiction of Dido and her tragedy.

Ovid's Dido likewise acknowledges and simultaneously deflates the most powerful symbol of *Aeneid* 4, the representation of Dido's passion as *vulnus*, which is metaphorically evoked at the beginning of book 4 (67) and becomes a literal wound at the end of the book when Dido has stabbed herself with Aeneas's sword ("infixum stridit sub pectore uulnus" [689]). In language that heightens the erotic values of this wound, Ovid's Dido refers to the metaphorical wound and the symbolic value of the wound she is about to inflict upon herself:

> Nec mea nunc primum feriuntur pectora telo:
> ille locus saevi vulnus amoris habet. (191–92)

> Nor is my heart pierced first by the sword: that place has the wound of cruel love.

Her assertion that her heart already has a wound betrays her awareness of this metaphor from *Aeneid* 4. Her crude use of this metaphor, "saevi vulnus amoris," however, minimizes its force in comparison to the *Aeneid*, where Dido's inability to think of her passion in metaphorical or abstract terms suggests her lack of vision and consequent vulnerability. By having Dido herself express the connection between the metaphorical and literal wound, Ovid again allows Dido a point of view that only the narrator or reader of Virgil's text possesses. Yet by allowing Dido the position of a reader whose literal interpretations emphasize the pathos in the narrative, and by frequently making the implicit explicit, *Heroides* 7 effectively deflates the metaphorical quality of Virgil's language.

At a critical moment in Virgil's *Aeneid* 4, when Mercury appears to Aeneas to command his departure, he tells Aeneas: "uarium et mutabile semper / femina" (4.569–70) (a variable and changeable thing is woman always). Although such an antifeminist statement is not a normative assertion for the entire text of the *Aeneid*, this pithy definition of *femina* nonetheless casts a long shadow over the *Aeneid*: much of the chaos and instability in the cosmos as well as in society is attributed to the feminine. Ovid's *Heroides* 7 depends on a discernibly different concept of *femina*, a definition of woman as a skeptical reader of language and meaning. Dido echoes Mercury's comment to complain of Aeneas and implicitly negate Mercury's comment: "Tu quoque cum ventis utinam mutabilis esses" (51) (Would that you too were changeable with the winds).

omc le fnÿne quât mozt luy eft pcbainc
Doulcem et chante et a Boix tresseraine
parillement re dido pour tout Boir.
Qui ne te puis par prier esmouuoir
Et plus nay en ta bie esperance
O: ce te fait scauoir ma doleance
Br scay pourtant que ma malheurete
Empeschera toute ma boulente
Haue puis que iay perdu ma renommee
Et le bon bruit dont ie fus estimee

1. Dido writes her letter with the sword on her lap. *Heroides* 7 in French translation by
Octovien de Saint-Gelais. Balliol MS 383, fol. 30v. Fifteenth century. By permission of the
Master and Fellows of Balliol College, Oxford.

The elegiac context of *Heroides* 7 emphasizes the pathos of Dido's lament detached from the narrative context of the *Aeneid;* the Ovidian focus thereby removes Dido from the political context of Virgil's narrative and erases her identity as *dux.* When Dido reads Virgil, she reads Dido as *amans.* Yet the politics of desire, and the politics of the Latin love elegy, provide a context from which to critique the problematic representation of epic deeds and values never quite fully understood by any of the characters in the text, least of all by Dido. From outside the text, as reader rather than character, she is able to question both deeds and values particularly with reference to gender and textuality. In this respect, Ovid's *Heroides* 7 appears representative of readers' responses to the *Aeneid* as well as an influential reading of the *Aeneid* that has encouraged such response.

Heroides 7 explicitly relies on the elegiac category of the *amans* in its exploration of desire; since this *amans* is a female reader of Virgil, hence a "cultivated" woman, *Heroides* 7 draws on the elegiac categories of the *domina.* As Paul Allen Miller observes, this period produced the *docta puella*—the skillful courtesan whose cultivated tastes and political influence represented no small threat in Augustan Rome.[64] A century after the Ovidian depiction of Dido as a reader of Virgil, the persistence of the stereotype of the "learned woman" was given its full misogynous interpretation in Juvenal's sixth satire. In that context, Juvenal assumes that for the woman reader (reading is a transgressive act comparable to the sexual transgressions cataloged in this diatribe), reading Virgil means reading Dido:

illa tamen gravior, quae cum discumbere coepit,
laudat Vergilium, periturae ignoscit Elissae. (6.434–35)

That woman, however, is more oppressive who, upon reclining at the table, praises Virgil, excuses Dido about to perish.

The Medieval Dido

The medieval Dido must initially be seen in relation to these variations on the figure of Dido in the ancient world: the historical, heroic Dido, rewritten by Virgil in his depiction of the tragic, angry queen of *Aeneid* 4, and Ovid's more affective—though, to many modern readers, less effective—Dido in *Heroides* 7. These overlaid traditions of Dido in Latin historical and poetic texts provide the landmarks by which we might orient our study of Dido's itinerary in medieval textual cultures; nevertheless, the trajectory of Dido's story often separates her from these classical texts. *Heroides* 7 occasionally generated texts in direct imitation that may be considered unadulterated versions of Ovidian influence, such as the fourth-century anonymous epistle from Dido to Aeneas, a 150-line North African text.[65] The Dido who writes this letter repeatedly suppresses her anger and emphasizes the desperate quality of her desire for Aeneas. Although several details in the text suggest an awareness of Virgil's *Aeneid* 4, the tone and treatment of emotional states are demonstrably Ovidian; indeed, several lines from *Heroides* 7 are evoked.[66]

Medieval versions of the Aeneas-Dido story frequently appear to conflate the Ovidian and the Virgilian Dido, a consequence of the fact that Ovid's *Heroides* 7 insinuates itself so intricately into the Virgilian pre-text that it complicates the attempt to assign responsibility for any one medieval representation of Dido to either classical poet. If the medieval Dido very often resembles Ovid's Dido in exhibiting less anger and more pathos than she does in the *Aeneid*, the plot of *Aeneid* 4 nonetheless provides the context for many vernacular treatments of Dido. The fact that the vernacular Dido is often a hybrid of the Virgilian and Ovidian figures reflects the complex issues of reception and readership of classical texts. Compared to the enormous cultural authority of Virgil's *Aeneid* throughout the late antique and medieval West, the *Heroides* remain relatively unknown and unread until the middle of the twelfth century. At that point, however, the *Heroides* begin to circulate widely, and during the next few centuries they become one of the most frequently read and cited texts from the Ovidian corpus.[67]

That medieval readers of *Heroides* 7 implicitly juxtaposed Ovid's Dido to Virgil's Dido is illustrated in an early school commentary produced in the third quarter of the twelfth century at the Benedictine monastery of Tegernsee in southern Germany.[68] In the three *accessus* to the *Heroides* that are preserved along with the commentary, the commentator presents the student of Ovid with a moral context by which to judge the desire of the Ovidian heroines: Penelope, whose epistle is first, programmatically represents the ideal of chaste marital love against which the illicit or foolish (*legitimus, illicitus, stultus*) love of the other heroines is measured.[69] Given the narrative context of the Trojan War in which Penelope's desire is performed, the *accessus* mentions the Troy story as an explanation for the separation of Penelope and Ulysses and the conditions in which she writes to Ulysses. Penelope's story thus provides both the moral and narrative framework for the rest of the *Heroides*; central to this framework is the issue of disciplining desire implied by the dogmatic intentions attributed to Ovid as author of these texts.

The initial gloss to *Heroides* 7 evokes the fall of Troy and notes that Aeneas is on his way to Italy under orders from the gods when he is carried by an adverse wind to Libya, a comment that loosely paraphrases *Metamorphoses* 14.77. However, for the rest of the narrative context, the commentator calls upon the plot of the *Aeneid* (without naming Virgil or his text) to fill in the details necessary to a reading of *Heroides* 7. This gloss explains that Dido fell in love with Aeneas and that he was admonished by the gods after one year to proceed to Italy against the wishes of Dido. Dido's story thereby exemplifies foolish love, "Ex intentione auctoris stultus amans arguitur" (by the author's intention, the foolish lover is denounced), a moral reading that obliquely points to the fact that Dido refers to herself as *stulta* at line 28.

The commentary provides a wealth of narrative detail. An early gloss describes Dido's background and her purchase of land from Iarbas through the trick of the ox hide. At line 95, the commentator explains Dido's situation by reference to Sychaeus's death, his appearance to Dido in a dream, and his instructions for her exile. The glosses are highly explanatory; nonetheless, they make possible something of an intertextual reading of *Heroides* 7 by presenting such a narrative context for Ovid's text. For instance, at line 94, when Ovid's Dido reconsiders her understanding of the cave scene, the commentator provides the essential details of *Aeneid* 4:

> IMBER AQVIS. Dido et Eneas ierant quadam die uenatum. contigit autem ut, tempestatem grandem fugientes omnes qui erant in uenatione, ipsi duo in antro conuenirent ubi primo cum ea concubuit.

> Dido and Eneas had gone hunting on a certain day. Moreover, it happened that, since everyone on the hunt fled a large storm, these two met in a cave, where he first lay with her.

The medieval reader of *Heroides* 7 who takes a cue from this commentary might well appreciate some of the irony in Dido's comments as she revises her sense of the significance of the events in the cave. The commentary itself does not, of course, force the sort of ironies that result from juxtaposing *Heroides* 7 to *Aeneid* 4; however, the explanation in the gloss suggests that Ovid's text at this moment refers to an event already narrated in an earlier text—and that earlier text, Virgil's *Aeneid*, would very likely already be well known to the student of Latin poetry. Since Ovid's Dido does depict herself as a *stultus amans*, and since she sees the cave scene as an example of her foolish blindness regarding Aeneas, this brief gloss on the cave scene at least makes possible a reading of Ovid's Dido as a figure extracted from the narrative context of *Aeneid* 4, yet still involved in a revision of that context.

The *Heroides* also circulated widely in medieval vernacular culture as part of the *Ovide moralisé*, a text that, as Rita Copeland puts it, "seems to contain and rehearse within its own boundaries the very practice and history of the textual transmission of Ovid in the Middle Ages."[70] Thus book 14 of the *Ovide moralisé* includes a version of *Heroides* 7 inserted after the brief summary of the *Aeneid* that appears in the Latin text at line 81.[71] The persistence of this tradition may be measured not only by the presence of the *Heroides* in the prose versions of the moralized *Metamorphoses* but also in Caxton's version of *Metamorphoses* 14, part of a text that appears to have been prepared for publication, yet never published.[72] As an "Englished" prose version of a French translation of Ovid, Caxton's *Metamorphoses* predictably includes a lament voiced by Dido in book 14. *Heroides* 7 has by now drifted very far from its Latin "origins."

The *Heroides* also appear in late medieval and early Renaissance vernacular culture as a distinct set of texts. They were translated into French in the last decade of the fifteenth century by Octovien de Saint-Gelais, a version that circulated widely in manuscript and print.[73] The particular appeal of *Heroides* 7 is evident in the "Letter of Dido," an English translation of a French version of *Heroides* 7 included in Richard Pynson's 1526 edition of several of Chaucer's works and indirectly attributed to Chaucer.[74] Since Ovid is not mentioned as the author of this text, the author-function implied by the title, "Letter of Dido," makes Dido the honorary author of her letter. The vernacular tradition of *Heroides* 7 has removed the text from its classical author and implicitly assigned it to the speaker of the poem.

This "Letter of Dido" is part of a collection that includes the *Book of Fame*, a text that provides the premise for the reader's interest in the "Letter of Dido." The "Letter of Dido" is framed by the translator's preface and envoy and introduced visually by a woodcut (see figure 2) that depicts Dido about to fall on the sword in front of a burning funeral pyre in the foreground; the outlines of a city appear in the background. The translator briefly notes the events leading up to the writing of this letter—the fall of Troy, the seven-year journey of Aeneas, the rescue of his men through divine influence, the intentions of Venus and Juno to marry him to Dido, and his decision to break his promise ("but this untrue man / brake the promise / wherefore thus she began"). Such introduction presents the narrative from the *Aeneid* story as the specific context in which the letter is composed, and the image of Dido's suicide visually enacts the end of *Aeneid* 4.[75] Although the "Letter of Dido" drops out of the Chaucer canon after Pynson—none of the black letter editions of Chaucer include this text—its presence in this edition alongside the text of Chaucer's *Book of Fame* illustrates the paradoxical situation evident in both the textual autonomy of *Heroides* 7 and its intertextual dependence on the Virgilian plot as context.

Throughout both the Latin and the vernacular traditions of medieval

2. Dido falls on the sword. Woodcut. "Letter of Dido," Pynson's edition of Chaucer's *Book of Fame* (1526). By permission of the Houghton Library, Harvard University.

literary culture, Dido's story (in its Virgilian/Ovidian form) circulates as a unit more or less detached from the larger narrative of the *Aeneid* and yet still identified with it.[76] If Dido is not routinely subsumed by the Virgilian story that sees her story as an episode in the travels of Aeneas, the outlines of the Aeneas-Dido story are necessary to activate Dido's status as an abandoned woman. In the *Carmina Burana* (ca. 1200), for instance, Dido's voice is heard in two *planctus*, similar in form but quite different in tone from the *Heroides*. If, like the *Heroides*, these *planctus* provide a performative text for female desire, they nonetheless lack the declamatory basis of Ovid's texts. Both *planctus* imply a narrative context for Dido's lament, though that context depends only on a rudimentary knowledge of the plot of the *Aeneid*; indeed, the reader needs only to recall that Dido was the queen of Carthage and that Aeneas abandoned her.[77] The *Aeneid* story is evoked, as in *Heroides* 7, as though Dido herself knew the plot of the entire narrative, such as when she names Lavinia:

> nam sitientis Libyae
> regina spreta linquitur,
> et thalamos Laviniae
> Troianus hospes sequitur![78] (46–49)

> For the spurned queen of arid Libya is abandoned, and the Trojan guest seeks the marriage bed of Lavinia.

This Dido has emerged from the *Aeneid* story and looks back on it.

In vernacular texts, the Dido story occurs as a brief, citational unit that makes some general reference to her position as a heroine abandoned by her lover. La Vieille in the *Roman de la Rose*, for instance, introduces a short (forty-line) version of the Dido story simply by reference to Dido's attempts to retain Aeneas:

> Onc ne pot Enee tenir
> Dydo, reïne de Cartage,
> qui tant li ot fet d'avantage
> que povre l'avoit receü
> et revestu et repeü,
> las et fuitif du biau païs
> de Troie, dom il fu naïs.[79] (vv. 13144–50)

> Dido, queen of Carthage, could not hold Eneas, though she had done so much for him; she had received him impoverished and restored and nourished him, an exhausted exile from the good country of Troy where he was born.

Similar exempla of the Dido story occur throughout medieval texts, so that Gower or Machaut,[80] for example, could allude to Dido as a particular kind of tragic, amatory heroine, an Ovidian treatment that marginalizes the interpretive framework of the *Aeneid* itself or the entire *Aeneid* story, but nonetheless relies on the basic outline of the Virgilian plot. As part of her instruction of Bel Accueil, La Vieille evokes Dido in a brief catalog of women from the *Heroides* that includes Oenone, Phyllis, and Medea, in order to illustrate the dangers women face when they base all their hope on one man. In Dido's case, her fatal error, as far as La Vieille is concerned, is that she trusts a lover's oath. Dido's skepticism in *Heroides*

7 is replaced in the *Roman de la Rose* by the skeptical figure of La Vieille (a male creation of a female skeptic), who reads the *Heroides* as exempla of women who love too much. La Vieille may not voice the normative discourse in the poem (indeed, she undercuts her own discourse),[81] but her long speech presents something of a skeptical critique of *fin amors* from a female point of view intended to suggest how the female object of desire can turn the situation to her advantage. In such a context, Dido's story as it is presented in *Heroides* 7—where she blames herself for her blind acceptance of Aeneas—becomes an exemplum of the dangers of love for women.

This tradition of exemplification derived from the *Heroides*[82] makes possible the placement of Dido in catalogs of women, such as Chaucer's list of betrayed women in the *Book of the Duchess*, where he pairs Dido and Phyllis:

And Phyllis also for Demophoun
Heng hirself—so weylaway!—
For he had broke his terme-day
To come to hir. Another rage
Had Dydo, the quene eke of Cartage,
That slough hirself for Eneas
Was fals—which a fool she was![83] (728–34)

The textual exempla of Dido's story constitute a tradition that is often evoked simply by a brief citation of her suicide, often (as we see in the *Roman de la Rose*) in graphic language that eroticizes her death. The visual representations of Dido that occur in manuscript illuminations of the *Roman de la Rose*[84] reflect this tradition of exemplification. The Dido story in the *Roman* draws particular attention to the phallic qualities of Dido's penetration by the sword, since La Vieille explicitly notes that the naked Dido placed the upturned sword between her breasts and fell on it: "L'espee prent, et toute nue / la drece encontremont la pointe, / souz ses .II. mameles l'apointe / seur le glaive se let choair" (13169–72) (she took the sword, and completely naked, encountering the upright point and inserting it beneath her two breasts, she let herself fall on the sword). This moment is frequently illustrated in the illuminated manuscripts of the *Rose*, though the illuminators never, to my knowledge, depict Dido as a nude figure. (See figures 3, 4, and 5.) The image of Dido falling on the sword functions as a visual gloss that pictorially interprets the suicide by aligning the reader's gaze with the phallic sword and its penetration of Dido's body; the gaze thereby implicates the reader in the aggressive penetration of Dido's body by the sword.[85] The miniatures in the *Rose* text are usually placed within the text and thereby function as a

3. Dido falls on the sword. *Roman de la Rose*. London, British Library, Egerton 881, fol. 101r. Fourteenth century. By permission of the British Library.

visual break in the textual portion of the narrative. Such images not only present a sexualized pictorial gloss on the texts they illustrate, but through the politics of the gaze they also construct the reader as a partic-ipant in the specular, sexual dynamics of reading.

The *Rose* miniatures appear as visual exempla that work to emblema-tize the Dido story. Like the textual personifications of figures such as Haine, Felonie, and Vilenie, who are visually rendered in the pictorial pro-gram that accompanies manuscripts of the first *Rose* text, the visual re-

4. Dido falls on the sword. *Roman de la Rose.* MS Douce 195, fol. 94v. Fifteenth century. By permission of the Bodleian Library, University of Oxford.

presentations of Dido reduce the text to a single visual meaning depicted in Dido's eroticized death. In Michael Camille's terms, "the visual is always much more explicit than the verbal because words bear no iconic resemblance to the things they signify."[86] As a text, the Dido story is rehearsed within the discourse of La Vieille—a potentially subversive discourse that is undermined; as an image, Dido becomes simply an object of the readerly gaze much as the rose is the object of allegorical desire. The

5. Dido falls on the sword. *Roman de la Rose*. MS Douce 371, fol. 87r. Fifteenth century. By permission of the Bodleian Library, University of Oxford.

visual, iconographic shorthand of the illumination transforms the critique of *amor courtois* presented by La Vieille into an erotized representation of Dido falling on the sword. This image—textual and visual—of Dido in the *Rose* functions as an important visual pre-text for Chaucer and Christine de Pizan, as we shall see.

The visual Dido—almost exclusively the product of vernacular texts[87]—is the extreme manifestation of the exempla tradition that separates Dido from the classical Latin texts of Virgil and Ovid. The Virgilian/Ovidian Dido acquires a certain amount of textual autonomy in the vernacular tradition. Although there is clearly no one reading of Dido —the commentators on *Heroides* 7 and La Vieille each exploit the foolishness of Dido's love for entirely different ends—Dido is nonetheless the focus of interpretive gestures that treat the *Aeneid* context of her story as background. In any case, the medieval tradition of reading Dido in vernacular culture disrupts the paradigm of medieval allegorical interpretation of the Virgilian Dido as *libido* in relation to the biography of Aeneas (traced in chapter 2), a tradition that stretches from Augustine to Dante; this approach reads the *Aeneid* as a masculinist narrative of the human soul or the brave man. Within vernacular culture, by contrast, readerly interest in the *Aeneid* story settles on Dido. However, as Petrarch's comment at the beginning of this chapter makes clear, the intertextual possibilities for reading Dido also depend on the historical tradition, first attested to in the texts of Timaeus and Justin; this series of texts, as we have already seen, explicitly depict Dido's story outside the context of the *Aeneid*. We must now consider the implications of the historical Dido to our understanding of the intertextual possibilities of Dido and the medieval *Aeneid*.

Countermemory and the Historical Dido

Although almost forgotten by modern readers, the historical Dido had her readers and her champions throughout the late antique period and into the Middle Ages. Justin's account from the second century demonstrates that the tradition of the historical Dido persisted in spite of Virgil's authoritative revision of her story. Late antique readers of *Aeneid* 4— Augustine, Jerome, Tertullian, and Macrobius, among others—frequently responded to Virgil's Dido by explicitly juxtaposing their experience of Virgil's text to their awareness of the historical Dido. In the *Saturnalia* 5.17, Macrobius (ca. 400) explicitly remarks upon the two traditions:

Thus he has modeled his fourth book of the *Aeneid* almost entirely on the fourth book of the *Argonautica* of Apollonius by taking the story of Medea's passionate love for Jason and applying it to the loves of Dido and Aeneas. And here he has arranged the subject matter so much more tastefully than his model that the story of Dido's passion, which all the world knows to be fiction, has nevertheless for all these many years been regarded as true (per tot tamen saecula speciem veritatis obtineat). For it so wings its way, as truth, through the lips of all men, that painters and sculptors and those who represent human figures in tapestry take it for their theme in preference to any other, when they fashion their likenesses, as if it were the one subject in which they can display their artistry; and actors too, no less, never cease to celebrate the story with gesture and in song. Indeed, the beauty of Vergil's narrative has so far prevailed that, although all are aware of the chastity of the Phoenician queen and know that she laid hands on herself to save her good name, still they turn a blind eye to the fiction, suppress in their minds the evidence of the truth (intra conscientiam veri fidem prementes), and choose rather to regard as true the tale which the charm of a poet's imagination has implanted in the hearts of mankind.[88]

In juxtaposing the fictionality of Virgil's narrative to the historical tradition, Macrobius must nevertheless acknowledge the power and affective quality of Virgil's representation of Dido, since it not only usurps the "true," historical version but inspires visual and performative versions that transcend the written text and result in pictorial and dramatic re-enactments. (See figure 6.) The survival of a mosaic among the Roman artifacts from a fourth-century villa at Lo Ham in Somerset, England, testifies to Macrobius's assertions regarding the popularity of *Aeneid* 4 as a visual text. The mosaic depicts the love affair from *Aeneid* 1 and 4. The interpretation of *Aeneid* 4 as a story of Dido's passion ("fabula lascivientis Didonis") is evident in the portrayal of the lovers: in each of the three scenes in which she appears (the banquet, the hunt, and the cave), Dido's partially clothed body is juxtaposed to Aeneas's clothed body, thereby connecting Dido to the nude image of Venus in the centerpiece and locating the sexual danger of the narrative in the physical attractions of the female body.[89] Although the text of the *Saturnalia* and this set of images were produced at entirely different locations, both attest to the popularity of Virgil's depiction of Dido. Nonetheless, Macrobius's explicit juxtaposition of this version of Dido's passion to the "chastity of the Phoenician queen" ("Phoenissae castitatis") demonstrates the extent to which the Virgilian tradition of Dido's story seemed to readers such as Macrobius to include the countermemory of the historical Dido.

Servius, Augustine, and John of Salisbury, among others, acknowledge this dual tradition, as we shall see in chapter 2. For a Christian writer like Jerome, the non-Virgilian Dido—given the authority of historical "truth" —could be read against Virgil. In the context of the early Christian church, the historical Dido fit neatly into discussions of female chastity. Her determination not to marry Iarbas—a conviction that leads to her dramatic suicide in Justin and Timaeus—could be made to illustrate the extent to which a "virtuous" woman might go to avoid a second marriage. Toward the end of the first book of *Adversus Jovinianum*, the influential discussion of female sexuality that was to reverberate throughout the tradition of medieval misogyny, Jerome briefly evokes the historical Dido as one of several pagan examples of chaste widowhood.[90] Jerome even reads her death on the funeral pyre as a pagan version of the Pauline doctrine, since it demonstrated that Dido "maluit ardere quam nubere" (she preferred to burn rather than marry). Jerome's privileging of the historical Dido in this section of the treatise is emphasized at the end of book 2 when he cites a line from *Aeneid* 4 ("conjugium vocat, hoc praetexit nomine culpam" [4.172])[91] that betrays his moral disapproval of Virgil's version of Dido's story. Thus the chaste Dido of the historical tradition could be recuperated for Christian efforts at circumscribing female sexuality within the reigning discourses of the late antique church.[92] By such mechanisms, the historical Dido becomes the "chaste" Dido fre-

6. Lo Ham Mosaic. The story of Dido and Aeneas from *Aeneid* 1 and 4. Right: Trojans arrive in Carthage. Top: Venus and Cupid flanked by Dido and Aeneas. Left: the Hunt. Bottom: the cave scene. Center: Venus with cupids. Fourth century. Taunton County Museum. By permission of the Somerset County Council Museums Service.

quently deployed by writers such as Tertullian in their discursive efforts at managing sexuality, particularly female sexuality.[93]

In medieval literary traditions, traditions dominated by misogynous and misogamous discourse,[94] Dido is essentially characterized by her sexuality—either by her ability to resist sexual temptation in the historical version or by her tendency to succumb to sexual desire in the Virgilian tradition. The misogynous strain in medieval literatures reflects the extent to which the institution of marriage was the building block of secular society, and marriage required the regulation of female sexuality—the explicit purpose of medieval misogyny as well as the standard aim of medieval discourse of chastity. Dido's status as a widow becomes the definitive marker for the medieval reader. At the end of the Middle Ages, Boccaccio's Latin prose writings repeatedly take the historical Dido as an exemplum of the chaste widow. Boccaccio's Dido makes evident the misogyny implicit in the Christian ideal of chaste widowhood.

Recognized as the "true" Dido by many readers, the historical Dido might be evoked to expose the fictionality of *Aeneid* 4 or to adjust the pagan text of the *Aeneid* to a Christian context. As a countermemory to the Virgilian Dido, the historical Dido was transmitted to the High Middle Ages by several means. Texts such as Servius's commentary on the *Aeneid*, Jerome's *Adversus Jovinianum*, Augustine's *Confessions*, or Tertullian's *De monogamia*, all of which circulated to some degree among learned medieval readers, provide some brief notice of the historical version of Dido's story. The outlines of the historical version even permeate the thirteenth-century French prose work, the *Histoire ancienne jusqu'à César*, as we shall see in chapter 3. But the historical Dido would be best known to readers of Justin's *Epitoma historiarum Philippicarum Pompei Trogi*, a text that survives in some two dozen medieval manuscripts and appears—via Servius—to have helped shape historical texts such as the *Histoire*.[95] But for our purposes, the most important late medieval reader of Justin's *Epitoma* was Giovanni Boccaccio, whose fourteenth-century Latin texts repeatedly rehearse the historical version of Dido's story as it appears in Justin's text. Boccaccio's interest in the historical Dido provides the conduit by which the non-Virgilian, historical Dido became known to late medieval vernacular readers and writers such as Christine de Pizan, John Lydgate, the author of the French prose *Eneydes*, or William Caxton.

As several scholars have noted, Boccaccio's Didos are multiple. He frequently evokes the Virgilian Dido in his vernacular poetry, yet in his late prose Latin texts he repeatedly dismisses the fiction of Virgil's text in preference for the historical truth of Justin's version of Dido's life;[96] that is, the historical Dido could facilitate the sort of moral reading that Boccaccio generally develops in his Latin writings, particularly those composed under the influence of his friendship with Petrarch.[97] Boccaccio's overt interest in the historical Dido is evident in *Genealogia deorum* 2; the historical Dido also provides the context for reading Dido in *De claris mulieribus*, *De casibus virorum illustrium* and the commentary on Dante. These are the texts that connect Boccaccio most explicitly with humanism, and the writing and rewriting of these texts occupied Boccaccio for the last few decades of his life. Janet Smarr has pointed out that Boccaccio's late texts "reveal a growing distrust of his readers' abilities to understand ironies and allegories," a distrust that perhaps reflects the fact that his final works also mark a "change in the audience itself as Boccaccio moved from the court of Naples to the bourgeoisie of Florence."[98] And, as Smarr notes, after he produced his last fictional (and most stridently misogynist) text, the *Corbaccio*, Boccaccio appears to have turned his attention solely to questions about "what fictions mean when they are read correctly."[99] In the context of his shift from the vernacular to the more authoritative Latin and his parallel shift in authorial concern from producing fictions to reading (and thereby rewriting) fictions, Boccaccio's treatment of Dido in his Latin texts provides a focus for his humanist angst about the dangers of poetry, especially pagan Latin poetry.

The last two books of Boccaccio's *Genealogia deorum* constitute a humanist defense of poetry, a defense intended to demonstrate the value and authority of poetry despite its status as fiction;[100] this defense of poetry relies heavily on the discourse of misogyny. In a key passage in Book 14 of his *Genealogia*, Boccaccio conflates the attractions of poetry and the attractions of women. In defending poetry against the charge that it leads to licentiousness, Boccaccio readily grants that some (normative male) readers, already enmeshed in the sexual attractions of women, will find poetry, particularly the poetry of Catullus, Propertius, and Ovid, seductive in and of itself ("tanquam in hoc toto inclinati pectore, volentes trahuntur, seducuntur, atque tenentur" [p. 729]) (with wholehearted inclination they surrender to its influence, are deluded, seduced, and enthralled [p. 77]).[101] Indeed, at one point in this discussion, Boccaccio suggests that not all readers are morally and intellectually capable of negotiating the dangers of poetry. Since such readers cannot resist the sexual temptations represented by women, Boccaccio does not consider them capable of negotiating the variable attractions of poetry:

Quid enim de his arbitrari possumus, si puella lascivis gestibus, petulcis oculis, blandis verbis spem polliceatur infaustam, postquam a mutis, seu tacitis carminibus seducuntur? Erubescant igitur miseri, et in melius insanum suum reforment consilium, prospectentque Ulixem, gentilem hominem, non mutorum carminum, sed mellifluos syrenarum cantus sprevisse tanquam nocuos atque transisse. (p. 730)

What might one expect of them in case a girl by licentious glance and gesture, and soft utterance, held out an unholy promise to them, if they are allured by unuttered verses perused in silence? Well may the wretches blush and revise their mad counsel, considering how Ulysses, noble soul, spurned the sound, not of songs read in the closet, but the dulcet music of the Sirens, whom he passed by for fear of harm at their hands. (p. 77)

The reader, figured as male, risks being seduced by the text-as-siren. Such emphasis on the predispositions of the reader in the face of the seductive risks of poetry is not original to Boccaccio; indeed, this formulation essentially restates the standard Augustinian approach to reading, which places moral responsibility on the reader.[102] Nonetheless, Boccaccio's statement clarifies the politics of reading that informs his particular reaction to Dido and his reading of Virgil throughout his scholarly texts.

Boccaccio's theory of reading as the negotiation of dangerous attractions (the risk that *carmen* might be a "puella lascivis gestibus, petulcis oculis, blandis verbis") depicts the reader as a male heterosexual subject whose desire for women/texts must be disciplined or controlled, since it might otherwise undermine his stability. In the reading of *Aeneid* 4 as it is developed in *Genealogia* 14, the reader is analogous to Aeneas, whose final resistance to sexual temptation is exemplary: "quod robur animi ad illudendas frangendasque amoris petulci catenas" (p. 728) (What strength of character in spurning and breaking the chains of an obstreperous passion! [75]). Within this paradigm, Boccaccio's interest in the psychology of female sexuality shapes his understanding of Virgil's Dido:

> Secundo, quod sub velamento latet poetico, intendit Virgilius per totum opus ostendere quibus passionibus humana fragilitas infestetur, et quibus viribus a constanti viro superentur . . . introducit Dydonem generositate sanguinis claram, etate iuvenem, forma spectabilem, moribus insignem, divitiis habundantem, castitate famosam, prudentia atque eloquentia circumspectam, civitati sue et populo imperantem, et viduam, quasi ab experientia Veneris concupiscientie aptiorem. (p. 722)

> Vergil's second purpose, concealed within the poetic veil, was to show with what passions human frailty is infested, and the strength with which a steady man subdues them . . . he introduces Dido, a woman of distinguished family, young, fair, rich, exemplary, famous for her purity, ruler of her city and people, of conspicuous wisdom and eloquence, and, lastly, a widow, and thus from former experience in love, the more easily disposed to that passion. (p. 68)

Dido's widowhood marks her as a sexually dangerous woman, a reading supported by the medieval assumption that widows were highly sexual women whose unattached status made them a particular threat to the social order.[103] Boccaccio repeatedly explores this cultural stereotype of the widow in his vernacular texts, and he exploits the misogynist anxiety regarding the widow most fully in the *Corbaccio*.

From Boccaccio's perspective, Dido's widowhood—a historical fact provided by Justin—gives verisimilitude to the passionate drama Dido enacts in Virgil's *Aeneid* 4, even if Virgil's text is technically a fiction. The reader, along with Aeneas, should spurn the temptations represented by Dido: "Et tunc nexum oblectationis infauste solvimus, quando, armati fortitudine, blanditias, lacrimas, preces, et huius modi in contrarium trahentes, constanti animo spernimus, ac vilipendentes omittimus" (p. 723) (Then we burst the bonds of unholy delight, and, armed with new fortitude, we unfalteringly spurn all seductive flattery, and tears, prayers, and such, and abandon them as naught [p. 69]). If Boccaccio sees *Aeneid* 4 as a reading of the sexual dangers represented by Dido particularly, and by female sexuality generally, his efforts at overcoming his anxiety about the attractions of pagan Latin poetry attempt to desexualize poetry, to read it so that its seductive powers are circumscribed by the moral context brought to it by the reader.

By contrast to Boccaccio's critical engagement with Virgil's *Aeneid* in his elaborate defense of poetry in the last two books of the *Genealogia*, his version of Dido's story in book 2 illustrates his interest in Justin's version. The first twelve books of the *Genealogia* constitute an encyclopedic effort at collecting and narrating the standard plots of classical myths—often arranged around the biography of a god or hero.[104] Boccaccio's interest in the historical Dido is understandable, since Justin's version of the story, which concludes that as long as Carthage stood, Dido was celebrated as a deity, lends textual support for the euhemeristic model that he adapts so thoroughly in his discussion of the pagan gods in the *Genealogia*. In book 2, Boccaccio's rehearsal of the basic "stories" connected to Dido illustrates his initial efforts at negotiating the conflicting textual traditions that his critical stance in book 14 is intended to resolve. Boccaccio's presentation of Dido (2.60)—a brief 270 words—shows traces of his struggles with the conflicting authorities of Virgil's *Aeneid* 4 and the historical account. In narrating Dido's story, Boccaccio betrays his preference for Justin's version of Dido's story.

The brief summary in *Genealogia* 2 notes that Virgil presented one version of Dido's death, but that story lacks the support of the historical texts: "Virgilio placet, eamque, discedente a se Enea, ob amoris impatientiam occisam. Verum Justinus et historiographi veteres aliter sentiunt" (p. 106) (And, according to Virgil, this one killed herself, Aeneas having departed from her, out of impatience with love. Truly, Justin and the other historians think differently). Such contradictions, acknowledged as they are at this stage of the *Genealogia*, become the basis of Boccaccio's conviction that the compelling version of Dido's story—particularly the version he would later present to women readers in *De claris mulieribus*—is the historical version.

In *Genealogia* 2, Boccaccio introduces Dido with a comment that her chastity made her a credit to married women ("Dydo precipuum matronalis pudicitie decus" [p. 106]), thus providing a moral interpretation for Dido's rejection of Iarbas and her suicide. Most of his narrative is a dense summary of Justin's text; indeed, he echoes Justin quite closely in places. Justin's version provides details that Boccaccio merely summarizes, however. As noted earlier, Dido's actions following the death of Pygmalion—her leadership in assembling ships and fleeing, in deceptively hoarding wealth, and in abducting women to serve as wives in the founding of Carthage—suggest a transgression of normative expectations for women in the sex-gender system of the ancient world or in Boccaccio's Italy. Thus Boccaccio, following a comment of Servius, literally characterizes her actions as masculine: he states that she took on the spirit of a man "sumpto virili animo" (p. 106). This pithy comment not only replaces a certain amount of detail in Justin's text; it also represents the basic characterization of the historical Dido for Boccaccio. Indeed, he essentially repeats the idea in *De claris mulieribus* and *De casibus*, and he includes it in his commentary on Dante. In Boccaccio's terms, Dido is essentially a credit to her sex because she has transcended its normative boundaries by refusing to perform as a sexual woman.

In *De claris mulieribus*, Boccaccio states his intention to produce a text that will encourage female virtue through a moral reading of classical figures: the text is dedicated to a woman, and Boccaccio's introductory comments concern the reception of his work by women. Nonetheless, given his raw material—women of antiquity—he can only consider a limited number of women who are *clarae* to be virtuous. Much of *De claris mulieribus* presents negative examples, such as Semiramis or Medea, whose failings—usually attributed to their rampant and uncontrollable sexuality—are loudly denounced by the narrator. In addition, throughout *De claris mulieribus*, Boccaccio betrays his hierarchical assumptions about gender and praise: he considers virtue to be inherently masculine so that praiseworthy women are simply measured by their male attributes and their rejection of the feminine. As one scholar characterizes his gender-based values: "Le modèle héroïque masculine est indispensable à l'éloge superlatif."[105] Working from such an assumption, Boccaccio accepts the anomalous nature of female virtue. In addition, in his preface Boccaccio states that women are weak and given to dangerous sexual excess. Throughout *De claris mulieribus*, the narrator praises women according to their adherence to a narrow range of moral expectations, chief among which is chastity. Boccaccio's reading of Dido in *De claris mulieribus* represents his most discursive deployment of the moral implications of the historical Dido for the female readers of his text.[106]

By contrast to his construction of the reader of Virgil's *Aeneid* as a male heterosexual subject in the *Genealogia*, Boccaccio's implied reader in *De claris mulieribus* is a woman, quite possibly a widow, whose sexuality must be disciplined through an identification with the historical rather than the Virgilian Dido; in the Dido exemplum, Boccaccio explicitly addresses female readers and attempts to influence their possible reactions to the chaste ideal Dido represents. The historical Dido receives a long and purposeful treatment in this narrative context, so that the narrator might be able to set the record straight concerning her praiseworthy chastity, which has been so routinely maligned ("Huius quidem in veras laudes, paululum ampliatis fimbriis, ire libet, si forte paucis literulis meis saltem pro parte notam, indigne obiectam decori sue viduitatis, abstergere queam" [p. 168]) (Of this one, in fact, it pleases me to go into the true praises a little, by enlarging on the threads, if by chance, by my few words at least to the best of my ability I might be able to wipe away the mark shamefully thrown on the glory of her widowhood). By contrast to the workaday prose of *Genealogia 2*, the style of *De claris mulieribus* is more intricate and rhetorically self-conscious, suggesting a more literary purpose.

The biography of the historical Dido, based on Justin's version as Boccaccio presented it in *Genealogia 2*, provides Boccaccio with a Dido story already detached from the problematics of the *Aeneid* that neatly suits the format and context of *De claris mulieribus* and functions as an exemplum that invites a moral reading. Boccaccio, however, does not leave anything up to the reader's moral imagination—particularly that of his female readers.[107] Rather, he insistently presents the specific lessons that a Christian widow should learn from Dido's story, particularly if she is contemplating a second marriage. *De claris mulieribus* first presents the standard plot. Dido is married to Sychaeus upon her father's death, a union that illustrates a Christian ideal of marriage ("Hi autem invicem sanctissime se amarunt" [p. 168]) (They loved each other virtuously). Pygmalion, out of greed, kills Sychaeus, and Dido, though distressed, plans to flee. At this point, Boccaccio emphasizes the heroics of the story by his comments on gender and agency: "Et posita feminea mollicie et firmato in virile robur animo, ex quo postea Didonis nomen meruit, Phenicum lingua sonans quod virago latina" [p. 170] (And, womanly suppleness having been set aside, and her spirit having been strengthened into manly hardness, she afterward earned the name Dido, signifying in the Phoenician language what is called "virago" in Latin). This assertion—an expansion of the comment in the *Genealogia* that Dido took on the strength of a man—demonstrates the extent to which masculinity is valued as a category of praise throughout *De claris mulieribus*; nonetheless, no matter how virile Dido's identity as a leader, her biography in *De claris mulieribus* emphasizes her political vulnerability as a woman who unintentionally attracts a threatening suitor.

In fairly detailed prose, Boccaccio narrates the standard tricks and devices by which Dido escapes her brother with all her wealth, abducts the virgins in Cyprus and acquires a priest of Jupiter, and finally purchases the land for her city by the trick of the ox hide. Once Carthage is built, however, the king of Musitanum demands that Dido marry him under threat of war; the *principes* of the city, knowing Dido's commitment to her chastity ("inflexibile castitatis propositum" [p. 174]), dare not ask her directly to accept the king's offer. Instead, they trick her: they tell her that the king has demanded, under threat of war, that the Carthaginians send them tutors, but that none of the citizens were willing to take on this dangerous mission. Upon hearing this, Dido declares that a citizen should be willing to risk anything—even death—for country. Once she has made this assertion, the *principes* proceed to demand that she marry the king of Musitanum for the sake of the country. Dido realizes that she has been tricked and asks for a delay. Boccaccio's only concession to the Virgilian story comes at this moment in the narrative, when he notes in passing that Eneas has arrived on the scene: "atque adveniente Enea troiano nunquam viso" (p. 174) (And so, Trojan Aeneas, never before having been seen, arrived). Dido now rapidly plans her suicide. She has a pyre built as if to placate Sychaeus. She ascends this structure, pulls out a knife she has hidden in her clothes, and says to the citizens: "Prout vultis cives optimi, ad virum vado" (p. 176) (As you wish, good citizens, I go to my husband); thereupon, she kills herself. (See figure 7.) Boccaccio's reading of the moral value of her deed is evident even in the description of her death: "cum perfodisset vitalia, pudicissimum effundens sanguinem, ivit in mortem" (p. 176), (She pierced her vitals and died shedding her most chaste blood).

At this point, the narrator abruptly shifts into moral commentary introduced by an apostrophe to Dido ("O pudicitie inviolatum decus!") and structured around direct address to his female readers, whom he assumes to be reluctant to accept the moral intent of the Dido exemplum. His comments emphasize that Dido, though a pagan woman, preferred to die by her own hand rather than to enter into a second marriage and thereby violate her vow to Sychaeus. These moral applications of Dido's story are specifically spelled out through the rehearsal of an imaginary dialogue with the recalcitrant reader. The power relations of this

7. Dido commits suicide. *Des cleres femmes.* London, British Library, Royal 16 G v, fol. 48v. Fifteenth century. By permission of the British Library.

dialogue are transparent. The narrator mimics the complaint of a woman who wishes to excuse her second marriage: "It had to be done, I was destitute, my parents and brothers were dead and suitors pursued me with flattery. I am flesh, not iron." The narrator, having quoted this hypothetical argument, completely undermines it by comparing this widow's situation to Dido's: as an exile with a hostile brother and an urgent suitor, Dido did not have much choice, yet she was willing to die rather than enter into a second marriage.

A second woman then protests that she had an estate that needed an heir, so she had to marry to bear offspring. The narrator predictably responds that Dido did not have an heir either, yet she effectively resisted the temptations of a second marriage, and the narrator declares that it is female concupiscence—unbridled desire—that makes women concede to such social pressures. Finally, a woman more sly than the others ("astutior ceteris" [p. 180]) invokes the doctrine of Saint Paul as support for a second marriage, since it is better to marry than to burn. "O scelestum facinus!" the narrator exclaims, noting again that Dido, a pagan woman, was able to attain Christian ideals of chastity. The narrator directs his female readers to—metaphorically—regard the dead body of Dido ("intuentes Didonis cadaver") and to make an effort to fulfill the office of widowhood. Within the disciplinary possibilities of the gaze, these widows are directed to contemplate a textual representation of a female body opened by the knife.

The rhetorical exchange between the narrator and these hypothetical widows regarding the correct reading of Dido's story forces an extremely narrow interpretation on the historical version of the text. Boccaccio's narrator places little faith in the untutored responses of his female readers; even when presented with an outstanding exemplum of chastity among pagan women—where one would not expect it—Boccaccio's widows still need coaxing to discard their assumptions and excuses regarding chastity and to control themselves in the face of temptation. In the direct discourse that focuses the possible interpretations of this section, Boccaccio leaves available only one possible reading of Dido for his female audience. This moral reading erases the heroic aspects of the story: the tricks and agency with which Dido directs her life and establishes her city receive no emphasis in this view of Dido as a martyr to chastity. Such an aggressive reading implies that the Dido exemplum might circulate as part of the discourse of chastity, particularly aimed at the regulation of female sexuality in the form of second marriages. Indeed, *De claris mulieribus* specifically directs women to think of second marriages as a form of concupiscence, no matter what the potential situation of the widow—young, possibly friendless, perhaps impoverished or pressured by relatives. In this text, widows are defined solely in terms of their sexuality, and the narrator directs them in their thinking toward a form of self-discipline modeled after Dido's performance.

But who are these recalcitrant widows who might be dissuaded from a second marriage after reading a Latin prose account of Dido's death? How does Boccaccio's distrust of his fictive reader—a widow who is literate in Latin?—exemplify his gendered and sexualized understanding of reading? As a text about illustrious (*clarae*) women, which is dedicated to a woman, *De claris mulieribus* implicitly addresses a female readership, yet Boccaccio's extended exploration of female responses to the Dido exemplum is explicit (and anxious) enough to invite a consideration of the social and cultural attitudes toward the widow in late fourteenth-century Florence in relation to the pointedly gendered politics of reading that underlie Boccaccio's Latin texts. By contrast to Boccaccio's stereotype of the licentious widow, the portrait of the widow that emerges from historical studies of late medieval Florence suggests that "young widows were in fact the target of a whole set of forces struggling fiercely for control of their bodies and their fortunes."[108] Although the Christian ideal of chaste widowhood urged by Boccaccio in the Dido passage retained a certain validity in this period, the institutions of marriage and the family in the generations after the plague made enormous claims on women and their fertility.[109] Widows constituted a sizable portion of the population, and their anomalous status in relation to kinship structures led to the perception that the widow who did not remarry was a threat to the social order. As Isabelle Chabot notes, "Widowhood could frequently be the moment in which latent tensions and competition erupted between families linked by marriage"; in addition, the legal inferiority of the widow contributed to the "process of impoverishment for the widow who could not or did not remarry."[110] The hypothetical situation of Boccaccio's widow—young, poor, and under pressure from relatives—aptly describes the status of widows in his day, though the sexual motivations and social autonomy he ascribes to this fictive female reader appear to be cultural stereotypes resulting from the anxious misogyny of the period.

But the most fictional element in his portrait of the widow is the degree of literacy in Latin implied by the structure of the imaginary dialogue. Although Boccaccio does not literally designate the widows whom he quotes as *readers*, they certainly represent an implied audience of women whose interpretive resistance is the occasion for the direct address that intrudes upon the narrative of Dido's story. Yet despite the gender-specific nature of this implied audience, Boccaccio's choice of Latin for this text makes a sizable female audience unlikely, given the very small portion of women even in the elite classes who would have had the ability to read this Latin text.[111] The learned widow depicted in this dialogue, however unrealistic she may be, allows Boccaccio to dramatize his distrust of readers and reading. If widows are the most dangerous women, then the widow is an appropriate figure for the most dangerous reader. For the male reader who "overhears" this fictive dialogue between Boccaccio and the widow, the text reinforces the connections between the dangers of reading and sexuality.

The contested status of the widow and the social privilege that marked Latin readership in fourteenth-century Florence form an important backdrop to Boccaccio's purposeful exploration of the meanings to be derived from Dido's choice of suicide over a second marriage. Just as the institutions of marriage and the family both create and exclude the widow, so the deployment of humanist Latin texts creates a specific, elite audience based on exclusionary practices.[112] The learned woman, the anomalous female trained to read classical languages and to participate in the discourses of humanism, was considered to be—much like the widow—a sexual predator.[113] Boccaccio's choice of the widow as a female interlocuter suggests that the learned woman and the widow occupy identical positions of social marginality, from which their sexuality represents a threat to the social order, a paradigm of gender and reader relations that clearly depends on the prevalent misogynist stereotypes of the widow and the learned woman. Since the widow and the learned woman reader are both defined by their dangerous sexuality, the widow in Boccaccio's *De claris mulieribus* figures the female reader. The narrator's tutorial on the interpretation of the Dido exemplum constitutes Boccaccio's disciplining of the female reader, but it works as a gesture toward disciplining female sexuality as well.[114] By connecting sexuality and interpretation, *De claris mulieribus* deploys a model of chastity as a female ideal that constrains women in order to manage their interpretive responses to textual meanings. In its anxious focus on female sexuality, the category of chastity that emerges from *De claris mulieribus* is a misogynist construct: it arises from an impulse to control rather than empower women. The celebration of the interpretive possibilities of Dido's suicide appears relentlessly brutal by the end of the dialogue.

Although some modern readers have been eager to trace a feminist subtext in *De claris mulieribus*,[115] the constraints placed on the reader by the dialogue between the narrator and the widow in the Dido episode leave no room to recuperate this text to a feminist point of view. The textual limits applied to the Dido episode become especially evident by contrast to the Dido chapter in book 2 of *De casibus virorum illustrium*. Composed as an exploration of the vicissitudes of fortune, *de casibus* implies a normative male readership; in this context, the historical Dido becomes an example of fortune's uncertainty. The Dido chapter in *De casibus* generally rehearses the same narrative as *De claris mulieribus*; in several places even the same phrases occur. The interpretive focus on women and sexuality takes a less emphatic form. In place of the hypothetical dialogue of *De claris mulieribus*, the narrator appends an apostrophe that valorizes feminine chastity ("O mulieris virile robur, o feminei pudoris decus perpetuis celebrandum laudibus" [142]) (Oh manly strength of woman, oh glory of feminine modesty deserving to be celebrated by universal praises!). *De casibus*, however, presents a more thorough version of the heroic aspects of the story and provides a detailed explanation of Dido's careful attention to the preservation of her city by fortifying its foundations before her suicide.[116] The Dido of *De casibus* is a heroic figure who manages to provide for her citizens despite her suicide. Although her chastity remains a significant feature of her story, the Dido of *De casibus* is much less a martyr to chastity than the Dido of *De claris mulieribus*.

Boccaccio's attention to the historical Dido as an alternative to the erotic implications of Virgil's *Aeneid* 4 is most evident in his commentary on Dante's *Inferno* 5. In explicating the Virgilian Dido who inhabits the first circle of Hell, Boccaccio carefully juxtaposes the historical version of Dido's story to the Virgilian version evoked by Dante, and he pointedly notes that the story can be recounted in two ways. He first provides a brief version of the historical account. The narrative details in the Dante commentary are the same as those found in the three Latin versions; in several places Boccaccio has merely translated one of his Latin accounts into Italian, so carefully does he reproduce many of the details and phrases, such as the assertion that Dido took on the spirit of a man ("preso virile animo").[117]

But the historical Dido does not explain Dido's presence in the circle of those who died for love. At the end of the carefully detailed narrative of the historical Dido, Boccaccio notes that the story that Virgil tells differs from the account he has just provided. He briefly comments on the Virgilian version of Dido's first marriage—carefully noting that it is Virgil's text (*Aeneid* 1) that inserts the detail of the dream whereby Sychaeus informs Dido of the narrative of her death. Boccaccio then comments extremely briefly on Aeneas and his role in the Virgilian plot. He simply says that Aeneas, after the fall of Troy, arrived in Carthage, where Dido received him and honored him. Then, after having been friendly for a time ("dimestichezza per alcun tempo" [p. 456]), he abandons her to go to Italy, whereupon she kills herself ("di che ella per dolore s'uccise" [p. 456]). After the carefully plotted version of Dido's death in the historical account—complete with the trick of the funeral pyre, the knife hidden in her clothes, and her final speeches—this brief, elliptical summary of the scenes and rhetoric of *Aeneid* 4 appears purposefully spare. Boccaccio's reading of the historical Dido is intended to replace the Virgilian figure and minimize her dramatic appeal. In addition, Boccaccio also notes in the commentary that the testimony of the historical authorities (particularly Eusebius) exposes the fictionality of Virgil's *Aeneid* 4, since Aeneas and Dido did not belong to the same century, and he notes that Macrobius explains the preference for Virgil's figure because of the eloquence with which her story is presented. But he concludes, almost petulantly: "Fu adunque Dido onesta donna: e per non romper fede al cener di Siceo, s'uccise" (p. 457) (Dido was always an honest woman, and she killed herself in order to avoid breaking her vow to Sychaeus).

Although Boccaccio's Latin texts are generally not ranked with his vernacular works in modern critical assessments of his achievements as an author, *De claris mulieribus* and *De casibus* were nonetheless extremely influential texts in late fourteenth-century and fifteenth-century vernacular cultures. Both texts found a wider audience as a result of vernacular translations. *De casibus* was twice translated into French by Laurent de Premierfait, once in 1400 and again in 1409.[118] *De claris* was translated into French in 1402 by an anonymous translator.[119] The French version of *De casibus*—*Des cas des nobles hommes*—exists in at least sixty-nine manuscripts from the fifteenth century; *De claris*—*Des cleres femmes*—in sixteen manuscripts, according to the catalog produced by Carla Bozzolo.[120] Both French texts were also produced in early printed editions. In addition, John Lydgate's *Fall of Princes* (1439) rendered *Des cas des nobles hommes* into English.[121] Since these French texts were often produced as luxury manuscripts that included extensive illustration, the proliferation of vernacular translations of these two Latin texts represents a pervasive process of visualization as well.[122] Manuscripts of *Des cleres femmes*, for instance, often include a visual image that accompanies each biography of each woman.

In the case of Dido, these vernacular texts with their strong visual component repeatedly reproduce the historical version of Dido's story—both text and image—in vernacular textual cultures. In pictorial terms, this vernacular tradition occasionally contributes images of Dido's heroic actions to the existing iconographic traditions of Dido's story as it is represented in illuminated versions of texts such as the *Roman de la Rose*, the *Eneas*, or the *Histoire*—texts that portray the Virgilian version of the story. For instance, one fifteenth-century version of *Des cleres femmes* depicts Dido as an onlooker at the murder of her husband by Pygmalion (figure 8); another late fifteenth-century text depicts the trick of the ox hide; and one Lydgate manuscript includes a marginal image of Dido leading her people into exile (figure 9).[123]

In addition, the illuminated texts of *Des cleres femmes* appear to generate a discernibly separate iconographic tradition, one that shifts the emphasis away from the erotic specularity of Dido's suicide by sword, best exemplified by the *Roman de la Rose*. Boccaccio's *De claris mulieribus* states that Dido killed herself with a knife that she had hidden in her clothes while her people looked on, a statement the French translator renders quite literally.[124] As Brigitte Buettner has shown, the early illustrations of *Des cleres femmes* often demonstrate an attention to the literal terms of the text, even when that might result in an image that does not fully comply with existing iconographic traditions.[125] In the pictorial program of *Des cleres femmes*, the illustration of Dido's suicide shows her stabbing herself with a knife in view of her people (see figure 7), an image that emphasizes the theatrical nature of her death. The unique quality of such a pictorial tradition becomes evident when juxta-

lennes. Le xi. chapitre contient le cas de dido royne et fonderesse de cartage. Et commence ou latin Si uetrz.

Elen doit adiouster foy aux escriptures des vielz hystoriens. len peuest a paines trouuer aultre nation de si grant

8. Dido sees Pygmalion kill her husband. *Des cleres femmes*. Bibliothèque publique et universitaire de Genève. Ms français 190/1, fol. 56. Early fifteenth century. By permission.

9. Dido leads her people into exile. Lydgate, *Fall of Princes*. London, British Library, Harley 1766, fol. 112v. Fifteenth century. By permission of the British Library.

posed to the more standard representations of Dido's suicide by sword, a tradition followed even in *Des cas des nobles hommes*, a text that employs the term *gladius* as well as *culter*.

The visual Dido that emerges from the vernacular appropriation and transformation of Boccaccio's Latin texts epitomizes the heterogeneous nature of the medieval Dido. In the pictorial tradition of the "vernacular Boccaccio," Dido is sometimes depicted in more heroic—and somewhat less erotic—images than she is in the iconography attached to the "Virgilian" tradition of Dido's story. And the tradition of the "vernacular Boccaccio," with its myriad visual effects and its relatively wide audience, runs counter to the implied audience of an elite group of humanist readers literate in Latin. Certainly, the French versions of *De claris mulieribus* and *De casibus* brought the chaste body of the historical Dido—both text and image—to the attention of many more women readers than had Boccaccio's Latin accounts. Among these women readers was one, a learned woman and a widow who found in the historical Dido of *Des cleres femmes* an important figure to include in an allegorical project of textual city building. As we shall see in chapter 6, Christine de Pizan appropriates *Des cleres femmes* to serve a feminist rhetorical strategy. In the long view of literary history, Boccaccio's anxieties about the interpretive responses of his female readers resonate ironically against the reading of Dido that develops in the *Cité des dames*.

The "poetic memory" of the historical Dido as it was available to Virgil and to his audience is seen by late antique and medieval readers as a countermemory to be juxtaposed to the authority of the *Aeneid* as a canonical text. Nonetheless, the medieval reception of the historical Dido is mediated by the pervasive presence of Virgil's *Aeneid* in the textual cultures of the Middle Ages. In order to appreciate the status of the historical Dido in late medieval vernacular texts, we must first consider the reading practices that emerge from academic cultures and that create subject postions for the Latin reader of Virgil's Dido.

CHAPTER 2

Dido as *Libido*
From Augustine to Dante

*Sed quia legendi uerbum aequiuocum est, tam ad docentis et discentis
exercitium quam ad occupationem per se scrutantis scripturas, alterum,
id est quod inter doctorem et discipulum communicatur, ut uerbo utamur
Quintiliani dicatur praelectio. Alterum quod ad scrutinium meditantis
accedit, lectio simpliciter appelletur.*[1]

John of Salisbury, *Metalogicon* 1.24

*But because the word for reading (*legendi*) refers as much to the exercise
of the person teaching and the person learning as to the occupation of the
person examining written texts in itself, the first, that which is shared
between teacher and pupil, may be called—to use Quintilian's word—praelectio (lecture, a reading aloud). The other, which resembles the investi-
gation of one studying, may simply be called* lectio.

As part of his larger discussion of the aims and methods of education, John of Salisbury carefully delineates and then defines various modes of reading the Latin language in this passage. Reading
(*legere*) may be either interactive or solitary, though solitary *lectio* was
probably still a vocal and highly physical activity.[2] *Lectio* performs a
significant role in the formation of a textual community—one is able to
practice *lectio* as an individual because one has been instructed by others
and thereby initiated into a distinct community defined by the activity of
readership. Such readership initially depends on the instruction of the
doctor, yet it eventually empowers the *discipulus* to read individually,
though even private study would still identify one with a larger community of readers. Throughout this treatise on education, John asserts the
political and moral value of philosophical inquiry, which depends on *lectio, doctrina, meditatio* and *assiduitas operis* (1.23) (reading, instruction,
contemplation, and practice). He emphatically describes reading as
scrutiny: "Lectio uero scriptorum praeiacentem habet materiam" (1.23)
(Reading in fact holds the written matter in front). He approvingly notes
the strict discipline and corporal punishment required from the teacher
as part of the overall training in grammar that forms the foundation of a
learned man's ability to scrutinize ancient texts for their contribution to

contemporary philosophical discussions; the proper education is a critical requirement for the statesmen.[3] John's discussion in the *Metalogicon* of the rudimentary training in grammar as part of the acquisition of the ability to read in Latin has its philosophical counterpart in the *Policraticus*, a text composed with the specific aim of political reform.[4]

This discussion of reading as a skill acquired under intense supervision in the context of the larger moral, political, and philosophical roles that await the learned reader allows us to glimpse the social and cultural forces that helped to shape the reading experience in the textual cultures from antiquity onward. The status of the *Aeneid* as a school text throughout the late antique and medieval period assured the circulation of the Virgilian Dido within such a structured regime of reading as disciplined scrutiny of written material. In the homosocial arrangement of medieval academic cultures, the written text of the *Aeneid* came under the scrutiny of schoolboys and learned men who participated in the academic dialogues recorded in centuries of glosses and allegories that testified to the canonicity of the *Aeneid* and assured its continued status as a master text. In such a scene of reading, Dido's pagan sexuality could be most easily recuperated as a figure of *libido*. From Augustine's experiences as a schoolboy who received a Roman education, through the comments of Servius and the allegorical readings of Fulgentius, Bernard Silvestris, and John of Salisbury, Latin readers of *Aeneid* 4—readers who are by definition the product of institutionalized educational practices—find the character of Dido most legible as a personification of desire. Dante's awareness of this tradition and his approach to Dido illustrate the extent to which learned readers of the *Aeneid* had come to identify Virgil's Dido with the seductive qualities of textuality.

Augustine's Tears

Augustine's description of his early education in the *Confessions* reads as a programmatic episode for the conflicts between between will and desire that structure the *Confessions* as a whole. In addition, his description of his grammatical and literary training provides a paradigmatic outline of the larger issues involved in the curricular use of the *Aeneid*. In *Confessions* 1.13, Augustine recounts his first experiences as a reader:

Nam utique meliores, quia certiores erant primae illae litterae, quibus fiebat in me, et factum est, et habeo illud ut et legam si quid scriptum invenio, et scribam ipse si quid volo, quam illae quibus tenere cogebar Aeneae nescio cujus errores, oblitus errorum meorum; et plorare Didonem mortuam, quia se occidit ob amorem, cum interea meipsum in his a te morientem, Deus vita mea, siccis oculis ferrem miserrimus.

Quid enim miserius misero non miserante seipsum, et flente Didonis mortem, quae fiebat amando Aeneam, non flente autem mortem suam, quae fiebat non amando te, Deus. . . . Non te amabam, et fornicabar abs te. . . . Amicitia enim mundi hujus, fornicatio est abs te. . . . Et haec non flebam, sed flebam Didonem exstinctam, ferroque extrema secutam. (13.20–21)[5]

For at least those first letters were better, because more fixed, by which it was being instilled in me, and was instilled in me, that I have the ability both to read what I find written and to write myself what I wish; [those were better than] those [requirements] by which I was compelled to memorize the wanderings of some Aeneas, forgetting my own, and to weep for dead Dido, because she killed herself for love, while meanwhile with dry eyes, I most miserable was myself dying to you, God my life.

Truly what is more pitiful than a wretch who does not pity himself, and weeping at the death of Dido, which came about by loving Aeneas, but not weeping at his own death, which came about by not loving you, God. . . . I was not loving you and I was committing fornication toward you . . . for love of the world is fornication toward you. . . . And I was not weeping for this, but I was weeping for Dido, destroyed and killed by the sword.

Augustine explicitly distinguishes between his first responses to Latin literature, presented in the form of Virgil's *Aeneid,* and the more elementary instruction in grammar. He notes that his acquisition of literacy ostensibly provided him with the autonomy to read and write what he wished, but his initial experiences of reading the *Aeneid* and committing it to memory threatened his autonomy as a subject and undermined his will. Augustine's reaction to the Virgilian plot is focused on the character of Dido. Aeneas's actions are categorized in an offhand manner ("Aeneae nescio cujus errores"), but Dido's story claims his responses as a reader, which inextricably links Dido to the experience of learning to read and the dangers inherent in that experience. In this context, the experience of reading the *Aeneid* is dominated by *Aeneid* 4 and the experience of weeping over the death of Dido.

Written in 397 at a critical point in Augustine's career,[6] the *Confessions* address the issues of interpretation across the cultural divide that separates pagan and Christian cultures.[7] If the ability to read was central to the disciplined interpretation of scriptural texts by the Christian reader—a topic that was to occupy Augustine throughout his writing—it nonetheless gave the promiscuous reader access to pagan texts and the attractive narratives they contain. In the *Confessions,* Augustine's concern that reading be disciplined by specific interpretive models is matched by his concern that sexuality be brought under the control of the will. Central to Augustine's conversion to Christianity is his distress at human sexuality, what Peter Brown has characterized as his awareness that "the disjunction between conscious will and sexual feeling seemed to betray a dislocation of the human person quite as shocking as the obscene anomaly of death."[8] The threat to the will represented by the experience of reading pagan literature is analogous to the disconcerting experience of sexuality.

Augustine's account of his own sexual experiences illustrates the heterosexual prerogatives available to a man of his class who could keep and discard a female partner according to his whims.[9] Before his conversion and his resulting commitment to chastity, Augustine had two concubines—one of whom bore him a child; neither of these women had any legal claims on him and neither arrangement stood in the way of the socially advantageous marriage contract to a young girl that his mother eventually negotiated for him (a contract he ultimately broke).[10] In James Brundage's words, Augustine "regarded women fundamentally as little more than troublesome, though enticing, purveyors of sexual gratification for men."[11] His male friendships, on the other hand, offer intense intellectual intimacy and comfort.[12] Throughout the *Confessions,* Augustine describes his sexual transgressions as an abuse against divine will rather than the abusive use of women as the objects of desire; the heterosexual paradigm casts the reified female sexual partner in the role of threatening other to the masculine will. By contrast, Augustine's intimate, second-person, direct address to God in the *Confessions* has a distinctly erotic cast at times; in 1.5.6, he says his *dominus*: "Angusta est domus animae meae quo venias ad eam; dilatetur abs te" (Narrow is the house of my soul through which you come to me; may it be enlarged by you).

In conflating sexuality and reading, Augustine—the mature Christian author of the *Confessions*—retrospectively interprets his early captivation with Virgil's Dido as fornication *(fornicatio).* As a Christian reader of pagan texts, the mature Augustine must specifically renounce Virgil's Dido as a figure who connects sexuality and death and who draws tears from the youthful, pagan Augustine. The passage from *Confessions* 1.13 three times repeats the phrase that narrates Augustine's response to Dido's death ("plorare Didonem mortuam"; "flente Didonis mortem"; "flebam Didon extinctam"). Peter Brown notes that Augustine's rhetorical education encouraged him to weep;[13] these tears take on a distinctively sexual meaning when interpreted as a form of *fornicatio.* Likewise, in the *Confessions* Augustine pointedly identifies Carthage with lust

(3.1),[14] so that the queen of ancient Carthage might figure female sexuality and pagan literature simultaneously, and Augustine's tearful attraction to the character of Dido becomes an emblematic enactment of the conflicts between will and desire that Augustine's efforts are generally intended to resolve.

Indeed, this section of the *Confessions* ends with Augustine's pointed juxtaposition of the affective experience of reading Dido in *Aeneid* 4 to the comforting knowledge of the fictionality of the affair between Aeneas and Dido. With an oblique reference to the historical Dido, he comments: "quia si proponam eis, interrogans utrum verum sit quod Aeneam aliquando Carthaginem venisse Poeta dicit; indoctiores se nescire respondebunt, doctiores autem etiam negabunt verum esse" (1.13.22) (If I ask them, putting the question whether it is true what the poet said, that Aeneas ever came to Carthage, the unlearned will respond that they do not know; but the learned will deny that it is true). This appeal to learned readers familiar with the historical texts that contradict Virgil's *Aeneid* 4 supports Augustine's view of his schoolboy self as a naive reader, seduced by the rhetorical veneer of pagan texts.

A teacher of rhetoric whose conversion to Christianity forced him to rethink his entire classical education, Augustine explored the issues of interpretation for the Christian in *De doctrina christiana* and then produced in *De civitate Dei* a reordering of history in accord with Christian needs. The attitude toward Virgil's *Aeneid* that emerges from *Confessions* 1.13 animates these two later works in very specific ways. As Augustine notes in *De doctrina christiana* 2.28, the study of history, even pagan history learned outside of Christian teaching, may be usefully applied to the proper interpretation of the Scriptures. But as the discussion of Virgil's *Aeneid* in the *Confessions* makes clear, the story of Dido and Aeneas does not belong to history, since it is technically not true. Augustine's vision of Christian history in *De civitate Dei*, a text that purposefully revises Virgil's historical vision concerning the City of Rome, does not include Dido. Unlike the pagan Augustine who wept when he read Dido, the elderly Christian Augustine manages to form an interpretive structure that might subsume Virgil's text yet simultaneously erase Dido.

Dido is never mentioned by name in *De civitate Dei*, despite the fact that Virgil is one of the most frequently cited of the classical poets and *Aeneid* 4 is cited seven times.[15] Indeed, at an early moment in *De civitate Dei* that appears to refer to *Confessions* 1.13, Augustine refers to the canonical status of Virgil in the Roman schools, where young boys are instructed so intensely in Virgil that "poeta magnus omniumque praeclarissimus atque optimus teneris ebibitus animis non facile oblivione possit aboleri" (1.3) (the great poet, the most distinguished and best of all, absorbed by young minds, cannot easily be abolished by forgetfulness). In such a Virgilian context, there are moments when Dido is conspicuously absent from the discussion, given Augustine's powerful reaction to her the first time he read the *Aeneid*. In 9.4, for instance, in his discussion of the offices of the pagan gods, Augustine mocks the Roman belief that the gods are present in the wedding chamber to assist the bridal pair in consummating their marriage. Such a discussion could have easily evoked the cave scene from *Aeneid* 4 and the curious presence of the deities at the "wedding" and consummation scene of Dido and Aeneas. Likewise, book 1.17–20 presents a discussion of suicide and a careful evaluation of Lucretia's suicide, complete with quotations from *Aeneid* 6—but no mention of Dido.[16]

Several direct quotations from *Aeneid* 4 allude to Dido, though she remains unacknowledged in the text. At the end of 9.4, Augustine cites *Aeneid* 4.449 ("Mens immota manet, lacrimae voluuntur inanes") to refer to Aeneas as an example of firmness of mind; he attributes the tears in this line not to Dido but to Aeneas.[17] In several places, speeches of Dido's from the *Aeneid* are quoted verbatim in *De civitate Dei* and yet recontextualized so that the identity of the original speaker is not basic to the issue discussed.[18] The erasure of Dido from the vision of history constructed in *De civitate Dei* is especially evident in book 18.19, which fits the historical narrative of the *Aeneid* into the overall framework of history developed by Augustine. In a brief reference to the lineage of Roman kings, Augustine mentions Creusa as the mother of Ascanius and Lavinia as the mother of Silvius. The historical understanding of Virgil's *Aeneid* at work in this passage exemplifies Augustine's program throughout the text: the troubling aspects of *Aeneid* 4 that elicited such an affective response from him as a pagan reader are removed from the vision of history that relies on reason, not emotion. Augustine's overall reading strategy appears to embrace the stoic gesture of Aeneas alluded to in 9.4: *mens immota manet*. Even in quoting Dido, in evoking topics and passages drawn from *Aeneid* 4, the Augustine of *De civitate Dei* has suppressed his earlier, affective responses to Dido and her death. In *De civitate Dei*, he demonstrates his ability to read Virgil without reading Dido, or perhaps to read Dido without weeping. Augustine's concern to discipline desires, both sexual and readerly, illustrates a set of negotiations evident later in medieval approaches to Dido as a figure of *libido*.

Medieval Textuality and Virgil's Dido

The commentary tradition on Virgil's *Aeneid* accompanies the text throughout the Middle Ages. The allegory tradition, likewise, begins with Fulgentius's fourth-century text and persists until the Renaissance.

Although these interpretive Latin texts illustrate several authoritative readings of Virgil's *Aeneid* and Virgil's Dido, their overall authority in relation to vernacular cultures must be carefully assessed. Scholars often assume that the vernacular tradition of the *Aeneid* in the late Middle Ages is indebted to these commentaries and allegories,[19] but the nature or extent of this debt is seldom articulated. The Latin prose commentaries on the *Aeneid* and the vernacular adaptations of the *Aeneid* represent two distinct traditions: the commentary and allegory tradition is clearly the product of the schools and circulates within learned, textual cultures, whereas vernacular texts such as the *Roman d'Eneas* derive from court cultures and circulate among a more heterogeneous audience less defined by the reading practices of academic institutions.

The Latin texts of the commentary and allegory tradition facilitate the reader's grasp of the *Aeneid* as an ancient text.[20] The interpretive impulses of commentary at once acknowledge the alterity of Virgil's text, particularly at the linguistic level, and simultaneously seek to negate that alterity by the creation of an interpretive context. The most local glosses, as in Servius's or Priscian's commentaries, rely on etymologies and syntactical explanations, and the context of these commentaries becomes quite diffuse. The general, more reductive readings produced by allegoresis—such as that of Fulgentius and Bernard Silvestris—appeal to a controlling allegorical context in the "ages of man" paradigm. Yet, whatever the interpretive intent of the commentary and the final, often didactic goal of the commentary, these texts are never meant to replace their "source" texts; their composers saw themselves as scholars and their role as ancillary. These commentators were content—in some cases, quite literally—to work around the margins of Virgil's text, supplementing but not supplanting the "original" text or Virgil himself.[21] Nonetheless, as Rita Copeland demonstrates, commentaries and allegories often result in textual appropriation when the "commentary reinvents the text through difference with it, proposing a counter-text even as it works through the given text."[22]

Medieval readers of the Latin Virgil frequently encountered texts encrusted with marginal glosses drawn from the commentaries. In addition, a standard feature of medieval manuscripts—and early printed books—of the *Aeneid* is a set of arguments in verse that is presented more or less as an integral part of the text. These arguments date from the fifth or sixth century; in some late medieval manuscripts they are attributed to Ovid.[23] The argument for *Aeneid* 4 directs the reader's attention to Dido's story as the organizing plot of the book:

Vritur in quarto Dido flammasque fatetur.
At regina gravi Veneris iam carpitur igni.

Consulitur soror Anna; placet succumbere amori.
Fiunt sacra deis, onerantur numina donis.
Itur venatum, Veneris clam foedera iungunt.
Facti fama volat. monitus tum numine divum
Aeneas classemque fugae sociosque parabat.
Sensit amans Dido, precibus conata morari.
Postquam fata iubent nec iam datur ulla facultas,
Conscenditque pyram dixitque novissima verba
Et vitam infelix multo cum sanguine fudit.[24]

In the fourth book, Dido is inflamed and confesses it.
The queen is devoured by the severe fire of Venus. Her sister Anna
is consulted; it pleases her to succumb to love; they make sacrifices
to the gods; the divinities are weighed down by gifts. She goes
hunting; they secretly enter upon the pact of Venus. Fame of the
deed flies. Aeneas, warned by the will of the gods, was preparing his
fleet and companions for flight. Dido, his lover, perceived it and
tried to delay him with prayers. When the fates decree that she no
longer has any power, she ascends the pyre, says her last words and
unhappy, pours out her life with much blood.

This argument for *Aeneid* 4 emphasizes Dido as a character who succumbs to passion even as it notes the role of Venus and fate in the plot.
Aeneas's role, according to this *descriptio*, is limited to his preparations
for his departure. The passion and its story belong to Dido. This view of
Aeneid 4 as Dido's story is in sharp distinction to the allegorical view, as
we shall see.

The prose commentaries on the *Aeneid* constitute a rich tradition that
is difficult to trace. As Domenico Comparetti vividly puts it, "the mass of
commentaries which has come down to us is like a swollen torrent, fed
by tributaries of every sort and origin. All have been condensed or
rearranged or interpolated from various sources; none has remained in its
original form."[25] For range and completeness, the best representative of
this tradition is clearly Servius's massive, line-by-line commentary on
the entire twelve books of the *Aeneid*.[26] Dating from the fourth century,
Servius's commentary is assumed by scholars to be a compendium of earlier grammatical commentaries, arranged, revised, and completed by Servius.[27] Servius has set out to explain almost every word of the narrative,
often by appealing to other texts or other parts of Virgil's own texts.

Nevertheless, the local aspect of such a commentary makes a general,
large interpretation impossible. Although the commentary does not
attempt an interpretive allegory, it contains moments of allegorical explanation, as J. W. Jones, Jr., describes them: "No perceptive person,

having examined Servius, would categorize his commentary as allegorical. However, scattered here and there are approximately one hundred eighty-five notes of the allegorical type."[28] Servius asks a limited range of questions about each word and line of the *Aeneid*. He wants to explain how the word makes sense within its immediate context, syntactically, and within the immediate focus on the narrative. He does not ask that the narrative as a whole be reduced to a single, synthetic vision. Servius dismantles the narrative piece by piece; he shows very little interest in the plot as it develops in the *Aeneid*. Instead, each piece is judged individually, largely by appeal to its immediate surroundings.

Servius approaches *Aeneid* 4 and the story of Dido with the same localized interest that characterizes his commentary throughout. He introduces his discussion of *Aeneid* 4 with the offhand comment that the book has an "almost comic style" ("nam paene comicum stilum habet") because it treats of love; nonetheless, beyond scattered rhetorical comments about the level of diction Virgil employs in book 4, such introductory remarks do not direct or organize the interpretive remarks on *Aeneid* 4 that follow.[29] His one recurring motif in explaining *Aeneid* 4 appears equally gratuitous: Servius glosses the relationship between Dido and Aeneas in terms of the religious roles of a *flamen* and *flaminica* (Roman priest and priestess), an aspect of the text that Jones sees as a valorization of "Roman rite and ritual" in the face of Christianity.[30] Servius's approach to Dido is not structured around the sort of moral concerns that animate Augustine's concern with Dido as a figure of *libido* and that dominate allegorical texts such as Fulgentius or Bernard Silvestris.

Servius's commentary, however, does preserve a cultural awareness of the historical Dido; like Augustine or Macrobius, Servius reads Virgil's poetic representation of the affair between Dido and Aeneas against his knowledge of the historical testimony that Dido died not because Aeneas abandoned her but to avoid an unwanted marriage to Iarbas.[31] In glossing *Aeneid* 4.36 when Anna refers to "despectus Iarbas," Servius inserts the story of the historical Dido in a passage that closely echoes Justin:

> DESPECTVS IARBAS rex Libyae, qui Didonem re vera voluit ducere uxorem et, ut habet historia, cum haec negaret, Carthagini intulit bellum; cuius timore cum cogeretur a civibus, petiit ut ante placaret manes mariti prioris, et exaedificata igitur pyra se in ignem praecipitavit. ob quam rem 'Dido', id est 'virago', quae virile aliquid fecit, appellata est; nam 'Elissa' proprie dicta est.

> Spurned Iarbas, the King of Libya, who in the true account wished to marry Dido, and as history tells it, when she refused this, made

war on Carthage; when her citizens, in fear of him compelled her [to marry], she asked first that she might placate the shade of her former husband, and then having built a pyre, she threw herself into it. Therefore, she was called Dido, that is, "virago," a woman who has done something masculine; for she was properly called Elissa.

Servius repeats a brief version of the comment at 4.335 to gloss the use of the name Elissa ("meminisse pigebat Elissae") and again at 4.674 to gloss a reference to Dido's name, emphasizing in both these later comments that Dido's name means "virago." Given the diffuse yet definite presence of the Servius commentary in medieval texts of the *Aeneid*, this outline of the historical version of Dido's suicide provided learned readers throughout the period with access to the countermemory that juxtaposes history to Virgil's text. The story of the historical Dido is part of the textuality of the medieval *Aeneid*.

Despite these momentary acknowledgments of the historical Dido, Servius is usually concerned to explicate the circumstances of *Aeneid* 4 as they affect Virgil's Dido. Although he repeatedly acknowledges that the historical Dido, as virago, has a masculine identity, he attributes the fact that Iarbas disparagingly refers to Dido as *femina* at 4.211 to "contemptu sexus inferioris" (contempt for the inferior sex). Likewise, he explains the reference to Dido as *furens* at 4.69 by asserting the nature of love: "in quo nihil est stabile" (in which nothing is stable). And once, at line 85, he notes that Dido is at the mercy of *libido*. Like all the threads that run through this commentary, glosses such as these do not add up to any synthetic characterization of Virgil's Dido.

The influence of this tradition on vernacular readings of the *Aeneid*, like its focus, could not have been more than locally attached to a particular word, scene, or episode. When vernacular poets, scribes, scholars, and schoolboys consulted Servius, they found a reference work on grammar, which provided local explanations of the episodes and scenes in the narrative. While such a set of localized glosses might preserve the story of the historical Dido (ut habet historia), Servius's commentary could not direct the medieval reader of Virgil toward an understanding of the *Aeneid* as a synthetic narrative poem—that task was undertaken by the allegorists.

Allegory and the *corpus* of the *Aeneid*

In the allegory tradition, we find the attempts of a commentator to synthesize one controlling view of the *Aeneid*, an attempt to interpret the *Aeneid* as a coherent narrative. The traces of this tradition are visible in

Fulgentius, Bernard Silvestris, John of Salisbury, and Dante. Fulgentius's *Virgiliana continentia*, dating from the late fifth or early sixth century, is a short and focused treatment of the entire *Aeneid*. In this allegory, Virgil's shade appears to Fulgentius the mythographer, and the ensuing dialogue provides an allegorical description of the text following a forcefully stated thesis, articulated by Virgil himself: "In omnibus nostris opusculis fisici ordinis argumenta induximus, quo per duodena librorum uolumina pleniorem humanae uitae monstrassem statum" (143.21–24) (In all my writings I have introduced themes of natural order, whereby in the twelve books of the *Aeneid* I have shown the full range of human life).[32] Virgil then explains the *ordo naturalis* of the events of the *Aeneid* by explicating the plot in terms of a biography of *unusquiuis*, everyman. Such an interpretive gesture applies the available schematic paradigm of the "ages of man" to the organization of meaning in the text.[33] As the male protagonist, Aeneas thus represents the normative masculine biography of everyman; female characters, especially Dido, are thereby seen in relation to such an androcentric reading of Virgil's text.

In order to achieve this allegorical summary of the *Aeneid*, Fulgentius had to construct elaborate moral interpretations of the episodes, whereby the shipwreck of Book 1 becomes a representation of childbirth: "Naufragium posuimus in modum periculosae natiuitatis, in qua et maternum est pariendi dispendium uel infantum nascendi periculum" (148.6–8) (I introduced the shipwreck as an allegory of the dangers of birth, which include both the pangs of the mother in giving birth and the hazards of the child in its need to be born). Likewise, Virgil's shade simultaneously summarizes and interprets Book 4:

> Feriatus ergo animus a paterno iudicio in quarto libro et uenatu progreditur et amore torretur, et tempestate ac nubilo, uelut in mentis conturbatione, coactus adulterium perficit. In quo diu commoratus Mercurio instigante libidinis suae male praesumptum amorem relinquit; Mercurius enim deus ponitur ingenii; ergo ingenio instigante aetas deserit amoris confinia. Qui quidem amor contemptus emoritur et in cineres exustus emigrat; dum enim de corde puerili auctoritate ingenii libido expellitur, sepulta in obliuionis cinere fauillescit. (152.16–25)

> In book 4 the spirit of adolescence, on holiday from paternal control, goes off hunting, is inflamed by passion and, driven by storm and cloud, that is, by confusion of mind, commits adultery. Having lingered long at this, at the urging of Mercury he gives up a passion aroused to evil ends by his lust. Mercury is introduced as the god of

the intellect: it is by the urging of the intellect that youth quit the straits of passion. So passion perishes and dies of neglect; burnt to ashes, it disintegrates. When it is driven from the heart of youth by the power of the mind, it burns out, buried in the ashes of oblivion.

Fulgentius has transformed Dido into the personification of *libido*—desire or lust; indeed, he does not even name her until Aeneas sees her in the underworld (157.18–20).

In the twelfth-century commentary doubtfully attributed to Bernard Silvestris, the commentator—whether Bernard Silvestris, some other Bernard, or somebody else entirely—sets out to unwrap the *integument* of Virgil's text.[34] This process of interpretive disclosure reveals a homosocial paradigm that structures the reading experience around a normative masculinity. Bernard (as I will refer to this commentator) summarizes Virgil's intention in the *Aeneid*: "modus agendi talis est: integumento describit quid agat vel quid paciatur humanus spiritus in humano corpore temporaliter positus" (p. 3)[35] (his agenda is this: in an *integument* he describes what the human spirit does or what it endures while placed temporarily in the body). Bernard goes on to define *integument*: "Integumentum est genus demonstrationis sub fabulosa narratione veritatis involvens intellectum, unde etiam dicitur involucrum" (p. 3) (*integument* is a sort of presentation wrapping the comprehension of truth in a fictitious narrative, whence it is also called a wrapper [covering, envelope]). The image of wrapping or covering represents the function of the *integument*, prompting one scholar at least to refer to the *integument* as a sort of "poetic cloak," and to describe the explication of a text as the activity of unwrapping or undressing the truth: "L'art du commentateur consiste à déshabiller la leçon philosophique, à lui enlever le manteau fabuleux qui la cache aux yeux du vulgaire et à la faire apparaître dans son authentique nudité."[36] Indeed, this characterization aptly describes the sexual politics of a sort of "embodied logic"[37] visible in this commentary on the *Aeneid*: in unwrapping the "truth" of this text, the commentator finds under the *integument* an allegory based on a Platonic vision of the gendered human body as a microcosm of the universe. Following twelfth-century allegorical practice, Bernard reads the universe represented in the *Aeneid* as a body, a reading informed by the vision of the world's body that dominates the *Timaeus*, especially the medieval *Timaeus*, which breaks off at chapter 53 of the Greek text.[38] In this reading context, the masculine body of Aeneas itself becomes the locus of interpretation for the world's body.

Bernard's commentary proceeds from the assumption that, as a philosopher, Virgil intends his text to be read according to a "natural order," which the commentator recuperates by reading the text as a representation of the development—psychologically and physically—of the male body of Aeneas.[39] Bernard glosses his etymological explanation of the name Aeneas to emphasize the thematics of the body: "Dicitur autem Eneas quasi ennos demas, id est habitator corporis" (p. 10), and Bernard justifies his interpretation of the *ordo naturalis* of Virgil's text as an allegory on the "ages of man." This adaptation of the interpretive framework of Fulgentius's fifth-century allegorical reading of the *Aeneid*[40] allows the commentator to impose a biographical order on the plot of Virgil's text, so that the temporal aspects of the plot of the *Aeneid* represent a biographical paradigm of the masculine body. This reading of the first half of the *Aeneid*—especially the Aeneas-Dido story of book 4—not only depends on the cultural constructions of masculinity as a normative framework for interpretation, but it also implicitly codes the text as masculine.[41]

The relationship between plot and interpretation is visible in the actual presentation of this commentary: generally the plot of the *Aeneid* is announced in a skeletal summary (*continentia fabulosa*), followed by an interpretation (*expositio*) of it. Such developmental reading of the *Aeneid* finds book 1 to be an account of early childhood or the first age; the shipwreck becomes a figurative account of childbirth, a reading drawn from Fulgentius's allegorical interpretation of Virgil's narrative. Book 2 chronicles the second age, "id est pueritie," the end of infancy when children begin to speak. Thus Aeneas's narration of his adventures at the beginning of *Aeneid* 2 marks his entrance into the second age. Book 3 illustrates the nature of adolescence, *natura adholecentie*, since the burning of the city in book 2 and the death of Anchises in book 3 represent the end of childhood. Book 4 chronicles the adventures of youth, *natura iuventutis*, in its account of Aeneas's affair with Dido. The funeral games for Anchises in book 5 become an allegory of the age of manhood, *natura virilis etatis*. And finally, in book 6, the newly matured Aeneas enters the underworld to seek his father and to strengthen his virility, that is, to control his wandering spirit and to attempt to rule his desires with reason. Book 6, however, is so densely glossed that it resembles an autopsy more than an allegory. In order to elucidate the philosophy of book 6, the commentator resorts to an extremely dense etymological explanation of the words, as much as of the plot, of *Aeneid* 6. The density of such glosses causes the controlling allegory—the developmental look at the text as biography—to break down almost entirely. The commentary breaks off before it reaches the end of book 6, in contradiction to the introductory statement that the the commentary would treat the entire twelve books of the *Aeneid*.

This commentary on the *Aeneid* is permeated by an analogy of the body, an analogy that operates not only through the structuring paradigm that allows the *Aeneid* to be read developmentally along the "ages of man" model, but also through the cosmological, Platonic vision by which Bernard reads the earth as a macrocosm of the human body. The commentary continually refers to the earth as a body:

> terre corpus ad modum humani corporis dispositum est. Quemadmodum in humano corpore sunt meatus humoris, id est vene, per quas sanguis desfluit et inde facto vulnere exilit, ita et in terra sunt vene quas cataractas vocant, per quas aqua deducitur et inde si fodiatur exilit. Item quemadmodum in humano corpore sunt arterie per quas hanelitus per corpus meat, ita in terra sunt caverne per quas aer immittitur. (p. 8)

> The body of the earth is arranged in the manner of the human body. Just as in the human body there are passages for humors, that is, the veins, through which blood flows and from which it pours when a wound has occurred, so there are veins in the earth, which they call cataracts, through which water is led and from which it springs if it is pierced. Likewise, just as in the human body there are windpipes through which the breath passes through the body, so there are cavities in the earth through which air is admitted.

At this point, the veins in the body are compared to the cataracts in the earth, a comparison that uses the human body to describe the world's body. Bernard also compares the moisture of the body, the humors, to the sea: "Mare corpus humanum intelligitur quia ebrietates et libidines que per aquas intelliguntur ab eo defluunt et in eo sunt commotiones vitiorum et per ipsum ciborum et potus meatus fit" (p. 10) (The sea is understood to be the human body, because inebriations and desires that are understood to be the waters flow from it, and in it are the excitements of vices, and through it are the passages of food and drink). This analogy of the body is central to the interpretive strategy developed here; such comparisons can be found throughout the commentary. By locating the meaning of the narrative of the *Aeneid* in the body of Aeneas and embedding the local concept of the body in a larger Platonic view of the world's body, the commentator produces a double focus by means of which he can elicit the philosophical meaning of the corpus of the *Aeneid*: he unwraps the corpus of the text to disclose a representation of the figurative and philosophical potentials for meaning in the body, both the masculine human body and the world's body.

The concept of the body that acts as a controlling analogy for this commentary also participates in a particular mythology of the body. In the twelfth century, as a result of certain advances in the study of medicine, the concept of the medical body began to take on new meaning and thus provided a new frontier for the study of philosophy. This medicalization of the human body was initiated and encouraged by the growing collection of medical texts in Latin, translated from Greek and Arabic, particularly those attributed to Constantine Afer in the late eleventh century.[42] Enriched by these texts, medical education and practice were transformed in the early twelfth century, leading to a practical interest in human anatomy and the study of surgery, especially at Salerno.[43] At Chartres, the study of medicine was a branch of the study of philosophy, an institutional approach that led to the development of Bernard's analogy of the medical body as a microcosm of the cosmological body.[44] The study of the medical body was supported by the study of the elements in philosophical discourse, as well as the study of human anatomy in medical texts.[45] In addition, the development and practice of surgery, and the practice of dissecting the bodies of animals,[46] produced a new discourse of the body that effectively complements the discourse of the world's body from Plato's *Timaeus*. The rather crude, nonpoetic concept of the medical body as it develops in Bernard's commentary on the *Aeneid*—especially compared to the more philosophical and poetic description of the body as it develops in the *Cosmographia*[47]—appears to result from the medical discourse of the twelfth century, a discourse that enhances the mythic possibilities of the masculine human body viewed as a microcosm of the world's body.

The medical body and the world's body—both the macrocosmic and the microcosmic corpus—thereby shape this commentary and its inherent construction of masculinity. The anthropomorphic qualities of this approach—reading the text as a *corpus* that participates in an elaborate macrocosmic view of the world—represent an interpretive application of a particular *embodied logic*, as defined in sociological terms: "Human beings think nature and society with their bodies. That is to say, they first think the world and society as one giant body. In turn, the divisions of the body yield the divisions of the world and of society, of humans and of animals. Primitive classifications, therefore, followed an *embodied logic* of division of gender and kinship and replication."[48] The elaborate analogy of the body structures Bernard's commentary and allows us to glimpse the gendered assumptions of a reading based on such *embodied logic* within the homosocial context of Latin textual cultures.

Throughout this commentary, Bernard emphasizes the perceptual potentials of the human body. This concept finds much fuller expression in the *Cosmographia*—a text securely attributed to Bernard Silvestris— where, as Brian Stock observes, "Bernard's view may be described as sensorial and empirical perception, since the data from the external world, reflected directly by the senses, are analyzed by the brain, which in turn sends messages to the various parts of the body. This is essentially a physical approach and Bernard's debt to Galen is clear."[49] Stock summarizes the philosophical potential of this approach: "Bernard, lastly, sees man as a *sensilis mundus,* a sensorial cosmos. Man's senses are also related directly to the mechanical arts."[50] The reader, in Bernard's terms, "thinks the text" through *his* own gendered body, and he simultaneously subjects the body to interpretation. Since the body is both an instrument of interpretation and a locus of interpretation, its masculine identity reflects the gender-specific nature of Virgil readership in the twelfth century.

Virgil's text certainly invites a corporeal reading in its emphasis on the physicality of Aeneas in the first six books of the narrative, from his initial vulnerability in the storm in book 1 (l. 92) to his weary comment in the underworld about the transmigration of souls that return to their sluggish bodies (6.719–21). But the corporeal drama of book 4, especially the elliptical quality of the cave scene as the consummate moment of desire for Dido and Aeneas, elicits the most extensive demonstration of Bernard's gendered, physiological interpretations. In Virgil's text, the lovers are brought together in the cave as the consequence of the storm, a cosmological incident clearly motivated on the "macrocosmic" level as the climatic personification of divine will. Nonetheless, the *Aeneid* likewise emphasizes Aeneas's humanity, his weariness, and his natural affinities with Dido, aspects of his character that are forcefully illustrated throughout *Aeneid* 1. This microcosmic causality opens up a space for Bernard to impose his own medicalized explanation of the microcosmic causality implicit in the text:

Tempestatibus et pluviis ad cavernam compellitur, id est commotionibus carnis et affluentia humoris ex ciborum et potuum superfluitate provenientis ad immundiciam carnis ducitur et libidinis. Que immundicia carnis cavea dicitur quia serenitatem mentis et discretionis obnubilat. Affluentia humoris ciborum et potuum taliter ad libidinis immundiciam ducit. In decoctione humoris quattuor sunt: liquor, fumus, spuma, fex. Decoctis ergo humoribus ciborum et potuum in cacabo stomachi fumus inde progrediens et, ut natura levitatis exigit, ascendens ascendendo et per arterias colando rarior factus ad cerebrum venit et animales virtutes facit. Liquore vero membra coalescunt. Fex vero per inferiores meatus in secessum emittitur; spuma vero partim per sudores partim per foramina sensuum fluit. Cum autem spume nimia est superfluitas, quod contingit in crapulosis comestionibus et ebrietatibus, per vi-

rilem virgam quia ventri proxima est et subdita in sperma, id est
semen virile, conversa emittitur. . . . Itaque ducunt pluvie Eneam
ad caveam iungiturque Didoni et diu cum ea moratur. (p. 24)

By storms and rain he is driven to the cave; that is, by the excitements of the flesh and the influx of moisture arising from an excess
of food and drink, he is led to the impurity of the flesh and of
desire. The impurity of the flesh is said to be a cave because it
clouds the clearness of the mind and the discretion. The influx of
the moisture of food and drink leads to the impurity of desire in the
following way. In the digestion of moisture, there are four things:
liquid, steam, foam, and excrement. Therefore, when the humors of
food and drink have been digested in the cooking pot of the stomach, steam is produced, and as the nature of lightness demands, it
rises and in the course of rising and filtering through the arteries, it
is thinned out; it comes to the brain and forms the animal powers.
The members grow strong by the liquid. The excrement is sent out
through the lower passages into the stool; the foam flows out partly
through sweat, partly through the openings of the senses. When,
however, the foam is too abundant, which comes to pass from glut-
tonous eating and drinking, then converted into sperm, that is,
male seed, it is emitted through the male member because it is
closest to the stomach and underneath it. . . . And so, the rains lead
Aeneas to the cave and he is joined to Dido and for a while he
remains with her.

This explanation is a classical description of the Galenic theory of the
humors and their effects on the body, a theory made available in the texts
translated by Constantine Afer, and basic to twelfth-century medical discourse.[51] In *Aeneid* 4, Aeneas is ostensibly the victim of two deities; in
Bernard's reading, he is a victim of his own body, a victimization emphasized by the medical/physiological explanations of the scene. Bernard's
commentary has taken the cosmological potential of the macrocosmic
explanation and translated it into a microcosmic one: the rain is a macrocosmic representation of the moisture in the body, since the theory of the
humors could be used to explain climatic as well as medical disorders.

The medical discourse evoked in this commentary allows Bernard to
ascribe a gender to this text, since the medicalized understanding of the
Aeneid renders the narrative as a textual body, a corpus whose gendered
nature as a normative, masculine body participates in the macrocosm of
the world's body. Such anthropomorphic gestures conflate the body of
Aeneas and the body of the text. In this paradigm, the sojourn with Dido

is understood mechanically; Dido must be overcome or dismissed. If the medical body and the world body are masculine, the sexed body is feminine. The gendered worldview of this commentary leads to the disposal of Dido as a figure for *libido*.

In glossing Aeneas's journey through the underworld, Bernard clarifies the relationship between Aeneas as rationality and Dido as *libido*. In a local comment on *Aeneid* 6.451–55, Bernard emphasizes the fact that Dido has been dismissed by Eneas, who now sees in her an example of his former error. He explains the encounter explicitly in these terms, such as his gloss on the word "AFFATUS: Eneas ad umbram Didonis loquitur dum rationabilis spiritus per retractionem libidinis naturas contemplatur" (p. 95) (Eneas speaks to the shade of Dido as the rational spirit, through hesitation, contemplates the natures of desire). Dido's flight from Aeneas is characterized as the flight of *luxuria* from wisdom. The normative male spirit, representing reason, has simultaneously purged himself of desire and the feminine. The construction of his adult virility is complete.

The performance of the reader is likewise structured around the acquisition of a masculinity in emulation of Aeneas and his successful negotiation of childhood and adolescence, denoted by gender-specific terms such as *pueritia, iuventus,* and *virilis aetas.* This text requires that its reader dismiss Dido in order to qualify for adult manhood; the implied reader is only allowed to read as a male; indeed, the text implies that the reader is initially a *puer.* In addition, the reader of this commentary occupies a homosocial subject position: the male reader identifies a masculine textual body as the object of interpretive desire. In this dynamic, the feminine is excluded as a consequence of the initiation rite of reading as a homosocial activity that conflates textuality and textual communities. Bernard's commentary is designed to discipline the sort of readerly desire that marked Augustine's tearful response to Dido and her story when he read her as a boy. As we have seen, Augustine conflates Dido's sexuality with the dangers of reading pagan texts; Dido thereby represents a very real danger to the careless, male, Christian reader who might be destabilized by her narrative presence and her story. Bernard Silvestris's commentary is constructed around a framework designed to avoid such readerly dangers.

As a school text, the commentary on the *Aeneid* attributed to Bernard Silvestris directed academic readers of Virgil in their understanding of Dido. Among these academic readers was John of Salisbury, a student in Paris between 1136 and 1147 and subsequently an administrator at Canterbury. John of Salisbury's political treatise, the *Policraticus* (1159), incorporates Bernard's allegorical reading of the *Aeneid* as a paradigm of the ages of man; as Seth Lerer notes, this reading has a particular value in the classroom: "The moral allegory has an explicitly pedagogic reference: the *Bildungsroman* transpires in the classroom."[52] In addition, the final two books of the *Policraticus* develop an elaborate "organic metaphor" of the body politic that drives John's arguments regarding the ideal society in which the king and the church cooperatively function for the good of all—an important issue for John of Salisbury, who was at that point engaged in the Becket controversy.[53] Like the medical body, the body politic depends on a physiological explanation of the body as a set of interdependent members. Although the concept of the body politic as it emerges in the *Policraticus* does not depend on the sort of medical discourse so evident in Bernard's commentary, the concept of the body as a metaphor for the state does assume a mechanical understanding of the workings of the body as a unit: the king corresponds to the head of the body, the soul is the priest, the knights are the hands, and so forth. John's metaphorical use of the body as a conceptual paradigm marks a more complex application of the corporeal thinking that can be traced to Plato's *Timeaus* and that made possible the medical understanding of the textual body in Bernard's commentary on the *Aeneid*.[54]

John summarizes an allegorical reading of the *Aeneid* at the end of his final book of the *Policraticus*, thereby adding a paraphrase of the allegorical summary of the first six books of Virgil's text to the wealth of exempla drawn from classical texts that fill the pages of the treatise.[55] The dense use of exempla and allusions to the classical texts in the *Policraticus* demonstrates the efficacy of his educational theories as they are developed in the *Metalogicon*, a text composed at the same time as the *Policraticus*.[56] The *Metalogicon*, as I noted at the start of this chapter, characterizes *lectio* as a careful scrutiny of written material, which forms the foundation of all philosophical exercises. Indeed, the philosophical reader finds a foundational meaning as a result of scrutinizing a classical text: "Excute Virgilium, aut Lucanum, et ibi cuiuscumque philosophiae professor sis, eiusdem inuenies condituram" (1.24) (Examine Virgil or Lucan and when you are a teacher of any philosophy whatsoever, you will find a foundation in them). *Lectio* as a skill allows the philosopher to buttress his own arguments with textual allusions that lend moral authority to his own treatise. John's reading of the *Aeneid* on the "ages of man" model—mediated as it is by Bernard's commentary—lends further corporeal support for his metaphor of the state as a human body.

But as a writer who is at pains to demonstrate wide reading in classical texts, John does not simply replicate the allegorical conflation of Dido with *libido*; John's reception of the *Aeneid* and his reading of Dido is mediated not only by the allegorical commentary of Bernard Silvestris but by a number of other texts as well. In his scrutiny of Justin,

Augustine, Macrobius, and Jerome, authorities on whom he relies throughout the intertextual project of the *Policraticus*, he encountered the historical or chaste Dido, a Dido who belongs to history and who exposes Virgil's poetic fiction:

> Virgilius Marcelli citra magna uirtutum merita perpetuauit gloriam et, poetica licentia fidem peruertens historiae, Didonem, licet pudicissima fuerit, hospitis, quem ex ratione temporum uidere non potuit, incesto amore posteris persuasit fuisse corruptam. (8.14)[57]

> Virgil perpetuated the glory of Marcellus, without regard to the great merit of his worth, and overturning the truth of history, by poetic license, he persuaded posterity that Dido, although she was extremely chaste, had been destroyed by a sinful lust for a guest whom, according to the calculation of time, she could not have seen.

A historically sophisticated reader such as John of Salisbury, despite his interest in the physiological focus of the "ages of man," cannot ignore the repeated testimony concerning the historical Dido—in reality a chaste woman. His summary of *Aeneid* 4, though true to the spirit of Bernard's commentary, does not name Dido:

> Quarta illicitos amores conciliat et ignem imprudenter conceptum in pectore ad amantis infelicem producit rogum. (8.24)

> The fourth part unites illicit loves and leads the fire unwisely conceived in the heart toward the unfortunate pyre of the lover.

Nonetheless, John's summary preserves the controlling analogy in Bernard's commentary on book 4 in its identification of the feminine with the dangers of illicit love, dangers that the mature, virile male reader should overcome.[58] Such assumptions are consistent with the long rehearsal of misogynist discourse (8.11), drawn largely from Jerome, that precedes the section on tyrannicide in the *Policraticus*.[59] If John seems to prefer Dido in her historical identity, he does not reject the homosocial performance of reading Virgil that emerges from Bernard's commentary.

Like John of Salisbury himself, the *Policraticus* was a product of medieval educational institutions that trained the clerical elite in the specialized skills of *lectio* as the careful scrutiny of ancient texts. Both the text and the biography of John of Salisbury illustrate the extent to which the ability to read Latin prepared one to mediate between classical culture and the demands of the governing elite. The *Policraticus* preserves the homosocial reader-relations produced by the gender-specific composition of the schools, and the reception and circulation of the *Policraticus* in the following centuries helped to maintain the dialogue between ancient texts and elite male readers.[60] Yet John's awareness of the historical Dido—also preserved in the *Policraticus*—constitutes something of a countermemory to homosocial consequences of the "ages of man" model of reading with its exclusion of the feminine. The existence of this countermemory of Dido later allows a reader such as Christine to read Dido against Virgil.

Virgil's Text and Dante's Dido

The academic traditions of reading Virgil that produce commentaries and allegories in Latin prose retain their curricular authority throughout the medieval period, yet the allegorical reading of the *Aeneid* cannot account, even partially, for the vernacular interest in Dido. Vernacular texts such as the *Roman d'Eneas* or Chaucer's *House of Fame* 1 are not shaped by the "ages of man" allegory and they do not reflect the corporeal arrangements of discourse that animate Bernard Silvestris's commentary or John of Salisbury's *Policraticus*. Among vernacular poets, perhaps Dante engages most directly in a dialogue with the allegorical tradition and its concomitant identification of Dido as *libido*. But even Dante's representation of Dido in *Inferno* 5, although it is mediated by the allegorical approach to Virgil's text, is not completely shaped by it. A look at *Inferno* 5, where Dido is placed in the second circle, and the brief allusions to Dido in *Convivio* 4.26 and *De monarchia* 2.3, demonstrates Dante's interest in Dido despite the allegorical tendency to dismiss her as an obstacle to be overcome by masculine reason.

Just before Dante set aside his vernacular treatise, the *Convivio* (1304–8), he discussed the necessity that in the noble man the appetite (*appetito*) must obey reason (*ragione*); this comment is part of a discussion of the developmental stages of human life that begins at 4.24. He refers to the allegorical reading of *Aeneid* 4 as support for this assertion:[61]

> E così infrenato mostra Virgilio, lo maggiore nostro poeta, che fosse Enea, ne la parte de lo Eneida ove questa etade si figura; la quale parte comprende lo quarto, lo quinto e lo sesto libro de lo Eneida. E quanto raffrenare fu quello, quando, avendo ricevuto da Dido tanto di piacere quanto di sotto nel settimo trattato si dicerà, e usando con essa tanto di dilettazione, elli si partio, per seguire onesta e laudabile via e fruttuosa, come nel quarto de l'Eneida scritto è. (*Convivio* 4.26)[62]

Vergil, our greatest poet, shows that Aeneas was unrestrained in this way in that part of the *Aeneid* in which this age of life is allegorized, the part comprising the fourth, fifth and sixth books of the *Aeneid*. How great was his restraint when, having experienced so much pleasure with Dido, as will be recounted below in the seventh book, and having derived from her so much gratification, he took his departure from her to follow an honorable, praiseworthy and profitable path, as is recorded in the fourth book of the *Aeneid!*

Dante proceeds to exclaim over the immense maturity and self-restraint that helped guide Aeneas through the underworld. Starting with a deferential nod to Virgil's status as a master poet, this reading not only employs the allegorical paradigm of the "ages of man" to interpret Aeneas as the hero of the epic, but it also places a high value on Virgil's poetic accomplishments as the creator of the noble figure of Aeneas. As reader of Virgil's text and author of this philosophical commentary on his own poems, Dante creates an intertextual triangle (Dante—Virgil—Aeneas) for the distribution of praise. Since Dido is depicted as the object of immature desire and the source of pleasure, she must be discarded for Dante as reader to participate in the developmental reading of nobility in the *Aeneid* made possible by the "ages of man" trajectory.

Dante's interest in the developmental "ages of man" model in the *Convivio* is transferred to the allegorical framework of life's journey in the *Commedia*, and in the *Commedia*, the interpretive tasks that Dante the pilgrim must perform take on an added complexity and difficulty.[63] Dido's placement in the *Inferno* locates her at the nexus of several interpretive traditions that Dante (both pilgrim and poet) must negotiate. Dante puts Dido in the second circle of the underworld, the circle reserved for those whose carnal appetite (*talento*) overcame their reason (*ragione*). As Dante's guide, Virgil explicates the figures before them; he particularly notes that two of Dido's companions, Semiramis and Cleopatra, are both explicitly known for the vice of *lussuria*. But Virgil is slightly less judgmental in his description of Dido—ostensibly a character of his own creation, about whose significance he might be expected to be the most authoritative interpreter. He identifies her for the pilgrim: "L'altra è colei che s'ancise amorosa, / e ruppe fede al cener di Sicheo" (61–62) (The next is she who slew herself for love and broke faith to the ashes of Sichaeus). Compared to Virgil's denouncement of the other women named in this circle—Semiramis, Cleopatra, and Helen—this descriptive identification is quite mild. Not only is Dido known for *amorosa* rather than *lussuria*, but she remains nameless at this moment in the canto. Twenty lines later, when Dante the pilgrim characterizes the entire group of carnal sinners as the "troop where Dido is" ("la schiera ov'è Dido"), he definitively

inscribes the entire group with Dido's name. Thus it is left to Dante to recognize and name Dido, the literary creation of his *maestro,* so that at this
point in the canto, Dido's destructive performance of desire becomes the
emblematic detail for her own story as well as the characteristic feature by
which Dante the pilgrim might understand an entire category of sinners in
the second circle.[64]

Dante the pilgrim is here positioned to dramatically enact a reading of
Dido as an early interpretive effort on this journey: like Aeneas in the
underworld in *Aeneid* 6, Dante must retrospectively interpret the events
that account for Dido's appearance here.[65] Such interpretive effort complements the centrality of reading to this canto, since canto 5 also
includes a sustained exploration of readers and reading in the story of
Francesca and Paolo, an episode that demonstrates, in Susan Noakes's
terms, "the instability of the meaning of the text and the unreliability of
the reader."[66] As a reader of Virgil's *Aeneid,* Dante must accommodate
his understanding of Virgil's text to the various intertwined traditions of
reading Virgil, such as the allegorical reading that he acknowledges in the
Convivio. In addition, as Giuseppe Mazzotta has shown, in this canto
Dante self-consciously cites the first book of Augustine's *Confessions*
and Augustine's reading of Dido as the intertext by which Virgil's *Aeneid*
is reinterpreted.[67] But although Dante may cite the scene of reading from
Confessions 1.14, he revises Augustine's understanding of the character
of Dido, and in the process he expands the textual possibilities available
to the Christian reader of the *Aeneid.*

Canto 5 draws on the tradition of Dido as a figure of *libido,* a meaning
alluded to by Virgil as the author who assigns meaning to his own character and by Dante as reader who simultaneously enacts and transforms the
interpretive roles of Aeneas—understood in the "ages of man" paradigm—as well as by the youthful Augustine in this confrontation with
Dido. This approach overall requires that Dido be discarded. However,
such an initial interpretive response becomes difficult to sustain in light
of the questions about the reliability of the reader that emerge toward the
end of the canto in the episode of misreading related to the pilgrim by
Francesca. As Dante's own texts demonstrate, Dido may mean different
things to different readers, or may mean different things to the same
reader at different times. For instance, in the passage in the *Convivio* discussed earlier, Dido is merely the object of desire, whereas Aeneas successfully becomes identified with the masculine qualities of reason in his
rejection of her. But *Inferno* 5 categorizes the sinners in the second circle
for the fact that they allowed their reason to be overcome by desire, a context that assigns Dido the position of subject rather than object of desire;
likewise, she is glossed by reference not to Aeneas but to Sychaeus,
which identifies *Aeneid* 6 (Aeneas's encounter with Dido in the under-

world) as the subtext for *Inferno* 5 rather than *Aeneid* 4, which directs the allegorical reading of Virgil in the *Convivio*. As subject, Dido engages the attentions of the reader(s)—both the pilgrim and the audience—more fully than the *Convivio* passage would allow.

In addition, Dante reads Dido altogether differently in *De monarchia* (1314), a Latin text that presents an imperial ideal as the model of history and leads to a fairly reductive interpretation of the *Aeneid* as a text of empire.[68] In the second book of *De monarchia*, Dante sees Aeneas's imperial nobility reflected in the geographical identities of his three wives (*coniunx*, consort). Creusa represents Asia, and Lavinia, this third wife, represents Europe. In order to place Dido—and Africa—in this picture, Dante sets aside the identification of Dido as *libido* and accords authority to Dido's own interpretation in the *Aeneid* that the incident in the cave constitutes a marriage ("nec iam furtiuum Dido meditatur amorem: coniugium uocat, hoc praetexit nomine culpam" [4.171–72]).[69] Although this approach to Dido's significance in the *Aeneid* does not entirely negate the view of Dido that emerges in the *Convivio* or the *Inferno*, it legitimates her interpretation of her affair with Aeneas as a marriage and places her within the imperial paradigm, an interpretation that makes it difficult for the reader to consider her simply as the personification of *libido*.

Dante's three approaches to Dido in these three different texts suggest the difficulty of assigning authority to any one reading of Dido, particularly since Dido appears in a canto that demonstrates the limitations of reading, limitations that circumscribed both Virgil's reading of history and Augustine's reading of Virgil.[70] In a discussion of the moment in *Purgatorio* 30.48 when Dante transposes Dido's speech to Anna ("agnosco ueteris uestigia flammae" [1.23]) into the pilgrim's mouth, Peter Hawkins suggests that "Beatrice is none other than the 'transvaluation' of Dido."[71] The limitations of reading are thus only a momentary obstacle for Dante or for his audience; the final experience of Virgil's text allows for its transformation within the providential model of reading that the *Commedia* enacts, and within this model there is room to transform Dido.[72]

Dante's engagement with Dido in *Inferno* 5 revises the model of reading Virgil that emerges from the allegorical tradition that he himself rehearses in the *Convivio*. The dynamic focus of *Inferno* 5 leaves room for a reading of Dido that accords her agency and holds her responsible for a crime of love more than lust. And although Dante the pilgrim must rethink the appeal of wordly love that he finds in the second circle, that process of revision will transform his reading of Dido. The intense engagement with Virgil's text and Dido as its female protagonist depicted in the *Commedia* illustrates how vernacular poets such as Dante, even when they have extensive acquaintance with the allegorical model of reading Virgil's *Aeneid* as a philosophical text that depicts Dido as a figure of *libido*, nonetheless betray their interest in Dido as a character detached from Virgil's text. Like Dante, most medieval vernacular poets who retell the *Aeneid* display an intense engagement with the figure of Dido, and most explore her story, to some extent, from her point of view. For instance, the *Eneas* poet shifts the medical explanation of the causes of *Aeneid* 4 to focus attention on Dido more than Aeneas, as we shall in the next chapter.

John of Salisbury's *Policraticus* and Dante's *Convivio* testify to the circulation of Bernard Silvestris's approach to the *Aeneid*. In the "ages of man" paradigm, Dido acts as a conduit for the homosocial reading of the *Aeneid*; for the schoolboy, such an interpretive paradigm directs him in a *lectio* designed to save him from dangerous responses (such as weeping at the death of Dido) to pagan texts and simultaneously to initiate him into a circle of learned readers. The social status available to a learned reader is evident in a figure like John of Salisbury, whose philosophical writings insist on the importance of schooling for statesmen. As a conduit for male desire as it is elicited and disciplined in the schools, the Virgilian Dido facilitates the formation of a privileged group of readers. Such a formation is replicated in the context of larger power networks as they are articulated in the wider social structures. But the Virgilian Dido was also shadowed by her historical double: Augustine, Servius, and John of Salisbury acknowledge the countermemory of the historical Dido. Although this knowledge of Dido's other story is not a richly developed tradition within these textual communities—especially within the schools—it was available to the most learned readers. And in the late Middle Ages, the historical Dido became available to vernacular readers.

CHAPTER 3

Dido in Courtly Romance
and the Structures of History

*Kinship is organization, and organization gives power. But who is orga-
nized? If it is women who are being transacted, then it is the men who
give and take them who are linked, the woman being a conduit of a relationship rather than a partner to it. . . . If women are the gifts, then it is
men who are the exchange partners. And it is the partners, not the presents, upon whom reciprocal exchange confers its quasi-mystical power of
social linkage. The relations of such a system are such that women are in
no position to realize the benefits of their own circulation.*

Gayle Rubin

*A woman was an object of value because she would bring forth children.
An object of exchange, rather; a pawn in a game where men were the play-
ers. They might be divided into two sides: those who took and those who
yielded the pawn. But the second of these groups was made up of several
teams. Among the makers of marriage in the middle of the twelfth century, among the castle dwellers conspiring to win as much as possible from
the game, the bride's parents or relatives were flanked on one side by their
lord and on the other by their vassals.*

Georges Duby

In these two passages, Gayle Rubin and Georges Duby extend the kinship theories developed by Lévi-Strauss into their own disciplinary
concerns—feminist theory and medieval history, respectively. Taken
together, these two excerpts articulate the cultural implications of European feudalism as a social order based on the "traffic in women."[1]
Twelfth-century feudal society developed around systems of land tenure
based on inherited vassalage; the practice of primogeniture resulted in vertical conceptions of kinship that stressed lineage and genealogy.[2] The
institution of marriage allowed each generation to renegotiate kinship
networks and land. The resulting power relations are most visible in the
arrangement of marriages, as well as the adjudication of incest prohibi-
tions and divorces. Aristocratic women—often contracted for marriage in
the cradle, married as soon are they were pubescent, and nurtured as wives
only as long as they could produce heirs—were the conduit by which the
power relationships between noble men were formed and maintained.[3]

That the church and the aristocracy often had conflicting interests in controlling the marriage market suggests the centrality of this traffic in women to the development of medieval cultural and social structures. The cultivation of *fin amors* in the courts of Provence during the twelfth century illustrates the values that emerge in a culture based so explicitly on the circulation of women. In the standard adulterous triangle of Provençal "courtly love," the poet pays homage to his *domna*, the spouse of his lord. Yet, as Julia Kristeva notes, "the lady is seldom defined and, slipping away between restrained presence and absence, she simply is an imaginary addressee, the pretext for the incantation."[4] Such poetic expressions of desire as homage generally remain unrequited. And, as Eve Kosofsky Sedgwick suggests, adultery is often an expression of bonds between men, bonds for which women are merely the conduits.[5] Given the *domna*'s status as conduit in a social structure based on kinship between men, the poet/vassal's service to his lady is a metaphorical expression of service to his lord. The idealization of such service—the conventional expressions that love makes a better poet—is perhaps the most codified expression of the homosocial values of feudalism.

By comparison to the Provençal traditions, the romances of Chrétien de Troyes, along with much of the Norman and French poetry of the twelfth century, focus more on idealized love or desire within the context of marriage than on adultery. Nonetheless, both the institution of marriage, in which a woman passes from father to husband, or the codified adultery so conventional in *fin amors*, in which a woman forms the link between lord and vassal, represent women as objects of desire within male networks of power and organization. Marriage and adultery both codify the homosocial values of feudal cultures, so that medieval French courtly romances were produced and then circulated within a social context where "men have certain rights in their female kin, and . . . women do not have the same rights either to themselves or to their male kin."[6] In such a system, desire must be carefully regulated. As Gayle Rubin notes: "If a girl is promised in infancy, her refusal to participate as an adult would disrupt the flow of debts and promises. . . . From the standpoint of the system, the preferred female sexuality would be one which responded to the desire of others, rather than one which actively desired and sought a response."[7] In courtly narrative, then, the normative role for female characters is to be the object of desire, not to be the desiring agent; women must ultimately circulate among men as the gifts whose exchange insures the social order.[8]

Courtly romances—both the *romans antiques* derived from classical sources and the Arthurian narratives derived from Celtic matter—explicitly rehearse the gendered ideologies implicit in feudalism. The reception of Virgil's *Aeneid* that is recorded in two French romances—the anonymous *Roman d'Eneas* and Chrétien's *Erec et Enide*—illustrates the extent to which social assumptions regarding gender might control and direct the textual and cultural appropriations enacted by medieval romance. Each of these texts, the one derived from classical, the other from Celtic sources, contains a representation of Dido as a romance character.

But Dido is not easily incorporated into medieval romance. Dido's role in the *Aeneid* transgresses the standard boundaries for female behavior within feudal ideology as it is reflected in twelfth-century texts. Virgil's Dido does not circulate among men; once in Carthage, she has lost husband and father, and has become estranged from her brother. There is no man to grant her as a gift to another man and thereby establish kinship. In the *Aeneid*, Dido acts on her own behalf, whether as leader or as lover. She welcomes Aeneas into Carthage and offers him her city; she also actively desires him and expresses her desire repeatedly, and in the end, of course, she suffers the consequences. Her lack of male defenders is illustrated in the fact that it is a woman, her sister Anna, who attempts to intervene and persuade Aeneas to remain in Carthage. Within a feudal context, Dido does not belong to any man, which limits her value as an object whose exchange would facilitate transactions among men; but since she decides to bestow herself on a man of *her* choice—Aeneas and not Iarbas—her presence in the text is disruptive to the social order. Dido's sexual agency challenges the economy of desire that structures feudal romance.

In the *Roman d'Eneas*, the status of Dido signals a particular sort of alterity. Until recently, one standard critical approach to medieval narratives such as the *Roman d'Eneas* denies that the poem—or medieval poetry in general—acknowledges the historical difference represented by the pre-text of Virgil's *Aeneid*. As Thomas Greene states this position: "The use of elements from Virgil and Ovid found in the *Roman de Thebes* or the *Roman d'Eneas* does not provide an etiological construct to deal with cultural discontinuity, to connect subtext with surface text; they fail to provide this because they fail to register the discontinuity. They lack historical self-consciousness."[9] However, to a medieval poet such as the anonymous poet of the *Roman d'Eneas*,[10] who, as we shall see, often self-consciously acknowledges his/her role as a mediator between the classical Latin text of Virgil's *Aeneid* and the vernacular text being produced, Dido's agency suggests the dangers inherent in a situation in which a woman does not circulate within the prescribed limits of exchange and kinship. In the poet's authorial experience of Virgil's *Aeneid* and Virgil's Dido as recorded in the construction of the *Eneas* and the brief allusion to the Eneas story in Chrétien's *Erec et Enide*, we do witness an awareness of cultural discontinuity and historical self-consciousness, since the social assumptions regarding gender in Norman culture make the appropriation of Dido a difficult matter. Dido's status in Virgilian narrative forces the medieval poet to articulate the assumptions regarding gender and power that are operative in the medieval text. In the process, the texts of the *Eneas* and Chrétien's *Erec* acknowledge, if only briefly, a discontinuity between the cultural assumptions about gender and power in classical texts and the medieval context into which they are imported. Dido plays the central role in the intertextual theatrics of cultural appropriation.

The Portable *Aeneid* in Chrétien's *Erec et Enide*

The circulation of the *Roman d'Eneas* as a textual artifact that comments on the sexual politics of Norman culture is perhaps alluded to in a brief passage from Chrétien's *Erec et Enide*, an Arthurian romance composed a decade later. *Erec et Enide* contains a neatly framed visual citation of the *Aeneid* story that would appear to evoke the *Eneas*: in this early romance, Chrétien depicts the Aeneas-Dido story on the bow of the saddle presented to Enide when she acquires a new palfrey about two-thirds of the way through the narrative. The story on the saddlebow is described in an expressive ekphrasis[11]—a verbal description of a work of graphic art—that invites the reader to visualize a pictorial narrative:

> La sele fu d'autre meniere,
> coverte d'une porpre chiere;
> li arçon estoient d'ivoire,
> s'i fu antailliee l'estoire
> comant Eneas vint de Troye,
> comant a Cartaige a grant joie
> Dido an son leu le reçut,
> comant Eneas la deçut,
> comant ele por lui s'ocist,
> comant Eneas puis conquist
> Laurente et tote Lonbardie,
> dom il fu rois tote sa vie. (5287–98)

> The saddle was of another sort,
> covered with a purple cloth;
> The saddlebows were of ivory,
> and there was carved the story,
> how Eneas came from Troy,
> how in Carthage with great joy
> Dido received him in her bed,
> how Eneas deceived her,
> how she killed herself on account of him,

how Eneas then conquered
Laurentum and all of Lombardy,
of which he was king all his life.

The text describes four or five separate, cartoonlike bas-relief panels in which the figures of Eneas and Dido pose in some characteristic fashion that identifies the role of each in the story. This description summarizes a story; the summary is large enough to suggest the outline of a complex plot and briefly evocative enough to suggest that the *Aeneid* story as a complete narrative already had some currency among vernacular audiences at the time *Erec et Enide* was produced.[12]

The repetition of *comant* frames the four episodes of the *Aeneid* story depicted on the ivory carving of the saddlebow. Each *comant* has an allusive quality: the word *comant* implies that the pictorial description itself is much more full and evocative than the linguistic representation of this description. Yet no one of these episodes could be more than a brief outline. Although the brevity of this pictorial outline makes it difficult to determine whether the text depicted on the saddlebow is intended to be a summary of the *Roman d'Eneas* or of Virgil's *Aeneid*, the suggestion that these images depict a well-known story would point to the *Eneas* as a pretext for this later vernacular text.[13] Both texts, however, foreground Dido. Most notably, the ekphrasis represents a specific reading of Dido's story: "comant a Cartaige a grant joie / Dido an son leu le reçut, / comant Eneas la deçut, / comant ele por lui s'ocist." In this extremely brief depiction, the adverb *comant* supplies the entire interpretive framework. The emphasis falls on Dido's agency in acting on her desire: how *she* receives him in her bed, and then how *she* commits suicide for him. This description emphasizes Dido's anomalous situation as a woman who acts on her own; indeed, the sequence of these assertions implies that Eneas can deceive Dido precisely because she is detached from any kinship networks. Dido's story is reduced to three emblematic motifs: desire, betrayal, and death. But the character of Dido that emerges from this narrative is the subject, not the object, of desire.

The last few lines of the ekphrasis emphasize Eneas's conquest of lands: "comant Eneas puis conquist / Laurente et tote Lonbardie, / dom il fu rois tote sa vie." These motifs would appear to be taken from the medieval romance tradition; they evoke the last half of the *Eneas* much more than the last six books of the *Aeneid*. Yet Lavinia is not named as the cause of these wars—a fact all the more surprising in light of her dominant role in the second half of the *Eneas*, where she is fully developed as the explanation for the events of the story. In the *Eneas*, Lavinia is also important as a counterpoint figure to balance Dido. Since Chrétien's repertoire of allusions clearly included Lavinia, who is specifically evoked in the Joy of the Court episode, her absence in this ekphrasis appears all the more deliberate.[14] The images on the saddlebow invite the viewer to consider the implications of the Aeneas-Dido story as a framed episode distinct from the larger *Aeneid* narrative.

The saddlebow provides a particular interpretation of Dido's story that has implications for the text as a whole. The narrative assumptions of *Erec et Enide* depend on feudal ideologies regarding marriage.[15] Erec acquires Enide from her father, a "povre vavasor," in order to display her in the contest of the sparrow hawk. Since marriage to Enide cannot bring Erec wealth or property, Enide's beauty is given as the currency that makes him forgo a more economically beneficial transaction. This process illustrates a feature of Chrétien's romances characterized by Roberta L. Krueger; in commenting on the narrator's manipulations in *Yvain*, she states: "The narrator calls our attention to the romance's mystification of woman's place at the same time he reveals the underlying reality of her status as an object of exchange."[16]

Yet marriage threatens Erec's standing in the social order based on chivalric pursuits, since his desire for his wife distracts him from male activities, particularly tournaments where prowess is demonstrated. In this respect, Erec's dalliance with his wife threatens the integrity of the male homosocial world. Once Erec overhears Enide lamenting Erec's decline, Erec takes her through a series of tests and "adventures" that subject her to threats—particularly the threat of rape—and the abuse of strangers; these adventures often put Enide at extreme risk.[17] Throughout these adventures, Enide is forbidden to speak. In the course of the narrative, the marriage of Erec and Enide becomes reconciled with the prevailing social order through the silencing of Enide. As the daughter of an impoverished noble, Enide has married into the aristocratic world; she has to be tutored in its social codes.[18] She has to learn not to speak; indeed, she has to learn to be the object reified by the male gaze, not the subject of desire.[19] Yet her circulation is idealized within the text.

In the context of the marital negotiations of Erec and Enide, the story on the saddlebow illustrates the ultimate dangers of socially unregulated female desire, which led to Dido's suicide. The description of the saddle occurs at a pivotal point in the narrative. Erec and Enide have just become reconciled, and Enide's acquisition of the new palfrey and the saddle with its carved story marks a new stage in the romance. She travels beside her husband in her newly achieved status. The otherness of this pagan Latin text of female desire and death in the context of Aeneas's victorious conquest momentarily suggests the "other" story that is always inherent in female sexuality if social controls fail to channel and direct female desire through marriage. If Enide's story essentially represents the disciplining of female speech and desire under the harness of aristocratic marriage, the "other" story is presented as a cautionary tale: for Dido, desire led to death. The reader's gaze fixes Dido as image carved in the ivory; Dido becomes an iconic representation of female sexuality that momentarily comes before the reader's line of vision. Although Enide does not glance at the saddle, the image on the saddlebow constructs the reader as a knowledgeable viewer who might recognize the saddle as an artifact whose circulation is emblematic of the circulation of the *Eneas* as a textual artifact in Norman culture.

The *Eneas* Poet as *Scriptor*

The reception of the *Aeneid* story in *Erec et Enide* is mediated by the transformation of Virgil's *Aeneid* into the Roman d'Eneas (1156) by an anonymous Norman clerk under the patronage of Henry II and his new spouse, Eleanor of Aquitaine.[20] The *Eneas* was one of several texts produced as part of a cultural program designed to legitimate the Plantagenet dynasty.[21] The author of the *Roman d'Eneas* most likely belonged to a clerical subculture similar to that of John of Salisbury, and the *Roman d'Eneas* and the *Policraticus* belong to the same decade. The reading of Virgil's *Aeneid* and the authorial approach to the interpretive issues posed by Virgil's Dido are nonetheless markedly different in the two texts. The *Policraticus*, as we have seen, follows the universal masculinity of the "ages of man" model for recuperating Virgil's text and essentially diminishes Virgil's Dido as an object of desire; as a Latin treatise, this text emerges from and circulates within the elite, gender-specific textual cultures whose reading practices explicitly acknowledge the priority and canonicity of ancient texts. By contrast, the Norman clerk who translated and transformed the *Aeneid* into the *Eneas* produced a vernacular text that is not limited to a gender-specific clerical audience, despite the fact that its author apparently belonged to the Latin-reading clerical elite. As a vernacular narrative, the *Roman d'Eneas*—the most sustained "imitation" or translation of Virgil's *Aeneid* in English or French until the end of the fifteenth century[22]—does not defer to its Latin source as an original master text, nor does it present itself in the exegetical role of a commentary intended to facilitate access to the Latin *Aeneid*. Nonetheless, the narrator's scribal voice invites us to acknowledge the intertextual status of this vernacular *Aeneid*.

The *Eneas* poet presents an author-function as *scriptor*, as a vernacular mediator who approaches the plot of the *Aeneid* as though it were a series of questions to which the vernacular text provides explanatory answers; in that respect, the narrative of the *Eneas* implicitly provides both text and commentary. Beyond plot, however, the *Eneas* could be said to be very little indebted to the Latin text: the octosyllabic line of the Old

French narrative imparts an altogether different tone than Virgil's somber hexameters; the characters—both mortals and immortals—are much less complex in the medieval vernacular *Aeneid* than in the Latin text, and the large ethical issues of the *Aeneid* barely survive in the *Eneas*. The *Eneas* subsumes and transforms the *Aeneid* to the extent that modern readers have—until very recently—often dismissed the *Eneas* as a pale, almost parodic, version of its anterior text.[23]

The narrative texture of the *Eneas* subtly acknowledges its status as a vernacular adaptation. In the narrator of *Eneas* we encounter the voice of a speaker who has a complex set of roles to perform, although this speaker is not as fully developed as other romance narrators, such as those found in the texts of Chrétien de Troyes. As the engineer behind the French vernacular version of the *Aeneid*, the narrator adopts several different rhetorical poses, which identify the speaker's role as a reader of ancient texts.[24] Sometimes the voice of this narrator is the voice of a scribe reacting to the text being "translated," as happens, for example, in the episode in which Dido realizes that Eneas's fleet is prepared for departure:

> Dido s'en monte a ses estres,
> laisus as plus haltes fenestres;
> quant aprester vit la navie,
> se el fet duel *ne mervoil mie*. (1875–78)

> Dido went up to her apartments, up to the highest windows. *I do not wonder* that she grieved when she saw the fleet made ready.

Conventional as such assertions may be, expressions such as "ne mervoil mie," which are scattered throughout the *Eneas*, remind us that the narrative itself is delicately framed by the narrator's perception of that narrative/story as it is being produced. This sort of reaction focuses attention on the scribal act of this narrator, and such comments articulate the "scriptural temporality" of this text—that is, the momentary awareness, from time to time, of the "activity of writing" as one aspect of its textuality.[25] In the *Eneas*, the narrator's scribal voice—faint and intermittent as it is—reminds us of the levels of mediation in this text. The language does not represent an event, but transforms an earlier linguistic representation of an event. In order to describe this scene, the speaker had first to read an earlier version of it. As a scribal narrator, this poet's response to Dido's grief is actually a response to a previous representation of Dido's grief, and the narrator occasionally records a reader's response in the process of transforming the Latin into French. The Dido episode elicits specific reactions from this *scriptor* as reader, who encounters in Dido a pagan woman who functions as the subject of desire.[26]

The *Eneas*, like the other *romans antiques*, makes the Latin texts of academic subcultures available to the vernacular audience. In the process, the *Eneas* poet obviously had to adapt the plot and characters of the *Aeneid* to the cultural expectations of a courtly context; most notably, the poet had to accommodate the Plantagenet desire for a historically inclusive rendering of the Roman mythic past celebrated by Virgil to suit the cultural constructions of Norman imperial power. As Lee Patterson characterizes the cultural context of the *Eneas*: "The *Eneas* contributes both to the myth of continuity that the Anglo-Norman ruling class promoted and to the privileging of lineage, and of primogeniture, that was so crucial to the Norman social and economic structure."[27] The reception of Dido as an anomalous woman in the *Eneas* is conditioned by a Norman vision of history as lineage and genealogy that legitimates its royal succession and power. In addition, the courtly patronage responsible for this text includes Eleanor of Aquitaine, a figure whose circulation simultaneously exemplifies and defies the cultural paradigm of traffic in women.[28] In terms of audience and patronage, the *Eneas* belongs to a textual community that relegated women to the role of object whose circulation insured the dynastic arrangement of social structures and culture.[29] As we shall see, in this context, the anomalous woman who might be perceived as subject of desire—whether Eleanor or Dido—elicits social comment.

In addition to the *scriptor*-function—the speaker's scribal role as a learned clerk rendering Latin into the vernacular—this narrator also acts in places as a *compilator* who collects writings from sources, both classical and contemporary, which are inserted into the narrative under production. Thus the *Eneas* contains exempla from the *Metamorphoses*,[30] descriptions of wondrous monuments and animals from the encyclopedic tradition,[31] and so forth. Such compilation frequently leads to commentary; in such respects, the *Eneas* in its entirety attempts to explain the events and allusions in Virgil's narrative. These two authorial roles, *scriptor* and *compilator*, account for the texture and discourses found in the *Eneas*. Within the social context of twelfth-century courtly culture, grounded as it is in the feudal exchange of women, the *Eneas* poet brings a specific set of perceptions based on gender and agency to the authorial task of reading Dido.

In twelfth-century Norman culture, the "traffic in women" intersects with two specific ideologies: the ideology of "predatory kinship," as Eleanor Searle characterizes the cultural legacy of the Norman expansion in the eleventh century,[32] and the twelfth-century concept of idealized love, which directs desire into specific alignments within kinship and vassal networks in support of basic feudal structures. The texture of the *Eneas* is animated by both ideologies. The discourse of "predatory kinship" is exemplified by the rhetorical stance adopted by both Turnus and

Eneas in relation to Lavine, and the discourse of love is expressed by both Dido and Lavine as well as by Eneas. The ten thousand lines of the *Eneas* eventually elide these two discourses, as though the discourse of love, particularly as it is voiced by Eneas and Lavine at the end of the poem, becomes an allegory for the "predatory" motives of Eneas. By contrast to Dido, Lavine expresses desire that reinforces the kinship networks represented by her betrothal to Eneas; as Barbara Nolan puts it, "Lavine and Eneas enter into a social, politically suitable love."[33]

The *Eneas* as a whole represents marriage as an institution that suits the needs of the conquerors, in this case Eneas, who must acquire kinship networks, along with land, in the selection of a wife and the negotiation of a marriage contract. Such assumptions frequently motivated the marriage practices of the Normans in their various settlements and conquests; as they did in Britain after 1066, the Normans frequently relied on selective intermarriage with women from the conquered groups in order to establish or stabilize their governments.[34] The structure of the *Eneas* opposes the destructive, basically unreciprocated desire of Dido (a desire not reinforced by or reinforcing a marriage settlement) to the constructive desire of Lavine (a desire that becomes fully reciprocated by Eneas and is reinforced by the entire system of vassalage and kinship that the marriage of Lavinia and Eneas represents). Dido's status in the *Eneas*—as later in the ekphrastic allusion in *Erec*—illustrates the dangers of socially unregulated female desire. In reading Dido, the *Eneas* poet has transformed *Aeneid* 4 into a twelfth-century cultural vision that reflects the feudal traffic in women on a cultural plane and the medical view of lovesickness on a narrative level.

In the first third of the poem, Eneas commands much less attention than Dido; from the first description of Carthage, the narrative is very much Dido's story. Upon introducing her, the narrator appreciatively compares her to male rulers:

Dame Dido tint le païs;
miaus nel tenist quens ne marchis;
unc ne fu mais par une feme
mielz maintenu enor ne regne. (377–80)

Lady Dido ruled the country better than any other count or marquis would have ruled it. No domain or realm was ever thereafter better governed by a woman.

Dido enters the text as a female leader; this introductory acknowledgment of her political role—noted as a transgression of standard gender roles—makes it difficult for Dido to be placed in the conventional status

of "object of exchange." In this respect, Dido's stature essentially defies
the nascent generic conventions of romance that often relegate women to
a (perhaps idealized) silent, central absence. Her anomalous agency elicits
the scriptural comments of the narrator, who implicitly acknowledges
the difficulty of recuperating Dido as *dux*—the initial image of the
Virgilian Dido in the *Aeneid*—to a feudal vision: the text notes that no
realm was ever again so well ruled by a woman, which defines this anomalous performance by its historical and cultural alterity rather than presenting it as a gendered performance of regal power possible at any time.

The *Eneas* poet likewise transforms the scene in *Aeneid* 1 when Venus
appears to Aeneas and explains to him the story of Dido's exile. In the
Eneas, Dido and Carthage are the focus of the narrative. The story of
Pygmalion and Sychaeus is briefly summarized:

> Sicheüs ot a non ses sire,
> uns suens frere lo fist occire,
> en essil chaça sa seror,
> por ce qu'il volt avoir l'enor. (383–86)

> Sicheus was her husband's name. One of her brothers had had him
> killed and had driven his sister into exile, because he wished to
> take possession of the realm.

The narrator notes that, as a widow, Dido takes wealth and companions
and sails to Africa, where she purchases land through the trick of the ox
hide. At this point, the *Eneas* poet embellishes the Virgilian narrative
with an explanatory detail from the historical tradition. Virgil elliptically
states that the Tyrians purchased as much land as could be encircled by
an ox skin or bulls' hide ("taurino quantum possent circumdare tergo"
[1.268]), a reference to the elaborate trick that is carefully described in
Justin's account. The *Eneas* poet, drawing on a Servian gloss, explains in
more detail how this trick was executed:[35]

> Dido trancha par correetes
> lo cuir, qui molt furent grelletes;
> de celes a tant terre prise
> c'une cité i a asise;
> puis conquist tant par sa richece,
> par son angin, par sa proëce,
> que ele avoit tot le païs
> et les barons a soi sozmis. (399–406)

> Dido cut the hide into very thin thongs; with these she took so
> much land that she founded there a city. Then she conquered so

much by her wealth, by her cleverness, and by her prowess, that she possessed the whole country, and the barons submitted to her.

The gloss leads to an assertion of Dido's noble qualities and her stature in relation to her place in the feudal hierarchy that depicts her as a woman receiving homage and submission from the barons beneath her in the social structure. The Norman Dido is initially a masculine figure whose greatness is evident in the splendor of her holdings, such as her fortified stronghold, which is extensively described in the text (407–70). In the *Aeneid*, the story of Dido's marriage and exile is succinctly summarized by Venus for Aeneas's benefit as well as the reader's; in the *Eneas*, the omniscient narrator presents Dido's past in such a way that it makes Dido the protagonist. By contrast to Virgil's text, Dido's story in the *Eneas* is not presented as though it were only a stage in the biography—or journey—of Aeneas. The first quarter of the text of the *Eneas* revolves around Dido: she is much more fully characterized than Eneas, and her passion and her story become the focus of the narrative.

Throughout the Dido episode, the *Eneas* poet, as *scriptor*, reads the Virgilian text within medieval contexts. The *Eneas* poet translates Dido's passion into medieval terms by transforming it into an illness. In this respect, the poet incorporates a twelfth-century understanding of erotic longing as a specific disease—lovesickness—a medical category that received authoritative treatment, as Mary Wack has demonstrated, in the *Viaticum* of Constantine Afer and its commentaries.[36] As Wack suggests, this medical category intersects neatly with Ovidian discourse on love. The academic interest in lovesickness is part of the medicalization of discourse and bodies that pervaded twelfth-century textual cultures. This medical understanding of eros is handily grafted onto the Virgilian depiction of Dido's passion as a form of erotic infection. Dido's sleeplessness in *Aeneid* 4 becomes an acute case of lovesickness, represented without the sinister coloration that Virgil gives it in the imagery of the wound and the fire in *Aeneid* 4. The *Eneas* poet depicts the internal sufferings in vivid, corporeal terms:

> An tel travail et en tel poine
> fu la raïne une semaine;
> ne nuit ne jor ne ot repos,
> ne por dormir ne ot l'oil clos.
> En dolor ert et en grant mal;
> al ne sot dire al vasal;
> ne garra mes ansi lonc tens,
> se al ne prent autre porpens:
> ou li an estovra morir

ou al vasal s'amor gehir.
Cele angoisse a lonc tans sofert,
qu'el ne l'osot dire an apert. (1433–44)

The queen was in such torture and such pain for a week that she had no rest, night or day, nor ever closed her eyes in sleep. She was in sorrow and great sickness, and did not know how to speak to the knight. She will not be cured for a long time unless she has other thoughts; either she must die of it or confess her love to the knight. For a long time she suffered this anguish which she did not dare to admit openly.

The depiction of desire as an illness ("grant mal," "angoisse") that causes sleeplessness is consistent with Virgil's text where Dido's passion is metaphorically depicted as an infection or a wound that keeps her from her rest. The medieval text, however, suggests that this case of "lovesickness" is less a metaphorical description of Dido's state of mind than a medical condition that, understood in clinical terms, may explain the events of the poem. The condition here is presented mechanically; in the medical understanding of this disease, the lover had to be distracted by other thoughts and experiences that might forestall or prevent the melancholy or excessive thoughts (*cogitationes nimias*) that mark the condition.[37] In the assertion that Dido needs to transfer her thoughts elsewhere ("se al ne prent autre porpens"), the poet as *scriptor* assertively diagnoses her as a patient—and suggests a cure.

This focus on Dido's story as a textbook case of lovesickness allows the poet to create space in which to depict and explore Dido as a subject of desire. By contrast to the medical explanation for the cave scene in Bernard's allegory, which explains the event by reference to Aeneas's body, the *Eneas* poet focuses on Dido's physical symptoms as the explicit cause of the cave scene. In the *Aeneid*, Virgil used Venus, Juno, Cupid, and a divinely orchestrated thunderstorm to get Dido and Aeneas into the cave to undergo the "wedding" rites. The *Eneas* poet, who consistently depicts events with a minimum amount of help from the gods, must detail Dido's suffering more fully and intensely in order to motivate Dido's actions without representing them as the result of divine manipulations. Dido's own suffering must compensate for the divine agency in this scene—within the outlines of the plot as Virgil frames it. The *Eneas* poet interprets Dido's inflammation in terms acute enough to motivate the cave-scene wedding. In such a context, the poet intrudes upon the narrative and inserts a proverbial comment to explain the medical reasons why she undertakes to go hunting:

A un matin formant li plest
qu'ira chacier an la forest,
por esbatre de sa dolor,
s'antroblïer porroit s'amor;
car amors est molt plus griés chose,
quant an loisonje et repose,
et qui s'an velt bien delivrer,
si ne doit mie reposer;
se l'en s'en velt bien esloignier,
autre antante li a mestier,
car quant an antant autre part,
se li sovient d'amor plus tart. (1445–56)

One morning she felt a great urge to go hunting in the woods, that she might divert herself from her sorrow and forget her love; for love is a much more grievous thing when one is lazy and rests, and he who wishes to escape well from it should never rest; and if one wishes to get far away from it, he must have another interest, for when one is occupied elsewhere, one recalls one's love more slowly.

General statements like those in the last eight lines again acknowledge the scriptural time of the text: the voice of the speaker inserts a proverbial statement, expressed in the present tense. The poet appeals to cultural generalizations that represent a clinical understanding of lovesickness as a disease whose cure depends on activities that distract the lover from erotic and passionate obsession. This comment is a vernacular paraphrase of medical discourse, asserted at a definitive moment in the narrative.[38] Most significantly, this assertion precedes the cave scene; in one twelfth-century gloss on the *Viaticum*, hunting is suggested as a distraction that assists the lover in finding a cure. In the *Eneas*, the decision to go hunting is specifically depicted as a consequence of Dido's lovesick condition.[39]

By comparison to the *Aeneid*, the poet simplifies the role of Venus and the immortals altogether in the inception of the Aeneas-Dido affair; indeed, the French poet, interested in the medical course of love, attributes Dido's inflammation and lovesickness to her fondling of Ascanius (803–22). The cave scene marks the fulfillment of human desires, not of a divine plan:

Tant vont fuiant ansanble andui,
a une crote sont venu.
Iluec sont andui descendu.
Estes les vos andos ansanble,

il fait de li ce que lui sanble,
ne li fait mie trop grant force,
ne la raïne ne s'estorce,
tot li consent sa volenté;
pieça qu'el l'avoit desirré. (1518–26)

They went fleeing together until they came to a grotto. There they
both dismounted. Here are the two of them together. He does with
her what he wishes, nor does he use very much force at all, nor
does the queen resist: she consents to him with all her will, for she
has long desired him.

This scene exemplifies a predatory understanding of sexuality: Eneas's
actions are measured by the amount of "force" required, Dido's responses
by the amount of *volenté*. Dido's willingness explicitly results from her
desire. Within the categories implied by such terminology, sexuality is
measured by masculine initiative and conquest. Dido's behavior is
measured by her responses, not her initiative, in spite of the narrative
emphasis that it is Dido who is the character caught in the throes of lovesickness, not Eneas. At a later judgmental moment in the text, the narrator reverses this position and comments on Dido's agency in the affair:
"Or a Dido ce qu'el voloit: / del Troïen fait son esploit / e son talant tot en
apert" (1605–7) (Now Dido has what she wanted: with the Trojan she
does her will and her desire all openly). Here Dido occupies the role
assigned to Eneas in the earlier passage ("il fait de li ce que lui sanble").
The gendered performance of desire appears to be available to either sex.
As Wack's study of medical texts on lovesickness demonstrates, *amor
hereos* often unmanned or feminized the male lover. In Dido's case, her
passion also feminizes her in the course of the narrative, since she is
eventually removed from her masculine role as leader.

In both texts, the cave scene marks the turning point in the narrative of
the Dido story, since its public nature allows for political interpretation
of the sexual involvement of Dido and Eneas. *Fama* immediately provides the meaning of the event: "Eneas l'a vergondee" (1540) (Eneas has
dishonored her). The report spread by Fame takes predictably judgmental
terms:

Par Libe nonce ceste fame
la felenie de la dame;
dit que de Troie estoit venu
uns hom, Dido l'a retenu
ansanble soi anz an Cartage;
or la maintient cil an putage.

An luxure andui se demeinent
lo tens d'iver, d'el ne se poinent. (1567–74)

Throughout Libya this Rumor announces the lady's misdeed: she
says that a man has come from Troy, that Dido has kept him with
her in Carthage, and that she now keeps him there in shame. Both
of them pass the winter season in lechery, and are not troubled
about it.

Although Eneas is depicted as the sexual predator in the cave scene, public report blames Dido, who is dishonored, guilty of "felenie," and held
responsible—as though she were the predator—for retaining Eneas in
Carthage. Several phrases in this passage are based on Virgil's Latin;
indeed, the French term *luxure* replaces the Latin *luxu* in this passage.[40]
In the context of the *Eneas*, the term *luxure* specifies the personal nature
of this desire. Dido's personal dishonor, however, reverberates throughout the realm, and Dido's rejected suitors see her affair with Eneas as a
dishonor to themselves ("molt se tienent por vergondez") (1585), since
Eneas has gained "terre et feme" for himself. The nature of this public
judgment is not much altered in the transformation of this passage from
Latin to French; however, the emphasis on honor and the explicit connection, frequently expressed, between the "terre et feme" that dominates the last half of the *Eneas* express the conflict in feudal terms.[41]
Dido's sexuality has disrupted the standard circulation of land and
women in terms of feudal ideology.

The interpretation of Dido that emerges from the *Eneas* removes the
agency of the gods from her downfall and contextualizes her tragedy in
purely personal terms, a characteristic of the *Roman d'Eneas* frequently
noted by scholars.[42] Dido's death results from the pathology of her
lovesick desire; consequently, she pardons Eneas (2066–74) and dies
much more peacefully than does Virgil's Dido. In the *Eneas*, the narrative
erases the anger that Virgil's Dido so eloquently expresses in broad political terms, particularly her references to the Carthaginian wars, which
close her life by setting it in the context of Roman history.[43] Instead,
Dido's death in the *Eneas* essentially removes her from history; her
funeral and the epitaph on her tombstone explain her life in personal
terms:

«Iluec gist
Dido qui por amor s'ocist;
onques ne fu meillor paiene,
s'ele n'eüst amor soltaine,

mais ele ama trop folemant,
savoir ne li valut noiant.» (2139–44)

Here lies Dido, who killed herself for love. There would have been
no better pagan if solitary love had not seized her: but she loved too
madly, and her wisdom availed her nothing.

The epitaph points to Dido's alterity as a pagan woman undone by *amor
soltaine*, whose lovesickness causes her to love foolishly. Within the
dynastic paradigm of Roman history implied by the *Eneas*, Dido has no
place in the ancestral lineage that emerges from Roman history and
merges with Norman kinship networks and the Plantagenet dynasty.
Unlike Virgil's Dido, the suicide of the Norman Dido has no global, proleptic meaning: no avenger such as Hannibal will appear to legitimate her
complaints. Within the view of history operative in this poem, a woman
without male protectors essentially has no claim on history.

Nonetheless, in the discursive space of the *Eneas*, Dido's story—with
its unfavorable depiction of Eneas—requires a narrative correction in the
story of Lavine. The extent to which the first section of the *Eneas* has
emphasized Dido's story to the detriment of Eneas's character is expressed by Amata when she presents a brief interpretation of the Aeneas-
Dido episode in her remark to Lavine: "N'as tu oï comfaitemant / il mena
Dido malement" (8579–80) (Have you not heard how he mistreated
Dido?). Such negative judgment of Eneas's actions momentarily assigns a
legitimacy to Dido's point of view in the text, since Amata's remark
holds Eneas accountable for his actions in Carthage. Although Amata's is
not a normative voice in the *Eneas*, this interpretation of Eneas's character must be counteracted by the final developments of the Lavine plot.

Eneas and Lavine

In feudal terms, the position of Virgil's Lavinia is easily explained. As the
daughter of a king, she has tremendous value as a conduit for feudal networks and the acquisition of a realm for the landless Trojans. Although
he has already promised his daughter to Turnus, Latinus nonetheless sees
compelling reasons to renegotiate a marriage contract with Aeneas. For
the Norman poet, this set of exchanges is easily recuperated within the
cultural assumptions of predatory kinship and traffic in women. However, in order to fully appropriate the final six books of the *Aeneid* into a
narrative plan that would impose a feudal ideology on Virgil's narrative
and restore Eneas to his central role in the plot, the *Eneas* poet had to
develop and give voice to the mute character of Lavinia.[44] The result is
Lavine, a feudal woman who speaks a language modeled on Ovidian

texts, particularly the textualized desire of the *Heroides*.[45] Throughout the last two-thirds of the poem, these Ovidian discourses, overlaid with the medical discourse of lovesickness, provide a consistent *amplificatio* that expands the plot of the *Aeneid* into a love affair between Lavine and Eneas. By contrast to Enide, whose disruptive speech is systematically silenced in the course of Chrétien's text, the *Eneas* gives a voice to the previously silent Lavine. Lavine's voice, however, is thoroughly implicated in the dominant patrilinear discourses of the poem, since, by comparison to Dido, Lavine's amatory language channels female desire into acceptable forms of expression.

Lavine's desire is activated by lovesickness, though by comparison with Dido's lovesickness, which proves to be fatal, Lavine's symptoms prompt her discourse on love by providing her with symptoms she can name and describe in language. Her illness thus allows her to articulate her desire. Since her desire is compatible with the social order in every respect, her speeches represent a social performance of female heterosexuality designed to meet the needs of a patriarchal, feudal order. Lavine's repeated exploration of lovesick desire transforms the last section of Virgil's *Aeneid* into a romance plot that culminates in marriage, so that Lavine's extensive speeches work as a textual antidote to the poisonous passion that destroyed Dido.

Furthermore, Lavine's emotional state is contagious. Within a thousand lines of her initial inflammation, she communicates her love to Eneas, who eventually reciprocates her passion. Eneas's desire for Lavine is expressly contextualized as the proper, socially productive form of desire, which will culminate in marriage, land, and lineage. Eneas explicitly compares his passion for Lavine to the less powerful desire he felt for Dido (9038–45), and his rhetorical rehearsal of such heterosexual desire stands in stark contrast to the supposed homosexuality that Lavine and Amata attribute to him.[46] Indeed, Amata's assertion (quoted earlier) that Eneas mistreated Dido is presented by her as evidence that he does not like women, but rather prefers boys: "il priseroit mialz un garçon / que toi ne altre acoler; / o feme ne set il joër" (8572–74) (He would prefer to embrace a boy rather than any other woman; he does not know how to play with women). Such assertions produce a regulatory discourse that enforces a normative heterosexuality within a homophobic regime. This narrative exploration of the compulsory heterosexual identity that Eneas must achieve suggests as well that his "proper" love for Lavine may channel his sexuality into the dominant homoerotic ideology enacted by the social paradigm of marriage as the "traffic in women."

The description of Eneas's lovesickness closely parallels Lavine's; the two lovers have all the same symptoms. However, Eneas is in a more privileged position than Lavine: he can act, and he resolves to do so as soon as he recognizes the source of his pain and the power of love. He tells himself:

Lai ce ester, ne t'entremet,
et si panse de ta bataille.
Ne sai que ceste amor te vaille,
car se tu voinz, ce puez savoir
que donc la t'estuet il avoir;
se vencuz es, se l'as perdue,
si an fera autre sa drue. (8982–88)

Let this be; do not occupy yourself with it, and think instead about your battle. I do not know what this love avails you, for if you win, you know that then you will surely have her; if you are defeated, then you have lost her and another will bear away your love.

Indeed, he then utters his resolve to find in his love the motivation to act even more resolutely to possess Lavine "et molt me metrai a grant fais, / ainz que la perde et que la lais" (8995–96) (and I will set myself to great feats, rather than lose or abandon her). In medical terms, the male victim of lovesickness has an advantage in searching for a cure, since he can shift his thoughts to battle and to the great feats he might accomplish. By comparison to Dido, whose passion feminized and destroyed her, Eneas's malady is the catalyst for his heroism. Within the regulatory terminology of this poem, his lovesickness assures that he abandon the status assigned by Amata when she calls him "un traïtor" and "un sodomite" (8583). In that regard, his passion contributes to an achievement of a normative masculinity.

The texture of the last section of the *Eneas* signals that the vernacular transformation of the *Aeneid* is complete. The scribal-like role adopted earlier by the narrator at places in the story of Dido gives way to a narrative that marks a synthesis of Virgilian plot and Ovidian rhetoric. Once Eneas and Lavine voice the normative discourses that support the feudal exchange of women, the narrator becomes transparent; once those characters voice the most productive ideology of love, the speaker's *scriptor*-role as cultural mediator is no longer required. The Ovidian speeches that replace the narrator's scribal voice elucidate a social paradigm that regulates sexuality by eliding marriage and desire within a homophobic regime.

The Norman Dido is a casualty of the gendered politics of conquest, and the imperial ideology at work in the *Eneas* ultimately mimics that of the *Aeneid* so that the Roman imperial vision is replaced by the dynastic vision of the Normans. In the process of *translatio studii*, the *Eneas* poet explores the connections between gender and conquest, since the progression of the poem finally idealizes the predatory gestures of the conquerors by eliding them with the idealized amatory discourses voiced by Lavine and Eneas toward the end of the poem. A text that ostensibly sets out to legitimize Norman imperial power results in a portrait of power and gender relations.

Although Dido's story disrupts the thematic focus on Eneas as an ideal prince, she does not subvert the ideal he eventually embodies at the end of the poem, particularly because Lavine, as her double, recuperates Eneas as a lover. But, taken together, Dido and Lavine rehearse the textual possibilities of female subjectivities, albeit female subjectivities that would appear to be produced by a male poet working out of the homosocial context of clerical cultures. But as a pagan leader who succumbs to a destructive passion, Dido forces the plot of the *Eneas* to accommodate a hybrid discourse. This quality of the *Eneas* is especially evident by comparison to the masculinist vision of Bernard's commentary on the *Aeneid*. Such hybridity perhaps reflects the liminal status of the *romans antiques* as vernacular appropriations of ancient texts for a courtly audience notable for its heterogeneous composition in terms of literacy and learning as well as gender.

The *Eneas* was produced in a court whose queen was known, even during her lifetime, for her resistance to the dominant gender ideologies that would subjugate married women, however aristocratic, to the demands of kinship networks and dynasties. Eleanor of Aquitaine's ability to divorce one king and then marry another without first obtaining royal permission was the stuff of legends by the time she had joined the Plantagenet court. In addition, when she accompanied Louis VII on a crusade, numerous inaccurate rumors circulated that she led armies as an Amazon queen and committed adultery.[47] Although Eleanor's autonomy as queen was severely circumscribed by existing power networks, she was nonetheless perceived by contemporaries as transgressing conventional gender roles. The paradoxes regarding gender and power in the *Roman d'Eneas* might best be viewed against the backdrop of Eleanor's biography as an anomalous woman who could transgress social conventions regarding gender roles but who could not transform them to suit her individual ambitions. As one of the earliest of the *romans antiques*, the *Eneas*—with its insistent scribal awareness of Dido as an anomalous woman—illustrates what Krueger has identified as "the displacement of woman and the appropriation of her power as a central problem—or project—in romance."[48] The gestures toward displacing Dido in the *Eneas* are replicated in the larger cultural appropriation of the *Aeneid* as an extension of the Troy story in medieval historiography.

The reception and transmission of the *Roman d'Eneas* illustrate the extent to which the kinship organization of Norman culture, with its emphasis on genealogy and dynasty, helped to shape a conception of history articulated as lineage. Not only did the *Eneas* provide a model of *translatio imperii* from ancient world, but, read in the context of the other *romans antiques*, this model could be extended in either direction to become a universal paradigm stretching from biblical times through to Norman genealogy. As Jerome Singerman has shown, the manuscript evidence persuasively demonstrates that the *Eneas* was read within such a genealogical/historical model, and that this paradigmatic placement of the *Aeneid* story was carried over into the composition of the French prose texts known as the *Histoire ancienne jusqu'à César*, a vast cycle of universal history produced in the early thirteenth century (ca. 1208–30).[49] Thus the social organization of gender visible in patrilineal power structures is imprinted on the structures of history, and Dido's anomalous status in terms of Norman ideology is reproduced in the cyclical vision of the Northern French *Histoire*, which paradoxically writes her out of history while simultaneously rendering her even more iconographically legible.

Dido and the Structures of History in the *Histoire ancienne jusqu'à César*

Geoffrey of Monmouth's *Historia regum Britanniae* (ca. 1135) and its French version, Wace's *Roman de Brut* (ca. 1155) illustrate the Norman desire for historical narratives structured around genealogy and lineage that appropriate Trojan ancestry for Norman identity. These two texts, along with Benoît de Sainte-Maure's *Roman de Troie* (ca. 1160–70), construct a paradigmatic *translatio imperii* from Troy to Rome by a brief rehearsal of the *Aeneid* story that describes only Aeneas's departure from Troy with Ascanius and his arrival in Italy and eventual marriage to Lavinia.[50] This standard epitome omits *Aeneid* 4 and Aeneas's sojourn with Dido in Carthage; consequently, many versions of the Troy story in its medieval transmutations do not mention Dido.[51] Nonetheless, as the production of the prose texts of the *Histoire* in Northern France illustrates, the circulation of the *Aeneid* and the *Roman d'Eneas* made it possible for historical narratives to acknowledge Dido, even if the structures of history provide no place for her—a North African queen—in the trajectory of this patrilineal, Eurocentric story.

The text known as the *Histoire ancienne jusqu'à César* is a vast compilation and translation of received narratives that move from Genesis through Greek, Theban, Trojan, and Roman history. A large number of manuscripts from the thirteenth and fourteenth century survive, many of which were illustrated, some lavishly.[52] The careful scrutiny of several scholars has shown that the compiler of the *Histoire* based the *Eneas* section of this text on the Latin text of Virgil's *Aeneid*.[53] Nonetheless, the *Histoire* author certainly knew the *Roman d'Eneas*, from which the compiler occasionally borrowed both local details of plot and the overall chronological placement of the *Eneas* story in the received manuscript order of the *romans antiques*.[54] Dido's story in the *Histoire* follows the outlines of *Aeneid* 1 and 4 and shows almost no influence from the *Roman d'Eneas*: the lovesick, vocal heroine of the French romance is depicted more sparely and her portrait and actions generally emphasize her regal beneficence.

However, scholars have noted that the visual material in the *Histoire* shares an iconographic tradition with the *Roman d'Eneas*, particularly in illustrations of Dido falling on Eneas's sword.[55] One standard representation of Dido's suicide in the *Histoire* shows Dido's suicide on the left and Eneas sailing away on the right (see figures 10 and 11).[56] This pictorial arrangement appears as well in a thirteenth-century manuscript of the *Eneas* (see figure 12), one of the earliest medieval illustrations of Dido's death, according to Pierre Courcelle.[57] Courcelle notes as well that the image of Dido's suicide is one of two privileged scenes from the text of the *Histoire* (the other is Camille in battle) that is repeatedly chosen as part of the visual program of the cycle.[58] The *Eneas* thus appears to have contributed to the visual tradition that would emblematize Dido's death, since as Jeanne Courcelle comments regarding the pictorial material in these vernacular texts: "les sujets retenus correspondent les plus fréquemment aux moments le plus pathétiques."[59] Although the text of the *Eneas*, with its rhetorical expressions of desire and loss, may not have shaped the text of the Dido story in the *Histoire*, the interest that illuminators demonstrate in the image of Dido's death would appear to sustain the affective focus of the *Roman d'Eneas*.

The brief treatment of Dido's story in the *Histoire* illustrates the contradictory demands of history on the Virgilian narrative. The *Histoire* author/compiler generally demonstrates a tolerance for conflicting and contradictory versions of "history" so that in several places alternate versions of a mythic or historical event are presented for the reader to resolve.[60] In the case of Dido's story, such tolerance for conflicting versions leads to an ingenious appropriation of the historical version of her death into the Virgilian narrative. In following the outlines of Virgil's narrative, the *Histoire* shapes the Dido story around the narrative focus on Aeneas and his journey from Troy to Rome. After the shipwreck, he goes to explore the territory where he has landed and he comes upon Dido's newly established city. The background of Dido's story is inserted into the narrative at this point—much like the insertion of Dido's past that appears in *Aeneid* 1 when Venus explains her story to Aeneas—but the

10. Left: Dido falls on sword; right: Eneas sails away. *Histoire ancienne jusqu'à César*. Bibliothèque Nationale, français 301, 172r. Fourteenth century. By permission.

Histoire compiler, like the *Eneas* poet, follows the passage from Servius's commentary on the *Aeneid* that explains more fully the trick of the ox hide. In this way, the explanatory material from Servius that uses Justin to explain (and contradict) Virgil's account of Dido is enfolded into the larger Virgilian narrative. Thus a gloss on the *Aeneid* that points to the historical tradition ("ut habet historia") becomes incorporated into a narrative in such a way that it loses its status as an explanatory gloss and becomes part of a relatively seamless narrative. But to accomplish such incorporation, the compiler had to make some adjustments to the plot.

The *Histoire* dedicates one section to the story of Dido's marriage and Pygmalion's murder, her arrival in Carthage, and her clever purchase of land. Then the narrative returns to Eneas's point of view as he enters Dido's city and sees the paintings on the wall of Juno's temple; his tearful responses to these scenes are recorded, and, in a close paraphrase of Virgil's text, Eneas's line of vision is traced as he looks at a representation of Penthesilea on the wall and then watches Dido emerge from the temple. Dido then generously receives Eneas into Carthage (see figure 17); she feasts him and he presents her with rich gifts. She kisses Ascanius and

11. Left: Dido falls on sword; right: Eneas sails away. *Histoire ancienne jusqu'à César.* Bibliothèque Nationale, français 9685, fol. 113v. Thirteenth century. By permission.

12. Left: Dido falls on sword; right: Eneas sails away. *Roman d'Eneas*. Bibliothèque Nationale, français 784 fol. 70r. Thirteenth century. By permission.

starts to acknowledge that she feels *amor* toward his father. She requests that he tell the story of the fall of Troy, which he then recounts in detail and concludes with weeping. At this point, enamored of Eneas, Dido seeks advice from her sister Anna, who makes a comment that compares Dido's interest in Eneas to her previous rejection of Iarbas.

Anna's comment is a cue for the *Histoire* compiler to incorporate the rest of the Servian gloss on the historical Dido that records her suicide to avoid marriage. The compiler very deftly weaves this material into the narrative; a rubric notes this explanatory flashback ("Comment la royne Dido refusa a mari iabar le roy de Cezile") (How the queen Dido refused to marry Iarbas the King of Sicily). The compiler tells how Iarbas, having heard of Dido's beauty, seeks to make her his wife. He sends messengers, but Dido refuses his offer. Iarbas then assembles his people to attack her city and Dido's own people (*hommes*) urge her to accept Iarbas rather than allow them to be destroyed. She yields to this pressure from both sides, but requests that she be permitted to make sacrifices to appease the soul of her husband. Once she has a great fire built, she throws herself into it and would have preferred to burn, but her people (*gens*) rescue her and agree that she does not have to marry against her will (see figure 13). When Iarbas hears this, he believes that she does not wish to have a new husband because of her love for Sychaeus. The section ends with several etymological comments, among them that her name, Dido, means *barnesse* or baroness, a noble woman.

After this clever insertion into the narrative of one suicide attempt and one deferred marriage, the focus returns to Eneas and Dido, who go hunting and find themselves alone in the cave. Upon their return to Carthage, the narrator deftly notes that their affair becomes public and that Dido thinks that Eneas wants to take her for a wife and remain in Carthage. However, Eneas has a dream that he should go on to Italy, and, despite his awareness of the difficulty this poses for Dido, he sadly arranges to leave her. He insists to her that the gods demand his departure and eventually, though she tries to persuade him to stay, he departs. Dido's second suicide attempt then follows: the narrator, rather matter-of-factly, states that in her grief and anguish she goes into her chamber and takes a sword that Eneas had left and kills herself (see figure 14).

In following the Servian glosses on Virgil's text, the compiler has combined the two conflicting versions of Dido's story and the reasons for her death into one narrative. Consequently, the historical version of Dido's story is written into Eneas's biography so that it actually loses its status as a separate, contradictory account that discloses the status of Virgil's text as a poetic fiction. The Virgilian narrative becomes more historically valid once the historical Dido has been incorporated into it, yet in the process, both Didos—the poetic and the historical—are removed from the structures of history as they are articulated in the *Histoire* with its relentless rehearsal of genealogy and lineage. Dido's interest in Eneas is expressed at one point as an appreciation for his excellent lineage, and her desire to be his wife is thus framed, in part, as her desire to be part of his genealogical placement in history. His departure and marriage to Lavinia transfer power to Rome, and her death effectively removes her from this broad canvas of Western history articulated in a linear structure that incorporates Troy and Rome but omits Carthage. In the *Histoire*, her life is monumentalized only in the sepulcher her people build for her after they have burned her body; she claims no place in the textual monuments of history.

Nonetheless, despite the narrative focus on a structure of history that does not finally make a place for Dido as a city builder and a leader, the fact that Dido's story is frequently chosen as a topic for illustration results in a visual program that includes images of Dido as a queen

13. Dido throws herself into the pyre, her people pull her out. *Histoire ancienne jusqu'à César*. Bibliothèque Nationale, français 1386, fol. 47r. Thirteenth century. By permission.

14. Left: Dido throws herself on the sword; Right: Eneas sails away. *Histoire ancienne jusqu'à César*. Bibliothèque Nationale, français 1386, fol. 47v. Thirteenth century. By permission.

receiving Eneas into her city (figure 17) as well as the proliferation of images of her death by falling on Eneas's sword. These images implicitly contradict the sense of erasure that the text of the *Histoire* enacts in its narrative emphasis on genealogy. Such a paradox is emblematic of the Dido that emerges from Norman culture in the *Eneas* and is then refigured in the *Histoire*: Dido does not fit the vision of history as genealogy, but any rhetorical attempt to work around her must result in a tradition that accommodates her story to some degree. Such a paradoxical tradition is fully explored in Christine's engagement with both history and Dido. Chaucer's Dido likewise shows an authorial investment in the reader's subjective remembering of Dido and encountering the problematics of that memory.

CHAPTER 4

Sely Dido and the Chaucerian Gaze

For sometimes, instead of riding off on his horse to inspect his crops or bargain with his tenants, Sir John would sit, in broad daylight, reading. There, on the hard chair in the comfortless room with the wind lifting the carpet and the smoke stinging his eyes, he would sit reading Chaucer, wasting his time, dreaming—or what strange intoxication was it that he drew from books? Life was rough, cheerless, and disappointing. A whole year of days would pass fruitlessly in dreary business, like dashes of rain on the window pane. . . . But Lydgate's poems or Chaucer's, like a mirror in which figures move brightly, silently, compactly, showed him the very skies, fields, and people whom he knew, but rounded and complete. Instead of waiting listlessly for news from London or piecing out from his mother's gossip some country tragedy of love and jealousy, here, in a few pages, the whole story was laid before him. And then as he rode or sat at table he would remember some description or saying which bore upon the present moment and fixed it, or some string of words would charm him, and putting aside the pressure of the moment, he would hasten home to sit in his chair and learn the end of the story.[1]

Virginia Woolf

Chaucer's narrators frequently exhibit an intense self-consciousness about their scribal roles; in this regard, they manifest some of the attributes evident in the *scriptor*-role adopted by the narrator of the *Roman d'Eneas*. In the dream visions especially, Chaucer's narrators meditate obsessively on the relationship between reading and writing, thereby thematizing the act of reading. In addition, these narrators explicitly present themselves as readers of classical Latin texts, texts whose authors and titles they often name. Chaucer himself appears to have been well acquainted with poets such as Virgil and Ovid as Latin *auctores* mediated by commentaries and pedagogical practices. Most likely, he would have known a commentary tradition on Virgil's *Aeneid* such as that of Servius, as well as the sort of Ovidian commentary on *Heroides* 7 that reads Dido as an exemplum of *stultus amans*.[2] Although his pedagogical experience of Virgil's *Aeneid* might mirror that of the schoolboy discussed in chapter 2, his intense engagement with Ovid's texts, particularly the *Heroides*, throughout his poetic career appears to have been a formative reading experience for his subject positions as a poet.[3] In the dream visions, the Chaucerian narrator characteristically foregrounds the reading of classical texts as significant pre-texts for vernacular narratives.

Chaucer's Dido appears exclusively in the context of the dream visions as part of the narrator's encounter with the alterity of classical texts and traditions. She is never invoked in the *Troilus* or the *Canterbury Tales* (beyond the summary of the Legends that appears in the Prologue to the Man of Law's Tale).[4] Dido's presence in Chaucerian narrative appears to derive from his narrator's self-conscious contact with Virgil and Ovid. Nonetheless, Chaucer was demonstrably acquainted with the medieval Dido as she appears in vernacular texts, particularly in the *Roman de la Rose* and the *Commedia*, perhaps as well in Machaut's *Jugement dou roy de Navarre* or the *Histoire ancienne jusqu'à César*.[5] Chaucer was also very likely to have known the historical version of Dido's story from Boccaccio's Latin texts.[6] Since Chaucer's narrators are often much less generous about citing medieval pre-texts than citing the *auctores*, the vernacular intertextualities of Chaucer's Dido must be seen in relation to his narrators' subject positions as readers and the tasks they explicitly undertake in narrating Dido's story. In the *House of Fame* 1 and the "Legend of Dido," the Chaucerian narrator in each explores the relationship between authorial positions he adopts as reader and translator, respectively, and the textualized desire he encounters in the figure of Dido. Since the "Legend of Dido" effectively revises the representation of Dido in *House of Fame* 1, these two texts, taken together, provide a composite portrait of Chaucer's Dido and Chaucer's responses to the interpretive difficulties she posed for the late medieval reader.

House of Fame 3: "The Fame of Pius Eneas"

In the passage from her essay "The Pastons and Chaucer," quoted at the beginning of this chapter, Virginia Woolf vividly imagines John Paston's interest and absorption in his copies of Lydgate and Chaucer. Woolf derived her understanding of reading habits in fifteenth-century England from her acquaintance with the Paston letters and not from any wider historical knowledge of medieval reading practices. Yet she depicts a particular experience of reading that makes the everyday world over into something more compelling—or "rounded and complete." Likewise, she pointedly contrasts the orality of women's gossip with the captivating power of the written text for this particular male reader, John Paston. Woolf's imaginative picture of John's "strange intoxication" is surprisingly close to the behavior of "Geffrey," the narrator of the *House of Fame*. In book 2 of the *House of Fame*, the eagle mockingly describes Geffrey's absorption in texts:

. . . that thou hast no tydynges
Of Loves folk yf they be glade,
Ne of noght elles that God made;
And noght oonly fro fer contree
That ther no tydynge cometh to thee,
But of thy verray neyghebores,
That duellen almost at thy dores,
Thou herist neyther that ne this;
For when thy labour doon al ys,
And hast mad alle thy rekenynges,
In stede of reste and newe thynges
Thou goost hom to thy hous anoon,
And, also domb as any stoon,
Thou sittest at another book
Tyl fully daswed ys thy look;
And lyvest thus as an heremyte,
Although thyn abstynence ys lyte. (644–60)

The correspondence between these two passages is instructive. By the eagle's account, "Geffrey," like John Paston, prefers reading to other forms of communication or experience. This potential of narrative and textuality to eclipse other experiences is central to the *House of Fame*. Indeed, the eagle's description of Geffrey's readerly behavior stands in marked contrast to other Chaucerian moments that represent reading as a community experience, as in the first book of the *Troilus*, where Criseyde and two other women "Herden a mayden reden hem the geste / Of the siege of Thebes" (2.83–84). Geffrey's silent reading completely isolates him from oral, community experience; he hears no news of his neighbors nor gossip from afar. Instead of participating in a textual community—of listening to a text read aloud or reading to others—he separates himself, alone in his house, a quiet and dazed consumer of books. The dream allegories connect the individual experience of reading classical stories to the dream visions of the male narrator. In the Chaucerian corpus as a whole, literacy and silent reading are usually presented as the prerogative of male readers like the Clerk.[7] *House of Fame* 1 carefully anatomizes Geffrey's experience of solitary or silent reading; in the process, the role of gender and representation in the construction of the reader is thoroughly explored through the interpretive matrix of dreams and memory as visual texts.[8] And Dido is the central figure in this textual experience.

The *Book of Fame*—as this text was also known during the Middle Ages and early Renaissance[9]—points to the connections between fame and textual traditions as the narrator perceives them in the text. Throughout the

allegory, the dramatized narrator (whom the eagle calls by the name
Geffrey in the second book) becomes almost completely consumed by the
conceptual task of narrating this dream. The narrative is so dominated by
verbs that enact the narrator's perception (*saugh, seemed, rede*),[10] that the
narrator's interpretive abilities (comically considered by the eagle to be
limited by his "bookishness") become the organizing principle of the text.
But although the eagle may laugh at Geffrey's bookishness, the readerly
skills implied by that label carried a particular set of values in relation to
gender and class in fourteenth-century England, where literacy functioned
as a "survival skill," in Janet Coleman's terms.[11] The growing literacy rate
in the course of the century contributed to a discernible pattern of upward
mobility for literate men in a bureaucratic social structure.[12]

In addition, the expanding book trade contributed to a wider readership
for vernacular texts, which led to an increase in the private consumption
of books.[13] If literacy provided men with opportunities for social advance-
ment, it also allowed more readers to have unmediated access to texts. As
Paul Saenger has shown, the late fourteenth century provided the lay
reader with substantial opportunity for silent reading, a mode of reading
that increasingly displaced the public experience of vernacular texts.
He comments: "Psychologically, silent reading emboldened the reader,
because it placed the source of his curiosity completely under his
personal control."[14] As an individual experience, silent reading encourages the reader's associative responses and thus activates or encourages
the intertextual experience of literature.[15] In addition, silent reading
emphasizes the visual qualities of texts and narrative.

Although the name Geffrey explicitly makes this narrator something
of a figure for the author, Geoffrey Chaucer, Geffrey's bookishness points
to the poet's activities as a reader rather than a writer. In *House of Fame*
1, Geffrey's dynamic confrontation with the ekphrastic text of Dido's
story enacts the textual shaping of the reader's subjectivity in relation to
the insistently pictorial nature of medieval textuality.[16] Geffrey becomes
a figure for the reader at large who confronts the text in all its "visuality,"
to borrow a term from Norman Bryson.[17] The "visuality" of texts in a
manuscript culture represents a significant arrangement of language. Late
fourteenth-century readers negotiated a chirographic textuality remarkable for its vividness; even the act of construing the meaning of mor-
phemes required visually decoding a handwritten script, a unique image
that could only imitate but never exactly duplicate other images. In addition, the presence of rubrics, historiated initials, decorated borders, illuminations, and glosses (whether marginal or interlinear) gives each page
of text in a manuscript culture a unique, vivid energy, visually encoded
and organized.[18] In the *House of Fame*, this visual aspect of textuality is
explored by reference to the memorial qualities of the canonical text of

the *Aeneid* and the visual dynamics inherent in the reader's response to the image of its female protagonist, Dido.

An awareness of narrative as visuality organizes our assumptions about written language in a manuscript culture not around categories such as "text and image," but rather around the concept of textuality *as image*.[19] Like the the cinematic experience in modern culture, the intensely visual aspect of reading situates the reader in relationship to a complex interplay of images to be decoded. And the cinematic apparatus, as Teresa de Lauretis has shown, is a "technology of gender," a technology that both constructs and represents gender. Film theory has been particularly attentive to the construction of the subject as a gendered viewer in relation to the cinematic narrative; in a manuscript culture, the reader is analogously constructed. Within such narratives, de Lauretis notes that "woman, *as* subject of desire or of signification, is unrepresentable . . . except as representation."[20] The visual qualities of the dreamer's experience of memory and reading in *House of Fame* 1 function cinematically so that the narrative foregrounds the dreamer's subject position as a viewer of images. Geffrey's vision of Dido's story in all its vivid but unrepresentable textuality illustrates the ways in which the act of reading and its apparatus of literacy, along with the technology of book production, functioned as a technology of gender in fourteenth-century England.

In order to understand this narrator's construction as a subject in the face of textuality and visuality, an important pre-text for the *House of Fame* is the *Roman de la Rose*, a highly rhetorical text that explicitly situates the male dreamer—and the reader—as a viewer of images.[21] Even in the fourteenth century the *Rose* was very frequently produced in highly decorated and illuminated editions, editions that actualize the pictorial qualities of the narrative and provide the reader with images as part of the text.[22] One standard image in the frontispiece to the *Rose* depicts the dreamer outside the walled garden gazing at the portraits painted on the wall, thereby dramatizing the role of viewer in relation to the pictorial qualities of the allegory (see figure 15). Though scholars recognize that the *Rose* is an important pre-text for much Chaucerian narrative, the material presence of the *Rose* as a carrier of images also forms an intertextual basis for Chaucer's engagement with the specular dynamics of reading and the textuality of narrative.[23] Indeed, another Chaucerian narrator, the dreamer in the *Book of the Duchess*, is momentarily depicted as a viewer of the *Rose* texts when he awakes in a room "And alle the walles with colours fyne / Were peynted, bothe text and glose" (332–33). To some extent, the sexual politics of the *House of Fame* replicates that of the *Roman de la Rose*. For the narrator of the *House of Fame*, as for the dreamer in the *Roman de la Rose*, the masculine identity of the viewer is essentially authorized and clarified by the iconic representation of

15. Frontispiece to *Roman de la Rose.* From top left: Dreamer in bed; Dreamer dressing; Dreamer buttoning his left sleeve; Dreamer looking at the garden wall. Fourteenth century; executed for Charles V. New York, the Pierpont Morgan Library M 48, fol. 1r. By permission.

women. In the *House of Fame*, Geffrey's construction as a masculine subject depends on the specular gestures of reading the images of Dido,
Venus, and Fame.

The visual activities of the narrator in the *House of Fame* parallel the
subject position of the narrator as eye/I in the opening segment of the
Roman de la Rose. The texture of the *House of Fame* appears indebted to
the fact that Chaucer translated Guillaume de Lorris's section of the
Rose. The language of Fragment A of the *Romaunt of the Rose* (the most
likely section of the surviving *Romaunt* to have been done by Chaucer) is
echoed throughout *House of Fame* 1 and 3, particularly in the repetition
of the phrase "saugh I." Likewise, the structure of *House of Fame* 1, the
emphasis on the dreamer's viewing of visual texts, is similar to the
dreamer's narration in the *Romaunt*. Consider the *Romaunt* dreamer's
description of the garden:

> I saugh a gardyn right anoon,
> Ful long and brood, and everydell
> Enclosed was, and walled well
> With highe walles enbatailled,
> Portraied without and wel entailled
> With many riche portraitures.
> And bothe the ymages and peyntures
> Gan I biholde bysyly,
> And I wole telle you redyly
> Of thilk ymages the semblaunce,
> As fer as I have in remembraunce. (136–46)

Such perceptual emphasis on the dreamer as viewer underlies the activities of the dreamer in the *House of Fame*:

> But as I slepte, me mette I was
> Withyn a temple ymad of glas,
> In which ther were moo ymages
> Of gold, stondynge in sondry stages,
> And moo ryche tabernacles,
> And with perre moo pynacles,
> And moo curiouse portreytures,
> And queynte maner of figures
> Of olde werk, then I saugh ever. (119–27)

The "riche portraitures" in the *Romaunt* and the "curiouse portreytures"
in the *House of Fame* 1 captivate the respective dreamers. The repetitive
use of the first person in each passage locates the perspective from the

narrators' points of view, and the images and "figures of olde werk" not only command the dreamers' attention but seem to require that the dreamers undertake a careful description of these images and artifacts. Both texts construct the dreamers as viewers whose visual experience organizes the narrative. The dreamer in the *House of Fame*—a would-be love poet who lacks experience in love (247–49)—resembles the *Rose* dreamer in his erotic quest, and the *Rose* texts constitute a sort of visual pre-text for the *House of Fame*.[24]

However, by contrast to the heterosexual quest that drives the dreamer in the *Rose*—a contract exposed for all its violence and brutality at the end of the allegory—Geffrey's quest is much more ambiguous and much more in the genre of visionary literature.[25] The *House of Fame* narrator is an "unstably gendered narrator," in Elaine Tuttle Hansen's analysis a narrator repeatedly threatened with feminization.[26] For this narrator, Fame—both abstract and personified—is the ostensible object of desire in the allegory; when the dreamer sees Fame in book 3, he presents a vivid description of *fama* that emphasizes her gender:

A femynyne creature,
That never formed by Nature
Nas such another thing yseye.
For alther-first, soth for to seye,
Me thoughte that she was so lyte
That the lengthe of a cubite
Was lengere than she semed be.
But thus sone in a whyle she
Hir tho so wonderliche streighte
That with hir fet she erthe reighte,
And with hir hed she touched hevene,
Ther as shynen sterres sevene,
And therto eke, as to my wit,
I saugh a gretter wonder yit,
Upon her eyen to beholde;
But certeyn y hem never tolde,
For as feele eyen hadde she
As fetheres upon foules be. (1365–82)

As the narrator gazes on this "femynyne creature," she changes size and he becomes aware of her strange and disturbing features; in fact, the only aspect of Fame that he can definitely ascertain is her identity as a "femynyne creature"—all other aspects of this creature are changeable. The protean qualities of this female emblematically connect textual uncertainty and feminine instability for the viewer of images and the reader of texts. Geffrey's uncertain and unfocused search for fame is particularly undermined by this sight: this female image that metamorphoses before his eyes challenges his authority as a viewer and makes a fixed interpretation impossible. This vision of Fame cannot contribute to a stable sense of gendered identity for this narrator—a male reader who depends on the context provided by tradition or fame in reading any one particular text.[27]

This instability of *fama* represents the gender-specific shape of knowledge and language in this poem. In its spatial and textual workings, the *House of Fame* attempts to impose order on the past, particularly the textual past, a past that can be recuperated and depicted through literary and rhetorical means that self-consciously rely on human memory. The narrator of the *House of Fame* makes several statements about the importance of memory in the narration of his dream. These references to the "treasury of the brain," and to "remembrance," explicitly point to the medieval understanding of memory within textual cultures. The *House of Fame* rehearses a memorial awareness of literary experiences as they are shaped by textuality; in the case of Dido, these literary experiences stored in the narrator's memory are visual as well as textual, and they are drawn from several traditions. As Mary Carruthers has shown, from the thirteenth century onward, medieval texts show a renewed engagement in the rhetorical properties of memory and what she calls the "architectural mnemonic."[28] Carruthers has traced the properties of the architectural mnemonic in the *House of Fame* itself;[29] she has also explored the intersections between memory, reading, and the visual arrangement of books in medieval textual cultures.[30] These various memorial practices in medieval textual cultures derive from Latin textual communities that are entirely masculine. Both practitioners and theorists of memory are male participants in monastic or scholastic communities.[31] When Geffrey alludes to memory as a mechanism for storage and retrieval of information, he refers specifically to a technology that records and rehearses masculine experience. In this context, the memorial textuality of Dido's story illustrates the preservation of knowledge by Latin readers equipped to read the Latin texts where she originates and equipped with the rhetorical skills to remember those texts; both of these activities are gender-specific.

Before we consider the relationship between memory and textuality in *House of Fame* 1 in Geffrey's vision of Dido, we need to consider the implications of the scene in *House of Fame* 3 when Geffrey sees the classical authors responsible for the Dido story. As he moves through the temple where famous poets are placed on pillars, he describes the sight of Virgil and Ovid:

Tho saugh I stonde on a piler,
That was of tynned yren cler,
The Latyn poete Virgile,
That bore hath up a longe while
The fame of Pius Eneas.
And next hym on a piler was,
Of coper, Venus clerk Ovide,
That hath ysowen wonder wide
The grete god of Loves name.
And ther he bar up wel hys fame. (1481–90)

Although this representation of Virgil and Ovid might appear to set these two *auctores* in some sort of oppositional pairing that leads modern scholars to see Chaucer's Ovid as an ironic figure,[32] it is rather part of a larger rehearsal of "olde gestes" (1515). The reception of Virgil and Ovid signified by their placement here in the House of Fame points to the arrangement of textual history as it emerges in the *Histoire ancienne jusqu'à César* and the manuscript tradition of the *Roman d'Eneas*, which enfolds "the fame of Pius Eneas" into the larger canvas of Theban and Trojan history. Virgil and Ovid are preceded by Josephus ("That of Jewes gestes tolde" [1434]); Statius ("That bar of Thebes up the fame" [1461]); and Trojan fame is figured by Homer, Dares, Dictys, Guido delle Colonne, and Geoffrey of Monmouth. Lucan and Claudian follow Ovid. The pattern traced by Geffrey's vision of poets roughly follows the outlines from the *Histoire* tradition: Judaic or biblical history—Theban— Trojan—Roman. Chaucer also acknowledges the difficulty of reconciling the tradition represented by Homer and that of Dares and Dictys (1476–77).[33] If Ovid's placement seems to interrupt this historical arrangement of the *auctores*, we must remember that several of Ovid's *Heroides* were included in texts of the *Histoire*;[34] Ovid's appearance here is meant to supplement rather than to supplant or subvert Virgil's authority. Nonetheless, the textual ordering of history around models of *translatio imperii* privileges the "fame of Pius Eneas" and presents the poets in relationship to a monumentalizing view of the past that has no room for Dido.[35] The "architectural mnemonic"—in Carruthers's terms—that shapes the experience of Fame's palace likewise enacts the textuality of history for Geffrey: the enfolding of biblical and classical texts into a vivid narrative (in the case of the texts of the *Histoire*, these narratives are frequently animated by pictorial images) that highlights characters such as Alexander (1413), Hercules (1413), Achilles (1463), and Eneas (1485). As we have already seen, Dido has no place in such constructions of history. But earlier, before Geffrey has been transported to Fame's palace, he had encountered the compelling textual memories of Dido in the temple of Venus. This earlier experience illustrates the difficulty of reconciling the readerly experience of the texts and images associated with Virgil's *Aeneid* and Ovid's *Heroides* to the totalizing discourse of historical fame momentarily foregrounded in book 3. If history has failed to remember Dido, Geffrey the reader cannot forget her.

Memory and Desire in Geffrey's Vision of Dido

House of Fame 3 not only focuses our attention on the figural representation of classical authors such as Virgil and Ovid in relation to "olde gestes," but it also emphasizes the embodied presence of the narrator, whose perceptions and memory organize the dream.[36] In *House of Fame* 1, the emphasis on the vivid narrative of Dido's story focuses on the sensorial experience of reading for this narrator who is very much at the mercy of the texts he reads. As reader, Geffrey encounters an ancient, authoritative text eventually attributed to Virgil. This experience of reading dramatized in *House of Fame* 1 nonetheless divorces these texts from their authors and directs our attention to the visual responses of the reader; through these visual responses the narrator is constructed as a subject. Most notably, in contrast to the insistent presence of male authors on the pillars in *House of Fame* 3, the narrator's perception in *House of Fame* 1 is particularly dominated by his reading of images of two women—Venus and Dido. The dreamer's response to Dido exemplifies the relationship between memory and textuality, or the sort of "textual overdetermination" described by Michael Riffaterre: "The intertext may be as written as the text, but being elsewhere, outside the text, the relationship between the two is memorial, as if the intertext had lost its written materiality and survived only in memory, to be read solely through the mind's eye."[37]

The "mind's eye" of this dreamer is certainly overdetermined. At the start of his dream, Geffrey acknowledges his intensely overloaded perception of the space in which he awakes. Surrounded by images and artifacts, he is disoriented until his gaze falls on one emblematic portrait:

> For certeynly, I nyste never
> Wher that I was, but wel wyste I
> Hyt was of Venus redely,
> The temple; for in portreyture
> I sawgh anoon-ryght hir figure
> Naked fletynge in a see,
> And also on hir hed, pardee,
> Hir rose garlond whit and red,
> And hir comb to kembe hyr hed. (128–36)

Although the source and valence of this representation of Venus as a naked swimmer have been the topic of scholarly inquiry,[38] the context of this image is perhaps as significant as its lineage: as the first pictorial text sighted in the temple, Venus's portrait allows the dreamer to locate himself—he decides that he is in the temple of Venus—which authorizes his reading of the "figures" and "ymages" around him. Although the dreamer sees this rather erotic portrait of Venus, he does not record his reactions.

Yet, as the dreamer observes the portrait of Venus, the *House of Fame* implicitly enacts the gendered dynamics of the gaze. The dreamer's experience of reading is initially structured by his view of Venus "naked fletynge in a see," an image that depicts the female—here a pagan goddess who explicitly personifies female sexuality—as an object fixed within the scopic economy of the gaze.[39] The sexual implications of such a specular representation of Venus are much more striking in the analogous portrait of Venus in the *Parliament of Fowls*:

And on a bed of gold she lay to reste,
Til that the hote sonne gan to weste.

Hyre gilte heres with a golden thred
Ibounden were, untressed as she lay,
And naked from the brest unto the hed
Men myghte hir sen; and, sothly for to say,
The remenaunt was wel kevered to my pay,
Ryght with a subtyl coverchef of Valence—
Ther was no thikkere cloth of no defense. (265–73)

The voyeuristic pleasure expressed by this narrator ("to my pay") that the image of Venus is covered with "no thikkere cloth of no defense" elucidates the sexual politics represented by the image of Venus in *House of Fame* 1. The gaze is basic to sexual identity. As Jane Gallop expresses it, "Sexual difference takes its actual divisive significance upon a sighting. The privilege of the phallus as presence, the concomitant 'disappearance' of any female genitalia under the phallic order, is based on the privilege of sight over the other senses."[40] In *House of Fame* 1, the image of Venus, naked, swimming in the sea—like the statue of Venus in the *Knight's Tale* (1955–65), covered from the navel down with "wawes grene"—is only slightly less eroticized than the Venus in the *Parliament*. All three versions of Venus enact for the viewers both the possibilities of discerning female sexuality as lack and simultaneously acknowledging the heterosexual dynamics of readerly desire. In *House of Fame* 1, this initial image of Venus authorizes the authorial role of the dreamer, whose masculinity is reaffirmed by the visual evidence of female castration as well as the heterosexual erotics of his readerly responses to the female as object of desire.[41] By such a mechanism, the embodied narrator whose perceptions constitute this dream vision is constructed as a male heterosexual subject by the sight of Venus.

This representation of Venus as a reified figure of female sexuality, sighted by the dreamer, conflates the sexual implications of the pictorial image with the experience of textuality. The image of Venus creates a particular subject position for the dreamer, who becomes constructed by his enactment of the gaze; unlike the protean sight of Fame that appears in book 3, this image of Venus allows the narrator to identify and definitively describe her characteristics. The text limits the dreamer—later identified by the eagle in book 2 as a loveless poet—to this one set of textual desires,[42] but it also rehearses the extent to which the visual nature of textuality constructs masculine subject positions for the reader at large. The ensuing vision of Dido is entirely framed by the masculine subject position of the dreamer.

Immediately after viewing the image of Venus that signals his masculine subjectivity, Geffrey the dreamer comes upon the *Aeneid* story "graven in this chirche" (473). This pictorial version of the *Aeneid*, 324 lines long, is the most elaborate example of ekphrasis found in Chaucer. This particular ekphrasis in the *House of Fame* represents a specific use of representation in narrative: the text describes a painting that itself depicts a text.[43] A representation of this sort is a form of citation: an earlier, well-known text is contained, depicted, and thus "cited" in a later text, as we saw with Chrétien's citation of the Eneas-Dido story on the saddlebow in *Erec et Enide*.[44] In addition, the status of this ekphrasis as citation depends on recognition, which depends on textual memories. As Chaucer's most extensive use of ekphrastic description, this citation of the *Aeneid* as a textual painting in the temple of Venus not only points to the visuality of texts for the medieval reader, but in the process, it enacts a specifically specular interpretation of Dido.

Chaucer's precise deployment of the rhetorical possibilities of ekphrasis explicitly points to the pictorial aspect of textuality within the memorial rehearsal of this dream vision, since the visuality of ekphrastic description intersects neatly with the structures of the "architectural mnemonic." The potential of textuality to include images within texts— well attested among continental pre-texts to the *House of Fame* such as the *Roman de la Rose* or the *Histoire*—is here transformed into a textual image through the ekphrastic narrative. This extended ekphrasis of the *Aeneid* story demands a complex perceptual effort on Geffrey's part, and the visual text of the ekphrasis arranges the narrative as though it were a pictorial illustration for the reader outside of the text. This particular description reads as though it might describe something like the frontispiece to the *Roman d'Eneas* (see figure 16); in this respect, the ekphrastic description mimics the role of textual illustrations, which themselves closely parallel the progress of an artificial memory and its use of image as aide-mémoire.[45] The structure of the narrative in *House of Fame* 1 dramatizes the ways in which images trigger memories—particularly literary memories. The painting of the *Aeneid* on the wall of the temple outlines a narrative, and the viewer—here, the dreamer—supplies the rest of the picture beyond the outline. And this dreamer is a reader: the experiences he brings to the ekphrasis are his experiences with other texts in all their visual richness so that the narrative in *House of Fame* 1 represents images that in turn cite texts.

In this pictorial narrative in *House of Fame* 1, the outline and development of the narrative are more fully developed than in any other ekphrasis in Chaucer; consequently, Geffrey's role as reader of the ekphrasis is especially foregrounded. The standard ekphrasis in Chaucer is a brief suggestion, or a list of characters, or a reference to a particular subject matter. The descriptions of paintings in the *Book of the Duchess*, the *Parliament of Fowls*, and the *Knight's Tale* refer to texts and traditions in a general, schematic way.[46] They allude and evoke more than they quote. The *House of Fame*, by contrast, begins an elaborate pictorial narrative with a quotation of the first lines of the *Aeneid*:

"I wol now synge, yif I kan,
The armes and also the man
That first cam, thurgh his destinee,
Fugityf of Troy contree,
In Itayle, with ful moche pyne
Unto the strondes of Lavyne." (143–48)

Although the dreamer then proceeds to describe a painting, he has found these first lines "writen on a table of bras" (142) on the walls of the temple. This ekphrasis initially cites the text of the *Aeneid* and then develops into a pictorial narrative that suggests the potential visuality of Virgil's text. Perhaps it suggests also how little distinction exists between text and image in the specularity of manuscript representation. But the addition of "yif I kan"[47] to the opening lines of Virgil's text immediately calls attention to the mediating role of the narrator and points suggestively to what this narrator later cannot tell regarding female sexuality and desire in his vision of Dido. Since throughout this passage, the dreamer repeatedly makes statements such as "sawgh I how" (163), "And I saugh next" (174), the mediating consciousness of this narrator—especially what he "kan" and "kan not" say—exposes the sexual politics of reading and the unrepresentability of woman, except as representation.

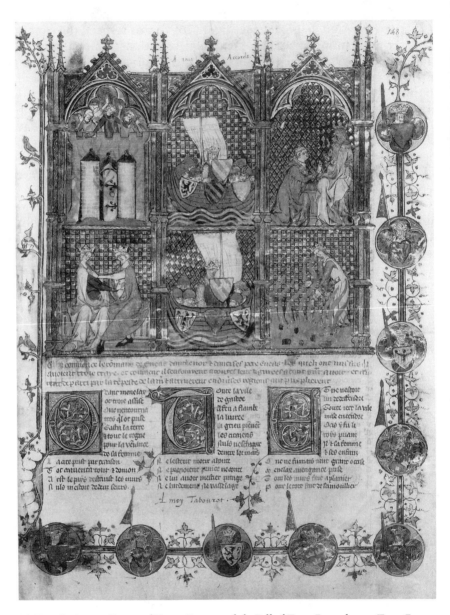

16. Frontispiece to *Roman d'Eneas*. From top left: Fall of Troy, Eneas leaves Troy; Eneas tells Dido his story; cave scene; Eneas leaves Dido; Dido's suicide. Bibliothèque Nationale, français 60, fol. 148r. Fourteenth century. By permission.

Since Chaucer presents the plot of the *Aeneid* as *ordo naturalis*, a fifty-seven-line summary of the second book of the *Aeneid* follows the translation of the opening lines. The summary represents each episode of the *Aeneid* as a panel or unit in a sequence of images; such textual images are similar to the visual images in texts such as the *Histoire*. (See figure 17, which depicts Dido receiving Aeneas into her city.) The narrative evokes the events of *Aeneid* 2: Sinon's false oaths and the wooden horse, Priam's and Polites' deaths, Venus's descent from Olympus and her advice to Aeneas to flee, the flight of the family, the loss of Creusa, the appearance of her ghost after her death, and the final departure of Eneas and his small band of Trojans. Throughout, the narrator records his reactions to this representation of a pictorial narrative text: "And aftir this was grave, allas!" (157). In Virgil's *Aeneid*, book 2 is a first-person narrative, recited by Aeneas, a fact that accounts for the pathos to which this dreamer and Chaucer are reacting, and for the curious comment, which occurs twice (once at line 180 and again nine lines later): "That hyt was pitee for to here." Ostensibly, the narrator is not hearing but seeing this text, but as Carruthers notes, the theories of the architectural mnemonic suggest that the memory image could speak.[48] The visual experience of reading this text leads him to ventriloquize the direct discourse that the text represents. As he narrates the visual experience of reading the *Aeneid*, he crosses the boundary of a purely pictorial representation to evoke the situation that existed in Aeneas's telling of the original, as though the narrator listened directly to Aeneas.

By contrast to such a narrative pace, *Aeneid* 4—Dido's story—explodes in the mind of the dreamer. The introduction to the story of Dido credits Venus (this story, of course, is painted in her temple) with the entire operation of the affair:

> And, shortly to this thyng to pace,
> She made Eneas so in grace
> Of Dido, quene of that contree,
> That, shortly for to tellen, she
> Becam hys love and let him doo
> Al that weddynge longeth too.
> What shulde I speke more queynte,
> Or peyne me my wordes peynte
> To speke of love? Hyt wol not be;
> I kan not of that faculte.
> And eke to telle the manere
> How they aqueynteden in fere,
> Hyt were a long proces to telle,
> And over-long for yow to dwelle. (239–52)

17. Dido receives Eneas into Carthage. *Histoire ancienne jusqu'à César.* London, British Library, Royal 16 G vii, fol. 82r. Fourteenth century. By permission.

This passage demonstrates Geffrey's inability to accommodate Dido as a subject of desire; at this point in the narrative, he sees a representation to which he cannot respond. Presumably the painting is on the wall before him, yet his narrative moves into a summary of a textual rather than a visual version: "Hyt were a long proces to telle, / And over-long for yow to dwelle." These frequent expressions of *occupatio* emphasize the unrepresentability of Dido at this point. This narrator's words cannot paint the picture he sees since he lacks the ability to "speke of love." Thus the initially neat ekphrasis, framed by the dreamer's perception of it and narrated by the dreamer's sequential view of the frames of the story, begins to break down when we approach the events of *Aeneid* 4 and the story of Dido. We momentarily lose sight of the ekphrasis since Geffrey's perceptions and reactions dramatically intervene between us and the pictorial text he is viewing: his own account emphasizes that he is no longer attempting to narrate the story on the wall but has begun to seriously distort the picture as a result of the associative responses to the visual textuality encoded in the ekphrasis.

The two hundred lines at the center of *House of Fame* 1 chronicle the dreamer's attempt to read Dido as she appears in Virgil's *Aeneid*: until line 265, he emphasizes his visual experience with the repetition of phrases such as "Ther saugh I grave," and the frequent use of "how" to introduce long descriptions. The repetition of "how" gives the impression of the sort of summary often found in rubrics, suggestive of the visual organization of textuality ("How Eneas / Tolde Dido every caas / That hym was tyd upon the see [253–55]). But the narrator's experience of this "text" does not clearly distinguish between rubric, image, or textual narrative proper. Just after the beginning of this section, the last marker that this story is actually a painting occurs; at this point, Geffrey introduces the more dramatic events of *Aeneid* 4:

> And after grave was how shee
> Made of hym shortly at oo word
> hyr lyf, hir love, hir lust, hir lord. (256–58)

During the presentation of *Aeneid* 4, such verbal reminders that the narrative describes a visual text disappear altogether. For this dreamer/narrator, reading Dido challenges any easy categories of understanding and any distinct boundaries between text and image, self and other. He refers to Dido's sexuality as "hir nyce lest" (287) (her foolish lust), a gloss that reads like a literal translation of the moral category by which *Heroides* 7 was read as a text that exemplifies *stultus amans*. Yet such attempts to intertextually categorize the Virgilian images on the wall cannot provide a stable subject position for this dreamer/reader, who seems unable to look at certain moments of Dido's story.

As the dreamer summarizes the next few panels of the ekphrasis, he responds emotionally to the scene he is presenting. He is elliptical about the event: "For he to hir a traytour was; / Wherfore she slow hirself, allas!" (267–68). This image introduces a long lament that functions as the dreamer's commentary or gloss on the painting. He comments not on Dido or her story but on its general applications: "Loo, how a woman doth amys / To love hym that unknownen ys!" (269–70). He considers the general condition of women, and such thoughts lead him into a series of proverbial expressions, and eventually he brings his commentary around to the example before him: "Al this seye I be Eneas / And Dido" (286–87). For almost two hundred lines the narrative emphasizes the dreamer's reactions rather than his perception: the dreamer is "saying" not "seeing" at this point. And what he says in response to what he does see dramatizes the visual experience of reading Dido for Geffrey. As he gazes on the female character whose sexuality threatened the mythic program of the *Aeneid*, Geffrey fails to fit her into an objectifying category, though he attempts to fit the specific story into his favorite commonplaces—as exemplified by his expression of proverbs that only tangentially relate to the story of Dido depicted on the wall before him.[49] His perceptions are easily thwarted and confused at the sight of Dido's image; the assumptions he brings to his pictorial version of *Aeneid* 4 do not enable him to appropriate the story.

Geffrey concludes this lament by eventually asserting that Dido's complaint got her nowhere. He then returns to a recognizable summary of the final events of Virgil's *Aeneid* 4.522–705:

> And when she wiste sothly he
> Was forth unto his shippes goon,
> She into hir chambre wente anoon,
> And called on hir suster Anne,
> And gan hir to compleyne thanne,
> And seyde that she cause was
> That she first loved him, allas,
> And thus counseylled hir thertoo.
> But what! When this was seyd and doo,
> She rof hirselve to the herte
> And deyde thorgh the wounde smerte. (364–74)

Like the earlier narrative summary before Geffrey's outburst, this descriptive segment can be easily visualized as a pictorial text: one panel might show Dido looking out at the departing ships, the next might depict Dido in her chamber complaining to her sister Anne, and the third might show her in the act of stabbing herself.

Within such a visual context, Geffrey narrates Dido's death in highly iconographic language. "She rof hirselve to the herte / And deyde thorgh the wounde smerte" (373–74) vividly describes the standard representation of Dido's suicide in the illuminations that accompany the Dido exemplum in the *Roman de la Rose*. In illustrated versions of the *Roman*, Dido's suicide by sword—both text and image—is followed immediately by the story of Phyllis; indeed, in one fourteenth-century *Rose* manuscript, both suicides are depicted in the same frame (see figure 18). The *House of Fame* shows the same visual organization of these two female suicides as if to suggest a visual memory of the textuality of the *Rose*; Geffrey's associative response to the depiction of Dido's death by sword leads him immediately on to Phyllis, whose suicide results from Demophon's betrayal: "And when she wiste that he was fals, / She heng hirself

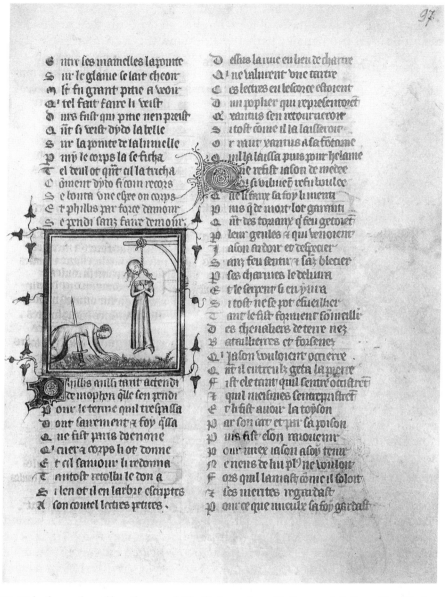

18. Dido throws herself on the sword; Phyllis hangs herself. *Roman de la Rose*. New York, the Pierpont Morgan Library, M 132 fol. 97r. Fourteenth century. By permission.

ryght be the hals" (393–94). Although Dido's affair with Eneas is almost impossible for Geffrey to describe, his narration of these suicides is highly pictorial, as though the memory of the *Rose* texts provides a scopic perspective that allows Geffrey to regain his narrative abilities at this point.

He may not be able to speak of love, but he can certainly describe Dido's death, a visual moment in both the *Rose* and the *House of Fame* that implicitly implicates the viewer in the penetration of Dido's body by the sword. Just as his contemplation of Venus earlier authorizes his masculinity, the reader/dreamer can reclaim his subject position as a male heterosexual when he envisions Dido's phallic death.

But Geffrey glosses Dido's suicide:

And al the maner how she deyde,
And alle the wordes that she seyde,
Whoso to knowe hit hath purpos,
Rede Virgile in Eneydos
Or the Epistle of Ovyde,
What that she wrot or that she dyde;
And nere hyt to long to endyte,
Be God, I wolde hyt here write. (375–82)

Geffrey does much more here than simply name the sources for the *Aeneid* story. He calls on them to complete and fill in what he has left indistinct or general; indeed, his evocation of these pre-texts implies a stabilizing context, based on textual authority, for the Dido story, as though his own position as reader, commentator, or mediator might be anchored in these texts.[50] But Ovid's Dido, as we have seen, implicitly functions as a reader who interrogates Aeneas's character and the mythic justification to which he appeals; when the dreamer appeals to the "Epistle of Ovyde" he appeals to a text that inscribes Dido's desire and lament within a readerly critique of *Aeneid* 4. *Heroides* 7 offers Geffrey an opportunity to read like a woman, an offer with which he momentarily grapples but resists in the end.[51]

The reference to *Heroides* 7, however, initiates a flood of associations—between what he sees depicted in the ekphrasis and what he has read and stored in his memory. The narrator is thus led from the *Aeneid* to the *Heroides* in general ("As men may ofte in bokes rede" [385]). The readerly position of Dido in *Heroides* 7 is duplicated by the other female victims in other texts of the *Heroides*. The text of Virgil's *Aeneid* engenders in his mind the memory of Ovid's Dido, whose story is repeated by the other women in the *Heroides*. As we have already seen, he presents an outline of *Heroides* 2 in his brief, nine-line account of the story of Demophon and Phyllis. Then, as his reaction carries him away, he mentally rehearses the plots of five more of the *Heroides*:

Eke lo how fals and reccheles
Was to Breseyda Achilles,

148

And Paris to Oenone,
And Jason to Isiphile,
And eft Jason to Medea,
As Ercules to Dyanira,
For he left hir for Yole,
That made hym cache his deth, parde. (397–404)

These betrayals are each the topic of one of Ovid's *Heroides* (3, 5, 6, 12, and 9, respectively). The *Heroides* arise from his reaction to the ekphrasis of the *Aeneid;* but the female-voiced commentary of the *Heroides*, evoked by Dido (*Heroides* 7), must complement the relatively monolingual text, characterized as the "fame of Pius Eneas" in book 3. As narrator/reader, Geffrey has experienced the subjectivity recorded in these female-voiced epistles; nonetheless, such intertextual memories, engendered by the pictorial version of Dido's story, are not fully voiced. These classical women—Briseis, Oenone, Hypsipyle, Medea—are simply readerly formulations in the mind of the dreamer; they are not present in the *House of Fame*, or even in the temple of Venus. There is nothing in the narrative to suggest that these stories are painted on the wall along with Virgil's *Aeneid*. In this instance, Ovid is in the eye of the beholder.

Geffrey completes his digression with the story of Theseus (*Heroides* 10), a nineteen-line summary of Theseus's broken oath that parallels *Heroides* 10—in some places quite closely. This summary then ends with a direct reference to the textuality of this story: "as the book us tellis" (426). Prompted by the wealth of material he has stored in his mind, this bookish narrator returns abruptly to the textual context of the *Aeneid*:

> But to excusen Eneas
> Fullyche of al his grete trespas,
> The book seyth Mercurie, sauns fayle,
> Bad hym goo into Italye,
> And leve Auffrikes regioun,
> And Dido and hir faire toun. (427–32)

Dido has not only threatened the stability of Aeneas, but Ovid's Dido as reader calls into question the *Aeneid* story, and by extension the stability of the dreamer/reader. The dreamer ultimately appeals to Virgilian authority to reorient himself.

After the dreamer has finished his digression on the texts of the *Heroides* and *Aeneid* 4, he literally begins to *see* more clearly the outlines of the pictorial text on the wall. The final bit of summary is punctuated by expressions that emphasize the dreamer's act of viewing the painting. The dreamer sees two events of *Aeneid* 5: the scene that opens the book

149

(Aeneas setting sail for Italy when a storm arrives [1–4]) and the very end of *Aeneid* 5 (the loss of Palinurus [827–71]). *Aeneid* 6 is compressed into a similarly static, visual image.

After a brief summary of the last six books of the *Aeneid*, the dreamer breaks off with a comment that emphasizes his subjective absorption in the textuality of the *Aeneid* story: "But not wot I whoo did hem wirche, / Ne where I am, ne in what contree" (474–75). The dreamer goes out of the temple and enters a large field of sand—a desert called Libya, and possibly meant to refer to Dido's Libya.[52] The vividness of the painting, which leads to his decentering involvement with Dido's story, when juxtaposed to the desert outside, dramatizes the effect of "awakening" from a text.[53] Throughout his viewing of the figures and scenes on the walls of the temple, Geffrey has been producing his own images as the product of his reading, especially in response to Dido: this narrator is little more than the sum of the texts he has read, and he cannot keep them out of the picture. The world outside the temple/text appears all the more stark to the dreamer, who, like a/the reader, is constructed by the text.

Given the technology of gender at work in this text, Dido is primarily represented as the object of the male gaze, and thereby the object of desire, despite the dreamer's insistent awareness of *Aeneid* 4 and *Heroides* 7 as a set of texts that situate Dido—and several other classical women—as the subject of desire. Nonetheless, the memory of Dido's story offers Geffrey a momentary subject position that calls into question the totalizing discourse identified as the mythic/historical program of the *Aeneid* ("the fame of Pius Eneas") in *House of Fame* 3. The interpretive gestures made by Geffrey the dreamer in response to the image/text of Dido suggest that reading—like dreaming—is an associative activity highly dependent on memorial process, and potentially given to repetitive critique rather than closure. Such reading—and remembering—appears to be a masculine gesture. Nonetheless, the specularity of Dido's suicide allows Geffrey to achieve some semblance of interpretive mastery. In book 3, after Geffrey has enumerated the poets of history on the pillars in the palace of fame, his final comment refers to their discourse as a "ful confus matere" (1517). This refers, of course, to the contradictions between these poets, but this comment also points to the memory of Dido and the exclusionary practices represented by this particular construction of history her memory exposes.

The subjectivity of this male narrator remains uncertain and unstable until the end of the poem. In her analysis of marginal male subjectivities, Kaja Silverman makes a connection between "historical trauma"—particularly that of war—and the difficulties the male subject might face within cultural discourses.[54] It is worth considering the cultural discourses at work when this text was produced. Chaucer may have purposefully depicted Geffrey's subjectivity "at the margins," as Silverman would say, as part of a portrait of cultural uncertainty. The *House of Fame* (1379–80) emerges from a decade marked by uncertainty; the 1370s saw the English effort in the Hundred Years War look increasingly impotent; the death of the Black Prince and Edward III within the decade brought the young Richard II to the throne in a period of economic distress due to the war.[55] Yet there existed a general cultural climate based on class mobility and the proliferation of texts, as we noted earlier. Cultural traumas—in the form of the Peasants' Revolt and the difficulties of Richard II—were yet to come in the decades that followed. Geffrey's experience of texts and traditions may fail to fully authorize a secure masculine subjectivity, yet the progress of the poem assures that, as Hansen notes, Geffrey is "finally *not* a woman."[56] Dido's critique, connected to the unrepresentability of female desire, contributes to the narrator's confusion as a reader in the face of history; but despite the confusions presented by dreams, reading, memory, fame, and history, the gender of this narrator is signaled by the specularity of his interpretive gestures, by his ability to enact the male gaze—particularly at the moment Dido falls on the sword—in the face of Dido's critique. In the context of the cultural anxieties of the 1370s, this narrator may not be able to achieve a completely stable masculinity, but in the course of the poem he nonetheless resists the dangers of feminization.

Although the medieval Dido drawn from the Aeneas-Dido story exists in a variety of texts and images, the ekphrastic image of Dido in *House of Fame* 1 is one of the most specular moments in the medieval reception and transformation of the Virgilian Dido. Since the *House of Fame*—along with most of the Chaucerian corpus—has no iconographic tradition of manuscript illumination, Dido's visual status in this text is striking. Compared to Dante's gentle glance at Dido in *Inferno* 5, Chaucer relentlessly explores the gendered politics of the gaze in relation to the subject position occupied by the reader, as if to follow the interpretive suggestions presented by Jean de Meun's Dido rather than Dante's Dido.[57] While Dido's status as a subject of desire remains all but unrepresentable in the *House of Fame*, her subject position as reader of the *Aeneid* in Ovid's *Heroides* 7 is momentarily explored by Geffrey. It is her status as representation—the image of Dido falling on the sword—that emerges most forcefully here. Her death provides the most vivid possibility for reading Dido. This complex set of responses to reading Dido in *House of Fame* 1 clearly contributes to Geffrey's confusion in the face of Virgil and his responsibility for pius Eneas in *House of Fame* 3. An entirely different set of issues regarding gender and representation animates the *Legend of Dido*.

"The Naked Text in English":
Gender and Translation in the *Legends*

The *Legends* narrator differs strikingly from the self-conscious, self-effacing Geffrey, whose uncertain status as a masculine subject is so carefully explored in the *House of Fame*. As Rita Copeland has shown, the narrator in the *Prologue to the Legend of Good Women* essentially works to position himself and claim authority as a vernacular *auctor*.[58] By contrast to the destabilizing conditions under which Geffrey rehearses the experience of reading Dido in *House of Fame* 1, the *Legends* narrator assertively states the authorial control necessary to his task when he authoritatively declares his intentions to translate "olde appreved stories":

> For myn entent is, or I fro yow fare,
> The naked text in English to declare
> Of many a story, or elles of many a geste,
> As autours seyn; leveth hem if yow leste. (G. 85–88)

One such "naked text," the *Legend of Dido*, represents an explicit repetition for Chaucer and his narrator; as a retelling not only of Virgil's *Aeneid* and Ovid's *Heroides* 7 but also of Chaucer's *House of Fame* 1, the *Legend of Dido* invites its readers to renegotiate an extremely familiar set of pretexts. As a revision of *House of Fame* 1, the *Legend of Dido*—contextualized by the playful discursions of the *Prologue*—provides a further commentary on the politics of reading Dido for Geffrey, for the *Legends* narrator, and for his audience.

The naked text of Dido's story (along with the stories of other classical women) results from a dream-vision encounter between the narrator, the God of Love, and Alceste. In this encounter, the narrator is put on trial as an author who is responsible for a series of Chaucerian texts.[59] The God of Love aggressively interrogates the Chaucerian narrator's intentions toward women as exemplified in his "translations." This narrator has especially offended in his selection of "source texts" that depict women such as Criseyde who are known for their "wikednesse" (G. 269). Besides the narrative of Criseyde's betrayal of Troilus, "Chaucer" is also held accountable for his naked text of the *Rose*:

> For in pleyn text, it nedeth nat to glose,
> Thow hast translated the Romauns of the Rose,
> That is an heresye agenyns my lawe. (G. 254–56)

The "naked texts" of the *Legends* and the "pleyn" text of the *Rose* depict these translations as texts that subsume the glosses and explanatory material of the pre-text into one seamless translation that supplants both text and commentary. The status of such "making" is clarified by Alceste when she defends his translator's work as a whole:

> Al be hit that he kan nat wel endite,
> Yet hath he maked lewed folk delyte
> To serve yow, in preysinge of your name.
> He made the book that hight the Hous of Fame,
> And eke the Deeth of Blaunche the Duchesse,
> And the Parlement of Foules, as I gesse,
> And al the love of Palamon and Arcite
> Of Thebes, thogh the storye ys knowen lyte. (F. 414–21)

According to the formulations of both Alceste and the God of Love, a translator's efficacy as a proponent of women depends as much upon his access to texts and his selection of source texts as on his abilities as a reader. In her defense of "Chaucer," Alceste even suggests that he remains unaware of his "matere":

> He may translate a thyng in no malyce,
> But for he useth bokes for to make,
> And taketh non hed of what matere he take,
> Therfore he wrot the Rose and ek Crisseyde
> Of innocence, and nyste what he seyde. (G. 341–45)

Alceste's humorous claim that "Chaucer" is innocent renders the task of translation entirely mechanical and unproblematic; both the God of Love and Alceste assume that the poet is a transparent agent who simply reproduces the material he selects. The foremost task of the *Legends* requires the narrator to select the most appropriate books available.

Since the *House of Fame* is not specified as one of the offensive texts, the *Legend of Dido* is not explicitly presented as a more appropriate version of its sources. Nonetheless, the *Legends* as a whole are intended to atone for the portrayal of Criseyde and the women in the *Rose*. Since Jean de Meun's Dido (and his *Rose* as a whole) forms an important pre-text for the *House of Fame*, the *Legend of Dido* is implicitly presented as a critique of the specular Dido from *House of Fame* 1. The ironic banter in the *Prologue* points to the Dido in the *Legends* as the more authentic figure.

The *Prologue* overall takes issue with the narrator's selection of his "matere," and the God of Love expounds in detail on the sources overlooked by the poet, particularly the classical sources such as Ovid's *Heroides* (G. 305–6), which would provide a different view of women. In his assignment that "Chaucer" revise his approach to gender and representation, he simply assigns "Chaucer" a new set of sources. The God of Love explains to the Chaucerian narrator that Alceste's story is found in a book, and that the other classical stories that the Chaucerian narrator should have "in mynde" are textual entities: "And in thy bookes alle thou shalt hem fynde" (F. 556). Whereas the *House of Fame* dramatizes the associative play of "reading" and the attendant difficulties for the reader's status as a subject, the *Prologue* suggests that a translator will act as a transparent vector for a text, unhampered by the intertextual memories that haunt Geffrey.

The *Prologue* in the end assigns the task of writing a "gloryous legende / Of goode women" (G. 473–74) as a penance for these earlier "mysseyde" translations (G. 430). The narrator is assigned a very pointed interpretive act in the process of "reading" these stories: he is to exemplify women "That were trewe in lovying al here lyves" and the "false men that hem betrayen" (G. 475–76). This task is also seen as part of a fictional reference to gender and patronage, for in the F version Alceste requires the male narrator to present the Legends to the queen (F. 496–97). This assumption that a female patron will appreciate a particular representation of "good" women is woven into the larger ironic fictions of the *Prologue*.[60] In the case of the *Legend of Dido*, the narrator returns to the texts of Virgil and Ovid, which had been the intertexts for the *House of Fame*, but on this occasion, he "translates" rather than reads them. Within the discussion of innocence and mastery throughout the *Prologue*, this process of "making" the legends creates a secure subject position for this narrator, whose purposeful approach to the "matere" of books should keep him from the sort of destabilizing experiences Geffrey faced.

The entire discussion of the gendered technology of translation in the *Prologue* turns on the assumptions that the poet works from a masculine subject position and approaches a set of texts that he reads and from which he "makes" his own text. These texts are explicitly categorized as texts that represent women. Thus the God of Love appeals to his law (G. 256) as part of the regulation of gender and representation, and the offenses with which "Chaucer" is charged all have to do with the proper portrayal of women through the appropriate selection of books and the proper reading practices. This gendered dynamic of translation practices revolves around the male poet as "maker" of representations of women. Within such an ironic set of fictional poetics, it comes as no surprise that the *Legend of Dido* renders Eneas as a traitorous, marginal character.[61] But the process of translation likewise creates a specific set of subject positions for Dido to perform a female, heterosexual desire. It is such textualized desire as it is traced in the *Legend of Dido* that I wish to focus on here.

In the *House of Fame,* Geffrey found Dido's story—particularly the nature of her "nyce lest" (285)—difficult if not impossible to narrate, as his repeated disclaimers about what he "could not say" emphasized. In the final analysis, he found Dido all but unrepresentable, except within the specular dynamics of the gaze, which rendered her a representation. The *Legends* narrator is specifically assigned to "spek wel of love" (G. 481). Thus the *Legend of Dido* presents itself as a narrative that tells what could not be told in the temple of Venus.

"That sely Dido hath now swich desyr"

The God of Love in the *Prologue* demands that the narrator tell a story "Of goode wymmen, maydenes and wyves, / That weren trewe in lovyng al hire lyves; / And telle of false men that hem bytraien" (F. 484–86). As scholars routinely note, "The olde appreved stories" do not fit this simple, fable-like moral, and consequently, the matter of the *Legends* is often dangerously at odds with the explicit rhetorical purposes of such a translation.[62] Clearly, the women praised in the *Legends* are not all equally good, nor are the men all equally traitorous. But the reference to these women is not simply a reference to their historical, folkloric, or legendary past, but a reference to their preservation in texts. Of all these women and all these texts, the *Legend of Dido* and its ostensible pre-text, the *Aeneid,* pose the most problematic relationship, since the *Legend of Dido* evokes and presupposes the most "appreved" of the "olde stories."[63]

Each of the legends is explicitly presented as a translation or adaptation of a classical story, the source of which is frequently named in the text.[64] Yet the stated purpose of the *Legends* means that the narrator must visibly adapt the "source" material he so self-consciously names to the rhetorical purpose of his own text. In the *Legend of Dido,* the narrator is more intrusively apparent than elsewhere in the *Legends:* he makes more self-referential comments, more exclamations about the difficulty of this task as redactor as well as translator, and refers frequently to his sources and authors as authorities to whom he defers. Indeed, the status of the *Aeneid* as well-read text and the possibility that the audience has Virgil's *Aeneid* "in mynde" produce the greatest amount of narrative tension in the *Legends.*

The first six lines of the *Legend of Dido,* for instance, acknowledge the politics of reception at work in this text:

Glorye and honour, Virgil Mantoan,
Be to thy name! and I shal, as I can,
Folwe thy lanterne, as thow gost byforn,
How Eneas to Dido was forsworn.

In thyn Eneyde and Naso wol I take
The tenor, and the grete effectes make. (924–29)

The explicit reference to the antecedent texts—those of Ovid and Virgil—from which this narrator must extract his legend (again, like Geffrey, "as I can") emphasizes that this text is a "translation" that functions interpretively. The deferential, Dante-like invocation of the first three lines is immediately undone by the narrator's statement of purpose; "How Eneas to Dido was forsworn" (927). The purpose of the legend dictates a particular view of Eneas as a "false" man, an interpretation that is implicitly imposed on the entire plot of the *Aeneid*, though the *Legend of Dido*, unlike the *House of Fame*, explicitly depends on *Aeneid* 4 as a detached unit. Consequently, the flight from Troy is briefly told in a summary that does not do Eneas much credit:

And Enyas was charged by Venus
To fleen awey, he tok Ascanius,
That was his sone, in his ryght hand and fledde;
And on his bak he bar and with hym ledde
His olde fader cleped Anchises,
And by the weye his wif Creusa he les. (940–45)

The careful survey (930–52) of the events of *Aeneid* 2—a book in which Dido does not appear and which consequently does not seem crucial to the progress of a "Legend of Dido"—suggestively adds to the profile of Aeneas as traitor. The loss of Creusa—a troubling and problematic moment in *Aeneid* 2, as Ovid's Dido is careful to point out[65]—is here noted in a brief comment that fails to get at the bitter irony of *Heroides* 7: "And by the weye his wif Creusa he les" (945).

When the narrator finally introduces Dido, almost one hundred lines into the text of her legend, he characterizes her in the regal splendor of medieval courtly discourse appropriate to a "glorious legend." Her identity as founder of Carthage is noted (1004–1114), although her heroic past as exile and leader is omitted by the narrator ("me lesteth nat to ryme" [996]). This may be Dido's story, but her story only takes on significance in relation to Eneas. However, unlike *House of Fame* 1, Dido's presence as queen of Carthage is given powerful notice:

This fresshe lady, of the cite queene,
Stod in the temple in hire estat real,
So rychely and ek so fayr withal,
So yong, so lusty, with hire eyen glade,
That, if that God, that hevene and erthe made,

Wolde han a love, for beaute and goodnesse,
And womanhod, and trouthe, and semelynesse,
Whom shulde he loven but this lady swete? (1035–42)

The narrator reads the *Aeneid* very closely here. The comment that if God would choose a lover, he might well select this "fresshe lady" appears to be a medievalized response to Virgil's *Aeneid* 1 (489–503), where Dido is compared to the goddess Diana. This simile never pleased commentators on the *Aeneid*, a fact that might have been available to Chaucer in a glossed text of the *Aeneid*.[66] Most notably, this description of Dido appears to give us the image of Dido that Eneas sees, though the gaze is not explicitly traced. Dido, however, looks directly at Aeneas:

The queen saugh that they dide hym swych honour,
And hadde herd ofte of Eneas er tho,
And in hire herte she hadde routhe and wo
That evere swich a noble man as he
Shal ben disherited in swich degre;
And saw the man, that he was lyk a knyght,
And suffisaunt of persone and of myght,
And lyk to been a verray gentil man;
And wel his wordes he besette can,
And hadde a noble visage for the nones,
And formed wel of braunes and of bones. (1061–71)

Dido sees in Eneas the idealized portrait of a courtly lover; to her he appears to be chivalrous and "gentil," though her look also acknowledges his physicality—that he is well made as to his "braunes" and "bones," a slightly fetishistic comment reminiscent of the Wife of Bath's when she notices the qualities of Jankyn's legs. We momentarily see Eneas through Dido's eyes; such a shifting point of view prepares the reader for Dido's response: "Anon hire herte hath pite of his wo / And with that pite love com in also" (1078–79). Dido here acknowledges Eneas's unimpaired masculinity and thereby performs the standard role for the female subject in upholding what Silverman terms the "dominant fiction": "the 'ideal' female subject refuses to recognize male lack ... disavowal and fetishism provide important mechanisms for effecting this refusal"; in her willingness to see in Eneas a courtly figure, she upholds his "phallic identification by seeing him with her 'imagination.'"[67] Of Eneas's responses, we are only obliquely informed, in a metaphorical comment (1103–5).

With its thematic focus on Dido and her perception, the *Legend of Dido* allows the narrator to explore the Eneas-Dido story as a narrative of female desire and expose the gaps that result from the specular approach to Dido's story in the *House of Fame*. Dido's response to Aeneas, to his "yonge sone Ascanyus," and to Eneas's narration of his deeds (1152–55) leads to her lovesickness:

Of which ther gan to breden swich a fyr
That sely Dido hath now swich desyr
With Eneas, hire newe gest, to dele,
That she hath lost hire hewe and ek hire hele. (1156–59)

Much like the responses of the *Eneas* narrator, who reads a medieval medical understanding of lovesickness into the text of Virgil's *Aeneid*, Chaucer here adapts the plot of *Aeneid* 4 to a symptomatic description of female desire. Dido expresses to her sister Anne that the Trojan has captivated her so much that she would "to hym ywedded be" (1179). Although the male narrator declines to "make rehersynge" of the entire conversation between the two sisters, the text gives voice to female desire in terms of marriage—an alliance that would have political advantages for Dido in addition to her personal desires. Although Virgil's Dido in *Aeneid* 4 and Ovid's Dido in *Heroides* 7 both voice their desire for Aeneas, the classical Dido is beyond control: her desire becomes a destructive force that rapidly undoes her and her city even before she consummates her passion for Eneas. For Virgil's Dido, marriage is an afterthought to her passion, despite her willingness to believe that a wedding takes place in the cave. Chaucer's Dido experiences a less dangerous desire that she wishes to channel within the social context of a marriage, which would domesticate Dido herself. In the *Legend of Good Women*, Dido is not automatically compromised as a ruler once she succumbs to desire; she merely loses her hue and her health—her city does not immediately decline.

The cultural assumptions of courtly discourse that permeate the legend function as the dominant fiction for the *Legend of Dido*. Within such a narrative context, the cave scene from Virgil's *Aeneid* is adjusted to suit a courtly romance. To the Chaucerian narrator, who had avoided retelling the cave scene in the *House of Fame* with an assertion of *abbreviatio* (1.239–44), the cave scene offers significant interpretive possibilities within the rhetorical context of the legends. In the *House of Fame*, by contrast, the cave scene is erased. Instead of the conflicting points of view so carefully presented by Virgil, the narrator of the *Legends* represents Aeneas as a false lover, who acts while the storm rages outside:

For there hath Eneas ykneled so,
And told hire al his herte and al his wo,

And swore so depe to hire to be trewe
For wel or wo and chaunge hire for no newe;
And as a fals lovere so wel can pleyne,
That sely Dido rewede on his peyne,
And tok hym for husbonde and becom his wyf
For everemo, whil that hem laste lyf. (1232-39)

This embellishment of the cave scene fits the interpretive framework of the *Legend of Dido*. Dido's response to Eneas's pleading depicts her as a beneficent host, so that Dido's desire for Eneas is understood as a courtly attribute. Consequently, when Eneas betrays Dido's faith, he betrays the conventions of this courtly world. When Dido looks at Eneas, she sees a courtly hero; the illusory nature of this perception later draws comment from the narrator, who asks women in general: "What maketh yow to men to truste so?"(1256).

In Virgil's *Aeneid* 4, the political as well as personal complications arising from Eneas's departure combine to overwhelm Dido and cause her suicide. The narrator of the *Legends* states that Dido "hath hire body and ek hire reame yiven / Into his hand" (1281-82), yet it is her body—not her realm—that bears the consequences of his betrayal. Eneas himself appears less motivated by the divine plan that he found Rome, and he tells Dido that he must leave because his father's ghost and Mercury have appeared to him and ordered his departure. Since Chaucer has Eneas voice such explanations, they become excuses for—rather than causes of—his departure. Unlike Virgil's Aeneas, who does not weep in *Aeneid* 4, Eneas breaks out in "false teres" at this point. In response to Eneas's statement that he must leave her, Dido initially appeals to their contracted union:

Have ye nat sworn to wyve me to take?
Allas, what woman wole ye of me make?
I am a gentil woman and a queen. (1304-6)

Since Eneas's departure may redefine her as a woman, her status as a queen is challenged by her inability to keep a man to his word that he will marry her.

In discussing the repercussions of Eneas's desertion, Dido first notes that the neighboring "lordes" will destroy her, but she bases her appeal to Eneas on her pregnancy: "I am with childe, and yeve my child his lyf" (1323). This detail glosses a moment in Virgil's *Aeneid* 4 when Dido wishes she were pregnant (4.328-29), a comment that Ovid's Dido amplifies into a possibility when she states that she is perhaps pregnant (*Heroides* 7.133-38). Chaucer, however, might well be following Machaut's lead in positively asserting that Dido *is* pregnant.[68] The *Legend of Dido* thereby

acknowledges one of the physical consequences of heterosexual performance for women, consequences that are generally erased in Chaucer's
poetry, where sexually active women such as Criseyde or the Wife of Bath
appear to be childless. Dido's pregnancy makes her body the central casualty of Eneas's departure. Moreover, she does not appeal to Eneas as a
dynast who should be interested in his lineage; rather, she refers to the
future life of her child, which adds considerable pathos to the act of throwing herself upon a sword.

The narrator's intrusive presence at the conclusion of the legend works
to mediate the interpretive possibilities of Dido's suicide. "And with his
swerd she rof hyre to the herte" (1351)—such a statement (which almost
echoes the *House of Fame*) would appear to conclude the legend, but the
narrator proceeds to present a close translation of Ovid's *Heroides* 7. This
letter provides textual evidence that Dido was "trewe in lovynge" until
the last moment in her life, and her letter continues to testify to and tex-
tualize her desire after her death. As Lisa Kiser has noted, throughout the
Legends the translations of the *Heroides* that are inserted into the narrative contrast markedly with the rest of the text: "Chaucer's Ovidian
translations represent the poet at his best. . . . the eleven lines of Dido's
letter end her legend with solemnity and grace. Ovid's Latin is closely followed there, his figurative language preserved along with the dignified
tone of his original."[69] The translation of *Heroides* 7 suggestively concludes with the invitation to read the text of the letter: "But who wol al
this letter have in mynde, / Rede Ovyde, and in hym he shal it fynde"
(1366–67). Of course, Dido's letter in the *Heroides* presents a skeptical
rereading of the plot this narrator has just presented in the *Legend of
Dido*. The attentive reader who would turn to Ovid's *Heroides* 7 at this
moment would find a reconsideration of such moments in this narrative
as the death of Creusa, the cave scene, and even Eneas's appeal to his
"destine" (1299).

Compared to the diffuse, associative texture of *House of Fame* 1, the
Legend of Dido has a much more coherent focus; this focus suggests that
Chaucer has purposefully attempted to dramatize a sort of interpretive
mastery, possibly to compensate for the uncertainty of Geffrey's subject
position as a reader in the face of the specular dangers of Dido and textuality. As Laura Mulvey comments, the "woman as icon . . . always threatens to evoke the anxiety it originally signified."[70] The contrast between
the two poems suggests that the anxious specularity of the *House of Fame*
might be countered through "translation." It appears more workable to
declare a "naked text" of Dido's story than to read a text that represents
the *Aeneid* in all the visuality inherent in "text and glose." As a "naked
text," the *Legend of Dido* implicitly subsumes its antecedent texts while
it simultaneously cites them. In light of the control that such "transla-

tion" makes possible, the narrator in the *Legend of Dido* can explore the nature of female desire within a paradigm of heterosexual, textual control. Instead of Geffrey's fear of what he "kan not" say about Dido's sexuality, the legend categorizes Dido and her desire by allowing her to voice it: she responds to Aeneas with pity, she wishes to marry him, she wishes to have his child. And such female desires obviously support the dominant fictions of normative heterosexuality—as Silverman puts it, "the preservation of two interlocking terms: the family, and the phallus."[71] Compared to the murderous rage of Virgil's Dido or the cynical attempts at deflation made by Ovid's Dido, Chaucer's Dido is a relatively complacent, domesticated figure. Of course, no reader can miss the parodic nature of the *Legends* as exempla that do not work. Nonetheless, in the *Legend of Dido*, the parodic texture works to expose the narrator's incapacities to make this portrait of Dido work as narrative; the parody is not directed at the assumptions regarding the representation of gender and sexuality that underpin the legend itself.

Although Chaucer almost certainly used Boccaccio's *De claris mulieribus* in his adaption of the legends of good women, he nowhere shows an awareness of the non-Virgilian Dido who never meets Aeneas and who died to preserve her status as a "chaste widow," so thoroughly embraced by Boccaccio in his Latin works, as we saw in chapter 1. Boccaccio's version of Dido's story would have fit the purpose of the *Legends*, since Boccaccio's Dido, in her commitment to Sychaeus, is particularly "true in loving all her life." As Mary Louise Lord has shown, on one occasion Chaucer seems to omit Dido from the standard catalog of chaste women where she is usually noted; it is quite likely, according to this argument, that Chaucer knew the historical tradition.[72] The non-Virgilian Dido would have been available as well in *De casibus*; the historical Dido, as we have seen, receives brief mention in Servius's glosses, in Jerome's *Adversus Jovinianum*, in Augustine's *Confessions*, in John of Salisbury's *Policraticus*, in the texts of the *Histoire*, and in the texts of the classicizing Friars. Chaucer's silence regarding the historical tradition perhaps testifies to his pedagogical experience of Virgil the *auctor*, an experience responsible for the authoritative discourses that the *Legends* narrator seems determined to deflate.

Chaucer refers to Dido only in her "Virgilian/Ovidian" identity. *Sely* Dido provided the Chaucerian narrator—a distinctively male narrator in both the *House of Fame* and the *Legend of Dido*—with a model for the specularity of medieval reading and textuality in the *House of Fame*. The *Legends* narrator attempts to achieve an interpretive mastery of Dido through translation practices that mirror the masculinist ideology of the courtly culture so thoroughly treated with irony in the *Prologue* scenes between Alceste and the God of Love. Gazed at, interpreted, and "read" by the Chaucerian narrator in the *House of Fame* and then "translated" in the *Legend of Dido*, Dido is constructed purely in terms of a masculine understanding of female sexuality. Although Chaucer's exploration of textuality and sexuality in relation to Dido would appear to embrace the female as "other" in a fairly productive model of reading and sexual difference, such a model—which channels as well as occludes female desire—relies on a binary set of heterosexist possibilities for the performance of gender.[73]

The citation of Ovid's *Heroides* 7 at the end of the *Legend of Dido* as a distinct document that supplements—and supports—the interpretation of Dido as a woman true in loving all her life endows Dido's epistle with a distinct status as a textual witness to the Eneas-Dido story. As Gower's brief exemplum of Dido's story in *Confessio Amantis* (1390) shows, this epistle and the desire it records could be read from an altogether different perspective, one that replaces Eneas's faults as a false lover with the sins of sloth. In Gower's account, Dido writes her letter to Eneas after his departure with every expectation that he will return to her from Italy:

> Bot sche, which mai noght longe abide
> The hote peine of loves throwe,
> Anon withinne a litel throwe
> A lettre unto hir kniht hath write,
> And dede him pleinly forto wite,
> If he made eny tariinge,
> To drecche of his ayeincomynge,
> That sche ne mihte him fiele and se.[74] (4.96–103)

In Gower's ironic glance at Ovid and Chaucer, Eneas's failure is due to the fact that "hise thoghtes feinte / Towardes love and full of Slowthe, / His time lette" (118–20).[75] Dido thereby thrusts a naked sword into her heart. Gower's self-conscious departure from Chaucer's interpretation of *Heroides* 7 derives from his contextualizing the epistle literally as a missive sent to Eneas so that he had time to return before Dido's suicide.

The status of *Heroides* 7 as a female-voiced text of desire in fourteenth-century literary cultures is perhaps best measured by an oblique reference in Langland's *Piers Plowman* concerning a piece of discourse that " 'It is but a dido,' quod pis doctour, 'a disourss tale.' "[76] The *Middle English Dictionary* glosses this use of "dido" as "A story of Dido, an old wives' tale." The textual authority of *Heroides* 7 was insufficient to grant cultural authenticity to female-voiced desire. In two efforts at translating Dido a century later, Caxton and Gavin Douglas both confront the textual legacy of multiple traditions and perpectives on Dido and what Douglas would call her double wound.

CHAPTER 5

Dido's Double Wound in Caxton's *Eneydos* and Gavin Douglas's *Eneados*

> My mastir Chauser gretly Virgill offendit.
> All thoch I be tobald hym to repreif,
> He was fer baldar, certis, by hys leif,
> Sayand he followit Virgillis lantern toforn,
> Quhou Eneas to Dydo was forsworn.
> Was he forsworn? Than Eneas was fals—
> That he admittis, and callys hym traytour als.
> Thus, wenyng allane Ene to haue reprevit,
> He haß gretly the prynce of poetis grevit.
>
> (Prol. 1.410–18)

> Bot sikkyrly, of resson me behufis
> Excuß Chauser fra all maner repruffis,
> In lovying of thir ladeis lylly quhite
> He set on Virgill and Eneas this wyte,
> For he was evir (God wait) all womanis frend.[1]
>
> (Prol. 1.445–49)

As we saw in the last chapter, the narrator in Chaucer's *House of Fame* 1 initiates his version of the *Aeneid* with the statement: "I wol now singen, yif I kan" (143). The addition of "yif I kan" to Virgil's stately opening lines—"arma virumque cano"—is a standard piece of Chaucerian irony, an irony that turns on questions of authorial authority in narrative. With his "yif I kan," the narrator invites us to contemplate his poses, his irony, and our susceptibility to his manipulative strategies. Such a comment reminds us, if we need reminding, that Chaucer's narrators continually draw attention to the intertextual nature of authorial performance.

In producing his 1513 Scottish translation of the *Aeneid*, the *Eneados*, Gavin Douglas confronts in deferential seriousness the very qualities of Virgil's text that this Chaucerian narrator exposes: the canonical authority attached to Virgil's *Aeneid* in the late Middle Ages. In the Prologue to the second book of the *Aeneid*, Douglas articulates his purpose and poetic stance as "followand Virgil, gif my wit war abill," (Prol.

163

2.10). Especially compared to the Chaucerian "yif I kan," Douglas's assertion, "gif my wit war abill," resonates with respect for Virgil's status as a
master poet.[2] Such a rhetorical stance is frequently evoked throughout
the *Eneados* and provides the interpretive framework for Douglas's translation of Virgil and his approach to Dido.

Douglas's *Eneados*—a text that includes prologues to each book of the
Aeneid—marks an early moment in the modern reception of Virgil's text.
In this chapter, I will consider Douglas's subject positions as a reader
(which he carefully delineates for us in the prologues). As a translator of
Virgil's *Aeneid*, Douglas explicitly works to make Aeneas the focus of the
epic and to displace Dido, whose thematic centrality in earlier vernacular
versions of the *Aeneid* greatly troubled him. In the *Eneados*, the first full-
length translation of Virgil's *Aeneid* into English, we can witness the formation of modern attitudes toward a monumentalizing view of Virgil's
text. Like the paradigm of "chaste thinking" that Stephanie Jed traces in
Salutati's text on the rape of Lucretia and the culture that produced it,[3]
the attitudes to Virgil's *Aeneid* and Virgil's Dido evident throughout
Douglas's *Eneados* continue to shape modern critical practices among
academic readers.

In the passages quoted at the beginning of this chapter, Douglas constructs Virgil as a master poet and censures Chaucer's version of *Aeneid* 4
in the *Legend of Dido*. In the process, he applies a gendered model of
interpretation when he asserts that Chaucer's text shows that "he was
evir (God wait) all womanis frend." Douglas bases these complaints on
the assumption that Chaucer intended to "follow" the text of the *Aeneid*
in the *Legend of Good Women*. Chaucer, of course, had no such intention, as the ironic narrative strategies in the *Legend of Dido* demonstrate.
Yet Douglas's criticism of Chaucer—that Chaucer does not "follow"
Virgil—illustrates Douglas's approach as translator of the *Aeneid*. To
Douglas, the *Aeneid* should be read for its "exemplarity," in Timothy
Hampton's terms, for its ability to provide "the reader with an image of
the self, a model of an ideal soul or personality which mediates between
ideals of public virtue and the reader's self-understanding."[4] As a master
text, the *Aeneid* exhibits a set of cultural norms framed by a masculine
point of view: Eneas is the hero of the epic, which is about the greatness
of Rome, a city founded with the gods' consent and under their direction.
Douglas articulates a reading of the *Aeneid* as a text "in praise of
Aeneas"—as one scholar characterizes the Italian humanist approach to
Virgil's text;[5] in both the *Legend of Dido* and *House of Fame* 1, Chaucer
implicitly questions these premises of the *Aeneid* plot by exploring
Dido's point of view and allowing her story to occupy the thematic center
of the narrative. Such a rhetorical strategy does not—at least in my analy-
sis—make Chaucer "women's friend," but it does exhibit a set of possi-

bilities for reading Dido in late medieval vernacular cultures that eventually culminates in Christine de Pizan's authorial exploration of Dido's story, as we shall see. But before we consider the implications of Christine's Dido in the context of early fifteenth-century texts, we must leap forward to two later texts—Caxton's *Eneydos* (1490) and Douglas's *Eneados* (1513). By contrast to Christine, Gavin Douglas's careful refusal to legitimate Dido's point of view illustrates a particularly influential model of reading Virgil in the early modern period.

Douglas's remarks about his own version of the *Aeneid* all betray his view of Virgil's text as the "original" against which his text must be measured. He expresses this relationship in a very rustic metaphor:

Quha is attachit ontill a staik, we se,
May go na ferthir bot wreil about that tre:
Rycht so am I to Virgillis text ybund. (Prol. 1.298–300)

In addition, Douglas asserts that he is bound to produce this vernacular Virgil in the "langage of Scottis natioun" (Prol. 103), a language kept as distinct as possible from more southern, "English" dialects: "Kepand na sudron bot our awyn langage" (Prol. 111).[6] At the same time, he states that he will follow Virgil, not word for word but sentence for sentence; such an assertion implicitly claims the benefits of textual appropriation for the cultural and linguistic idiom of the Scottish translator.[7] Douglas's concern about language and national identity points to the cultural role he wants his "wlgar Virgil" to play as a translation that creates vernacular textual authority within the late medieval court culture of James IV.[8] As a court poet whose entire poetic career spans the court of James IV, Douglas also had personal motives for undertaking the task of translating the *Aeneid*; as Denton Fox observes: "It seems very probable that at least one of his motives in translating the *Aeneid* was to increase his reputation for learning and so put him in the way of higher offices."[9] When we consider that after the death of James IV at Flodden, Douglas turned his attention solely to politics, his career as a poet appears to be constructed within the court and defined by his roles in relation to James IV.[10]

Douglas's French contemporary, Octovien de Saint-Gelais, produced a translation of Virgil's *Aeneid* in French verse in 1500 that appears to have an explicitly political goal as propaganda in support of the French conquest in Italy.[11] Gavin Douglas's translation appears to have a less specific purpose, but he nonetheless demonstrates an ideological aim in his attempts to claim Virgilian eloquence for the Scottish language and Scottish identity.[12] Such a set of cultural goals is consistent with the literary features of the Scottish courts—as James Goldstein has demonstrated—and it exemplifies some of the self-conscious courtly theatricality Louise Fradenburg traces in James IV's court in particular.[13] Douglas himself states that his translation could serve an educational purpose as well: "Thank me tharfor, masteris of grammar sculys, / Quhar ȝe syt techand on ȝour benkis and stulys" (Direction, 47–48). In light of the Education Act of 1496, which required Scottish grammar schools to instruct students in Latin,[14] Douglas's stated interest in assisting students and teachers in approaching Virgil's text illustrates the broader cultural and social aims suggested by his translation: to enrich the language of the "Scottis natioun," to claim a high level of learning and "humanist" culture for the Scottish court in its appropriation of Virgil's text, and perhaps to advance aims of the Education Act, by which a larger segment of the population could contribute to the administrative or legal needs of Scottish society.[15]

Douglas juxtaposes his Scottish *Eneados,* an exemplary text about Eneas and Rome, to Caxton's *Eneydos* "of Inglis natioun," a text about Dido. In his first prologue, Douglas judges both Caxton's and Chaucer's versions of the *Aeneid* by their faithfulness to or deviation from the plot of Virgil's text as a narrative of exemplarity. Caxton incurs considerable wrath for "perverting the story": condensing the first three books of the *Aeneid,* changing details of geography and the sequence of episodes, and—most serious of all—letting the story of Dido run away with the text. Douglas laments that Caxton

So schamefully that story dyd pervert.
I red his wark with harmys at my hart. (Prol. 1.145–46)

Douglas specifically complains that Caxton allowed Dido's story to usurp the text:

Me lyst nocht schaw quhou thystory of Dydo
Be this Caxtoun is haill pervertit so
That besyde quhar he fenys to follow Bocaß,
He rynnys sa fer from Virgill in mony place,
On sa prolixt and tedyus fasson,
So that the ferd buke of Eneadon,
Twichand the lufe and ded of Dido queyn,
The twa part of his volume doith conteyn
That in the text of Virgill, traistis me,
The twelt part scars contenys, as ȝe may se. (Prol. 1.163–72)

This "flyting" with Caxton illustrates the competing models for the reception of Virgil's text in late medieval culture, particularly in relation to the discourses of vernacular humanism. In many respects, Caxton's

Eneydos demonstrates the medieval interest in Dido—both the historical Dido and the Virgilian figure—to the exclusion of Aeneas. Moreover, as a text translated and printed by Caxton, the *Eneydos* allows us to assess the gendered models for the vernacular reception of Dido in the context of print technology as well as translation practices.

Reading Dido in Caxton's *Eneydos*

In reading Caxton's *Eneydos*, Douglas encountered a text that records the multiple traditions of Dido's story and makes Dido the central figure in the *Aeneid* narrative; indeed, the *Eneydos* almost defiantly refuses to provide a synthesis of these contradictory traditions. Such an ambiguous narrative texture was nearly intolerable to Douglas in his determination to resolve any contradictions in the reception of the *Aeneid*. But Caxton's *Eneydos* represents a complex set of traditions regarding Virgil and Dido that shaped its contradictory plot. Caxton's text—printed in 1490—is a very close translation of a French prose text, the *Livre des Eneydes*, printed in Lyons by Guillaume Le Roy in 1483, though the author and date of composition are unknown.[16] As a loose paraphrase of the *Aeneid* story that contains an acknowledgment of the tradition of the historical Dido, the *Eneydes* is best considered a vernacular compilation of various interpretive traditions engendered by Virgil's text, including the material from the *Histoire ancienne jusqu'à César*.[17] Following the *Eneydes*, Caxton's *Eneydos* presents a paraphrase of the *Aeneid* story and several related stories, most notably Boccaccio's version of the chaste Dido from *De casibus*, which it simply juxtaposes to a detailed version of the narrative of *Aeneid* 4. Taken together—as Douglas complains—the two Dido narratives occupy a major portion of the text and Eneas seems to be a minor character.

The *Eneydos* is one of the last books printed by Caxton before his death in 1491.[18] As one of the texts Caxton himself had translated as well as printed, the *Eneydos* marks an important moment for the intertextual horizons of the early printed book. Natalie Zemon Davis comments that we might "consider a printed book not merely as a source for ideas and images, but as a carrier of relationships."[19] In his prologue to the text, Caxton carefully depicts his relation to the ideas and images of the *Eneydes*:

After dyuerse werkes made / translated and achieued / hauyng noo werke in hande, I, sittyng in my studye where as laye many dyuerse paunflettis and bookys, happened that to my hande came a lytyl booke in frenshe, whiche late was translated oute of latyn by some noble clerke of fraunce, whiche booke is named Eneydos / made in latyn by that noble poete & grete clerke vyrgyle / whiche booke I sawe ouer and redde therin, How, after the generall destruccyon of the grete Troye, Eneas departed, berynge his olde fader anchises vpon his sholdres / his lityl son yolus on his honde, his wyfe wyth moche other people folowynge / and how he shypped and departed, wyth alle thystorye of his aduentures that he had er he cam to the achieuement of his conquest of ytalye, as all a longe shall be shewed in this present boke. (p. 1)

This synopsis of the *Eneydes* outlines the general story of the *Aeneid* without mention of Dido; rather, Caxton is captivated by the vivid tableau of the patrilineal Trojan family in its departure from Troy and the heroics of the male protagonist that result in the Trojan conquest of Italy. He thereby articulates the subject position of the humanist reader as one who looks to a text for its exemplarity—his initial assumptions about the "grete clerke" Virgil and his heroic narrative are quite similar to the assumptions articulated by Douglas.[20] Consequently, his description of the *Eneydos* as a text that follows this plot and ethos ("as all a longe shall be shewed in this present boke"), fails to account for the significant place of Dido in the narrative; yet in the process of presenting a translation of the *Eneydes*, Caxton becomes inextricably enmeshed in conflicting stories about Dido.

Caxton has actually imposed his expectations of exemplarity on the text of the *Eneydes* through the rhetorical framing of readers' expectations in his prologue. The *Eneydes* presents a distinctly different focus than the one attributed to it by Caxton. The 1483 edition of the *Eneydes* opens with a prologue—preserved in Caxton's version—that sets the story of the *Eneydes* in relation to contemporary strife; in Caxton's translation it reads:

And also this present boke is necessarye to alle cytezens & habytaunts in townes and castellis / for they shal see, How somtyme troye the graunte / and many other places stronge and inexpugnable, haue ben be-sieged sharpely & assayled, And also coragyously and valyauntly defended / and the sayd boke is atte this present tyme moche necessarye / for to enstructe smale and grete, for euerych in his ryght / to kepe & defende / For a thynge more noble is to dye / than vylanously to be subdued. (p. 10)

In Caxton's version, this introduction is overshadowed by the translator's long prologue, which contextualizes the *Eneydos* by reference to the linguistic difference between the two texts and the general problems of dialects and languages for the translator. In the *Eneydes*, this initial introduction sets up the siege of Troy "and many other places stronge and inexpugnable" as the moral frame of reference for its readers, themselves preoccupied with "keeping and defending" their castles and towns. By contrast to Caxton's attention to the male figure of Eneas, this narrator focuses on the city of Troy as the protagonist in the narrative; consequently, the attention in the text to Dido's establishment of Carthage and her subsequent fall localizes one of the "places stronge" referred to in the introduction as an alternate story to the Troy story.

The 1483 Lyons edition of the *Eneydes* contains a series of woodcuts that emphasize this particular focus on Troy and other cities; although Caxton may not have actually worked from the printed version of the *Eneydes*, these woodcuts nonetheless provide an alternate interpretive framework for the *Eneydes* that contradicts the one Caxton is at pains to emphasize. Of the sixty-one woodcuts that appear in this text, twenty span the section that covers Dido's stories.[21] The woodcut that introduces the historical Dido depicts her founding Carthage (see figure 19); the rubric to the image explains: "Comment dydo en libie pais estrange achata terre du large cuyr de beuf on elle edifia la cite de cartaige" (how in the foreign country of Libya Dido purchased land by means of a large hide of an ox on which she established the city of Carthage). As Michael Camille has observed, the images in a printed text are incorporated into the reading experience "precisely because the image has the same black and white structure as the word, and although it is read in space, is also read in time, following a linear pattern just as in the flow of language."[22] The woodcut depicts Dido in the center of the activities directing the founding of Carthage, the building of the walls, and the discovery of the horse's head. Such a visual component to the narrative of the *Eneydes* makes the story of Dido a story of Carthage and thematically connects this image to the frontispiece, which depicts the founding of Troy.

In the *Eneydes*, Dido's two deaths are illustrated by the same woodcut (see figure 20), which serves to punctuate the end of Boccaccio's version of Dido's story and appears again at the end of the Virgilian section, after fourteen intervening woodcuts, to conclude her story. This repetition forms a visual link between the two disparate stories, enfolding the historical version of Dido's death into the Virgilian one.[23] But this repetition also works to subsume the Dido story under the story of Carthage. Thus the *Eneydes*, in its printed form at least, provides specific visual clues that work to incorporate the contradictory texts of Dido's life into the larger design. Although Caxton has provided a close duplication of the *Eneydes* in English, the addition of Caxton's prologue with its focus on Eneas and the absence of any illustration in Caxton's edition make the *Eneydos* an entirely different experience for the reader than the *Eneydes*; in the Caxton version, Dido's story seems much more of a disruption.

19. Dido establishes Carthage. Woodcut. Guillaume Le Roy, *Eneydes* (1483). From the Lessing J. Rosenwald Collection, Rare Book and Special Collections Division, Library of Congress.

Caxton produced his *Eneydos* to meet a particular demand for texts in English. By 1490, Caxton's career as a translator and his business role as a printer were long established. Caxton's commitments to translation and printing are indeed inseparable: his own press authorized his twenty-six translations by printing them, and his translations fed his press and his business.[24] As a translator, Caxton demonstrates his concern to choose a specific readership through his choice of styles, so that Caxton's choice of a middle style ("not ouer rude ne curyous" [p. 3]) explicitly targets a specific audience, identified by the language he employs as a class-specific dialect:[25] "This present booke is not for a rude vplondyssh man to laboure therin ne rede it / but onely for a clerke & a noble gentylman that feleth and vnderstondeth in faytes of armes, in loue, & in noble chyualrye / Therfor . . . I haue reduced & translated this sayd booke in to our englysshe" (p. 3). Likewise, as a printer marketing his product in his pro-

170

20. Dido throws herself on the sword. Woodcut. Guillaume Le Roy, *Eneydes* (1483). From the Lessing J. Rosenwald Collection, Rare Book and Special Collections Division, Library of Congress.

logue, he openly appeals to a specific audience. Caxton's *Eneydos* is explicitly characterized as a close translation of the *Eneydes* ("For I haue but folowed my copye in frenshe as nygh as me is possyble" [p. 4]).[26] In translating and echoing the French compiler's stated intentions, Caxton acknowledges the narrative problems posed by the story of Dido when he sets out "firste to shewe the dyfference of Iohn bochace and of vyrgyle, to putte in bryef the falle of the sayd dydo recounted by bocache / and after by the sayde virgyle" (p. 22). Caxton's text preserves an "authorial" comment from the *Eneydes* on the problems posed by Boccaccio's version:

I fonde the falle of dydo, somtyme quene and foundresse of the noble cyte of cartage; the whiche in redynge, I was abasshed, and had grete merueylle / how bochace, whiche is an auctour so gretly renommed, hath transposed, or atte leste dyuersifyed, the falle and

caas otherwyse than vyrgyle hath in his fourth booke of *Eneydos* /
In whiche he hath not rendred the reason / or made ony decysion,
to approue better the his than that other. And yf ony wolde excuse
hym, and saye that he hadde doon hit for better to kepe thonour of
wymmen . . . This reason hath noo place: For he hath putte in
many places other grete falles, ouermoche infamous . . . By the
whiche partyculerly he sheweth the dyssolucyons and peruerse
condycyons that ben in the sexe femynyne. (p. 23)

Despite such pointed comments, which Caxton reproduces from the
French text, the *Eneydes* did not constitute Caxton's first acquaintance
with Dido in either historical or Virgilian form. In 1482, Caxton had
printed John Trevisa's English translation (ca. 1380) of Ranulf Higden's
Polychronicon (ca. 1360); Caxton's text includes an eighth book in addition to Trevisa's text. The first book of the *Polychronicon* contains the
story of the historical Dido, based directly on Justin's Epitoma historiarum Philippicarum Pompei Trogi 18:

> Dido, þat hiȝte Elissa also, went oute of Phenicia wiþ a grete com-
> panye of ȝonglynges i-chose, and seilede first into Cyprus. And þere
> þis womman Dido toke wiþ hir foure score maydens for to brynge
> forþ children, and com into Affrica, and þere fore ese and reste of
> here men, þat were wery of seillynge, sche bouȝte as moche lond as
> sche myȝte byclippe wiþ an oxe hide, and kutte þe hyde into a þong
> þat was ful long and ful smal, and biclipped þerwiþ a grete place,
> and cleped it Byrsa, þat is a þwong. . . . oþer Carthada, þat was a
> newe town.[27] (1.21)

After this description of Dido's settlement in Africa, there follows a discussion of the exact historical year in which the city of Carthage was
founded, a discussion that concludes with an editorial comment on Virgil
and the Aeneas-Dido story:

> Þan it may nouȝt stonde þat Virgilius and Phrygius Dares in his sto-
> rie of þe bataille of Troye seiþ, þat Eneas sih þat womman Dido, for
> Eneas was dede þre hondred ȝere and more or Cartage was i-founded
> þat Dido foundede; oþer þere was anoþer Dido, an elder þan sche;
> oþer Cartage was raþer i-founded. Þerfore Seynt Austyn, libro primo
> Confessionum, seiþ þat wise men denye þþat Eneas siȝ Carthago
> oþer Dido þat womman. (1.21)

In printing the *Polychronicon*, Caxton had contributed to the circulation of the historical Dido in the context evoked by Higden, which challenges the historicity of Virgil's *Aeneid*.

Caxton's press had also produced several English texts that include an extended exemplum of the Aeneas-Dido story. In 1483, Caxton printed Gower's *Confessio Amantis*, which contains a sixty-line version of *Aeneid* 4 at the start of book 4. In 1483, Caxton printed Chaucer's *Book of Fame* with its ekphrastic version of the *Aeneid* in book 1. By contrast to this awareness of the historical Dido, the thematic focus of the *Recuyell of the Historyes of Troye*—Caxton's first effort at translation and printing—straightforwardly valorizes Aeneas; in describing Priam's family, Caxton's text reads: "The eldest of the doughters of kynge Pryamus was named Cheufa whiche was wyf vnto Eneas. And this Eneas was fone of Ancifes and of venus of mundie" (1.506).[28] Eneas is later described: "Eneas had a grete body difcrete meruaylloufly in his werkis well befpoken and attempryd in his wordes. . . . Full of good counceyll and of fcience connyng He had his vifage Ioyoufe / and the eyen clere and graye" (543). Caxton had also translated Ovid's *Metamorphoses*, a text that appears to have never made it into print. In this translation, drawn heavily on the *Ovide moralisé*, the brief exemplum of the *Aeneid* in *Metamorphoses* 14 has been expanded into a fully voiced lament by Dido.[29] And by the time Caxton remarks on Boccaccio's "diversification of Dido," the historical Dido was available in English, in Lydgate's *Fall of Princes*—a text that was not printed by Caxton, though other Lydgate texts were. Thus Caxton's efforts as a printer, translator, and merchant of books frequently brought him into contact with the historical as well as the Virgilian Dido. His comments about the "difference" of Boccaccio's Dido acknowledge these contradictory traditions. In such a context, the publication of the *Eneydos*—one of the last books from his pen and press—might be viewed as an extended commentary on texts that Caxton had previously translated and/or printed.

Caxton's prologues and epilogues testify to the editorial agency he often assumed as a printer concerned about the relationships between texts.[30] Comments about the role of the editor as a compiler of texts are scattered throughout Caxton's prose additions to his translations and the editions he printed.[31] As printer, Caxton presents himself as a mediator ("symple persone William Caxton"), who is concerned about the relationship between texts and his responsibilities as a compiler and translator. Each text off his press bears a specific, visible relationship to other texts, whether in English, French, or Latin. The *Eneydos*—as a late edition to his textual merchandise—marks an amplification of Chaucer's *Book of Fame* 1 and Ovid's *Metamorphoses* 14. Likewise, it engages in a sort of textual dialogue with the passages just quoted from the *Polychronicon* and the *Recuyell*. But Caxton also saw the *Eneydos* in relation to Virgil's originary Latin *Aeneid* and Ovid's *Heroides* 7, as he notes in the prologue he composed to the *Eneydos* that echoes a similar passage in Chaucer's *Book of Fame*: "And yf ony man wyll enter-mete in redyng of hit, and fyndeth suche termes that he cannot vnderstonde, late hym goo rede and lerne vyrgyll / or the pystles of ouyde" (p. 3).

In translating and printing the *Eneydos* at a late stage in his career, Caxton situates the *Aeneid* story in reference to other texts in circulation; his production of the *Eneydos* openly acknowledges the interconnectedness as well as the contradictions between texts. The introduction to Boccaccio's Dido, for instance, suggests the varied textual experiences a reader might encounter: "That other daye, in passyng tyme, I redde the faĦ of noblys / of who mĪhoñ bochace hath spoken" (p. 22). Boccaccio's Dido receives full coverage in the *Eneydos*. Of the twenty-one chapters that record the story of Dido, the first four present a relatively faithful version of the historical Dido from *De casibus*, introduced by the passage quoted earlier that comments on the disparity between Boccaccio's and Virgil's versions. Chapters 6 to 8 rehearse the standard details of the historical tradition: Dido's marriage to Sychaeus, Pygmalion's murder of Sychaeus, Dido's departure from Tyre and her journey to Cyprus, the deception of Pygmalion's men by throwing overboard the bags of sand, the settlement in Carthage, and so on. The story of Iarbas's proposals and Dido's suicide by sword follows the text of *De casibus* very closely. The story closes with the information that Dido was honored as a goddess.

Boccaccio's moral conclusions regarding the chaste Dido are presented in chapter 9, which translates Boccaccio's apostrophe: "O the fortytude viryle of wymmen, or loos & pryce of chastyte femynyne" (p. 36). The *Eneydos* then presents a transition to the Virgilian Dido: "I shall reherce here after now in a nother maner" (p. 38).[32] The seventeen chapters that follow present a very detailed version of *Aeneid* 4 drawn from the *Histoire ancienne jusqu'à César*. Caxton's version of the cave scene illustrates the mechanical rehearsal of the plot of *Aeneid* 4:

> For the whiche cause, the tyryns and the troiens, wyth the hunters / and other of the sayd chasse . . . were constrayned for to flee / and to seche, euery one after hys power, some vyllages or habitacyons for to wythdrawe theym selfe, whiles that the fallyng of the reyne russhynge doun from the mountaynes descended in to the valeyes. Also of a nother parte, the quene dydo and Eneas, in fleeynge, founden a caue vnder a grete roche, in whiche they hidde theym selfe bothe togyder alone. (p. 56)

174

The narrative, however, is eventually structured around a specular view of Dido's corporeal mortality, such as at the moment when her distress at Eneas's departure is explicitly compared to a corpse: "After ye whiche thinges, dydo kept herself still, without eny wordes more to speke, ał pale & discoloured as a body that is taken out of ye erthe" (p. 87). Yet when the narrative focuses on Dido's death, her "corpse" becomes refigured in an ideal form.

The death scene is punctuated by Iris's description of Dido, which follows the standard rhetorical formula of *descriptio*:

> As in beaulte corporelle / yongthe, well made of her membres, eche in his qualyte, and ryght egall in proporcyon, without eny dyfformyte / the hede well sette by mesure vpon the nek, fayre heerys and long yelowe tresses . . . her forehed brod and highe ynoughe / the browes traytice and broun, and the lydes of the eyen acordyng to the same; the eyen grene, & open by mesure, lawghynge and of swete loke. (p. 112)

This extended description of Dido's physical characteristics—presented as it is at the point of her death—focuses the gaze of the reader on a serenely specular image of Dido that offsets the long, angry speeches of the previous chapters. In Caxton's unillustrated version of this text, this textual image attains significant force. In addition, this rhetorical portrait erases the violence of Dido's suicide—visually encoded in the illustration to the *Eneydes* (figure 20)—and replaces it with the icon of "woman."[33] The long, detailed version of the Virgilian Dido gives ample space for Dido to voice her rage before her suicide. By comparison to the more restrained death speeches of the historical Dido, the speeches of the Virgilian character—her "grete cursynges" (p. 72)—impart a rhetorical intensity to Caxton's narrative: "Whan the colde deth shall haue separed me, and taken awaie the soule from the body, my spyrite shall aproche the nyghe in all the places of thy flagellacyons, peynes & tormentes, for to see thy sorowes, and to here thy wepynges and sobbynges, and grete lamentacyons" (p. 73). Once the dead Dido has been emblematized as a portrait, the narrative shifts purposefully to Eneas: "But now I shall telle of Eneas" (p. 114).

Dido's two stories occupy a little over one-third of the *Eneydos*; this juxtaposition of the two versions makes Dido central to the *Aeneid* story as Caxton tells it. Neither the French text nor the English text explicitly resolves the contradictory nature of the two versions, though the images in the *Eneydes* provide a link between the two Didos that is missing in the *Eneydos*. Caxton's prologue, moreover, presents an advertisement for the *Eneydes* as a heroic narrative about Eneas within the rhetoric of exemplarity. Yet the text of the *Eneydos*, in its focus on a double rehearsal of Dido's story, clearly undermines the prologue's valorization of Eneas and his mission. The *Eneydos*, with its rhetorical prologue, works as a single text to demonstrate the contradictions that arise in medieval textual traditions from the various versions of the Dido story and the tendency of Dido to disrupt the thematic centrality of Aeneas. Caxton's decision to translate and print the *Eneydes* suggests not only his own tolerance for the multiple and contradictory traditions of reading Dido, but it also demonstrates his mercantile assumptions that an audience and a market existed for this text as well. Dido's textual presence in both French and English text intervenes to disrupt the reception of the *Aeneid* story as a monologic narrative of conquest and patrilinear Trojan survival. It is this disruption that Gavin Douglas responds to so vehemently.

"The dowbill woundis and the mortale wo"

Gavin Douglas's *Eneados* (1513) illustrates many of the cultural complexities posed by the existence of script and print as alternate media in the late fifteenth and early sixteenth centuries.[34] The pace of the geographical spread of printing throughout Western Europe perhaps accounts for the liminal quality of this particular Scottish text: books printed on the Continent or in London circulated in Scotland, but the first Scottish press was not established until 1507.[35] Consequently, as a reader of Virgil, Douglas encountered the *Aeneid* (as well as Caxton's *Eneydos*) in several printed editions. According to Priscilla Bawcutt, he quite possibly would have known Sebastian Brant's luxuriously illustrated and handsomely designed edition of Virgil's collected works, though Bawcutt has demonstrated on textual evidence that he almost certainly based his translation on the 1501 Paris edition of Virgil that included Ascensius's commentary on the text.[36] Yet, as translator of the *Aeneid*, Douglas did not appear to intend his text for the printing press.[37] Since the first printed version of Douglas's *Eneados* is dated 1553—long after Douglas's death in 1522—the *Eneados* circulated in manuscript throughout the first half of the sixteenth century.[38]

Douglas's Virgil bears the imprint of the vast commentary tradition as it had been codified by the early sixteenth century. Both the 1502 Brant edition and the 1501 Paris edition of Virgil's collected works printed the text of the *Aeneid* along with several separate commentaries (those by Servius, Donatus, Cristoforo Landino, etc.). Each page is designed to give immediate visual access to both text and "gloss." The texture of the *Eneados* and the presence of the prologues for each book act as a vernacular synthesis of this complex set of textual traditions. In the Brant edition, for instance, the layout is extremely handsome: Virgil's text is centered in the middle of the page, its letters and lines evenly and generously spaced. The various columns of commentary—in much smaller type and much more closely spaced than the text proper—are placed as large borders around the outer sections of the page. The commentary provides a visual frame for the text. In addition, the Brant edition includes numerous woodcuts that act as visual interpretations of the narrative of the *Aeneid*; as Eleanor Winsor Leach notes, the succession of these images "gradually builds toward a self-consistent visual essay on the poems."[39] (See figure 21.) The overall effect of the Brant edition presents a highly visual readerly experience, yet the text is organized to present the commentary material as a frame for the text proper. Although the Paris 1501 edition lacks the images of the Brant edition, the page layout works to frame the text by the commentary.

Bawcutt places Douglas within humanist traditions by characterizing him as a "vernacular humanist," a term intended to reflect his sympathy for the interpretive gestures of the Italian humanists of the fifteenth century but simultaneously acknowledging that he wrote in a vernacular language for a courtly audience.[40] The circulation of books such as the 1501 Badius Virgil or the Brant edition, which contained a wealth of commentary material (along with the thirteenth book of the *Aeneid*) provides a conduit by which the textual cultures of the Italian humanists might permeate early sixteenth-century court culture in Scotland. In translating such a heavily glossed text so vividly framed by commentary—and, in the Brant edition, so frequently punctuated by visual texts—Douglas would have felt invited, if not compelled, to present a certain amount of ancillary material for his readers. The verse prologues that he composed for each book of Virgil's *Aeneid* provide a forum for his own commentary (and his paraphrase of existing commentary) on Virgil's text. In addition, the Cambridge manuscript contains glosses for the first book, in Douglas's hand; he apparently intended to synthesize much of the material from the Latin commentaries for the Scottish reader, though he obviously did not persist in this intention, since the glosses do not go beyond the first book, nor do they appear in any other manuscripts.[41]

In the prologues, in the glosses (incomplete as they are), and in the text itself, Douglas visibly attempts to mediate between the canonical authority of Virgil's text and the vernacular reader. This effort of textual mediation is expressed in the prologue to the first book as respect for Virgil the poet ("Gem of engyne and flude of eloquens" [Prol. 1.4]), whose embodied identity is specifically invoked by Douglas:

Forgeif me, Virgill, gif I the offend.
Pardon thy scolar, suffir hym to rhyme
Sen thou was bot ane mortal man sum tyme. (Prol. 1.472–74)

Liber   Quartus   CCXXVIII

21. Dido throws herself on the sword. Woodcut. Sebastian Brant edition of Virgil (printed at Strasbourg by Johann Gruninger, 1502). By permission of the Spencer Collection, New York Public Library, Astor, Lenox, and Tilden Foundations.

Douglas here comments on the apprenticelike role that a translator might adapt in relationship to a master poet. By invoking Virgil as a "mortal man," he suggests that his translation represents his allegiance to the embodied author behind the text; the textual relationship is thereby figured in terms of a hierarchical relationship between men. Douglas asserts his judgment of Caxton's *Eneydos* and Chaucer's *Legend of Dido* in language that emphasizes such embodied intertextuality, evident in comments such as "my mastir Chauser gretly Virgill offendit" (Prol. 1.410), or his descriptive evocation that "Quharin Virgill beris the palm of lawd, / Caxtoun, for dreid thai suld hys lippis scald, / Durst nevir twich" (1.257–59). Douglas, of course, represents himself as the better apprentice because he is more attentive to Virgil the poet; his translation of the *Aeneid* pays homage to its author.

This singular reverence of Virgil, however, marks a significant shift from Douglas's allegiance to Ovid in his earlier composition, *The Palice of Honour* (1501). The allegory of the *Palice of Honour* is highly reminiscent of Chaucer's *House of Fame*. Like Chaucer's text, the intertextual horizon for the *Palice of Honour* is one of plenitude: it cites and appears to critique a large number of texts and traditions, including the *House of Fame* itself. Perhaps in imitation of Chaucer's position in *House of Fame* 3, Douglas negotiates a complex set of relationships between several precursor poets—the "greit Latine Virgilius," the "famous Father Poeit, Ovidius" (898–99), as well as Chaucer, "as A per se sans peir" (919), moral John Gower, and Lydgate, among others. Since the *House of Fame* foregrounds *Aeneid* 4 and the story of Dido, Douglas's *Palice of Honour* must come to terms with Dido as a literary figure.

Unlike the one-on-one relationship constructed for the poet as translator of the *Aeneid*, the authorial role of the dreamer/narrator in this earlier text allows Douglas to grapple with the multiplicity of poets, traditions, and texts that constitute the scholarly inheritance of late medieval vernacular humanism. And this intertextual pageant is vividly arranged for viewing, both by the poet/dreamer and the larger audience of the text. In her study on court culture in late medieval Scotland, Louise Fradenburg contextualizes the *Palice of Honour* within the "arts of rule" such as tournaments and pageantry. She characterizes the *Palice* as a poem that explores the "dependence of the poetics of honor on exhibitionism, theatricalization and phenomenalization."[42] Like an intensified version of the *House of Fame*, the *Palice* presents a series of embodied poets, characters, and scenes enacted out of classical, biblical, and medieval texts; it includes a series of processions, an ekphrastic description, and a magical mirror in which the textualized history of the world is visible. As Fradenburg's study demonstrates, such visual wealth is central to the "arts of rule" that court culture deploys. The *Palice* vividly depicts its intertextual horizons in visual and dramatic terms; that is, the poem enacts and displays texts and traditions and represents poets—as well as their literary and historical characters—as embodied presences in the allegorical vision. For the narrator as poet, this experience allows him to work toward a sort of poetics of poetic identity.

One notable feature of the *Palice of Honour* is the prominent strain of misogyny that runs through the text. At various moments, the poet/ dreamer, Venus, and the "nimphe" all voice antifeminist statements, which generally appeal to the normative values of the text. This antifeminist discourse appears completely gratuitous within the context of the allegory, and it is never evoked—as antifeminism is in Chaucer—within a dialogic structure that simultaneously allows for its critique. Behavior that is considered weak or cowardly is straightforwardly categorized as feminine. In the prologue, for instance, the dreamer describes his fainting spell: "Amyd the virgultis all in till a fary / As feminine so feblit fell I doun" (107–8). In part 3, the nymph accuses the dreamer of cowardice with a comment that he has "ane wyifes hart" (1937). Likewise, the dreamer comments that in his age, faithful women are rare (592), and he challenges Venus's authority with an assertion that "Ladyis may be Iudges in na place" (695). Venus herself rehearses the standard formulations of antifeminist propaganda:

A Lady, fy, that vsis tyrannie
Ane vennome is rather and a serpent fell,
A vennemous dragoun or ane deuill of hell.
Is na compair to the Iniquitie
Of bald wemen, as thir wise Clerkis tell. (983–87)

The frequent references to Virgil, Dido, and the *Aeneid* story are implicitly contextualized within such antifeminist discourse.

Each of the three parts of the *Palice of Honour* refers to a large number of classical poets, texts and stories as part of the dreamer/poet's narrative experience. In part 1, as the poet cowers in the woods looking at the procession of the court of Venus, among the mythological figures he notices are "The Quene Dido with hir fals lufe Enee, / Trew Troilus, vnfaithfull Cressida" (564–65). In this procession, Dido is paired with true or constant women—particularly the women identified with Ovid's *Heroides* (Helen, Penelope, Ariadne, Briseis, Phyllis, Medea, Phaedra, Hypsipyle) and all but one of the figures from Chaucer's *Legend of Good Women* (Lucrece, Thisbe, Philomela, Phyllis, Medea, Ariadne, Hypsipyle, Cleopatra, Alceste). Although the categories implied by this procession of lovers are rather loose, the inclusion of Dido specifically evokes the

Chaucerian and Ovidian Dido, whose passion and feelings of betrayal dominate her story.

But this Dido occurs early in the story, before the poet's instructive experiences in the Court of Poets, where he sees a parade of poets contextualized very closely to Chaucer's representation of the poets in *House of Fame* 3. The Ovidian Dido from *Heroides* 7 is omitted from the Court of Poets, despite the fact that *Heroides* themselves are evoked by name:

> The Ladyis sang in voices dulcorait
> Facund Epistillis, quhilks quhylum Ouid wrait—
> As Phillis Quene send till Duke Demophoon,
> And of Penelope the greit regrait
> Send to hir Lord, scho douting his estait,
> That he at Troy suld loisit be or tone. (808–13)

The Court of Poets gives voice to Ovidian heroines and later eulogizes Ovid ("He was expert of all thing as it semit" [1224]). Yet the progress of the *Palice of Honour* eventually takes the reader in part 3 to a garden in the first ward of the "Palice of Honour," where Venus and Cupid hold up "ane fair Mirrour" (1476), framed by gold and jewels. When the poet looks in the mirror, he sees a rehearsal of history as though it unfolded before his eyes: ("All thingis gone like as thay war present" [1497]). He narrates his vision with a Chaucerian-like repetition of the formula "I saw," which introduces every new stanza in this 233-line synopsis of universal history. The Old and New Testaments, the Theban story, and the Troy story are all visible in the mirror; the Troy story introduces a three-stanza summary of Virgil's *Aeneid* that represents the narrative as a story about Eneas:

> Sine out of Troy I saw the Fugitiues,
> How that Eneas, as Virgill weill discriues,
> In countreis seir was be the seyis rage
> Bewauit oft, and how that he arriues
> With all his Flote, but danger of thair liues,
> And how thay war resset, baith man and page,
> Be Quene Dido, remanand in Carthage,
> And how Eneas sine, as that thay tell,
> Went for to seik his Father doun in hell. (1630–38)

This exemplum states that the purpose of the trip to the underworld was for Eneas to see "all his successioun" (1646), and ends with the triumph of the Trojan hero: "And how he faucht weill baith on landis and seyis, / And Turnus slew, the King of Rutileis" (1655–56).

This visual text of the *Aeneid* is followed by a summary of Roman history that represents the Punic Wars as the legacy of Dido's curses on Aeneas when he abandons her:

> The Punik battellis in that Mirrour cleir
> Betwene Carthage and Romanis mony ʒeir
> I saw, becaus Eneas pieteous
> Fled fra Dido be admonitiounis seir.
> Betwene thir pepill rais ane langsum weir. (1666–70)

This reading of the *Aeneid* is consistent with Dido's own interpretation of her role in Roman history as she states in *Aeneid* 4.615–19, when she predicts an avenger in Hannibal and she swears that the Romans and Carthaginians will always be enemies. But Douglas would have also found support for this interpretation in the commentary tradition, since Ascensius glosses Dido's curses in exactly such terms, when he states that Virgil here refers to the future of Carthage ("i quibus poeta subtiliter alludit ad futuras Carthaginem"), and he notes that Donatus's commentary supports this view.[43] Douglas interprets the Punic Wars from Virgil's —and Dido's—perspective, thereby reading Roman history through a mythic lens, one that makes an abandoned queen responsible for the rise of Hannibal. Although Douglas emphasizes a reading of Dido's role in history as Ascensius contextualized it, he also exculpates Eneas by identifying him as "Eneas pieteous" and remarking that he left Dido due to many admonitions, again echoing one of Ascensius's glosses.[44] This reading of the Aeneas-Dido story emerges more clearly in the *Eneados*.

The narrator describes his vision of history as inclusive:

> And breiflie euerie famous douchtie deid
> That men in storie may se or Chronikill reid
> I micht behald in that Mirrour expres. (1693–95)

Nonetheless, this ostensibly universal reading of history as a mirror of culture is—in Douglas's own terms—quite gender-specific. His use of the term "men" ("That men in storie may se") specifically refers to male readers, since he notes in a gloss to *Eneados* 1 that there is no term in English like the term *homo* in Latin to represent all human beings: "Homo betakynnys baith a man and a woman, and we haue na term correspondent tharto, nor ʒit that signifyis baith twa in a term alanerly" (p. 13). Middle English "men" is a gender-specific term; as John Fyler has shown, Chaucer frequently exploited the gender-specific nature of statements, much like "men in storie may se or Chronikill reid," in order to dramatize the effects of male interpretation of events or traditions.[45] Although

Douglas—a male reader of tradition—sees a reflection of "universal" history in the mirror, his nymph has a different view of the mirror:

"I the declair," quod scho, "ȝone Mirrour cleir,
The quhilk thow saw befoir Dame Venus stand,
Signifyis na thing ellis to vnderstand
Bot the greit bewtie of thir Ladyis facis,
Quhairin louers thinks thay behald all graces." (1760–64)

If the mirror in which Douglas has viewed the traditions of history "signifies" female beauty, then the act of historical interpretation is here explicitly represented as a masculine gesture. In the *Palice of Honour*, Douglas has insistently focused on reading as a masculinist encounter with the specularity of texts. In this regard, Douglas carefully articulates his position as a reader and a poet who is not, as he said of Chaucer, "evir . . . all womanis frend."

The gendered politics of reading as explicitly presented in the *Palice of Honour* is implicit in the prologues and the translation of the *Eneados*. Whereas Caxton as a "compiler" can acknowledge multiple, contradictory traditions that explore the role of Dido in the *Aeneid* story, Douglas as "translator" must authorize one thematically consistent reading of the *Aeneid* that deauthorizes other traditions, particularly those traditions represented by Caxton's or Chaucer's Dido. Each of the prologues acts to contextualize the subject positions of the reader that account for Douglas's translation.[46] In the prologue to the fifth book, Douglas characterizes his experience of the Latin hexameters of Virgil's text:

The hie wysdome and maist profund engyne
Of myne author Virgile, poete dyvyne,
To comprehend, makis me almaist forvay,
So crafty wrocht hys wark is, lyne by lyne.
Tharon aucht na man irk, compleyn nor quhryne.
For quhy? He altyrris hys style sa mony way,
Now dreid, now stryfe, now lufe, now wa, now play,
Langeir in murnyng, now in melody,
To satyfy ilk wightis fantasy. (Prol. 5.28–36)

Douglas notes the indeterminacy of Virgil's narrative, specifically the ambiguity that develops line by line—or between the lines—of the text. As a reader, he fears that he might go astray in the face of such textual possibilities or narrative uncertainties. Within a stanza, however, he gets his bearings when he asserts that Virgil's text is full "Of morale doctryne, that men suld vycis fle" (42).

The prologues function as commentary to direct the reader through the text. In the "Prologue of the Saxt Buke," Douglas addresses the cultural difference that *Aeneid* 6 represents for the Christian reader. In the process, he makes an allegorical conflation of the Sibyl and the Virgin Mary ("Thow art our Sibill, Crystis moder deir" [145]). As a reader of the *Aeneid*, he invokes the Sibyl as a guide through the text: "To follow Virgil in this dyrk poyse / Convoy me, Sibil, that I ga nocht wrang" (7–8). Throughout the prologues, Douglas acknowledges the dangers of reading, and he cautions readers of the *Eneados* against hasty responses: "reid oftar than anys; / Weill at a blenk sle poetry nocht tayn is" (Prol. 1.107–8). In the prologue to the sixth book he repeats such a comment: "Reid, reid agane, this volume, mair than twyß: / Considir quhat hyd sentence tharin lyis" (12–13). Douglas constructs his role as a translator whose poetic efforts in the prologues help to situate the cautious reader, who must carefully chart a course through the uncertain terrain of Virgilian narrative.

In all the ancillary material Douglas presents as a context for his vernacular *Aeneid*, he nowhere refers to the "historical" tradition of the Dido story—the version that presents Dido's suicide as an act of heroic defiance in the face of an unwanted marriage proposal from Iarbas. Douglas does refer to the fact that Caxton's *Eneydos* "follow Bocaß" (165), though he does not even briefly allude to the fact that this "Bocaß" text represents the countermemory of Dido's death. But Douglas himself must have been well aware of the tradition of the "historical" Dido. Besides Caxton's *Eneydos*, Douglas would have known the outlines of the story from Boccaccio's *Genealogia*, a text he mentions in the prologue to the first book of the *Eneados*. In addition, his frequent references to Lydgate would certainly suggest his acquaintance with the historical Dido from Lydgate's *Fall of Princes* (2.1898–2233). Servius's commentary also includes a brief outline of the historical version of the Dido story—a tradition Douglas would have literally in the margins of his Latin Virgil.[47]

In his *Eneados*, Douglas not only avoids any mention of this alternate tradition, he soundly criticizes Caxton for his deviance from the Virgilian version of the story, as we have seen. Instead, his thematic approach to the character of Aeneas as the central figure in Virgil's text directs his reading of Dido's story in the fourth book of the *Eneados*. And this approach to the text of the *Aeneid* results in a highly moral reading of book 4. The 270-line "Preambill of the Ferd Buke"—one of the longest of all the prologues—presents an extended discussion (214 lines) on the nature of love before it acknowledges the content of book 4 ("Thy dowbill wound, Dido, to specify" (215), as he translates the monostichon found in Ascensius). The thoroughness with which this prologue articulates the discourse of love is highly significant, since Douglas's choices as translator throughout book 4 reflect his critical judgments as he expresses them in the prologue.

Much of the "Preambill of the Ferd Buke" is dedicated to a general discussion of the various categories of desire. The central distinction that operates throughout the prologue is an Augustinian understanding of the "two loves," as the marginal note in the Cambridge manuscript explicitly acknowledges: "De duplice amore vide Augustus de ciuitate de li. xv. c.xxii." Douglas initiates this discussion by invoking the power of Venus and Cupid in highly pejorative language, supported by classical and biblical figures undone by desire: Solomon, Samson, David, Aristotle, Alexander, Hercules, and so on. Even the tradition of Virgil's unfortunate love affair is evoked in the assertion that love "crelyt vp the flour of poetry" (1.32) ("crelyt" = "hoisted in a basket").[48] This discussion includes a reference to the force of desire as it is manifest in the natural world, notably by horses and bulls, for which Virgil's *Georgics* are cited as the authority. This section of the prologue emphatically represents the "cheyn of luf" (1.36) as a negative force whenever it exerts too much pressure.

The framework set up in the prologue by such references to ancient figures and texts then gives way to a consideration of the various natures of love. At this point, Douglas presents a series of categories and definitions. Although the prologue and the fourth book of the *Eneados* do not apply these definitions with unwavering precision, they do present the outlines of distinctions that are critical to Douglas's rendering of Dido's story in the *Eneados*. These distinctions frequently rely on categories of gender to make them operable:

Lust is na lufe, thocht ledis lyke it weill;
This furyus flambe of sensualite
Ar nane amouris bot fantasy ʒe feill;
Carnale plesance, but syght of honeste,
Hatis hym self forsuyth, and luffis nocht the.
Thare beyn twa luffis, perfyte and imperfyte,
That ane leful, the tother fowle delyte. (107–13)

In this passage and in several others throughout the prologue, Douglas asserts that women are particularly vulnerable to *lust*—the imperfect love that defouls and disgraces fair ladies (102).

By comparison to *lust*, "Lufe is a kyndly passioun" (114), but even in its positive manifestation, *lufe* must be constrained:

But quhar that lufe is rewlyt by messure,
It may be lyknyt to ane hail manis estait,
In temperat warmneß, nowthir to cald nor hait. (125–27)

185

In considering the risks of "inordinatly luffand" (122), Douglas directly asserts the Augustinian moral behind his definitions: "Lufe euery wyght for God, and to gude end" (133). Drawing on this framework, Douglas goes on to rail against those who transgress against these moral boundaries. Much of his venom is directed specifically at women, such as "Venus henwyffis" (188; bawds), whose persuasive speech is responsible for enticing women away from their proper role in wedlock.

The first two hundred lines of this prologue have little to do with the specifics of plot or character in reference to *Aeneid* 4; rather, the narrator has taken up this discussion of desire because it relates thematically to the fourth book of the *Eneados*, as he notes in his invocation to Venus at the beginning: "ʒour ioly wo neidlyngis most I endyte" (5). Douglas does refer to "myne author" in reference to the discussion of the *Georgics*, followed by a generalized reference to Virgil on love: "Be nevir our set, myne author techis so, / With lust of wyne nor warkis veneryane" (92–93). Beyond these comments, the prologue does not engage directly with the text of *Aeneid* 4 until the last eight stanzas.

This long preamble on love contextualizes the final comments on Dido that close the prologue and provide a transition into the story of *Aeneid* 4. The specificity and judgmental tone of the prologue purposefully frame the reader's moral response to Dido. Douglas authoritatively applies his discussion of desire to the case of *Aeneid* 4:

> Allace, thy dolorus cayß and hard myschance!
> From blys to wo, fra sorow to fury rage,
> Fra nobylnes, welth, prudens and temperance,
> In brutell appetite fall, and wild dotage;
> Danter of Affryk, queyn foundar of Cartage,
> Vmquhil in rycheß and schynyng gloyr ryngyng,
> *Throw fulych lust wrocht thine awyn ondoyng.* (1.222–28; emphasis added)

The term "fulych lust," like the similar reference to "nyce list" in the *House of Fame*, echoes—perhaps accidentally—the medieval glosses on Ovid's *Heroides* 7 that see Dido as an exemplum of *stultus amans*. In assigning Dido's experience of desire to the category of *lust* Douglas straightforwardly applies the categories and judgments that his prologue has so carefully set up. The reader of his *Eneados* is given specific moral guidance in approaching the difficulties of *Aeneid* 4. Indeed, the female reader is explicitly directed to construct a moral reading of Dido:

> And sen I suld thy tragedy endyte,
> Heir nedis nane othir invocatioun:

Be the command I lusty ladeis quhyte,
Be war with strangeris of onkouth natioun
Wyrk na syk wondris to thar dampnatioun;
Bot til attayin wild amouris at the thai leir:
Thy lusty pane begouth on this maneir. (264–70)

There is not a moment in the prologue to book 4 that expresses an ide-
alizing attitude toward love—and, by extension, the role women play in
love affairs. Rather, every aspect of love as a condition or an experience is
considered in terms of risk. Such an approach allows little room for the
reader to be captivated by Dido's story or dismayed by her fate. At the
moment when Douglas takes up Dido's story, he appears to note the
affective nature of *Aeneid* 4:

Thy dowbill wound, Dido, to specify,
I meyn thyne amouris and thi funeral fait,
Quha may endyte, but teris, with eyn dry?
Augustyne confessis hym self wepit, God wait,
Redyng thy lamentabill end mysfortunat. (215–19)

These particular comments about Augustine's tearful reaction to Dido's
story may have been prompted by Ascensius, who notes in his commentary that Augustine relates in the *Confessions* that he wept when he read
of Dido's death.[49] But Douglas refers to such an affective reading of Dido
in order to bracket it; his own rhetorical question concerning his stance
as translator ("Quha may endyte, but teris, with eyn dry?") does not work
to suggest that he has been even momentarily seduced (as he says
Chaucer was) by Dido's plight. Augustine's reactions provide a negative
example: the reader of the *Eneados* is spared the temptation to empathize
with Dido by the relentlessly gruesome picture of desire that the
"Preambill of the Ferd Buke" presents in such detail. The rhetorical
thrust of the prologue presents a judgmental reading of Dido; nowhere is
the reader invited to sympathize with her plight.[50]
The narrative of *Eneados* 4 presents the Aeneas-Dido story from a singular vantage point. Dido's *lust* is identified as the cause of her downfall,
and at every possible turn, Eneas is exculpated, so that Douglas's choices
in translating *Aeneid* 4 explicitly support the views he develops in the
prologue.[51] The fourth book of the *Eneados* likewise illustrates his overall understanding of Virgil's *Aeneid* as a text about the exemplary hero
Eneas, an interpretive approach that is specifically stated in the introductory prologue to the *Eneados* when he asserts that Virgil's text is a narrative about "ane prynce, ane conquerour or a valȝeant knyght" (Prol.
1.332). In *Eneados* 4, Dido first describes Eneas to Anna in exactly these

terms: "Quhou stout in curage, in weir quhou vailȝeand!" (4.1.23), a passage that translates *Aeneid* 4.11 ("quam forti pectore et armis!").

Throughout the fourth book, Douglas constructs Eneas's identity around clusters of abstract virtues that reinforce the central values of the text. Thus, when Jupiter sends Mercury to Aeneas in Carthage to ask him whether he has forgotten the promised city in Italy, the question is phrased entirely in terms of his duties:

> non illum nobis genetrix pulcherrima talem
> promisit Graiumque ideo bis uindicat armis;
> sed fore qui grauidam imperiis belloque frementem
> Italiam regeret, genus alto a sanguine Teucri
> proderet, ac totum sub leges mitteret orbem. (4.227–31)

Douglas's version shifts the emphasis from duties to abstract characteristics:

> His derrest moder promist ws not that he
> Of hys gydyng sa faynt a man suldbe,
> Nor, for syk causys, hym delyverit twyß
> Furth of the Grekis handis, hys ennemyß;
> Bot at he suld haue beyn *wyß, sage and grave,*
> Hie senȝeoreis and gret empyre to have,
> And Itale dant, quhilk brandysis in battell,
> And, by his dedis, declair and cleyrly tell
> Hym cummyn of Teucreis hie genealogy,
> And to subdew the warldis monarchy. (4.5.99–108)

Douglas embellishes this passage to delineate these features of heroic identity—that Eneas is *wyß, sage,* and *grave*—that have no precedent in the Latin "original." In the process, he asserts a normative reading of Eneas's character that erases the central thematic conflict of *Aeneid* 4—the fact that Eneas is neither guilty nor entirely innocent, but is implicated in a conflicting set of allegiances that only his duty to found Rome can clarify. At this moment in Douglas's version, as Eneas is given direction from the gods, he is constructed in highly positive terms that foreclose Dido's critique of his behavior upon his abandonment of her. Douglas subtly presents Eneas's decisions as less open to criticism than does Virgil; consequently, Dido's final speeches appear to lack any legitimate grounds and her behavior appears to be hysterical.

Likewise, at the moment when Aeneas's lack of response to Anna's appeal on behalf of Dido is compared to the roots of an oak tree, Virgil characterizes Aeneas's predicament:

haud secus adsiduis hinc atque hinc uocibus heros
tunditur, et magno persentit pectore curas;
mens immota manet, lacrimae uoluuntur inanes. (4.447–49)

Douglas's version explores the implications of this passage quite fully:

The sammyn wyß was this gentil baroun,
Now heir, now thar, with wordis ombeset,
And in his stout breist, ful of thochtis het,
Of reuth and amouris felt the perturbance.
Bot euer his mynd stude ferm, for ony chance
Onmovyt, quhar hys fyrst purpoß was set,
That al for nocht the teris war furth3et. (4.8.82–88)

Douglas glosses the Latin *heros* with the phrase *gentil baroun*, which gives a chivalric set of associations to the noun and suggests that Eneas exhibits a set of characteristics that result from class, breeding, and socialization. He also outlines exactly the nature of the *curae* that torment Aeneas in this scene: "Of reuth and amouris felt the perturbance." As Bawcutt has shown, this glossing or amplification of Virgil's text results from Douglas's tendency to translate Ascensius's gloss—which identifies the *curae* felt by Aeneas—as though it were part of the text.[52] In identifying pity and love as the foremost emotions at this moment, he follows Ascensius in naturalizing a complex and indeterminate scene in Virgil and recuperates Virgil's Aeneas as an altogether responsive and exemplary figure. Douglas's translation works to subdue the problematics of *Aeneid* 4 as a disturbing episode that can only be understood by reference to the plot of the *Aeneid* as a whole.

Douglas's understanding of *Aeneid* 4 reflects the rhetorical approach of the Italian humanists, who framed their interpretations of Virgil's text in terms of epideictic rhetoric, a rhetoric that "relies on praise and blame as its distinctive elements and directs these elements toward attaining virtue and vice."[53] As Craig Kallendorf has shown, such an approach, which derives ultimately from Donatus, explains the interpretive framework of Cristoforo Landino's commentary on the *Aeneid*, Mapheus Vegius's thirteenth book of the *Aeneid*, as well as the reading practices of Petrarch, Boccaccio, and Salutati. Given the presence of Laudino's commentary and Mapheus Vegius's thirteenth book in Douglas's *Aeneid*, Douglas's approach to *Aeneid* 4—to praise Aeneas and to blame Dido—participates directly in the Italian humanists' reading of the *Aeneid* as a text "in praise of Aeneas."[54] Douglas's debt to Boccaccio is specifically noteworthy; Jerome Singerman has demonstrated that "Douglas' whole way of reading Virgil seems, in fact, to be heavily influenced by the discussion of the *Aeneid* in book XIV of the *Genealogia*."⁵⁵ And, as I discussed in chapter 1, Boccaccio's approach to Virgil in *Genealogia* 14 explicitly creates a subject position for a reader as a male heterosexual whose attractions to women/textuality must be carefully regulated. Douglas's understanding of "the manfull Troian Eneas" (1.81) and his approach to Dido in the prologue to the fourth book replicate Boccaccio's understanding of sexuality, gender, and reading as developed in *Genealogia* 14.

In this context, Eneas appears quite innocent of any blame and Dido appears straightforwardly guilty; Douglas does not hesitate to emphasize the transgressive nature of her desire. Early in *Aeneid* 4, Dido expresses her conflict between loyalty to her murdered husband and her desire for Aeneas:

si non pertaesum thalami taedaeque fuisset,
huic uni forsan potui succumbere *culpae*. (4.18–19)

Douglas's translation of this passage makes the issue much more explicit:

War not alsso to me is displesant
Genyvs chalmyr or matrymone to hant;
Perchans I mycht be venquist in this rage,
Throu this a *cryme* of secund mariage. (4.1.37–40)

This rendering of *culpa* as *cryme* occurs again when Douglas translates the resonant comment of the Virgilian narrator concerning Dido's misinterpretation of her affair with Aeneas following the cave scene ("coniugium uocat, hoc praetexit nomine culpam" [4.172]). Douglas states that Dido "clepis it spousage, and with that fayr name / Clokyt and hyd hir cryme of oppyn schame" (4.4.89–90).

The occurrence of *culpa* in these two early passages in *Aeneid* 4 illustrates Virgilian ambiguity of the most difficult sort. *Culpa* generally denotes, as the *Oxford Latin Dictionary* glosses it, "the responsibility for something," "to be to blame, to be at fault." The term suggests a self-conscious awareness on the part of an individual. By contrast, the *Oxford Latin Dictionary* glosses *crimen* in terms of a wider, social context: "an indictment, charge, accusation; a matter for accusation, a misdeed, a crime." Douglas appears to be aware of this distinction; of the four occurrences of the word *culpa* in the *Aeneid*, he once (*Aeneid* 2.140) translates it as "gilt." His choice of *cryme* (derived from Latin *crimen*) would appear deliberate. Indeed, Dido's own speeches make possible an understanding of the distinction between *culpa* and *crimen*. Although she initially refers to her potential involvement with Aeneas as *culpa* in the passage just quoted, upon Aeneas's departure, she reclassifies her transgression as *crimen*: "non licuit thalami expertem sine crimine uitam / degere more ferae" (550–51). In the *Aeneid*, Dido only retrospectively at the end of the book considers her affair with Aeneas to be a *crimen*, at line 550, when she must face the devastating political implications of his departure and her personal choices are thereby seen in a larger context. For Douglas, the desire Dido feels for Aeneas is always a *crimen*—a misdeed or a crime— from the moment she gives it a name. He does not allow his readers to entertain the slightly less judgmental connotations of *culpa* as guilt or blame.

In assigning all the blame to Dido, Douglas explicitly corrects Chaucer's reading of the *Aeneid*. In his comments on Chaucer's *Legend of Dido* in the prologue to the first book, Douglas exculpates Aeneas from any "spot of cryme" (420) imputed to him in Chaucer's text by explaining Aeneas's motivations in book 4 as the result of his obedience to divine commands:

Certis Virgill schawys Ene dyd na thing
From Dydo of Cartage at hys departyng
Bot quhilk the goddis commandit hym beforn,
And gif that thar command maid hym maynsworn,
That war repreif to thar diuinyte
And na reproch onto the said Enee. (Prol. 1.425–30)

A critique of this approach to *Aeneid* 4 is recorded by a dissenting gloss (not attributed to Douglas) to this passage found in the Cambridge manuscript: "This argument excusis nocht the tratory of Eneas na his maynswering, considering quhat is said heir afoir in the ii c. of this prolog. . . . It follovis than that Eneas vrocht nocht be command of ony goddis, bot of his awyn fre wye. . . . He falit than gretly to the sueit Dydo, quhilk falt reprefit noucht the goddeß diuinite, for thai had na divinite, as said is befoir" (p. 15 no. 425). The existence of this gloss shows that Douglas's approach to *Aeneid* 4 could not completely foreclose his readers' engagement in Virgilian ambiguity; nevertheless, as a translator, he takes great pains to exculpate Eneas and blame Dido.

In his depiction of the cave scene, Douglas adds an explanatory comment that amplifies and purports to explain the motivations involved as Dido and Eneas enter the cave (the additional phrases are italicized):

Within a cave is entrit Dido queyn,
And eik the Troiane duke, *al thame alane,*
By aventur, as thai eschewyt the rane.
Erth, the first moder, maid a takyn of wo,
And eik of wedlok the pronuba Iuno,

And of thar cuplyng wittering schew the ayr:
The flambe of fyreslaucht lychtnyt heir and thar
And on the hillys hie toppis, but leß,
Sat murnand nymphis, hait Oreades. (4.4.74–82)

Douglas's own narration of the conversation between Juno and Venus a few lines earlier makes it clear that the goddesses are behind this storm and that Dido and Eneas cannot be said to enter the cave entirely "by aventur." The explanation that they need to escape the rain appears quite gratuitous, especially in comparison to Virgil's spare depiction of this scene. Douglas's text naturalizes a rich, problematic moment in Virgil's text in such a way that Dido's choices appear less significant.

The fourth book of the *Eneados* generally reflects the attitudes toward desire expressed in the preamble, even to the point of distinguishing *lufe* and *lust*. The vivid corporeal imagery of *Aeneid* 4 allows Douglas to represent Dido's passion in somewhat rustic terms, such as the description of her consuming desire ("est mollis flamma medullas / interea et tacitum uiuit sub pectore uulnus [66–67]):

In this meyn sesson byrnyng hait as gleyd:
The secrete wound deip in hir mynd gan spreyd,
And of hoyt amouris the subtell quent fyre
Wastis and consumys merch, banys and lyre. (4.2.35–38)

Although early in book 4 Douglas frequently uses *lufe* to describe Dido's passion, he inserts *lust* to translate *luxu* at *Aeneid* 4.193, when *fama* characterizes the behavior of the lovers as self-indulgent: "And how the wyntir sesson betwix thame tway / Thai spend in lang reffell, lust and play" (4.5.37–38). This use of *lust* resonates powerfully when Douglas translates Aeneas's pithy assertion about Italy: "hic amor, haec patria est" (347): "Thar is my lust now and delyte at hand, / Thar is my cuntre and my natyve land" (4.6.131–32). The choice of *lust* for *amor* recalls the categorical assertion from the prologue, "lust is na lufe." Dido's fault—her *cryme*—is reduced from its rich Virgilian ambiguity to a simple matter of mistaking the nature of Eneas's desire. The complex significations of Virgilian narrative, especially the problematics of interpretation for Dido and the reader, are removed from the vernacular text. Douglas's translation repeatedly demonstrates the moral reading of Dido expressed in the prologue: "Throw fulych lust wrocht thine awyn ondoyng" (228).

The fourth book of the *Eneados* consequently illustrates the implicit misogyny of the prologue that precedes it and the explicit misogyny of the *Palice of Honour*. Rather than portraying Dido as a tragic figure who might be seen as a victim of her own greatness, Douglas presents Dido's

story as a cautionary tale. Her final speeches are those of a fallen woman
rather than an abandoned queen:

Thus lang I levyt haue, and now is spent
The term of lyfe that forton heth me lent;
For now my gret gost vndir erth mon go.
A richt fair cite haue I beild alsso,
Myne awyn wark and wallys behald haue I,
My spowß wrokyn of my brothir ennemy,
Fra hym byreft hys tressour, and quyt hym weill.
Happy, allace! our happy, and ful of seyll,
Had I beyn, only gyf that neuer nane
At our cost had arryvit schip Troiane. (4.12.19–28)

The rhetoric of this lament emphasizes Dido's state of mind more than
her achievements; indeed, her city building seems almost insignificant in
this version. Earlier in the book, at *Aeneid* 4.95, Douglas translates Latin
femina (in a passage that refers to Dido) as "a sylly woman" (4.3.11), possibly emphasizing the character of *sely* Dido from the Chaucer tradition.[56] This is not the portrait of a defeated leader.

Douglas's description of Dido as "a sylly woman" illustrates some of
the categories of gender that are operative in his translation, particularly
evident at the level of single words or brief phrases used as interpretive
glosses. The most commonly cited example of this impulse comes from
his gloss on the word *virago* used at *Aeneid* 12.468 to describe Juturna:

Of Iuturna, the verray virago
(Quhilk term to expone, be myne avyß,
Is a woman exersand a mannys offyß). (12.8.56–58)

Douglas does not present Dido as a "woman exersand a mannys offyß,"
despite the fact that Ascensius introduces his transcription of the arguments to book 4 with the assertion that Dido was a virago: "virago illa cui
elisse nomen est."

Douglas's reading of *Aeneid* 4 and his interpretive approach to Dido's
story illustrate the extent to which antifeminist discourse—along with
the epideictic rhetoric of the humanists—shaped his translation practices. Unlike Chaucer and Caxton—rather, in a direct critique of their
reading of Dido—Douglas constructs a rhetorical framework for *Aeneid* 4
designed to limit the intertextual space the reader might want to explore.
In its explicitly deferential refiguration of Virgil's poem as an exemplary
text about Aeneas and Rome, the *Eneados* is purposefully juxtaposed to
Caxton's text "of Inglis natioun"—a text about Dido. The *Eneados* thus

represents the sort of efforts at cultural appropriation—aimed ultimately at cultural imperialism—that would align the court of James IV with the learning and ideology of the Italian humanists. This particular intersection of ideologies was especially facilitated by print technology, which had made the vast commentary tradition on Virgil's *Aeneid* readily available in the printed book. Likewise, the emphasis on Latin learning and the pedagogical usefulness Douglas envisions for his vernacular Virgil suggest that the *Aeneid* could perform an important role in claiming cultural preeminence and authenticating the Scottish identity in opposition to the English, who are symbolically feminized in Douglas's view by their identification with their pro-Dido translator Caxton and their pro-woman poet, Chaucer.

The politics of vernacular humanism as exemplified in Douglas's *Eneados* relies on a gendered model of interpretation that is antifeminist in origin and practice, so that translation itself becomes something of an antifeminist gesture in its attempt to limit the reader's responses to gender and sexualities. In addition, the intersections of such gendered discourses and the explicit claims to cultural preeminence in Douglas's *Eneados* demonstrate the extent to which imperialist thinking relies on hierarchical models of gender. Compared to praising Aeneas, the medieval paradigm of reading Dido offers more open, intertextual space for the modern feminist reader. And Christine de Pizan, working in a somewhat different version of late medieval humanism, provides an opportunity to consider that readerly space.

CHAPTER 6

Christine de Pizan's Feminist Self-Fashioning and the Invention of Dido

Vous diray qui je suis, qui parle,
Qui de femelle devins masle
Par Fortune, qu'ainsy le voult;
Si me mua et corps et voult
En homme naturel parfaict;
Et jadis fus femme, de fait
Homme suis, je ne ment pas.
    La Mutacion de Fortune (141–46)

I will tell you who I am, who speak, who from female became male by for-
tune, who willed it so; she changed me, both body and will into a perfect
natural man; and I am made a man who once was a woman. I do not lie.

In this programmatic passage from the beginning of the *Mutacion de Fortune*, Christine de Pizan (1364–1430) represents her entry into literary activity as a change of gender, a formulation repeated later in her autobiographical text the *Avision*.[1] As Christine narrates her life story, the death of her husband, which made her a widow at the age of twenty-five, thrust upon her a set of responsibilities that ostensibly made a man out of her; most specifically, her widowhood made it necessary for her to support herself, and to that end, she turned to writing and the patronage it offered.[2] Christine sees authorship as a masculine performance, and in the *Mutacion* she fashions her authorial identity accordingly.

Throughout her writing, Christine explicitly connects her biography—specifically her widowhood—to her emerging authorial roles. The gender-specific aspects of her authorial self-fashioning are most striking by contrast to the self-fashioning impulses of sixteenth-century men so vividly characterized by Stephen Greenblatt; for men such as Thomas More, or Christopher Marlowe, "self-fashioning is achieved in relation to something perceived as alien, strange or hostile. This threatening Other—heretic, savage, witch, adulteress, traitor, Antichrist—must be *discovered* or *invented* in order to be attacked or destroyed"[3] (emphasis added). Greenblatt's model for a cultural poetics is quite obviously gendered. The fact that he characterizes the threatening Other as adulteress or witch

195

enacts the standard gestures of Western culture in aligning the Other with the female, but Greenblatt's inclusion of these two gender-specific terms in his list of Others also implies analogous categories of marginality: the savage is to the civilized as the adulteress is to her husband, and so on. In such a model, the marginality of the Other becomes easily elided with the marginal otherness of the female within social structures and cultural paradigms. In Greenblatt's terms, self-fashioning is a male prerogative, often accomplished at the expense of the female, as both categories are defined in English Renaissance culture. For instance, Gavin Douglas's self-fashioning as a translator of Virgil—and thereby a learned administrator with a claim to royal favors—depends on his reading of Aeneas's exemplary rejection of Dido as "threatening Other."

By contrast to Gavin Douglas and the men in Greenblatt's model, the self-fashioning construction of a female author more than a century earlier suggests an entirely different paradigm:[4] Christine de Pizan does not achieve her authorial identity in relation to "the threatening Other." Instead, it is her identity as a woman—and her culture's identification of woman with the Other—that must be negotiated and renegotiated in each of her texts. The relationship between gender and authorship consequently takes different forms in the various texts Christine composed, which accounts for her shifting subject positions as reader and writer of texts and traditions.[5] As Kevin Brownlee has shown, her early writings on the *Roman de la Rose* allowed her to "establish and to authorize her new identity as a woman writer—poet and clerk—within precisely those traditional literary discourses that had seemed to exclude this possibility."[6] Although the passage from the *Mutacion* presents the self that speaks as a female who becomes male, in other texts—most notably, the *Livre de la Cité des dames*—she represents the self that reads as female. As poet and clerk, Christine repeatedly encountered medieval versions of the *Aeneid* story and the contradictory figure of Dido, whose presence in medieval texts—whether as queen and virago, as chaste victim of Iarbas, or victim of her own desire for Aeneas—challenges any fixed categories of gender. In her authorial performance as a reader of Dido, a performance that demonstrates her rhetorical skill with antiphrasis and *inventio*, Christine achieves a "feminist" identity in the process of her textual negotiations.

The Author as Female Reader: Feminism as Textual Strategy

To claim any sort of feminist identity for Christine de Pizan engages the modern scholar in a divisive set of debates within Christine scholarship. Although the literary career of Christine de Pizan challenges the standard assumptions of many modern readers that women did not gain access to the means of literary production until the dawn of the novel,[7] the literary texts of this early woman writer have not held up under the scrutiny of modern feminists.[8] That she is far from radical needs no explanation, but many a modern feminist has expressed dismay at her straightforward acceptance and even endorsement of such patriarchal constructs as marriage or chastity.[9] Nonetheless, one frequently finds her labeled a feminist by modern readers.[10] From one point of view, such disagreement is easily explained: Christine's writing shows moments of resistance and revisionary critique, especially in relation to textual traditions, yet her overall rhetorical position seldom allows her adequate space to criticize the social institutions of her world and the resulting power relations in reference to gender or class.[11] Although a "feminism" also emerges from time to time in her responses to political or social institutions—particularly the practices of war—she does not sustain a feminist consciousness on political or social topics, and she remains a more contradictory figure when viewed in this light than when seen in the context of late medieval humanism. Her feminism is largely identifiable as—and limited to—a textual strategy, a result of her readerly engagement in narrative and historical texts and her performance as a woman reader.

Readership is central to authorship throughout the texts of Christine de Pizan, a fact that is visually emphasized by the variations on the "humanist" portrait of the author as reader that frequently accompany her works; such portraits literally depict her as a woman "avironnee de plusieurs volumes de diverses mateires," as she describes herself at the start of the *Cité des dames*.[12] The "humanist" portrait of Christine-as-reader points to the fact that she had access to books and libraries, and she possessed the education and learning that made it possible for her to make use of them. As Christine herself frequently notes, she was quite unusual in this respect.[13]

In the context of late medieval humanism as it develops in French court culture as a result of the extensive translation efforts and library building patronized by Charles V, vernacular textual culture was a vast and complex construct. In the rhetoric of reading dramatized by the *Cité des dames*, Christine the reader confronts the misogyny of these textual cultures and offers a revision of history in allegorical prose. the *Cité des dames* dramatizes the relationship between reading and writing in its introductory chapters, which describe Christine's perusal of a copy of Matheolus's *Lamentations*. Translated and amplified by Jean Le Fevre, this text exemplifies the medieval antifeminist polemic. Matheolus organized his diatribe around a series of general complaints about women—particularly as wives—and the institution of marriage. In fairly conventional rhetoric supported by the standard exempla, Matheolus insists that women are disobedient, quarrelsome, envious, cruel, proud, incapable of keeping secrets, and so forth. Christine's reading leads her to formulate questions concerning the origins and purpose of the misogynist tradition, which she finds patently false, but nonetheless pervasive:

> Mais la veue d'icelluy dit livre, tout soit il de nulle auttorité, ot engendré en moy nouvelle penssee . . . que tant de divers hommes, clercs et autres, ont esté, et sont, sy enclins a dire de bouche et en leur traittiez et escrips tant de diableries et de vituperes de femmes et de leurs condicions. Et nom mie seulement un ou deux ne cestuy Matheolus . . . mais generaument aucques in tous traittiez philosophes, pouettes, tous orateurs . . . semble que tous parlent par une meismes bouche et tous accordent une semblable conclusion, determinant les meurs femenins enclins et plains de tous les vices. (1.1)

> But just the sight of this book, even though it was of no authority, made me wonder . . . that so many different men—and learned men among them—have been and are so inclined to express both in speaking and in their treatises and writings so many wicked insults about women and their behavior. Not only one or two and not even just this Mathéolus. . . . but, more generally, judging from the treatises of all philosophers and poets and from all the orators . . . it seems that they all speak from one and the same mouth. They all concur in one conclusion: that the behavior of women is inclined to and full of every vice. (pp. 4–5)

Christine's comment that Matheolus's book was "de nulle auttorité" illustrates the variable horizons a didactic text might occupy in late medieval culture. The authority of any one interpretive tradition or text would appear provisional in contrast to alternative traditions or in the face of the multiplication or embellishment of meanings brought about by translation and commentary.[14] Textual authority implicitly depends on context. Nonetheless, she cannot overlook the authoritative tradition in which Matheolus's book participates, a tradition that includes Jean de Meun's *Roman de la Rose*. In following up the implications of these thoughts, Christine is filled with self-loathing and remarks upon her gendered identity: "Helas! Dieux, pourquoy ne me faiz tu naistre au monde en masculin sexe" (1.2) (Alas, God, why did You not let me be born in the world as a man? [p. 5]). Despite her earlier comments in the *Mutacion* about being turned into a man by fortune, her lament suggests that her experience as a reader of misogynist texts inescapably constructs her as female. She concludes: "par ma foulour me tenoye tres malcontente de ce qu'en corps femenin m'ot fait Dieux estre au monde" (1.2) (and in my folly I considered myself most unfortunate because God had made me inhabit a female body in this world [p. 5]). By contrast to the performance of masculinity in her authorial role, Christine states that her experiences as a reader of misogynous texts activate a corporeal awareness as a person "en corps femenin." Like the self-conscious evocation of a masculine identity in the *Mutacion*, these assertions of femaleness programmatically foreground the interpretive issues faced by the reader who occupies a feminine subject position.[15] The author of the *Mutacion* may have been forced into masculine roles by fortune, but in the *Cité des dames* she will rhetorically read like a woman.

The literary experience narrated at the start of this text is, in many respects, a conventional introduction, since medieval dream visions often begin with a representation of reading.[16] But Christine's specific construction as a female reader—and her reaction to her reading as a woman—dramatizes the dangers of misogynistic texts for the woman reader, since it depicts the paralysis of self-hatred that results.[17] At this critical juncture, the three ladies appear, and Raison intervenes, chiding Christine for her uncritical acceptance of the terms of misogynistic discourse and then presenting her with an interpretive model of resistance. She appeals to the tradition of commentary and the revisionary gesture implied by that tradition, to the distrust of poetic fictionality, and finally to a principle of rhetoric as a means of destabilizing the perceived authority of misogynistic discourse:

Regardes se les tres plus grans phillosophes qui ayent esté que tu argues contre ton meismes sexe, en ont point determiné faulx et au contrairc du vray, et se ils respunent l'un l'autre et reprennent . . . Et il semble que tu cuydes que toutes les parollcs des phillosophes soyent article de foy et qu'ilz ne puissent errer. Et des pouettes dont tu parles, ne sces tu pas bien que ilz ont parlé en plusieurs choses en maniere de fable et se veullent aucunes foiz entendre au contraire de ce que leurs diz demonstrent? Et les puet on prendre par la rigle de grammaire qui se nomme antifrasis qui s'entant, si comme tu sces, si comme on diroit tel est mauvais, c'est a dire que il est bon, et aussi a l'opposite. Si te conseille que tu faces ton prouffit de leurs diz et que tu l'entendes ainsi, quel que fust leur entente, es lieux ou ilz blasment les femmes. (1.4)

Consider whether the greatest philosophers who have lived and whom you support against your own sex have ever resolved whether ideas are false and contrary to the truth. Notice how these same philosophers contradict and criticize one another. . . . It also seems that you think that all the words of the philosophers are articles of faith, that they could never be wrong. As far as the poets of whom you speak are concerned, do you not know that they spoke on many subjects in a fictional way and that often they mean the contrary of what their words openly say? One can interpret them according to the grammatical figure of *antiphrasis*, which means, as you know, that if you call something bad, in fact, it is good, and also vice versa. Thus I advise you to profit from their works and to interpret them in the manner in which they are intended in those passages where they attack women. (pp. 6–7)

In this pithy summary of several interpretive issues concerning language, tradition, and authority in medieval culture, Raison provides the female reader with the means to enter the dialogic tradition of textual commentary and thereby problematize, if not subvert, the authority to which misogynistic discourse appeals. Such interventions are made possible by the early fifteenth-century textual cultures within which Christine worked: the texts that Christine read are highly mediated versions of textual dialogues, stretching back through complex traditions and textual transformations.[18] With the appropriation of the figure of antiphrasis, however, Raison authorizes the resisting reader. According to the preceptive grammarians, antiphrasis is a trope considered to be a subsection of allegory. Antiphrasis is included by name in the popular medieval treatises by Alexander of Villedieu and Evrard of Bethune; it can be traced to Donatus, who uses the term.[19] Donatus initially states that allegory is a trope by which another thing is meant than what is stated. As one of seven major categories of allegory, antiphrasis is a form of irony: irony is a trope that expresses a statement by its opposite, though its effectiveness depends on the seriousness of its proposition. Antiphrasis is "irony" of one word.[20] Raison's explanation, "that if you call something bad, in fact, it is good," specifically reproduces this rhetorical discussion of antiphrasis from the grammatical tradition; Christine no doubt based this passage on the discussion of antiphrasis in the section on grammar from the *Etymologia* of Isidore of Seville, a text Christine used in the process of composing the *Mutacion*.[21] By presenting the possibility of straightforwardly inverting the categories of antifeminist discourse, particularly when those categories are labeled by a single term, Raison makes it rhetorically legitimate to invert the terms of misogyny, to say that women are prudent rather than foolish, chaste rather than wanton, and so forth. To a large degree, the *Cité des dames* literally follows this principle in its interrogation of Matheolus's *Lamentations*.

Yet the rhetorical possibilities of antiphrasis are not limited to the revision of Matheolus's *Lamentations*, a text that Christine admits she cannot take seriously. The narrative of the *Cité des dames* engages just as pointedly in a commentary on the representation of women in historical texts and in medieval conceptions of history. Nowhere is this revisionary approach so obvious as it is in the story of Dido. The multiple possibilities the reader might encounter in the case of a literary figure such as Dido would empower the reader-as-author to formulate a revisionist stance toward misogyny and the masculine bias of textual traditions, without explicitly challenging textual authority as a cultural given. Of the pagan women who are numbered among the residents of Christine's city, Dido best exemplifies Christine's antiphrastic approach to competing textual traditions and her consequent formation of an authorial position identifiable as feminist. To begin with, Christine's thematic interest in Dido might be seen as a feminist revision of Dante's authorial relationship with Virgil.

Earl Jeffrey Richards asserts that Christine essentially saw herself as a French—and female—Dante. According to Richards, "Christine envisaged her literary vocation in the vernacular in similar terms as Dante: that is, both viewed their poetic calling as emerging from a confrontation with Virgil, whose work they understood as the essential embodiment of poetry."[22] Richards points to a passage in the *Chemin de long estude* in which Christine specifically refers to the moment in *Inferno* 1 when Dante names Virgil as his *maestro* and *autore*. As several scholars have noted, Christine takes the Sibyl—Aeneas's guide to the underworld in *Aeneid* 6—as her own guide in the *Chemin de long stude*, thereby replacing the masculine model implied by the Dante-Virgil partnership with a model of feminine partnership.[23]

In constructing an authorial position centered on her experiences as a female reader in writing the *Cité des dames*, Christine substitutes Dido—a city builder known to her in a variety of contradictory texts—for the Virgil Dante invokes as an embodied guide. The *Cité des dames* implicitly evokes the same Virgilian subtext that stands behind the first two cantos of the *Inferno*, where the history of Italy, Rome, and Christendom is seen as the historical fulfillment of the mythic agenda of Aeneas. In these sections, Dante specifically names Lavinia and Camilla. Within such a "Virgilian" context in the *Cité des dames*, several women from the *Aeneid* are prominently featured: Camilla, Lavinia, and Dido are all represented in Christine's text, and Dido's story especially represents a culmination of the thematic issues at play throughout the *Cité des dames*. Christine's interest in these characters thematically locates the text of the *Cité des dames* in relation to the specific, literary traditions derived from Virgil's *Aeneid* and his depiction of Dido. Dante the poet expresses the complex set of textual relationships at work in the *Commedia* when Dante the pilgrim insists that he is neither Aeneas nor Paul. Within her allegorical program, Christine-as-reader, by contrast, appears to figure her authorial self in the act of reading Dido.

Of course, to Christine the "Virgilian" context was highly mediated. There is nothing in Christine's poetry or prose to suggest that she had direct experience with the Latin hexameters of the *Aeneid* itself.[24] Christine's awareness of the *Aeneid* story appears to be based on her experience with the texts of the *Histoire ancienne jusqu'à César*. As we have seen, this vast narrative of universal history from the thirteenth century subsumes the plot of the *Aeneid* within the structures of medieval history. Consequently, the Virgilian Dido, as Christine might recognize her, did not belong to a fixed, authoritative Latin text, since the textual authority of the *Aeneid* takes a much more ephemeral form in the French prose summaries of the *Aeneid* story found in the various redactions of the *Histoire*.

In addition to such an explicitly "Virgilian" context, the *Cité des dames*—and Christine's reading of Dido—is mediated by several textual and historical traditions that are related, however indirectly, to Virgilian traditions. Central to these relationships is the complex textuality represented by Augustine's *De civitate Dei* in late medieval French humanism. Augustine's *De civitate Dei*—a literary and philosophical confrontation of Virgil's *Aeneid*—is generally recognized as a primary "pre-text" for the *Cité des dames*, particularly since Christine's title evokes Augustine's *Cité de dieu*, the title she would have known from the 1375 French translation by Raoul de Presles.[25] Charles V commissioned this French version of Augustine's *De civitate Dei* as part of his efforts at establishing a large body of traditional texts, both religious and secular, in French translations that would form the material basis of a *translatio studii*.[26] At least fifteen richly illustrated manuscripts of Raoul de Presles's *Cité de dieu*—which included commentary material in addition to Augustine's original text—were produced in Paris or northern France between 1375 and 1410; several appear to have been specifically produced for by Charles V or Jean, duc de Berry.[27]

This version of Augustine's *De civitate Dei*, supplemented as it is by the insertion of historical information and illustrated by miniatures representing historical and biblical incidents, exhibits a historical rather than a theological interest in the city of God, as Alexandre de Laborde noted in his massive study of the manuscript traditions of Raoul de Presles's text. The translator's Prologue dramatizes the historical immediacy of this reading of the city of God in Raoul de Presles's deferential emphasis on the lineage of Charles V in relation to a medieval construction of history and kingship.[28] The status of the *Cité de Dieu* in the decades immediately preceding the composition of the *Cité des dames*, we might see Augustine's text, in all its textuality, as an important mediating text for the production of the *Cité des dames*. Yet Augustine's *De civitate Dei*, though it essentially appropriates and re-presents the thematics of the city from

Virgil's *Aeneid*, notably omits any mention of Dido.[29] Christine's interest in Dido implicitly critiques Augustine's erasure of her. Christine's handling of traditional material in her Dido exempla demonstrates how Christine's the *Cité des dames* is positioned to interrogate the powerfully authoritative tradition dominated by Virgil and Augustine on the one hand, and Jean de Meun, Dante, and Boccaccio on the other.

Dido and History: The Self-Fashioning of the Author

Dido's story, as told within a historical paradigm in the *Mutacion* and then retold in the revisionary allegory of the *Cité des dames*, is emblematic of the relationship between these two texts, particularly since Dido's identity as city builder makes her central to the allegorical program of the textual city under construction in the first two books of the *Cité des dames*. Christine's interest in recontextualizing and retelling Dido's story in relation to the founding of Carthage foregrounds the thematic value of cities as a cultural construct central to French consciousness at the start of the fifteenth century.

By 1404, when she came to write the *Cité des dames*, Christine the writer/reader had had ample exposure to the textual traditions of Western culture, and in particular to medieval historical narratives, the reading of which formed the basis of a large segment of her long (23,636-line) poetical treatise, the *Livre de la Mutacion de Fortune* (1403). The seven parts of this poem are organized around a Boethian meditation on Fortune. The last three parts present a "universal history" that envelopes Christine's account of her own personal misfortunes in part 1 and concludes with a commentary on the contemporary historical events to which she is a witness. In this vast, conventionally narrated framework of ancient and biblical narrative drawn largely from the texts of the *Histoire ancienne jusqu'à César*, two themes from the historical traditions converge: the genealogical narrative of lineage and the destruction of cities.[30] The recitation of lineage—whether a biblical sequence of *patriarchs* drawn from the Old Testament or the history of kings—shapes the narrative of the *Mutacion* 4–7.

Dido's presence in the *Mutacion* is subject to the thematic priorities of history as it was conventionally written in the Middle Ages. The removal of Dido from Trojan lineage and Roman history is reflected in the genealogical structure that framed the medieval historical consciousness in the tradition of texts such as the *Histoire ancienne jusqu'à César*. As we have seen, since Dido plays no role in the transference of power and civilization from Troy to Rome to France, she is omitted from the genealogical framework of medieval history, and frequently eliminated from historical narrative as well. Lavinia's name, by contrast, often occurs in narratives of lineage since she contributes to the genealogy of Roman emperors, and then by extension, to the lineage of European emperors and kings, including those of France. In the *Livre du Chemin de long estude* (3110–36), Christine presents a linear model for the history of European civilization and adapts the Virgilian story to the narrative of universal history, which results in the complete omission of Dido's name and story, while Lavinia's role and story become visible. Of Aeneas's arrival in Italy, Christine comments: "Le roy Latin a moult grant joie / Le receut, et pour son lignage / Il lui donna par mariage / Sa fille" (3552–55) (The Latin king received him with great joy, and for his lineage, he gave his daughter in marriage to him). Likewise, the *Mutacion* includes Lavinia's name in the description of Roman lineage, since she gives birth to Silvius, who becomes the ruler after Ascanius (18342–47). In this respect, Lavinia's significance—which results from her male descendants—stands in direct opposition to Dido's place in history. Not only does Dido fail to leave an heir—a male descendant—but her city is eventually destroyed as well.

The contrast between Dido and Lavinia is explored in the *Mutacion*, which juxtaposes the stories of the two women, the Dido story preceding the Lavinia story in the text. Following the bare outline of the Virgilian version, available in the *Histoire ancienne jusqu'à César*,[31] Christine narrates the destruction of the queen:

Ceste dame a Eneas donne
Tous ses avoirs et habandonne,
Et cuer et corps en ses mains met,
Car cellui lui jure et promet
Qu'il l'espousera, sanz jamais
Avoir autre en sa vie, mais,
Il lui menti, et s'en parti,
Sanz congié, dont en tel parti
Fu Dido que piteusement
S'occist de dueil; et ensement
Mourut Dido, au cler visage,
Qui tant ot esté preux et sage
Qu'aultre dame ne la passoit!
Mais sage et folz Amours deçoit!
Eneas, qui la refusa,
D'ainsi la laissier s'excusa,
En disant que les dieux l'avoient
Amonnesté que ilz vouloient
Qu'en Ytalie s'en alast,
Et en ce lieu femme espousast;

Sebile l'ot prophetisié,
Qui parmi Enfer l'atisié
Le convoya et adestra,
Et l'ame Anchisés lui monstra.
Si lui dist que de lui vendroient
Lignees, qui el monde tendroyent. (18283–308)

This lady had given Eneas all of her possessions and herself; and put her heart and body in his hands, because he swore to her and promised that he would marry her, never to have another in his life. But he lied to her, and he departed without taking leave. Dido had such grief over this departure that she piteously killed herself. And in this manner Dido died, Dido of bright visage, who had been so valiant and wise that no other lady could surpass her! But love deludes both wise and foolish. Eneas, who rejected her, then excused himself for abandoning her thus, by saying that the gods had announced that they desired that he go to Italy, and in that place marry a wife. The Sibyl had prophesied it to him, the excited one who had accompanied and guided him through Hell, and shown to him the soul of Anchises. This one said to him that from him would come a lineage that would extend throughout the world.

This passage illustrates some of the paradoxes of gender and history that Christine confronted in the composition of the *Mutacion*. This "Virgilian" segment of the Troy story names Dido and elegiacally comments on her nobility and value ("Qui tant ot esté preux et sage / Qu'aultre dame ne la passoit"). Nonetheless, the historical framework of the *Mutacion* implicitly privileges Lavinia's place in history as the divinely promised bride whose role as wife ensures the lineage of the Roman empire. That Lavinia is not named in this particular passage illustrates the fact that even women—such as Lavinia—who belong to history might remain nameless in such historical paradigms; the focus on Dido illustrates as well the extent to which Dido's story defies standard categories of gender in terms of history and lineage.

Throughout the *Mutacion,* Dido is thematically connected to Carthage, a city whose complete destruction by the Romans in the third century B.C.E. received thorough coverage, via Livy, in medieval texts of universal history. In the seventh part of the *Mutacion de Fortune,* "qui parle de l'istoire des Rommains abrigee," Christine inserts an elegiac comment about the fall of Dido into her narration of the destruction of Carthage. Her comment laments Dido and her city and simultaneously acknowledges that Dido is omitted from the lineage of Rome:

.IXᵉ ans avoit que fondee
L'ot celle, qui dure souldee
Hot, par Eneas trop amer,
Ce fu Dido, lorsque, par mer,
De Troye s'en aloit, a nage.
Celle dame ot fondé Cartage,
Bien estoit drois que fust destruicte
Par la ligne Eneas et suite. (20599–606)

It had been 900 years since she had founded it (Carthage), who had
suffered retribution because she loved Aeneas too much—this was
Dido—when he sailed by sea on his way from Troy. This lady had
founded Carthage. It was only fitting that it was afterward
destroyed by the lineage of Eneas.

In the corresponding passage in the *Histoire ancienne jusqu'à César,*
Dido is noted briefly as the founder of Carthage.[32] Christine has amplified
that comment to connect the Aeneas-Dido story to the fall of Carthage, a
connection that emphasizes the survival and power of the lineage of
Aeneas, and elegiacally notes the destruction of the city of Carthage:

Mais grant pitié fu de destruire
Tel cité, qu'on veoit reluire
En toute beaulté et richece,
En force, en valour, en noblece. (20609–12)

But it was a great pity to destroy such a city, which could be seen
to shine in complete beauty and wealth, in power, in courage, and
in nobility.

Even as she acknowledges the conventional view[33] that sees Rome's conquest of Carthage as the historical consequence of the Aeneas-Dido story,
Christine nonetheless laments the fall of this city.

Although essentially left out of history, Dido is not completely erased
in the *Mutacion.* As Christine's reading of history clearly demonstrates,
the story of Dido and her connection to Carthage may not be represented
in the Eurocentric, masculine construct of history, but like the Amazons
(who are well represented in Christine's city), Dido and Carthage represent a persistent countermemory that cannot be completely suppressed
or erased from historical consciousness. In the *Mutacion,* Christine is
ambivalent toward Dido, an ambivalence that hints at her discomfort
with the patriarchal construct of history that she received from texts and
transmitted in the task of writing the *Mutacion;* it points as well to her
problems with the rhetoric of war that such historical constructs were

often used to serve.[34] Moreover, Christine frequently refers to Carthage (without mention of Dido) in several texts, particularly in discussions of warfare, as in her later treatise *Epistre de la prison de vie humaine* (1415). The destruction of Carthage casts a long shadow over the textual history she formulated in response to her sources; to Christine, the destruction of Carthage must have figured Dido's fate, writ large.

The thematic emphasis on the destruction of cities such as Carthage in the *Mutacion* illustrates the commonplaces of medieval historiography: the city as a unit functions as a protagonist in medieval historical narratives. Christine's narrative of the destruction of cities in the *Mutacion*—soon followed by her allegorical construction of a city in the *Cité des dames*—reflects the textual traditions that give such prominence to the city as a cultural entity. In addition to the obvious cultural context suggested by literary and historical traditions, the *Mutacion* and the *Cité des dames* reflect the political and social understanding of the city as a unit of defense, as it was for the French during the Hundred Years War. To French writers and readers of the early fifteenth century, the construction and destruction of textual cities would have had an immediate and resonant meaning beyond the traditional allegorical or historical connotations.

Although the last quarter of the fourteenth century was marked by a series of truces between the kings of France and England that brought relative peace and stability to the French, the first four decades of the conflict had left significant traces on the French landscape and consciousness.[35] The military practices of the English focused attention on cities, resulting in a war marked less by decisive battles between armies than by sieges of cities and walled towns—the sort of warfare in which the non-combatants who reside in contested territory are heavily implicated and suffer accordingly. The French responded to the initial campaigns of the English by investing enormous resources in fortifying cities, especially by building city walls and strengthening existing strongholds.[36] Throughout the fourteenth century, but especially during the reign of Charles V, the French landscape was transformed by these defensive measures aimed at turning urban settlements into walled fortresses.

Christine arrived in France in 1368, soon after the inception of such efforts toward the fortification of cities, and she grew into adulthood in a culture poised and prepared for invasion. Although the *Mutacion* and the *Cité des dames* were composed before the English invasions began again in the fifteenth century, these two texts reflect the cultural awareness of warfare and the anxieties of the French at the start of the reign of Henry IV.[37] The ostensible source of conflict was the English claim to the throne of France—a claim based on the construction of the royal genealogy in such a way that the English king, Edward III, would be placed more directly in the line of succession to the French crown than Philip VI, the successful claimant. Edward's claim depended on the fact that his mother, Isabella, the spouse of Edward III, was the daughter of Philip IV, who held the French throne from 1285 to 1314. Although Edward's genealogy made him the grandson of one French monarch (Philip IV) and the nephew of three succeeding French kings (Louis X, Philip V, and Charles IV), his claim depended on tracing descent through the female line. Christopher Allmand summarizes the issue as it was understood at the time:

> Edward appeared to have a good claim, indeed perhaps the best claim, to succeed him [Charles IV]. His right, however, had been transmitted to him through his mother, and it was this transmission through the female, later explained as the inability of a woman to pass on a claim which, as a woman, she could not herself exercise, which worked against Edward's ambition. When the French nobility, in whose hands the resolution of such a crisis lay, made its choice, that choice was to make one of their number, Philip, Count of Valois, king. The grounds were essentially those of suitability: Philip was French; he was eighteen years older than his English rival (then aged only fifteen); and he had always lived in France. Although not, as Edward III was, a direct descendant of Philip IV, he was at least his nephew through his father, Charles of Valois. In the circumstances, the degree of kinship was sufficiently close to secure him the support he required.[38]

Although Edward's claim was a rhetorical gesture intended to give an ideological justification to an essentially feudal conflict, his claim resulted in a proliferation of statements concerning the place of the female in the construction of royal lineage; most notably, by the time of Charles V, the French had appealed to the "Salic law" as justification for excluding Edward's claim on the grounds that it depended wholly on descent through the female line.[39] While the battles and sieges of the fourteenth century resulted from multiple economic and social causes, this debate around lineage and gender remained the stuff of war propaganda for the entire period of conflict.[40]

The composition of the *Mutacion* took place within such an ideological context: given the historical moment that produced these traditions and this text, this thematic emphasis in the *Mutacion* on lineage and the destruction of cities is especially significant. The textual construction of history around a masculine genealogy that essentially excluded women from the structures of history mirrors rather closely the appeal to the Salic law as an ideological defense for the French claim. Although Christine does not completely omit women from her narrative—many of the women in the *Cité des dames* appear in the *Mutacion*—in composing the *Mutacion*, she was participating in the construction of history around narratives of male lineage punctuated by the fall of cities. In this regard, the *Mutacion* is an important pre-text to the *Cité des dames*.

The English atrocities in France, well remembered in 1403 from the campaigns of Edward III and the Black Prince several decades earlier, undercut any possible chivalric concepts of war or idealization of military practices from the point of view of the noncombatant.[41] Christine must have been aware of the difficult position of the noncombatant: the military practices of the war brought incredible suffering to French women as well as to men. Townswomen and peasants often starved while a city was under siege, only to be raped and then butchered when the city fell.[42] Men in arms could potentially be taken prisoner (rather than killed) and held for ransom—a chivalric "courtesy" grounded purely in economic terms that offered the noncombatant very little protection in siege warfare;[43] Christine frequently mentions the vulnerability of women to rape during warfare.[44] In the *Mutacion*, Christine confronted a vast textual tradition that constructed history around lineage—traced through biblical, ancient, and medieval times—that either omitted women or subsumed them around a male genealogy punctuated by the fall of cities. As the collective French experience of the fourteenth century demonstrated, although women were omitted from lineage, they were not protected from the suffering of war that such lineages were used to justify. It is this disjunction between ideology and practice that best contextualizes the visible shift in emphasis from the *Mutacion* to the *Cité des dames*.

The thematic emphasis on the destruction of cities, so relentlessly rehearsed in the *Mutacion*, is replaced in the *Cité des dames* by the allegorical structure of city building: the narrator metaphorically constructs a city that will house the literary, historical, and religious women who are otherwise suppressed, overlooked, or misrepresented in history. In the *Cité des dames*, the detailed emphasis on architectural details and metaphors counteracts the cyclical destruction of cities that emerged from the *Mutacion*. The siege mentality of the *Mutacion* gives way to a serene framework of assembly rather than a narrative of genealogy. Although the *Mutacion* acknowledges an architectural and visual arrangement of texts, especially in the castle of Fortune and the hall of Fame where historical texts are depicted, it does not develop a coherent spatial order. By contrast to the model of linear history, which forms the narrative paradigm in the *Mutacion*, the exempla and anecdotes of the *Cité des dames* organize a spatial rather than temporal allegory.

The manuscript context of the *Cité des dames* visually reinforces the textual city as an allegory articulated in spatial terms. Like most of

Christine's works—most notably the *Epistre d'Othea* with its one hundred-plus illuminations—the early editions of the *Cité des dames* were all richly illuminated and produced under Christine's direction as luxury editions. As Sandra Hindman has shown, Christine herself generally took responsibility for the selection and execution of the miniatures in her texts, and careful attention to such miniatures and their "pictorial antecedents" demonstrates "the intervention of an author whose sensibility was highly attuned to visual imagery."[45] In contemporary manuscripts, each of the three books of the *Cité des dames* is introduced by one lavishly executed miniature, which, in Hindman's terms, provides "an intelligible visual summation of the book that it prefaces."[46] Such summation not only illustrates the spatial arrangement of the allegory, but it also shows the complex issues of specularity and textuality that are negotiated in Christine's invention of Dido, as we shall see.

The initial miniature that introduces book 1 of the *Cité des dames* in Harley 4431 (see figure 22) has a bipartite structure: the left half represents Christine at her desk; before her stand Dames Raison, Droiture, and Justice. Christine as author reads from an open book; on the desk lie three other books depicted as large luxury editions. This half of the miniature evokes the tradition of the "humanist portrait" of Christine the author as reader/writer that we have already noted.[47] Although the number of books depicted in such authorial presentations might vary, they are a common feature of pictorial representations of Christine the author—a constant visual reminder of her confrontation with texts, specifically with illuminated texts produced as bulky commodities. The right half of the miniature depicts the allegorical focus of the *Cité des dames* through the city-building activities of Christine and Raison, who are employed in fashioning a city wall. As Hindman notes, "The two scenes also give visual form to the metaphor that underlies the *Cité des dames* by reinforcing the association between the enterprises of authoring and building."[48] In addition, the scene insists that the activities of authoring and building depend on reading, and that the allegory of city building results from the author's status as a reader who must rely on texts and textual traditions in the "invention" of her city.

That the architectural metaphors so prominent throughout the prose of the *Cité des dames* are visually emphasized in each of the three miniatures that introduce the three books is obvious; however, it is significant that Christine's visual plan for the *Cité des dames* is limited to these three illuminations. This limited program of illustration marks a departure from the extensive visual text of the *Epistre d'Othea*, and it stands in sharp contrast to one of the most important "source" texts for the *Cité des dames*, the French versions of Boccaccio's *De claris mulieribus*, *Des cleres femmes*, which, as we have seen, contain an illustration for each

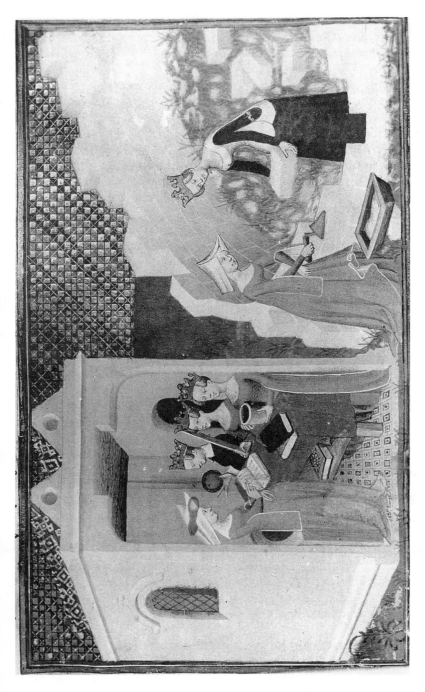

22. Christine at her desk; Christine builds her city. The *Cité des dames*. London, British Library, Harley 4431, fol. 288r. Fifteenth century. By permission of the British Library.

exemplum. As if to refuse the specular economy of the texts of *Des cleres femmes*, the textual exempla in the *Cité des dames* are not illustrated with individual images for each woman and each exemplum. Rather, taken together, the women in the *Cité des dames* are incorporated into the thematics of city building, since the exempla represent "lesquelles dites dames ont par si longtemps esté delaissies, descloses comme champ sans haye, sans trouver champion aucun qui pour leur deffence comparust souffisantment" (1.7) (those ladies who have been abandoned for so long, exposed like a field without a surrounding hedge, without finding a champion to afford them an adequate defense [p. 10]). Consequently, the focus of book 3 on a city that can provide a safe haven for women is visually reinforced in the third miniature, which depicts the entrance of the queen of heaven and a group of female saints into the city of ladies (see figure 23). This image visually enacts the textual revision that shapes Christine's allegorical city.

The density and architectural mass of the city walls that fill most of the illumination form a visual citation of the illustrations of the celestial city (see figure 24) found in the manuscripts of Raoul de Presles's *Cité de dieu*, two of which were illuminated in the same workshop as the *Cité des dames*.[49] Such visual intertextuality replaces the images of the church fathers with a female assembly of saints led by the queen of heaven.[50] The substitution of female saints for the male figures of church authority suggests that the masculine models for cities, history, and civilization, particularly as found in textual traditions, have failed to provide adequate champions or defense for women. Instead of the distributed authority suggested by the placement of the four church fathers in the four corners of the illumination—each figure is engaged in the authoritative act of writing—the *Cité des dames* illumination is less hierarchical. The queen of heaven is clearly distinguishable from the saints, but there is no rank visible in the dense group of women who form a procession behind her. By contrast to the church fathers, the female saints do not each singly represent authority. As a group, however, these saints are about to claim the protection offered by Christine's *Cité des dames*. The visual images in the *Cité des dames* do not merely cite the pictorial program of the *Cité de dieu*, they revise the masculine images of traditions and hierarchy that are part of the Augustinian tradition. Like the pictorial revision of Augustine's celestial city, the revision of the Dido story in the *Cité des dames* challenges the masculine bias of textual authority.

Rhetorical Invention and the Sources of the *Cité des dames*

In addition to the model of the resisting reader made possible by the practice of antiphrasis, Christine's role as author required that her reader-

23. Christine welcomes the saints into the city. The *Cité des dames*. Book 3. Paris,
Bibliothèque Nationale, français 607, fol. 67v. Fifteenth century. By permission.

responses be transferred into her textual constructions. In the authorial
subject position that emerges in the *Cité des dames*, the rhetorical
process of *inventio* provides the means by which Christine could incor-

24. The celestial city. Augustine, the *Cité de Dieu*, translation by Raoul de Presles. Paris, Bibliothèque Nationale, ms français 23, fol. 4r. Fifteenth century. By permission.

porate her readerly experiences into her writing. That Christine's writing is all drawn from her reading illustrates several traditional aspects of medieval rhetoric as a descriptive and prescriptive discourse; medieval rhetorical treatises essentially assume the intertextual basis of discourse, particularly narrative, almost to the extent of eliding the reader and the writer. In such a context, the use of "sources" becomes an important theoretical issue; indeed, the process of finding or discovering exempla to support the assertions of a rhetorical argument was known as invention (*inventio*). In the *Mutacion*, Christine lists the five parts of rhetoric: "la primeraine, invencion, / Et l'autre, disposicion, / Elocucion et memoire, / Prononciacion nottoire" (8043–46). This comment (almost a commonplace) was probably drawn from Bruneto Latini's *Livor de tresor*; its presence in this discussion of rhetoric suggests the extent to which a writer such as Christine might see narrative as commentary, as an opportunity to re-present and gloss earlier texts and traditions. This connection between reading and writing allowed Christine, in her authorial role, to adapt her narrative voice to her experiences as a reader.

In the *Cité des dames*, the process of invention is paramount: having framed her allegory, so to speak, by her architectural metaphors and the proverbial assertions of Dames Raison, Droiture, and Justice, Christine proceeds to "populate" her city through the discovery of appropriate female figures in source texts that provided the standard narratives regarding these *dames*. As a rhetorical strategy, *inventio* yielded up traditional stories to be adapted to her purpose. Although most of Christine's writing shows a fairly obvious adaptation of earlier texts to her own contexts, the revisionist plan of the *Cité des dames* required more careful discovery and use of sources than any of her earlier texts. The "invention" of Dido demonstrates the revisionist possibilities of such rhetorical strategies.

In reading Matheolus, Christine confronted the tradition of Dido as a lustful woman. In a predictably conventional fashion, Matheolus includes Dido in a list of wanton women of antiquity (Semiramis, Phasiphaë, Scylla, Myrrha, Byblis, Caunus, Phaedra, and Phyllis) undone by *libido*.[51] In Jean Le Fèvre's French version of the *Lamentations* of Matheolus, Dido is presented as an example of a "femme luxurieuse" (1571). Le Fèvre provides a thirteen-line summary, which notes Dido's "grant outrage" for Eneas when he arrives as her guest, her subsequent lament over her "fole amour," and her suicide. In addition to Matheolus, Christine had encountered several different versions of Dido's story by the time she came to include her so prominently in the *Cité des dames*. In the *Mutacion*, as we have seen, she adapted the Eneas-Dido story from the French prose synopsis of the *Aeneid* in the French *Histoire*.[52] Elsewhere in her poetic texts she refers to Dido as an abandoned woman, suggesting her acquaintance with the Ovidian Dido of *Heroides* 7—available to her in a

French poetic paraphrase that was interpolated into book 14 of the *Ovide moralisé*, as we have seen.

In addition, Christine would have been aware of the standard versions of Dido as an abandoned woman undone by desire in Dante's *Commedia* and Jean de Meun's *Roman de la Rose*—two texts she implicitly rewrites in the construction of the *Cité des dames*.[53] And her text of the *Roman de la Rose* might have included an image of Dido falling on the sword, a particularly graphic version of the specular Dido, as we noted in chapter 1. Christine's representation of Dido and her story in the *Cité des dames* also evokes the "historical" Dido as she encountered her in *Des cleres femmes*, the illustrated French version of Boccaccio's *De claris mulieribus*. Christine drew a good deal of her material on classical women from *Des cleres femmes*, but in every case she appears to have carefully revised and adapted Boccaccio's version to her purposes.[54] Christine's Dido in the *Cité des dames* is a textual response to Boccaccio's privileging of the historical over the Virgilian version of Dido's story.

Dido and the Reader

In addition to her frequent encounters with Dido in a variety of vernacular texts, Christine also comments that she herself had already told Dido's story on several occasions; as Droiture notes in book 2: "toy meismes autreffoiz en tes dittiez en ayes parlé" (2.219) (you yourself have spoken of [her] earlier in your works). Christine had mentioned Dido frequently in her poetry, not only in the *Mutacion de Fortune* but also in her lyric poetry and in her *Epistre au dieu d'amours*.[55] In all these other references, the Dido referred to is essentially the "Virgilian" Dido—the figure known for her passion for Aeneas and her suicide upon his departure. Yet in constructing the *Cité des dames*, Christine's reliance on *Des cleres femmes* provided her with a fairly authoritative account of the non-Virgilian, "historical" Dido.

Boccaccio's Dido has some attractive features for the context of the *Cité des dames*. She is initially identified as a wise, powerful city builder —a woman who possesses masculine qualities and strengths—a figure much like the author Christine constructs in the *Mutacion*: a widow whose widowhood turns her into a man. Had Christine's immersion in a medieval humanistic tradition that privileged the Virgilian version of the Dido story not been so complete, she might have simply presented her invention of the Boccaccian Dido as a straightforward exemplum. However, given her own experience of the Virgilian version of the Dido story—which she had frequently rehearsed in her own writing—she clearly had to reconcile the Dido Boccaccio provides her with the more traditional one she already knew.

For Christine's purposes in the *Cité des dames,* Boccaccio's Dido made possible a revision of her traditional counterpart, a revisionary perspective that is exemplified in Christine's two-part arrangement of the Dido narrative in the *Cité des dames.* The exemplum drawn from Boccaccio's text is placed in book 1 to illustrate the virtue of prudence, and the more recognizably "Virgilian" Dido appears in book 2, in a shorter, less elaborate exemplum that represents her as a woman remarkable for "amour ferme." This division into two parts is reinforced by the placement of each version: the first version occurs near the end of book 1; the second version is placed approximately two-thirds of the way through book 2; the locations of these two exempla are suggestive.

The placement of Dido's story in book 1 of the *Cité des dames* addresses the problems of lineage and history that Christine confronted in the composition of the *Mutacion.* Book 1 contains the stories of forty-two women, the majority of them from the classical tradition. These women are grouped in three general categories: warrior women, women associated with writing or other "civilizing" skills, and women who exemplify prudence, according to Christine's categories. Camilla's story, including her support of Turnus's cause, occurs in the first category; Dido and Lavinia— separated only by the story of Ops—conclude the narrative of book 1. These three Virgilian women suggest that the *Aeneid* story forms a significant subtext for the narrative of book 1; indeed, Christine explicitly comments on Virgil's preeminence as a poet and appears to consider the *Aeneid* story a fairly authoritative version of history that her own text implicitly challenges or corrects. Lavinia's story (based on Boccaccio's version), contains a brief synopsis of the *Aeneid* and extols Lavinia's prudence in raising her son, Julius Silvius, so that he remained safe from the threats of Ascanius, a jealous stepbrother (1.22). Christine notes that Lavinia governed the realm in her son's minority, and this act insured the lineage and founding of Rome: "Duquel enffant dessendirent puis Remus et Romulus, qui puis fonderent Romme, et les haulx princes rommains quis puis vendrent" (1.122) (From this child descended Romulus and Remus who founded Rome, as well as the great Roman princes who came later [p. 97]). The short exemplum on Lavinia inserts female agency into the foundation myth of the *Aeneid* story. In this regard, Lavinia's role complements Dido's: both are extolled for their prudence.

The textual city of Christine's allegory appears analogous to Dido's founding of Carthage so that the placement of Dido's story in book 1 responds explicitly to the problems of lineage and history that Christine confronted in the composition of the *Mutacion.* Throughout book 1, Raison stresses the inventiveness and agency of the women discussed. In general, book 1 showcases the role of women in the establishment of civilizations or in the discovery of civilizing arts: Christine notes the contribution of warrior women to their civilizations (Lampheto, Marspasia, Thamiris, Orithyia, Zenobia, Artemisia, Penthesilea); the contribution of city builders (Semiramis, Dido); the contribution of women to the arts of writing (Proba, Sappho, Carmentis, Minerva); and the contribution of women to the settlement of civilization (Nicaula, Ceres, Isis). All these women share the qualities of resourcefulness and agency, so that their contributions overlap in the sequence of the text. The arts of writing, exemplified by women such as Proba—who rewrote the *Aeneid*—and the arts of civilization that contribute to the establishment and defense of cities are given equal value. The texture of book 1 emphasizes the importance of writing/textuality and city building to give the overarching allegory of the *Cité des dames* a powerful resonance; this texture contextualizes the city-building activities of Dido, queen of Carthage, in a way that suggestively represents the textual city as a whole.

Dido is the most eminent of the city builders mentioned in book 1 of the *Cité des dames*. The Dido exemplum, which emphasizes the *prudence* and *avis* needed to found Carthage, is itself an exceptionally prudent rearrangement of Boccaccio's exemplum; many of the phrases and some complete sentences in Christine's Dido exemplum are lifted directly from *Des cleres femmes*.[56] Yet this compilation transforms Boccaccio's version and results in a subtle but purposeful revision of the figure of Dido. Christine's "invention" of Dido demonstrates the revisionary potential of "compilation" in the production of narrative: by relying closely on a textual antecedent, Christine ostensibly presents the Dido story as she found it in her sources. By presenting her transformation of the Dido exemplum as though it were traditional, Christine claims textual authority for her revision and essentially denies its status as a revision. The rhetorical possibilities of *inventio* facilitate a compilation of textual antecedents from a revisionary perspective.

In the *Cité des dames*, the standard details of the "historical" version of Dido's story are all subtly adjusted so that they emphatically support the thematics of Dido's agency, especially her intellectual feats. Many of these revisions are simply a matter of adjusting small details of plot. For instance, the text of *Des cleres femmes* states that Sychaeus, Dido's husband, knew that Pygmalion was covetous, and he consequently hid his treasure and money. In the *Cité des dames*, it is Dido who recognizes the covetous nature of her brother and who consequently advises her husband to hide his treasure, advice that he accepts, so that his vulnerability results from his failure to follow all of Dido's advice: "mais ne garda pas bien sa personne des agaiz du roy, si que elle luy avoit dit" (1.119) (but [he] neglected to protect his person against the king's ambushes, as she had advised him [p. 92]). Whereas the text of *Des cleres femmes* states that after Sychaeus's death, Dido made her decision to flee either on the advice of someone or "du propre conseil de sa pensee," the text of the *Cité des dames* removes any doubt about Dido's decisive agency; she simply "fu admonnestee par sa meismes prudence." The Dido exemplum throughout shows such small shifts in emphasis, each of which might seem minor in itself; but taken together they present a substantial revision of the story.

A standard anecdote in the historical versions of Dido's story relates how Dido shrewdly hides the treasure she takes with her on her flight and substitutes worthless objects instead in order to deceive her brother's men. The revisionary gestures of the *Cité des dames* are particularly evident in Christine's treatment of this incident. She rearranged and changed the plot slightly in order to stress the intellectual agency of Dido in her role as leader. The comment "plus grant malice fist ceste dame" (1.119), a phrase borrowed directly from *Des cleres femmes*, where it is used as a summary statement toward the end of the anecdote, is moved to an introductory position in order to direct the interpretation of the anecdote that follows. In addition, many of the narrative elements of this incident are amplified. This anecdote had been transmitted more or less intact from Justin to Boccaccio to the French text Christine knew. In Boccaccio's version, Dido hides her treasure and substitutes bags of sand, which she orders her followers to throw overboard once the ship is at sea. Once they have done so, she advises her followers that they might find it difficult to return to the greedy Pygmalion now that the treasure he coveted is lost. In the *Cité des dames*, this incident is more elaborate and contains a more sustained demonstration of Dido's cleverness. Dido, having hidden her treasure, places heavy, worthless items in the bags, which she then presents to Pygmalion's men who pursue her, so that they will allow her to go on her way undisturbed. Later, after she has landed in Africa and is involved in building her city, they return to demand the treasure, having discovered the deception. At this point, Dido provides them with two possible interpretations of the missing treasure: either the messengers stole the treasure and substituted the worthless items or "pour le pechié que le roy avoit commis de son mari faire occire, les dieux n'avoyent pas voulu que il jouyssist de son tresor, sy l'avoyent ainsi tresmué" (1.120) (because of the sin committed by the king in having her husband murdered, the gods had not wanted him to enjoy her husband's treasure and so had transmuted it [p. 94]). This incident constitutes the most extended departure from *Des cleres femmes*; while it simply amplifies an anecdote that existed in the anterior text, it does so in a way that purposefully highlights Dido's wit and intellectual abilities. Such emphasis on Dido's agency shifts the focus of the narrative to enhance the significance of Dido's role in the events depicted.

The details of the ox hide and the negotiations over the purchase of land—standard elements in the story of the historical Dido that survive even in *Aeneid* 1—lent themselves naturally to this interpretive framework; throughout, the *Cité des dames* presents an intensified version of the plot narrated in *Des cleres femmes*. But this intensified version is contextualized differently in Christine's version. This contextual shift is most evident in the placement of the most synthetic statement made about Dido's character in Boccaccio's version: the assertion that occurs early in the exemplum that Dido puts aside her feminine nature ("condicion feminine et couraige de femme") and takes on the power and force of a man. In Christine's text, this assertion is positioned at the end of the exemplum, where it acquires the force of a conclusion:

> et ne parloit on se d'elle non, tellement que pour la grant vertu qui fu veue en elle, tant pour la hardiesce et belle entreprise que fait avoit comme pour son tres prudent gouvernement, luy transmuerent son nom et l'appellerent Dido: qui vault autant a dire comme *virago* en latin, qui est a dire celle qui a vertu et force de homme. (1.120)

> She was spoken of only in terms of her outstanding strength, courage, and her bold undertaking. Because of her prudent government, they changed her name and called her Dido, which is the equivalent of saying *virago* in Latin, which means "the woman who has the strength and force of a man" (p. 95)

Whereas Boccaccio's praise of Dido in *De claris mulieribus* all builds to her suicide to avoid a second marriage and to protect heroically her status as a chaste widow, Christine's version has retained only the narrative details of Dido's agency and cunning; of course, Christine's narrative omits any mention of Iarbas or of Dido's suicide, since her story is taken up again in book 2. Christine's revision of Boccaccio's Dido in the *Cité des dames*, book 1, makes use of selection and rearrangement to eliminate the implicit misogyny that contextualizes Boccaccio's praise of Dido.

Dido's qualities as a virago in book 1 give way to her attributes as a lover in the exemplum that appears two-thirds of the way through book 2. Following the model of antiphrasis, book 2 features a series of women who are named and discussed by Droiture in order to illustrate a series of virtues that explicitly act as counterexamples to the series of vices consistently named in the misogynistic tradition represented by Matheolus. In book 2, the women named tend to exemplify virtues rather than accomplishments, though in some cases, especially in the case of the Sibyls, the virtues possessed by women lead to significant accomplishments as well. As an example of women's constancy in love, Dido's story follows a long discussion of thirteen women from the classical and Judaic tradition, as well as from historical accounts, who are exemplars of chastity (Susanna, Sarah, Rebecca, Ruth, Penelope, Mariannes, Antonia, Sulpitia, Lucretia, the Queen of the Galatians, Hyppo, the Sicambrian women, and Virginia). At this point in book 2, Droiture briefly rehearses the Virgilian version of the Dido story as it appeared in the *Mutacion*; this passage of the *Cité des dames* would almost appear to be a prose redaction of the earlier poetic text. In the context of book 2, where the stories of chaste women are presented as counterexamples to the charge that women are lustful, the Virgilian Dido—usually noted for her destructive desire—becomes an exemplum of constancy that is implicitly elided into the category of chastity.

Throughout her writing, Christine extols chastity as the preeminent feminine virtue, the one quality that allows women to defeat all enemies and to transcend the trials of this world.[57] By contrast to the inherent misogyny of Boccaccio's model of female chastity as a category that made possible the masculine control of female sexuality, Christine's presentation of chastity reflects her convictions, often repeated in her writing, that women might be empowered through chastity. The militant value of chastity is clearly represented in the *Cité des dames*, book 3, where female, Christian martyrs and saints transcend torture and repeated attempts at sexual assault through their steadfast commitment to chastity.[58] Although book 3 of the *Cité des dames* repeatedly celebrates the importance of chastity among Christian women, this group of pagan women known for their chastity and their resistance to rape in book 2 is emphatically placed to suggest that chastity is not a virtue found only among Christian women, but a universal female virtue.

The Virgilian version of Dido's story, however, cannot be presented as an example of chastity, since, in her sexualized relation to Aeneas, Dido misses an opportunity for a life of chaste widowhood. Boccaccio's Dido, who explicitly exemplifies the potential of chastity for widows—and whom Boccaccio rhetorically holds up as a model for widows contemplating marriage—lacked the textual authority accorded to the Virgilian Dido, and Boccaccio's version ultimately becomes absorbed into the Virgilian version in the course of the *Cité des dames*. But Christine does not rehearse the standard versions of the Virgilian Dido as she knew it from texts such as Matheolus or the *Roman de la Rose*, in which Dido's is a cautionary tale of "fole amour." In the *Cité des dames*, book 2, Christine adjusts the Virgilian story to exemplify "d'amour ferme en femme": constancy replaces chastity and thematically connects Dido's stories to those of chaste pagan women in book 2. In such an appropriation of the Dido story from its Virgilian readings, Christine not only recontextualizes the love affair between Dido and Aeneas in order to extract an appropriate reading of it for her purposes but also implicitly comments on the entire tradition that had categorized Dido in terms of her sexuality, the tradition represented by Dante and Jean de Meun. In the process, Christine revises the notion of chastity in relation to Dido's story. Thus she manages to recuperate Dido from the contradictory set of texts and traditions where she found her, without completely denying her sexuality.

The two Dido exempla of the *Cité des dames*, taken together, represent the negotiation of a complex set of traditions necessary to the formation of a textual city. Traces of this process of negotiation are visible in the dual citation evoked in the narration of Dido's suicide. The text first states that Dido killed herself by throwing herself into a fire, but this assertion is immediately modified by the acknowledgment of an alternate tradition, based on *Aeneid* 4: "Et autres dient que elle se occist de la meismes espee de Eneas" (2.220) (Others say she killed herself with Aeneas's own sword [p. 189]). This dual set of endings for the story constitutes Christine's adaptation of the version found in the *Histoire ancienne jusqu'à César*. As we saw in chapter 3, the *Histoire* includes a brief encapsulation of the historical version of the story sandwiched into the narration of Dido's affair with Aeneas: at this point, while Dido is contemplating what she should do about Aeneas, Iarbas demands that she marry him. She constructs a large pyre and prepares to throw herself into it but is saved from suicide at the last moment by her people. She then proceeds to become involved with Aeneas, whose departure causes the suicide by sword. In the *Cité des dames*, Christine acknowledges both possibilities for Dido's death—suicide by fire or by sword—as a reaction to the narrative in the *Histoire*. Christine's exemplum concludes, however, with the remark that the figure of Dido enjoyed more renown than any other woman of her time. The contradictory versions of Dido's death support this assertion that Dido enjoyed textual fame as a woman who "passoit en renommee toutes les femmes de son temps" (2.220). That this textual fame also replaces the specular circulation of Dido in Boccaccio, Jean de Meun, and the *Histoire* is emphasized by the fact that none of Christine's texts contain an image of Dido.[59]

Christine's "invention" of Dido not only illustrates her revisionist self-fashioning as a female reader of antiquity, but it also demonstrates her awareness of the connections between gender and interpretation. In the *Mutacion*, where she explicitly notes that she has become a man, she presents a version of Dido that is consistent with the construction of history and narrative found in texts such as the *Histoire*. In the *Cité des dames*, where she programmatically reads history from a female subject position, she "invents" a version of Dido that is quite distinct from any other representation. This Dido illustrates the politics of self-fashioning for Christine as an author. A figure such as Dido—whether Virgilian or historical—represented the selfsame more than the other. As a woman of wit and agency, a widow who constructs a city, Dido effectively figures Christine's textual construction of her authorial self. Not only does Christine's representation of herself as a woman who becomes a man upon her husband's death in the *Mutacion* and the *Avision* replicate the tradition of Dido putting aside her female nature in order to go into exile, but the standard statement that Dido is a virago resonates powerfully with the fact that Jean Gerson labeled Christine "virilis illa femina" and "illa virago" during the *Rose* debate.[60] In addition, Christine's emphasis upon her role as the builder of a textual city, vividly represented in the pictorial tradition that accompanies the *Cité des dames*, invites a comparison between Christine the author and Dido the city builder.

In reading Dido as part of her authorial self-fashioning, Christine's affinity for this classical figure would be consistently mediated by the masculine bias of textual traditions. The Virgilian Dido is most prominent in the historical traditions that privilege the thematics of lineage based on masculine genealogy, such as the *Histoire*. Although prominent, the Virgilian Dido is essentially removed from the meaningful structures of medieval history, as the *Mutacion* demonstrates. Likewise, Boccaccio narrates the biography of a woman who commits suicide as an act of self-preservation. In the textual realities of late medieval humanism, it appears that for the female reader to recognize herself in the "other" of the masculine text is to risk erasure. The pro-female reader, fashioned in the writing of the *Cité des dames* and tutored by Raison, Droiture, and Justice, is Christine's response to such risk. And Christine's "invention" of Dido is emblematic of the rhetorical possibilities that make that response an identifiably feminist textual strategy.

Such feminist subjectivity depends nonetheless on textual cultures, and Christine's feminist self-fashioning is produced only within the revisionary potentials within such cultures. The rhetorical figure of antiphrasis allowed Christine the author to invert the categories of textual misogyny experienced by Christine the reader. The rhetorical process of *inventio* allowed Christine the reader to discover the exempla of history that might support the process of antiphrasis as narrative strategy. However, Christine's construction of herself as reader is not always consistent with her construction of herself as author. One aspect of her authorial identity required that she become a man; another required that she represent herself—both textually and visually—as a female reader. Within these shifting identities, her readerly experience authorizes rhetorical resistance to textual misogyny, as we have seen, although her writerly self seldom critiques the sexual politics of contemporary institutions. When writer and reader become closely identified, as in the *Cité des dames*, the resulting narrative appears closest to a modern concept of feminist writing. That such feminist identity is not sustained—in fact it disappears from Christine's sequel to the *Cité des dames*, the *Livre de la tresor des dames*—does not negate the interventionist potential of the *Cité des dames*; rather, it suggests that the authorial identity found in the *Cité des dames* is a self-conscious construction, fashioned within the social context of courtly culture and the late medieval humanism specific to the French courts of the late fourteenth and early fifteenth centuries.

Christine's feminist self-fashioning results from the rhetorical strategies implicit in her invention of Dido. Conversely, the complexity of Dido's textual presence in medieval culture—specifically in the manuscript culture of late medieval humanism within which Christine worked—made possible the sort of compilation and subtle revision of her story in the *Cité des dames*. To the extent that Christine's authorial identity is fashioned in response to the discursive textuality of her culture, her feminist self-fashioning results rather directly from her invention of Dido and the textual strategies at work in such inventions. Dido's significance for Christine's self-fashioning is emblematic of the feminist possibilities Dido represents in literary history. By contrast to Dante's reliance on Virgil, and the elaborate intertextuality implied by Virgil's presence as Dante's guide in the *Inferno*, Christine's reliance on Dido, especially on the countermemory represented by the historical Dido, makes Dido rather than Virgil the central figure in the textual drama. Dido thereby becomes the originary literary figure who engenders the late medieval feminist writer.

Epilogue

✣

On Reading Dido

Miss Julia Hedge, the feminist, waited for her books. They did not come. She wetted her pen. She looked about her. Her eye was caught by the final letters in Lord Macaulay's name: And she read them all round the dome— the names of great men which remind us—"O damn," said Julia Hedge, "Why didn't they leave room for an Eliot or a Brontë?"

Unfortunate Julia! Wetting her pen in bitterness, and leaving her shoe laces untied. When her books came she applied herself to her gigantic labours, but perceived through one of the nerves of her exasperated sensibility how composedly, unconcernedly, and with every consideration the male readers applied themselves to theirs. That young man for example. What had he to do except copy out poetry?

Virginia Woolf, Jacob's Room

Like the entire section of *Jacob's Room* set in the British Library from which this passage is drawn, the scene depicted here ironizes in every direction: the complacency of Jacob and the predictable bitterness of Julia Hedge are soon enveloped in the larger ironies of museums, monuments, and culture. Woolf's look at textual traditions monumentalized in the Round Reading Room is scathing. The energetic resentment of Julia Hedge (Unfortunate Julia) offers no more direction (and commands no more sympathy) than the complacency of Jacob Flanders. And ultimately the social apparatus that supports the entire enterprise of Western culture is evoked: "The night-watchmen, flashing their lanterns over the backs of Plato and Shakespeare, saw that on the twenty-second of February neither flame, rat, nor burglar was going to violate these treasures— poor, highly respectable men, with wives and families at Kentish Town, do their best for twenty years to protect Plato and Shakespeare, and then are buried at Highgate."

And yet that reading room draws one into its cavernous, monumental seriousness ("No one laughed in the reading room"), a room whose design uncomfortably echoes Bentham's panoptic model for the perfect prison, which Foucault reads as the emblematic gesture toward our own, complicit self-imprisonment in institutions and in knowledge.[1] Indeed, the Reading Room in the 1990s—in the final years that the British Library will occupy the Round Reading Room in the British Museum on Great Russell Street—is a space where readers are literally under direct surveillance all the time, since library staff continually circulates in order to ensure that readers do not deface or steal books. Disciplined by tradition and policed by society, the modern reader encounters the textual past preserved and cataloged within monumental edifices.

And yet, in *Jacob's Room*, Julia Hedge's presence in the Reading Room demonstrates that the British Museum admitted women readers at the same time that Woolf was denied access to the Bodleian. But even when admitted, women are apt to remain bitter—or so it would seem from the depiction of Julia.

But I would have dared to be Dido. This is where I begin to suffer in a woman's place. Reading Virgil again, in the Aeneid *(books 3 and 4); one sees how the venerable Aeneas, who is destined to found a city, is kept from the feminine danger by the gods.*

Women readers. In light of the cultural implausibility and theoretical difficulties evoked by the very term "women readers," it is easy enough to echo the sentiments of Julia Hedge, or to attempt to shore up that bitterness with the sense of difference that seventy years has made since Julia's remark, "Why didn't they leave room for an Eliot or a Brontë?" I might easily insert here a narrative of my own sense of intellectual comradery as I researched this book and came upon the dazzling work of women scholars in classical studies such as Maria Rosa-Lida de Malkiel, Mary Louise Lord, Judith Hallett, or Christine Perkell who suggest ways of revising traditional approaches to classical studies. Or I might acknowledge that there is now, near the end of the twentieth century, an astonishing group of established women medievalists whose work has shaped my own in ways I cannot begin to fully credit or disentangle. I could also mention the vast number of feminist theorists, scholars, and critics who work to open up possibilities of reading and writing in new modes. But reading itself remains a technology that genders those who perform it, and texts remain embedded in traditions central to cultural identities.

This study shows how much modern critical approaches to Virgil are indebted to the social organization of readership throughout Western history. Modern academic cultures resemble the elite arrangement of reading and textual communities traced in chapter 2, and modern approaches to *Aeneid* 4 and the character of Dido echo Boccaccio's approach to the *Aeneid* in *Genealogia* 14 or Gavin Douglas's Prologue to book 4 of the *Eneados*. Christine's careful negotiation of the textual contradictions represented by Dido and her interest in Dido as one who "passoit en renommee toutes les femmes de son temps" have almost no counterpart in Virgil criticism, just as Christine herself has had almost no place until very recently in the textual traditions represented by the canon.

But twentieth-century readers are not limited to academic readings of Virgil and Dido any more than vernacular medieval readers were restricted to the pedagogical view of Dido as a figure of *libido*. A popular novel about Dido circulated in English at the same time that T. S. Eliot published his essays on Virgil as the poet of empire and W. F. Jackson Knight produced *Roman Vergil*.[2] And writers as diverse as Carolyn Heilbrun and Hélène Cixous frequently evoke Dido in contemporary discourses.

Alternate textual possibilities for the twentieth-century reader are offered by a gesture of refusal such as that of Monique Wittig's *Virgile, Non* (1985), which re-visions Dante's dependence on Virgil as a guide through the underworld, or Fawzi Mellah's *Elisa, la reine vagabonde* (1988), which reinstates the historical Dido as the founder of Carthage in Tunisian history.

In Dido's place. But I am not Dido. I cannot inhabit a victim, no matter how noble. I resist: detest a certain passivity, it promises death for me. So who shall I be? I have gone back and forth in vain through the ages and through the stories within my reach, yet find no woman into whom I can slip.

Dido's presence in Western textual cultures might be read as a challenge to the mythical celebration of empire, a discourse central to the construction of Eurocentric identities, though Dido cannot be said to consistently subvert the idea of empire in every reading of every text. But as part of the *Aeneid*, a text that has historically been part of the European and North American curriculum, Dido has been on view throughout the construction of imperial ideologies, a potential reminder to readers that the cultural discourses of colonization are not seamless myths but narratives structured around silencing (in Christine Froula's terms) and forgetting (in Homi Bhabha's terms). In light of Cixous's assertions that "literary history has been homogeneous with phallocentric tradition, to the point of being phallocentrism-looking-at-itself, taking pleasure in repeating itself,"[3] Dido presents the possibility of interrupting that repetition.

Dido's trajectory in medieval culture invites us to reread Virgil's *Aeneid* and revise our understanding of gender, national identity, and literary history in the light of the politics and possibilities of reading Dido. If the medieval Dido lacks the incandescent splendor of Beatrice or the haunting subjectivity of Criseyde, she circulates more pervasively as a discrete character throughout medieval vernacular cultures. For medieval poets such as Dante and Chaucer, Dido made possible a negotiation of Virgil's *Aeneid* and Ovid's *Heroides* 7 that perhaps engendered the construction of Beatrice and Criseyde. Beatrice and Criseyde, however, are ultimately used to reflect the subjectivities of Dante pilgrim and poet, or

Troilus and the *Troilus* narrator. The medieval Dido has become detached enough from the *Aeneid* that her position is not solely seen in relation to Aeneas. At some moments, such as in the *Cité des dames*, Aeneas becomes a reflector to Dido.

But let us look at the dangers implicit here. As Cixous's meditation on Dido illustrates, Dido may also figure danger for the female reader. Despite her alterity, Dido has all too often been reabsorbed into a stabilizing vision that connects desire to death for the female reader. And beyond the larger challenges posed by Woolf's "night-watchmen" in the material organization of cultural monuments is the connection between libraries and the cultural imperialisms they celebrate. *Reading Dido* is intended to be provisional in every respect, especially since it leaves us positioned in that Reading Room under the gaze of watchmen, surrounded, literally, by the artifacts of that past.

My sympathy, my tenderness, my sorrow, however, are all hers. But not me, not my life. I can never lay down my arms. —Hélène Cixous

Notes

Introduction

1. Rachel Blau DuPlessis, "For the Etruscans," in *The New Feminist Criticism: Essays on Women, Literature Theory*, ed. Elaine Showalter (New York, 1985), p. 272.

2. Walter J. Ong, S.J., "Latin and the Social Fabric," *The Barbarian Within and Other Fugitive Essays and Studies* (New York, 1962), p. 211.

3. Thomas Greene, "The Descent from Heaven: Virgil," in *Virgil*, ed. Harold Bloom (New York, 1986), p. 55. For a standard discussion of the *Aeneid* as a poem about empire, see Frank O. Copley, *Latin Literature: From the Beginnings to the Close of the Second Century A.D.* (Ann Arbor, Mich., 1969), pp. 188–240. See also note 22. Since this is a study of medieval texts, I have chosen to employ the spelling "Virgil" throughout, a spelling that first appears in the fifth century and reflects medieval vernacular practice; see Marbury B. Ogle, "The Later Tradition of Vergil," *Classical Journal* 26 (1930), p. 66.

4. See Paul Allen Miller, "*Sive Deae Seu Sint Dirae Obscenaeque Volucres*," *Arethusa* 22 (1989), pp. 47–79; for an anthropological reading of the *Aeneid* that demonstrates the pattern of substitution whereby Dido replaces Creusa and Lavinia replaces Dido, see Mihoko Suzuki, *Metamorphoses of Helen: Authority, Difference, and the Epic* (Ithaca, N.Y., 1989), pp. 92–149.

5. For a brief survey of the popularity of the Dido episode, see Alain Michel, "Didon du Moyen-Âge à la renaissance: Le lamento et l'allégorie," in *Énée et Didon: Naissance, fonctionnement et survie d'un mythe*, ed. René Martin (Paris, 1990), pp. 71–77; see also Steven Farron, "The Aeneas-Dido Episode as an Attack on Aeneas' Mission and Rome," *Greece and Rome* 27 (1980), pp. 34–47. For a discussion of medieval perceptions of Aeneas as a traitor, see Meyer Reinhold, "The Unhero Aeneas," *Classica et Mediaevalia* 27 (1966), pp. 195–207. Seventy years ago, Arthur L. Keith remarked: "It is no exaggeration to say that for the great majority of readers Dido looms up far above Aeneas and her melancholy story far outweighs the interest felt in the founding of imperial Rome." And he notes that his experiences in the classroom particularly support this aspect of reader-response: "I have taken more than twenty classes of students through their Vergil, students good, bad, and indifferent. . . . they never fail to show some interest in the story of Dido" ("The Dido Episode," *South Atlantic Quarterly* 21 [1922], p. 68).

6. For a survey of reader's citations of the *Aeneid* book by book, see Pierre Courcelle, *Lecteurs païens et lecteurs chrétiens de l'Énéide*, vol. 1: *Les témoignages Littéraires* (Paris, 1984).

7. On the relation of the *Aeneid* to later imperial ideologies, see David Quint, *Epic and Empire: Politics and Generic Form from Virgil to Milton* (Princeton, N.J., 1993), p. 24. See also Richard Waswo, "The History that Literature Makes," *New Literary History* 19 (1988), pp. 541–64.

8. The best survey of the non-Virgilian Dido is Mary Louise Lord's "Dido as an Example

of Chastity: The Influence of Example Literature," *Harvard Library Bulletin* 17 (1969), pp. 22–44 and 216–39. On Dido's Semitic identity, see Arthur Stanley Pease, *Publi Vergili Maronis Aeneidos: Liber Quartus* (Cambridge, 1935), p. 26. For an extended discussion of the Semitic identity of the Phoenicians and the consequent implications for our modern construction of Ancient Mediterranean cultures, see Martin Bernal, *Black Athena: The Afroasiatic Roots of Classical Civilization,* vol. 1: *The Fabrication of Ancient Greece 1785–1985* (New Brunswick, N.J., 1987), pp. 337–99. For a discussion of Bernal's work in relation to classics as a discipline, see Molly Levine, ed., *The Challenge of Black Athena* (Buffalo, N.Y., 1989), special issue, *Arethusa;* see especially, Sarah P. Morris, "Daidalos and Kadmos: Classicism and 'Orientalism' ": "Classical scholarship was nourished by specific European attitudes towards the past and the East, incorporating explicitly racist assumptions about the ethnicity of culture" (p. 40). See also Shelley P. Haley, "Black Feminist Thought and Classics: Re-membering, Re-claiming, Re-empowering," in *Feminist Theory and the Classics,* ed. Nancy Sorkin Rabinowitz and Amy Richlin (New York, 1993), pp. 23–43.

9. Trinh T. Minh-ha, *Woman Native Other: Writing Postcoloniality and Feminism* (Bloomington, Ind., 1989), p. 79.

10. Fawzi Mellah, *Elissa, la reine vagabonde* (Paris, 1988); see also Alya Bacca, "Survie d'Elissa-Didon dans la Tunisie contemporaine," in *Énée et Didon,* pp. 241–49.

11. Gayatri Chakravorty Spivak, *The Post-Colonial Critic: Interviews, Strategies, Dialogues* (London, 1990), p. 9. For an explicit discussion of the relationship Spivak sees between postcoloniality and feminism, see Spivak, "Feminism in Decolonization," *Differences* 3 (1991), pp. 139–70. The intersections of discourses of gender and colonization require theoretical formulations in which feminism and decolonization are interdependent. See also Haley, "Black Feminist Thought," pp. 23–43.

12. On the role of the *literati* in the consolidation of power and the concomitant persecution of subjugated groups, see R. I. Moore, *The Formation of a Persecuting Society: Power and Deviance in Western Europe 950–1250* (Oxford, 1987), pp. 124–53. Of course, the precise nature of Latin education of the male elite in medieval culture must be understood in terms of the various segmentations of the secular and clerical elites. On the acquisition of Latin for practical purposes by nobility and clergy, see M. T. Clanchy, *From Memory to Written Record: England 1066–1307,* 2d ed. (Oxford, 1993), especially chapter 7, "Literate and Illiterate," pp. 224–52. On the potential acquisition of Latin by the aristocracy, see Nicholas Orme, *English Schools in the Middle Ages* (London, 1973), p. 34, and Jo Ann Hoeppner Moran, *The Growth of English Schooling 1340–1548: Learning, Literacy and Laicization in Pre-Reformation York Diocese* (Princeton, N.J., 1985), p. 150. For a general discussion of literacy and culture, see Brian Stock, *The Implications of Literacy: Written Language and Models of Interpretation in the Eleventh and Twelfth Centuries* (Princeton, N.J., 1983).

13. Quintilian records the centrality of Virgil in the Roman curriculum: "Ideoque optime institutum est, ut ab Homero atque Vergilio lectio inciperet, quanquam ad intelligendas eorum virtutes firmiore iudicio opus est sed huic rei super est tempus, neque enim semel legentur. Interim et sublimitate heroi carminis animus adsurgat et ex magnitudine rerum spiritum ducat et optimis imbuatur" (*Institutio oratoria* 1.8.5.). (It is therefore an admirable practice which now prevails, to begin by reading Homer and Vergil, although the intelligence needs to be further developed for the full appreciation of their merits but there is plenty of time for that since the boy will read them more than once. In the meantime, let his mind be lifted by the sublimity of heroic verse, inspired by the greatness of its theme and imbued with the loftiest sentiments.); text and translation from Quintilian, *Institio oratoria,* trans. E. H. Warmington (Cambridge, Mass., 1920). On the place of Virgil in Roman and late antique education, see H. I. Marrou, *A History of Education in Antiquity,* trans. George

Lamb (New York, 1956), pp. 229–352. About Roman education, Marrou remarks: "An educated Roman was a man who knew his Virgil" (p. 252). Marrou demonstrates the centrality
of education to the structures of the state: "Roman culture . . . had always had an 'academic' tinge, and this became more marked as time went on . . . most of the work of preservation fell on the schools as guardians of tradition, and on books as ennobling influences.
More than ever, classical education was regarded as the embodiment of the ideal of perfect
humanity" (p. 310). See also Pierre Riché, *Les Écoles et l'enseignement dans l'Occident
chrétien de la fin du Ve siècle au milieu du XIe siècle* (Paris, 1979). As James J.
Murphy com-
ments on the connection between education and empire: "By the time Augustine was a
schoolboy in the 350's we find him undergoing a schooling not radically different in
methodology from that undergone by Cicero a hundred years before the birth of
Christ. . . . It was the system exported throughout the Roman world along with soldiers and
the merchants of colonial expansion" ("The Teaching of Latin as a Second Language in the
Twelfth Century," *Historiographia Linguistica* 7 [1980], p. 163).

14. The following studies suggest something of the shape of medieval educational practices: Philippe Delhaye, "L'Organisation scolaire au XIIe siècle," *Traditio* 5 (1947), pp.
211–68; Orme, *English Schools*; Paul F. Grendler, *Schooling in Renaissance Italy: Literacy
and Learning, 1300–1600* (Baltimore, Md., 1989), especially pp. 3–41, 111–271; Moran, *The
Growth of English Schooling 1340–1548*; Tony Hunt, *Teaching and Learning Latin in 13th
Century England* (Cambridge, 1991), vol. 1, pp. 59–79; Ralph J. Hexter, *Ovid and Medieval
Schooling: Studies in Medieval School Commentaries on Ovid's* Ars Amatoria, Epistulae ex
Ponto, *and* Epistulae Heroidum (Munich, 1986); William J. Courtenay, *Schools and
Scholars in Fourteenth-Century England* (Princeton, N.J., 1987), pp. 3–146.

15. Our knowledge of medieval educational practices remains incomplete, though a
number of recent studies have begun to revise existing paradigms and enrich our understanding of the variations in pedagogy. In a discussion of fourteenth- and fifteenth-century
grammar schools in England, for instance, John N. Miner points out: "Contrary to wide
belief, the literature of the later medieval grammar program in England did not consist of
excerpts from classical authors. Rather the literature consisted of a number of didactic
poems originating in or modified by a later Christian Europe" (*The Grammar Schools of
Medieval England: A. F. Leach in Historiographical Perspective* [Montreal, 1990], p. 166; see
especially "The Grammar Program: The Teaching of Latin," pp. 133–73). Such assertions
are supported by Hunt's research on the teaching of Latin in England. He comments: "The
Aeneid seems to have been a more advanced text in English schools and rarely provided
with vernacular glosses, though more work needs to be done on the transmission" (vol. 1, p.
65). Orme states that Virgil's *Aeneid* was part of university training in England (*English
Schools*, p. 106). Orme elsewhere summarizes the curricular shifts that suggest that Virgil
was not central to English schools in the thirteenth and fourteenth centuries but became so
by the fifteenth: "During the thirteenth century a set of six Latin poets, the *Sex Auctores*,
frequently appears in manuscripts and was probably widely read in schools. The authors
were late and post-classical Latinists, and their works included the collection of wise pre-
cepts known as the *Distichs of Cato*, the *Ecologue of Theodulus* . . . Avianus's fables,
Maximian's love poems, Claudian's *Rape of Proserpine* and Statius's account of the youth of
Achilles. Thirteenth-century pupils were therefore exposed to poetry mostly by Christian
authors, but including pagan and amatory subjects. By the fourteenth century tastes were
changing, and the *Sex Auctores* seemed too difficult linguistically or too unsuitable culturally. The first two, the most Christian, were retained but the others dropped out and were
replaced by twelfth- and thirteenth-century moral and religious poems. . . . This group of
texts was dominant in schools until about 1490–1520 when (except for Cato) it was discarded in its turn for the classical pagan authors introduced by the humanists: Cicero, Horace,
Livy, Ovid and Virgil" (*Education and Society in Medieval and Renaissance England*

[London, 1989], p. 29]. See also Moran, *Growth of English Schooling*, p. 183. In his study of Italian education, Paul Grendler finds a similar set of practices, and he likewise suggests that Virgil became a central part of the grammar-school curriculum only in the second half of the fifteenth century; until then the *Aeneid* was read by advanced students (pp. 111–14, 236–50). A safe generalization appears to be that after the humanist transformation of the curriculum in the fifteenth century the *Aeneid* is much more uniformly found in the curricula of the grammar school as a Latin primer, a position it more or less holds until the end of the nineteenth century.

16. Ong, "Latin and the Social Fabric," pp. 206–8. See also, Walter J. Ong, *Orality and Literacy: The Technologizing of the Word* (London, 1982), pp. 112–15. On the acquisition of Latin by medieval readers, see Grendler, *Schooling in Renaissance Italy*, Hunt, *Teaching and Learning Latin*, and Murphy, "The Teaching of Latin."

17. For studies on the place of Virgil in medieval curricula, see Eva Matthews Sanford, "The Use of Classical Latin Authors in the *Libri Manuales*," TAPA 55 (1924), pp. 200–201; Aldo Scaglione, "The Classics in Medieval Education," in *The Classics in the Middle Ages: Papers of the Twentieth Annual Conference of the Center for Medieval and Renaissance Studies*, ed. Aldo S. Bernardo and Saul Levin (Binghamton, N.Y., 1990), pp. 343–62; Jean Leclercq, *The Love of Learning and the Desire for God: A Study of Monastic Culture* (New York, 1982), pp. 137–43; M. Louis Holtz, "La Survie de Virgile dans le haut moyen age," in *Présence de Virgile: Actes du colloque des 9, 11 et 12 décembre 1976* (Paris, 1978), pp. 209–22; Birger Munk Olsen, "Virgile et la renaissance du XIIᵉ siècle," in *Lectures médiévales de Virgile: Actes du colloque organisé par l'École française de Rome* (Rome, 1985), pp. 31–48.

18. See R. Fowler, " 'On Not Knowing Greek': The Classics and the Woman of Letters," *Classical Journal* 78 (1983), pp. 337–49. Fowler's survey of women's attempts to acquire some acquaintance with classical languages during the eighteenth, nineteenth, and early twentieth centuries demonstrates the extraordinarily exclusive nature of education. For the current status of women in the discipline of classics, see Amy Richlin, " 'Is Classics Dead?' The 1988 Women's Classical Caucus Report," in *Classics: A Discipline and Profession in Crisis?*, ed. Phyllis Culham and Lowell Edmunds (Lanham, Md., 1989), pp. 51–65.

19. On women's exclusion from the learning of Latin, Ong comments: "This pattern is closely connected with the position of women in society and with the fact that until recently the learned professions, where Latin was used, were closed to them" ("Latin and the Social Fabric," p. 211). See also Fowler. On current issues of gender and classical studies, see Marilyn Skinner, "Classical Studies vs. Women's Studies: *Duo moi ta noemmata*," *Helios* 12 (1985), pp. 3–17; Judith P. Hallett, "Feminist Theory, Historical Periods, Literary Canons, and the Study of Greco-Roman Antiquity," in *Feminist Theory and the Classics*, pp. 44–101.

20. Virginia Woolf, *Three Guineas* (New York, 1938), p. 85. The fact that Woolf evokes Pindar in this passage perhaps reflects the British interest in Greek Antiquity that was especially strong at the end of the nineteenth century. See Frank M. Turner, *The Greek Heritage in Victorian Britain* (New Haven, Conn., 1981), pp. 1–14. Woolf's classic commentary on women and the classics is "On Not Knowing Greek," *The Common Reader* (New York, 1925), pp. 24–39.

21. Virginia Woolf, *A Room of One's Own* (New York, 1929), p. 8.

22. Virginia Woolf, *Jacob's Room and the Waves* (New York, 1950), p. 121.

23. Virginia Woolf, *To the Lighthouse* (New York, 1927), p. 189.

24. T. S. Eliot, "What is a Classic?" in *Selected Prose of T. S. Eliot*, ed. Frank Kermode, (London, 1975), pp. 128–29.

25. W. F. Jackson Knight, *Roman Vergil* (London, 1944), p. 304. Indeed, it is interesting to note that Eliot appears to have assisted the publication of Knight's book by Faber and Faber,

and Knight appears to have been responsible for Eliot's presidency of the Virgil Society (Knight was secretary). See G. Wilson Knight, "T. S. Eliot: Some Literary Impressions," in *T. S. Eliot: The Man and His Work*, ed. Allen Tate (New York, 1966), pp. 251–52. For a discussion of Eliot's influence on classical scholarship, see W. R. Johnson, *Darkness Visible: A Study of Vergil's Aeneid* (Berkeley, Calif., 1976), pp. 6–10. For a discussion of Eliot's changing responses to Virgil's *Aeneid* over time, especially his debt to Theodor Haecker's *Virgil, Father of the West*, see Gareth Reeves, *T. S. Eliot: A Virgilian Poet* (New York, 1989), pp. 96–116.

26. For Eliot's emphasis on Christian empire, see "Virgil and the Christian World," in *On Poetry and Poets* (New York, 1957), pp. 135–48; Eliot sees Aeneas as the prototype of the Christian hero (p. 143). In "Modern Education and the Classics," he makes the following appeal: "It is only upon readers who wish to see a Christian civilization survive and develop that I am urging the importance of the study of Latin and Greek. If Christianity is not to survive, I shall not mind if the texts of the Latin and Greek languages became more obscure and forgotten than those of the language of the Etruscans" (*Selected Essays* [London, 1932], p. 515). For a discussion of Eliot's "extreme right-wing authoritarianism," see Terry Eagleton, *Literary Theory: An Introduction* (London, 1983), pp. 38–42. See also Judith Perkins, "Literary History: H. G. Gadamer, T. S. Eliot and Virgil," *Arethusa* 14 (1981), pp. 241–49; and Elizabeth Watson, "Virgil and T. S. Eliot," in *Virgil in a Cultural Tradition: Essays to Celebrate the Bimillennium*, ed. Richard A. Cardwell and Janet Hamilton, University of Nottingham Monographs in the Humanities, 4 (1986), pp. 115–33.

27. Greene, "Descent from Heaven," p. 63. For a slightly nuanced view of the imperial Virgil, see Niall Rudd, "The Idea of Empire in the *Aeneid*," in *Virgil in a Cultural Tradition*, pp. 25–42, and Jasper Griffin, *Virgil* (Oxford, 1986), pp. 58–106. See also A. Michel, "Virgile et la politique impériale: Un courtisan ou un philosophe?" in *Vergiliana: Recherches sur Virgile*, ed. Henry Bardon and Raoul Verdière (Leiden, 1971), pp. 212–45. For an excellent study of the *Aeneid* in the context of the Roman concept of empire, see Philip Hardie, *Virgil's Aeneid: Cosmos and Imperium* (Oxford, 1986). Hardie's study indirectly exposes the extent to which the concept of "empire" is historically and culturally specific; the imperial themes examined by Hardie have little or nothing in common with the concept of empire employed by Eliot, Knight, Greene, or Kermode. On the modern appropriation of the concept of empire, see J. S. Richardson, "*Imperium Romanum*: Empire and the Language of Power," *The Journal of Roman Studies* 81 (1991), pp. 1–9.

28. Frank Kermode, *The Classic: Literary Images of Permanence and Change* (New York, 1975; rpt. Cambridge, 1983), pp. 17–26.

29. Ibid., p. 141.

30. On the feminist challenge to these "c" words, see Hallett, "Feminist Theory."

31. Quint, *Epic and Empire*, p. 30. Quint notes that "if Virgil is a propagandist for emperor and empire—the position that he and his epic have occupied for the ensuing epic tradition—he is far from an uncritical one" (p. 11).

32. Homi K. Bhabha, "DissemiNation: Time, Narrative, and the Margins of the Modern Nation," in *Nation and Narration*, ed. Homi K. Bhabha (London, 1990), p. 311.

33. See especially Gary B. Miles and Archibald W. Allen, "Vergil and the Augustan Experience," in *Vergil at 2000*, ed. John D. Bernard (New York, 1986), pp. 13–41; Katharine Toll, "The *Aeneid* as an Epic of National Identity: *Italiam Laeto Socii Clamore Salutant*," *Helios* 18 (1991), pp. 3–14.

34. Johnson, *Darkness Visible*, p. 11.

35. W. R. Johnson, "The Broken World: Virgil and His Augustus," *Arethusa* 14 (1981), p. 50.

36. On the "second voice," see Adam Parry, "The Two Voices of Virgil's *Aeneid*," in Steele Commager, ed., *Virgil: A Collection of Critical Essays* (Englewood Cliffs, N.J., 1966),

pp. 107–23. On the "doubleness of vision," see James E. G. Zetzel, "Re-creating the Canon: Augustan Poetry and the Alexandrian Past," *Critical Inquiry* 10 (1983), p. 102.

37. Diana Fuss, *Essentially Speaking: Feminism, Nature and Difference* (London, 1990), p. 35.

38. See Walter J. Ong, S.J., "Latin Language Study as a Renaissance Puberty Rite," *Studies in Philology* 56 (1959), pp. 103–24.

39. Ibid., p. 122.

40. Judith Fetterley, *The Resisting Reader: A Feminist Approach to American Fiction* (Bloomington, Ind., 1978). See also the collection of essays entitled *Gender and Reading: Essays on Readers, Texts, Contexts*, ed. Patrocinio Schweickart and Elizabeth A. Flynn (Baltimore, Md., 1986).

41. See Ronald Mellor, "Classics and the Teaching of Greek and Roman Civilization," in *Classics: A Discipline and Profession in Crisis?*, pp. 99–105.

42. Bloom's most recent collection of Virgil criticism, *Virgil's Aeneid: Modern Critical Interpretations* (New York, 1987), includes an excerpt on Dido by Barbara Bono entitled "The Dido Episode," pp. 103–27; this excerpt is reprinted from her book *Literary Transvaluation: From Vergilian Epic to Shakespearean Tragicomedy* (Berkeley, Calif., 1984).

43. Bloom, ed., *Virgil*, p. 5.

44. E. R. Curtius, "Virgil in European Literature," in *Virgil*, ed. Harold Bloom, p. 16.

45. See Eve Kosofsky Sedgwick, *Between Men: English Literature and Male Homosocial Desire* (New York, 1985), p. 1. My own characterization of reading and homosocial desire is much indebted to Sedgwick's formulation and discussion, and to my own experience, so effectively evoked by Rachel Blau DuPlessis: "Always: I have heard this story from many sources—they bond and clump outside your door and never 'ask you to lunch' or they talk and can be wonderful, lambent, but when you walk up 'they turn away' or 'they turn on you, teasing, making sexual jokes' " ("For the Etruscans," p. 272).

46. Eve Kosofsky Sedgwick, *Epistemology of the Closet* (Berkeley, Calif., 1990), p. 185.

47. Ibid., p. 58.

48. Donatus's *vita* describes Virgil as "libidinis in pueros pronioris" (more disposed to desire boys); see R. Ellis, ed., *Appendix Vergiliana* (Oxford, 1957), p. 4. Donatus's *vita*, from the fourth century, preserves much material from a second-century *vita* by Suetonius that has been lost.

49. John Boswell, *Christianity, Social Tolerance, and Homosexuality: Gay People in Western Europe from the Beginning of the Christian Era to the Fourteenth Century* (Chicago, 1980), p. 73. See also Paul Veyne, "Homosexuality in Ancient Rome," in *Western Sexuality: Practice and Precept in Past and Present Times* (Oxford, 1985), pp. 25–35; Saara Lilja, *Homosexuality in Republican and Augustan Rome* (Helsinki, 1983).

50. Boswell, *Christianity, Social Tolerance, and Homosexuality*, p. 73.

51. Ibid., p. 74.

52. Sedgwick, *Epistemology of the Closet*, p. 58.

53. See Tina Passman, "Out of the Closet and Into the Field: Matriculture, the Lesbian Perspective, and Feminist Classics," in *Feminist Theory and the Classics*, pp. 181–208.

54. See Robert Graves, "The Virgil Cult," *The Virginia Quarterly Review* 38 (1962), pp. 13–35.

55. Knight, *Roman Vergil*, pp. 113–14.

56. Curtius, "Virgil in European Literature," p. 15. See the same comment by R. D. Williams, *The Aeneid* (London, 1987), p. 1.

57. Mario A. Di Cesare, *The Altar and the City: A Reading of Vergil's Aeneid* (New York, 1974), p. ix. Another critic, in a discussion of the second eclogue, refers to the "good deal of foolishness that has been spoken about Vergil's sexual habits"; see Copley, *Latin Literature*, p. 175. Both comments appear to cite the judgment that appears in Bruno Nardi's

The Youth of Virgil (Cambridge, 1930) regarding the "array of silly gossip concerning the Poet" (p. 62). Nardi later comments: "As to the moral portrait, I think we must make allowances for what Donatus and the scholastics say, especially as regards the Poet's pretended penchant for boys. Except for this fault, Servius tells us, his life was blameless" (p. 108).

58. See M. Owen Lee, *Fathers and Sons in Virgil's* Aeneid: *Tum Genitor Natum* (Albany, N.Y., 1979), pp. 108–13. For another view that refutes Lee's position, see John F. Makowski, "Nisus and Euryalus: A Platonic Relationship," *Classical Journal* 85 (1989), pp. 1–15. As Marilyn Skinner observes, "The impact of both homosexuality and homophobia upon classical scholarship is a complicated topic deserving extensive treatment . . . no study of this kind presently exists" ("Classical Studies vs. Women's Studies," p. 16 n).

59. L. P. Wilkinson, "Classical Approaches IV: Homosexuality," *Encounter* 51 (1978): "In the *Aeneid*, though Dido is effective, if sometimes too rhetorical, as a tragic queen in the literary tradition of Medea, I feel it is with those young men killed in the flower of their youth while fighting in Italy, such as Lausus and Pallas, that the poet is really involved; and particularly with Nisus and Euryalus" (p. 30). Jasper Griffin makes a similar set of comments: "The scandal which ancient gossip had to tell about Virgil was of a homosexual sort, and the sensibility of the *Aeneid*, as we shall see, does not, to say the least, contradict the implication" (*Virgil*, p. 26); such an observation leads him to a repetition of Wilkinson's and Curtius's point: "The *Aeneid* is pervaded by beautiful youths, most of whom are killed; the eye of the poet lingers on them with an almost amorous tenderness. . . . We seem to see him trying to put that essentially homosexual sensibility at the service of the patriotic purposes of his poem" (p. 94).

60. Brooks Otis, *Virgil: A Study in Civilized Poetry* (Oxford, 1963), pp. 90–91.

61. Ibid., p. 94.

62. R. D. Williams, *The Aeneid* (London, 1987), p. 108. For a survey of attitudes toward Dido's guilt, see Niall Rudd, "Dido's *culpa*," in *Lines of Enquiry: Studies in Latin Poetry* (Cambridge, 1976), pp. 32–53. For a reading that sees Dido as guilty, see Viktor Pöschl, "Dido und Aeneas," in *Festschrift Karl Vretska*, ed. Doris Ableitinger and Helmut Gugel (Heidelberg, 1970), pp. 148–73.

63. The one woman who is not left behind at the end of book 5 is the mother of Euryalus, who is present in the Trojan camp in book 9 to mourn the death of her son; see *Aeneid* 9.473–502.

64. Suzuki, *Metamorphoses of Helen*, p. 11.

65. Christine Froula, "The Daughter's Seduction: Sexual Violence and Literary History," *Signs* 11 (1986), p. 633.

66. Di Cesare, *The Altar and the City*, p. 37.

67. Christine G. Perkell, "On Creusa, Dido, and the Quality of Victory in Virgil's *Aeneid*," in *Reflections of Women in Antiquity*, ed. Helene P. Foley (New York, 1981), p. 370.

68. Ibid., pp. 370–71.

69. For an example of a recent essay that purports to explore the multivalent nature of loss and sacrifice in relation to history and the foundational narrative of the *Aeneid* and yet never mentions the loss of women, see Sanford Budick, "The Prospect of Tradition: Elements of Futurity in a Topos of Homer and Virgil," *New Literary History* 22 (1991), pp. 23–37.

70. Joan Wallach Scott, *Gender and the Politics of History* (New York, 1988), pp. 44–45. For an excellent recent study of gender as a construct in medieval cultures, see Kathleen Biddick, "Genders, Bodies, Borders: Technologies of the Visible," *Speculum* 68 (1993), pp. 389–418.

71. Trinh T. Minh-ha, *Woman Native Other*, p. 113.

72. See Sarah B. Pomeroy, *Goddesses, Whores, Wives, and Slaves: Women in Classical Antiquity* (New York, 1975), chapter 1: "Goddesses and Gods," pp. 1–15.

73. Boswell, *Christianity, Social Tolerance, and Homosexuality*, p. 58.

74. Boswell notes: "Opportunities for erotic expression were organized around issues of class and age or marital status rather than gender. . . . A wealthy and powerful adult male citizen, for example, at the top of the status hierarchy, could penetrate any other person without loss of social status. . . . But for the same male to be penetrated—by anyone—would incur disrespect if it were known, and might even subject him to loss of civil privilege. By contrast, although a slave (or even a freedman) would lose no status for being penetrated by someone more powerful, he might suffer greatly (a slave could forfeit his life) if he penetrated a citizen" ("Concepts, Experience and Sexuality," *Differences* 2 [1990], pp. 67–87; here, p. 72).

75. All quotations from Virgil are from R. A. B. Mynors, *P. Vergili Maronis Opera* (Oxford, 1969). Translations are my own.

76. Judith Butler articulates this theoretical premise: "Gender ought not to be conceived merely as the cultural inscription of meaning on a pregiven sex . . . gender must also designate the very apparatus of production whereby the sexes themselves are established" (*Gender Trouble: Feminism and the Subversion of Identity* [London, 1990], p. 7).

77. Ibid., p. 6.

78. "Technologies of Gender" is Teresa de Lauretis's term; see *Technologies of Gender: Essays on Theory, Film and Fiction* (Bloomington, Ind., 1987).

79. Butler, *Gender Trouble*, pp. 6–7; see also, Monique Wittig, *The Straight Mind and Other Essays* (Boston, 1992); Teresa de Lauretis, "Sexual Indifference and Lesbian Representation," in *Performing Feminisms: Feminist Critical Theory and Theatre*, ed. Sue-Ellen Case (Baltimore, Md., 1990), pp. 17–39; Luce Irigaray, *This Sex Which is Not One* (Ithaca, N.Y., 1977), pp. 170–72; Adrienne Rich, "Compulsory Heterosexuality and Lesbian Existence," in Ann Snitow, Christine Stansell, and Sharon Thompson, eds., *Powers of Desire* (New York, 1983), pp. 177–205.

80. See James A. Brundage, *Law, Sex, and Christian Society in Medieval Europe* (Chicago, 1987).

81. For instance, in an exploration of the implications of compulsory heterosexuality in modern Western cultures, Judith Butler observes: "The institution of a compulsory and naturalized heterosexuality requires and regulates gender as a binary relation in which the masculine term is differentiated from a feminine term, and this differentiation is accomplished through the practices of heterosexual desire" (*Gender Trouble*, pp. 22–23). On modern categories of gender and the binary tendency of modern thinking, see, for instance, Alfred C. Kinsey, *Sexual Behavior in the Human Male* (Philadelphia and London, 1948): "Males do not represent two discrete populations, heterosexual and homosexual. . . . It is a fundamental of taxonomy that nature rarely deals with discrete categories. Only the human mind invents categories and tries to force facts into separated pigeon-holes" (p. 639). See also John Boswell, "Categories, Experience and Sexuality," in *Forms of Desire: Sexual Orientation and the Social Constructionist Controversy*, ed. Edward Stein (New York, 1990), pp. 133–73; Gayle Rubin, "Thinking Sex: Notes for a Radical Theory of the Politics of Sexuality," in *Pleasure and Danger: Exploring Female Sexuality*, ed. Carole S. Vance (London, 1984), pp. 267–319; Hélène Cixous, *New Born Woman* (Minneapolis, 1986), p. 83; Eve Kosofsky Sedgwick, "A Poem Is Being Written," *Representations* 17 (1987), pp. 110–43; and Sedgwick, *Epistemology of the Closet*, pp. 1–63.

82. See Kaja Silverman, *Male Subjectivity at the Margins* (London, 1992), chapter 1, "The Dominant Fiction," pp. 15–51; here, p. 50.

83. For recent discussions of the sexual politics of reading, see Carolyn Dinshaw, *Chaucer's Sexual Poetics* (Madison, Wisc., 1989).

84. "The commonest word for parchment was *membrana*, simply meaning animal skin" (Clanchy, *From Memory to Written Record*, p. 120). On the prevalence and status of parchment in medieval textual cultures, see chapter 4, "The Technology of Writing," pp. 114–44. See also Susan Noakes, *Timely Reading: Between Exegesis and Interpretation* (Ithaca, N.Y., 1988), chapter 4, "From Boccaccio to Christine de Pizan: Reading the Corpus," pp. 98–134; and Michael Camille, "The Book of Signs: Writing and Visual Difference in Gothic Manuscript Illumination," *Word and Image* 1 (1985), pp. 133–48.

85. Mary Carruthers, *The Book of Memory: A Study of Memory in Medieval Culture* (Cambridge, 1990), pp. 221–57. See also Camille, "Book of Signs," and "Seeing and Reading: Some Visual Implications of Medieval Literacy and Illiteracy," *Art History* 8 (1985), pp. 26–49.

86. Julia Kristeva, "Women's Time," *Signs* 7 (1981), p. 17. Robert Young, in a discussion of Sartre and Lévi-Strauss, summarizes the issue: "The use of chronology in historical writing, or in literary history, gives the illusion that the whole operates by a uniform, continuous progression, a linear series in which each event takes its place. History is thus a process of continuous unfolding" (*White Mythologies: Writing History and the West* [London, 1990], p. 45).

87. See Joan Kelly's essay "Did women have a Renaissance?" in *Women, History and Theory* (Chicago, 1984), pp. 19–50.

88. For definitions of intertext and intertextuality, see Michael Riffaterre, "Intertextual Representation: On Mimesis as Interpretive Discourse," *Critical Inquiry* 11 (1984), pp. 142–43. See also Michael Riffaterre, "L'Intertexte Inconnu," *Littérature* 41 (1981), pp. 4–7; and Julia Kristeva, *Desire in Language: A Semiotic Approach to Literature and Art* (New York, 1980), pp. 36–63.

89. For an example of a text of literary history organized around the aesthetic appreciation of both Virgil and Dante, see Domenico Comparetti, *Vergil in the Middle Ages* (London, 1895; rpt. 1966), trans. E. F. M. Benecke. The product of nineteenth-century philological study, Comparetti's study is unmatched both in the scope and the thoroughness of its survey and the heavy-handed judgments regarding literary value that organize the book.

90. See Pierre Courcelle and Jeanne Courcelle, "Énéc dans quelques manuscrits de l'«Histoire ancienne»," *Lecteurs Païens et Lecteurs Chrétiens de l'Énéide*, vol. 2: *Les manuscrits illustrés de l'Énéide du Xᵉ au XVᵉ siècle* (Paris, 1984), pp. 89–107.

91. As Jeanne Courcelle notes, "Les manuscrits virgiliens illustrés sont rares. Entre le Vᵉ siècle et le Xᵉ siècle, nous n'avons trouvé aucun jalon. Nous ne pouvons aligner, pour l'Énéide proprement dite, qu'un manuscrit du Xᵉ siècle, deux du XIVᵉ siècle, douze du XVᵉ siècle" (p. 395) ("Les illustrations de l'*Énéide* dans les manuscrits du Xᵉ siècle au XVᵉ siècle," in *Lectures médiévales de Virgile: Actes du colloque organisé par l'École française de Rome*, [Rome, 1985], pp. 395–416). For a complete survey of medieval illustrations of Virgil manuscripts, see the magisterial collection of images in Courcelle and Courcelle, *Lecteurs païens et lecteurs chrétiens de l'Énéide*, vol. 2. I have relied heavily on this volume in tracing the visual traditions of Dido that emerge from Virgilian texts.

92. Gayatri Chakravorty Spivak, *In Other Worlds: Essays in Cultural Politics* (London, 1988), p. 25.

93. Pease, *Publi Vergili Maronis Aeneidos*, pp. 68–69. See René Martin, "Didon de l'antiquité à nos jours: Inventaire des œuvres littéraires, scéniques et cinématographiques," in *Énée et Didon*, pp. xxi-xxv; Maria Rosa-Lida de Malkiel, *Dido en la Literatura Española: Su Retrato y Defensa* (London, 1974); Don Cameron Allen, "Marlowe's *Dido* and the Tradition," in *Essays on Shakespeare and Elizabethan Drama in Honor of Hardin Craig*, ed. Richard Hosley (Columbia, Mo., 1962), pp. 55–60; Adrianne Roberts-Baytop, *Dido, Queen of Infinite Literary Variety: The English Renaissance Borrowings and Influences* (Salzburg,

1974); and Bono, *Literary Transvaluation*. On the interpretive understanding of Dido among the Italian allegorists of the Renaissance, see Grendler, *Schooling in Renaissance Italy*, pp. 237–38. On Dido in medieval Spanish literature, see Judith Miller Ortiz, "The Two Faces of Dido: Classical Images and Medieval Reinterpretation," *Romance Quarterly* 33 (1986), pp. 421–30.

94. Roberts-Baytop, *Dido, Queen of Infinite Literary Variety*, pp. 104–18; Bono, *Literary Transvaluation*.

95. Edward W. Said, *Orientalism* (New York, 1979); *Culture and Imperialism* (New York, 1993). On the formation of racialized identities in the ancient and late antique world, see Lellia Cracco Ruggini, "Intolerance: Equal and Less Equal in the Roman World," *Classical Philology* 82 (1987), pp. 187–205.

96. Edward Said, "Representing the Colonized: Anthropology's Interlocutors," *Critical Inquiry* 15 (1989), p. 215.

97. Some of the commemorative collections include *Arethusa* 14, (1981), "Virgil: 2000 Years"; John D. Bernard, ed., *Vergil at 2000: Commemorative Essays on the Poet and His Influence* (New York, 1986); Charles Martindale, *Virgil and His Influence* (Bristol, 1984); Cardwell and Hamilton, *Virgil in a Cultural Tradition*; Viktor Pöschl, ed., *2000 Jahre Vergil: Ein Symposion* (Wiesbaden, 1983).

98. A significant study of Dido is Richard C. Monti, *The Dido Episode and the Aeneid: Roman Social and Political Values in The Epic* (Leiden, 1981). See also Martin, ed., *Énée et Didon*; Perkell, "On Creusa"; Bono, *Literary Transvaluation*; and Suzuki, *Metamorphoses*.

1. Dux Femina Facti

1. Text from Petrarch, *Opera* (Venice, 1501). I am grateful to Aldo Bernardo and Saul Levin for permission to consult their working transcription of this text. For a translation of the *Seniles*, see Francis Petrarch, *Letters of Old Age: Rerum Senilium Libri*, 2 vols., trans. Aldo S. Bernardo, Saul Levin, and Reta A. Bernardo (Baltimore, Md., 1992). Petrarch also mentions the historical Dido in *Africa* 3.524 and *Trionfo Della Castita*, lines 10–12, 154–59.

2. Petrarch notes that Augustine, Justin, and Macrobius knew that Aeneas and Dido could never have met, since they lived at different times.

3. For a description of *Seniles* IV.5, see Craig Kallendorf, *In Praise of Aeneas: Virgil and Epideictic Rhetoric in the Early Italian Renaissance* (Hanover, N.H., 1989), pp. 43–44, and Pierre de Nolhac, *Pétrarque et l'humanisme* (Paris, 1907), pp. 133–38.

4. For a general survey of the "historical" Dido, see the magisterial essay by Mary Louise Lord, "Dido as an Example of Chastity: The Influence of Example Literature," *Harvard Library Bulletin* 17 (1969). Lord's survey is much fuller than my own, and I have relied heavily on her citations in charting my own course through this material. See also Jean-Michel Poinsotte, "L'Image de Didon dans l'antiquité tardive," in *Énée et Didon: Naissance, fonctionnement et survie d'un mythe*, ed. René Martin (Paris, 1990), pp. 43–54. See also the brief discussion in Don Cameron Allen, "Marlowe's *Dido* and the Tradition," in *Essays on Shakespeare and Elizabethan Drama in Honor of Hardin Craig* (Columbia, Mo., 1962). I have taken the term "historical Dido" from Lord and Allen. See also Arthur Stanely Pease, *Publi Vergili Maronis Aeneidos: Liber Quartus* (Cambridge, 1935), pp. 16–17.

5. For an account of Timaeus, see Truesdell S. Brown, *Timaeus of Tauromenium* (Berkeley, Calif., 1958). See also Louis Foucher, "Les Phéniciens à Carthage ou la geste d'Élissa," in *Présence de Virgile: Actes du colloque des 9, 11 et 12 décembre 1976*, ed. R. Chevallier (Paris, 1978), pp. 1–15.

6. See Pease, *Publi Vergili Maronis Aeneidos*, p. 16.

7. For the text of Timaeus, see Felix Jacoby, *Die Fragmente der Griechischen Historiker*, 3B (Leiden, 1950), p. 624 (No. 566 F82). See also Pease, *Publi Vergili Maronis*

Aeneidos, 16. For an English translation, see Lord, "Dido as an Example of Chastity," pp. 33–34. The text is also preserved intact in an anonymous tract on women; see *Paradoxographoi: Scriptores Rerum Mirabilium Graeci,* ed. Antonius Westermann (Amsterdam, 1963), p. 215.

8. Pompeius Trogus's history probably belongs to the first decade of the first century. C.E. As Merle M. Odgers puts it, "His [Trogus's] account of Dido probably goes back ultimately to one which antedates or is contemporary with the *Aeneid*" ("Some Appearances of the Dido Story," *Classical Weekly* 18 [1925], pp. 145–48; here, p. 146).

9. M. Iuniani Justini, *Epitoma Historiarum Philippicarum Pompei Trogi,* ed. O. Seel (Leipzig, 1972).

10. On the implications of rape as part of a foundation myth, see Julie Hemker, "Rape and the Founding of Rome," *Helios* 12 (1985), pp. 41–47, and Stephanie Jed, *Chaste Thinking: The Rape of Lucretia and the Birth of Humanism* (Bloomington, Ind., 1989).

11. For the cultural implications of the concept of "traffic in women," See Gayle Rubin, "The Traffic in Women: Notes on the 'Political Economy' of Sex," in Raynar Reiter, *Towards an Anthropology of Women* (Stanford, Calif., 1972), pp. 157–210.

12. See Nicole Loraux, *Tragic Ways of Killing a Woman* (Cambridge, 1987), trans. Anthony Foster. Loraux notes that in Greek tragedy, suicide by the sword is a man's death, and women who choose the sword over the noose, "a womanly way of ending her life," are choosing a man's death (p. 17). However, she notes further that "in Latin texts, women generally kill themselves with a sword" (p. 88 n. 45).

13. See Rudolf Helm, *Die Chronik des Hieronymus. Band 7 Eusebius Werke* (Leipzig, 1913); Eusebius gives 1039, 1014, and 850 as the three possible dates (pp. 69–81). According to Eusebius, Aeneas was established in Italy by 1181. See also Pease, *Publi Vergili Maronis Aeneidos,* p. 58 n. 468. Lord, "Dido as an Example of Chastity," p. 217 n. 1.

14. Text from Beryl Smalley, *English Friars and Antiquity in the Early Fourteenth Century* (Oxford, 1960), p. 320. Translations are my own. Robert Holcot also alludes briefly to the historical Dido in citing Jerome's catalog of chaste women (*English Friars,* p. 322). As Smalley notes, Ridevall's knowledge came from Papias's *Vocabularium* (C. 1045). Ranulf Hidgen's *Polychronicon* (C. 1350) also preserves notice of the historical Dido (see chapter 5).

15. For a discussion of the various possibilities that Naevius invented the Aeneas-Dido romance, see Pease, *Publi Vergili Maronis Aeneidos,* pp. 18–21; Lord, "Dido as an Example of Chastity," p. 40; Michael Wigodsky, "Vergil and Early Latin Poetry," *Hermes: Zeitschrift für Klassische Philologie. Einzelschriften* Heft 24 (Wiesbaden, 1972), pp. 29–34; Odgers, "Some Appearances of the Dido Story."

16. For a thorough discussion of the ancient sources of the Dido story, see Jerzy Kowaloski, *De Didone Graeca et Latina* (Cracow, 1929).

17. Gian Biagio Conte, *The Rhetoric of Imitation: Genre and Poetic Memory in Virgil and Other Latin Poets,* trans. Charles Segal (Ithaca, N.Y., 1986), p. 152.

18. See Lawrence Lipking, *Abandoned Women and Poetic Tradition* (Chicago, 1988). Lipking refers to Virgil's Dido, in passing, throughout his book.

19. "When poetic memory works upon culture, it transforms the fragments of specific factual or historical material into an essential component of a systematically organized poetic discourse" (Conte, *Rhetoric of Imitation,* p. 50).

20. The concept of Dido's formidability might profitably be seen in the context of Judith P. Hallett's discussion in *Fathers and Daughters in Roman Society: Women and the Elite Family* (Princeton, N.J., 1984). Hallett's study of the position of women in the Roman family leads her to articulate the following paradox about classical Roman culture: "Many well-born women are remembered as possessing forceful personalities and exerting a substantial impact on men's public affairs, despite their society's extolling of domesticity as women's only proper concern, and despite their own legal disabilities and formal exclusion from

political participation. This paradoxical formidability is imputed to well-born Roman women both as individuals and en masse; it is imputed as a result of both actual conduct by female members of Rome's classical elite and contemporary perceptions of how elite Roman women were capable of acting" (p. 6).

21. Francis Cairns, *Virgil's Augustan Epic* (Cambridge, 1989), p. 38.

22. For Cairns's list of "the elements of the good king stereotype," see pp. 19–21. Justice, self-control, wisdom, and courage are four cardinal virtues of the "good king."

23. See Viktor Pöschl, *The Art of Vergil: Image and Symbol in the Aeneid*, trans. Gerda Seligson (Ann Arbor, Mich., 1962), pp. 60–91; Wendell Clausen, *Virgil's Aeneid and the Tradition of Hellenistic Poetry* (Berkeley, Calif., 1987), pp. 53–58.

24. For an analysis of the issues of interpretation here, see Charles Segal, "Art and the Hero: Participation, Detachment, and Narrative Point of View in *Aeneid* 1," *Arethusa* 14 (1981), pp. 67–83.

25. For commentaries on *Aeneid* 4, see Pease, *Publi Vergili Maronis Aeneidos*; and R. G. Austin, *P. Vergili Maronis Aeneidos Liber Quartus* (Oxford, 1955).

26. Richard C. Monti, *The Dido Episode and the* Aeneid: *Roman Social and Political Values in the Epic* (Leiden, 1981), p. 7. For a discussion of the cave scene as a conflict between the social expectations derived from a distinction between the public sphere and the private sphere, see Susan Ford Wiltshire, *Public and Private in Vergil's Aeneid* (Amherst, Mass., 1989), pp. 90–93. Ford notes: "For Dido the disaster evolved from her assumption of a public status for the personal relationship conceived with Aeneas in the cave during their retreat from the storm. The difference between a love affair and marriage is that one is private and the other is public. Dido's great yearning was for the one to be the other" (p. 91).

27. Eugene Vance, "Sylvia's Pet Stag: Wilderness and Domesticity in Virgil's *Aeneid*," *Arethusa* 14 (1981), "Virgil: 2000 Years," p. 135. Vance sees Dido as "willing to assume the role of predator when she had abandoned her role as majestic city builder and gone off into the woods to 'hunt' with Aeneas" (p. 135). Vance's point of view, in amplifying the judgmental tone of the narrator, allows no sympathy for Dido.

28. Gordon Williams, *Tradition and Originality in Roman Poetry* (Oxford, 1968), pp. 372–73.

29. Ibid., p. 372.

30. See, for instance, R. P. H. Green, "*Conubium* in the *Aeneid*," *Studies in Latin Literature and Roman History* 4 (1986), pp. 393–421. For the opposite view, see D. Fenny, "The Taciturnity of Aeneas," *Classical Quarterly* 33 (1983), pp. 204–19. Concerning this scene, W. R. Johnson notes: "I doubt that we can tell what is going on here precisely. All we know is that a real wedding is pictured; that the bride and groom cannot see what we can see; and, finally, that the image of the wedding which we have just witnessed is obliterated" (*Darkness Visible: A Study of Vergil's Aeneid* [Berkeley, Calif., 1976], p. 163 n. 42); and Austin: "Virgil thus makes the wedding ritually correct, as one would expect him to. But it remains a supernatural ceremony, and an uncanny one for all its seeming correctness" (*P. Vergili Maronis Aeneidos*, p. 69). See also Monti, *The Dido Episode*, pp. 45–47; Philip Hardie, *Virgil's* Aeneid: *Cosmos and Imperium* (Oxford, 1986), p. 273; and Clausen, *Virgil's Aeneid*, pp. 22–25.

31. See Saara Lilja's discussion of "Love as a Disease," *The Roman Elegists' Attitude to Women* (New York, 1978), pp. 100–109. For a general discussion of Roman attitudes toward love, see R. O. A. M. Lyne, *The Latin Love Poets: From Catullus to Horace* (Oxford, 1980), pp. 1–18.

32. As Hardie comments, this passage is "an example of the *topos*, common in amatory poetry, of the neglect of accustomed occupations because of erotic obsession. The novel feature here is that the actions neglected are those performed by others than Dido her-

self. . . . There is, in fact, an implicit identification of the queen, Dido, with her subjects and her city" (*Virgil's* Aeneid, p. 271).

33. Monti, *The Dido Episode*, p. 35.

34. As Barbara Pavlock describes her death, "she symbolically experiences sexual penetration when she falls on Aeneas' sword on their bed, which is now her funeral pyre" (*Eros, Imitation, and the Epic Tradition* [Ithaca, N.Y., 1990], p. 84). On the phallic quality of Dido's death, in the contexts of an epic emphasis on swords and blood, see Daniel Gillis, *Eros and Death in the Aeneid* (Rome, 1983).

35. On the connection between Dido and Ajax, see Clausen, *Virgil's Aeneid*, p. 56.

36. See Cairns, *Virgil's Augustan Epic*, chapter 2 "Kingship and the Love Affair of Aeneas and Dido," pp. 29–57. For a discussion of Aeneas's Trojan identity within the ethnographic vision of the Romans, see Richard F. Thomas, "Cultural Polemics in the *Aeneid*," in *Land and Peoples in Roman Poetry: The Ethnographic Tradition* (Cambridge, 1982), pp. 91–107.

37. "Virgil dramatizes at once his need and the need of Augustus' empire to destroy or exorcize woman as Other" (Mihoko Suzuki, *Metamorphoses of Helen: Authority, Difference, and the Epic* [Ithaca, N.Y., 1989], p. 149).

38. Judith P. Hallett, "Women as *Same* and *Other* in Classical Roman Elite," *Helios* 16 (1989), pp. 59–78.

39. Lilja, "Love as a Disease," p. 108.

40. Cairns, *Virgil's Augustan Epic*, p. 149.

41. On the destruction of Carthage as a major disgrace in Roman history, see Steven Farron, "The Aeneas-Dido Episode as an Attack on Aeneas' Mission and Rome," *Greece and Rome* 27 (1980), pp. 39–40.

42. Pease, *Pubii Vergili Maronis Aeneidos*, pp. 24–28; David Quint, *Epic and Empire: Politics and Generic Form From Virgil to Milton* (Princeton, N.J., 1993), p. 28.

43. For a discussion of the Roman ethnographic vision as it is manifest in the *Aeneid*, see István Borzsak, "Von Hippokrates bis Vergil," in *Vergiliana: Recherches sur Virgile*, ed. Henry Bardon and Raoul Verdière (Leiden, 1971), pp. 41–55.

44. Ronald Syme, *The Roman Revolution* (Oxford, 1939), p. 270. On Augustus's description of Cleopatra, see pp. 270–300.

45. For a discussion of the shield, see Quint, *Epic and Empire*, pp. 24–31.

46. Lillian S. Robinson, *Monstrous Regiment: The Lady Knight in Sixteenth Century Epic* (New York, 1985), p. 30.

47. Certainly the status of *Aeneid* 4 and the Aeneas-Dido story as Virgil's revision of an existing tradition is suggested by the version of the Roman foundation myth as presented by Livy's *Ab urbe condita* I.i.—a text produced at the same time as Virgil's *Aeneid* (see Lord, "Dido as an Example of Chastity," p. 40) and in circulation during the period in which the *Heroides* were composed. Livy's account of Aeneas's flight from Troy chronicles briefly his stop at Macedonia and Sicily before landing at Laurentum. Livy makes no mention of Dido or Carthage in the context of Aeneas's story.

48. As Saara Lilja comments: "Roman elegy, although its main subject is woman, looks at things from a man's point of view. Only Ovid's *Heroides*, and Arethusa's letter and the Cornelia elegy of book IV of Propertius, seek to represent the woman's point of view" ("Love as a Disease," p. 107).

49. Warren Ginsburg, "Ovid and the Problem of Gender," *Mediaevalia* 13 (1989), p. 11.

50. Judith Butler, *Gender Trouble: Feminism and the Subversion of Identity* (London, 1990), p. 6.

51. See Harold Bloom, *The Anxiety of Influence* (New York, 1979, p. 69). Brooks Otis succinctly expresses one critical position on the *Metamorphoses*: "Virgil is turned inside out and this is true whether we consider the indirect parody of the *Perseus*, the direct parody of the *Orpheus* and *Achaemenides* or the truly comic ellipses of the later 'summaries' of

the *Aeneid"* (*Ovid as an Epic Poet* [Cambridge, 1970], p. 351). See also Charles Segal, "Ovid: Metamorphoses, Hero, Poet," *Helios* (1985), pp. 49–63. Indeed, many modern scholars introduce their discussions of Ovid with reference to the opinion that "Ovid's poetry directly opposes Vergil's" (John Fyler, *Chaucer and Ovid* [New Haven, Conn., 1979], p. 17). However, not all scholars look sympathetically on Ovid's treatment of Virgil's *Aeneid*: "In this poem we hear not simply Dido struggling with Aeneas, but Ovid waging war against Vergil; and he is doomed to defeat from the start because of his incapacity and unwillingness to appreciate the Vergilian position" (Howard Jacobson, *Ovid's Heroides* [Princeton, N.J., 1974], p. 90). For studies of *Heroides* 7, see W. S. Anderson, "The 'Heroides,' " in *Ovid*, ed. J. W. Binns (London, 1973); Joachim Adamietz, "Zu Ovids Dido-Brief," *Würzburger Jahrbücher für die Altertumswissenschaft* 10 (1984), pp. 121–34; A. Michel, "Rhétorique et poésie dans le maniérisme des Héroïdes: Didon chez Ovid," in *Acta Conventus Omnium Gentium Ovidianis Studiis Fovendis*, ed. N. Barbu, E. Dobroiu, and M. Wasta (Bucharest, 1972).

52. I have used the following editions of Ovid: William S. Anderson, ed., *Metamorphoses* (Leipzig, 1982); S. G. Owen, *Tristium Libri Quinque* (Oxford, 1978); H. Dorrie, ed., *Epistulae Heroidum* (Berlin, 1971). Translations from Ovid are my own.

53. For a general discussion of Ovid's rehearsal of the *Aeneid* story in the *Metamorphoses*, see G. Karl Galinsky, *Ovid's Metamorphoses: An Introduction to the Basic Aspects* (Oxford, 1975), pp. 217–51; on this passage that summarizes *Aeneid* 4, see pp. 248–49.

54. Barbara Herrnstein Smith describes the epigrammatist's manner as follows: "To epigrammatize an experience is to strip it down, to cut away irrelevance, to eliminate local, specific, and descriptive detail, to reduce it and fix it in its most permanent and stable aspect, to sew it up for eternity" (*Poetic Closure: A Study of How Poems End* [Chicago, 1968], p. 208). Ovid elsewhere presents epigrammatic summaries of *Heroides* 7; see *Ars Amatoria* 3.39–40, *Amores* 2.18.25, and *Fasti* 3.545–50.

55. As Eleanor Winsor Leach argues, "In the *Heroides*, the past time of mythology is more specifically grounded in literature than it is in either of the other books . . . the *Heroides* use their elegiac context to reopen questions of the literary incarnations of myth . . . in re-interpreting their own histories, the heroines allude to events that have happened to them in other works by other authors" ("A Study in the Sources and Rhetoric of Chaucer's *Legend of Good Women* and Ovid's *Heroides*" [Diss., Yale, 1963]). And Florence Verducci characterizes the relationship between the *Heroides* and earlier texts as follows: "The words of most of Ovid's heroines exercise a calculated challenge, by way of parody, to an earlier literary prototype" (*Ovid's Toyshop of the Heart: Epistulae Heroidum* [Princeton, N.J., 1985], p. 82).

56. On the theoretical issues implied here, see Christine Froula, "When Eve Reads Milton: Undoing the Canonical Economy," *Critical Inquiry* 10 (1983), pp. 321–47.

57. W. S. Anderson effectively describes the rhetoric of Virgil's Dido: "Whatever she says, he has circumscribed it with his narrative frame, and no audience should . . . surrender its objectivity and view the epic situation as Virgil's Dido does" ("The 'Heroides,' " p. 54). By contrast, describing Ovid's Dido, he notes: "Ovid abstracts his Dido from that total drama, and freezes her in a single moment" (p. 54).

58. As Verducci describes the rhetorical basis of the *Heroides*: "The epistle can combine, often in radical tension, the privacy of the interior monologue and the publicity of would-be persuasion. This combination simultaneously encourages rhetorical and expressive motives" (*Ovid's Toyshop of the Heart*, p. 16). For a consideration of the rhetorical conventions exploited in *Heroides* 7, see Nicholas P. Gross, "Rhetorical Wit and Amatory Persuasion in Ovid," *Classical Journal* 74 (1979), pp. 305–18. Gross proposes that *Heroides* 7, while not simply versified *suasoria* (p. 309 n) demonstrates Ovid's attempt to "under-

mine the traditional rhetoric of heroic speech" (p. 314). See also Michel, "Rhétorique et poésie dans le maniérisme des Héroïdes."

59. The epitaph from the *Aeneid* is briefly evoked earlier in *Heroides* 7 at lines 121–22, where much of the monumentalizing quality of Virgil's text is undermined. For a discussion of these two passages, see H. Akbar Khan, "Dido and the Sword of Aeneas," *Classical Philology* 63 (1968), pp. 283-85.

60. On the implications of Aeneas's treatment of Creusa, see Christine G. Perkell, "On Creusa, Dido, and the Quality of Victory in Virgil's *Aeneid*," in *Reflections of Women in Antiquity*, ed. Helene P. Foley (New York, 1981), pp. 355-77. About 2.741–43, Perkell notes: "In this critical moment, Aeneas plans effectively for his father, son and household gods but not for his wife. May we infer that he is more concerned for them than for her?" (p. 360).

61. Besides the passages I have discussed, see, for instance, *Aeneid* 4.4–5 and *Heroides* 7.25b-26; *Aeneid* 4.66–67 and *Heroides* 7.37–38; *Aeneid* 4.373–74 and *Heroides* 7.89–90; *Aeneid* 4.433–34 and *Heroides* 7.180–82; *Aeneid* 4.504–7 and *Heroides* 7.101–2. For a careful comparison of the two texts, see the commentary by A. Palmer, *P. Ovidii Nasonis Heroides* (Oxford, 1898); see also J. N. Anderson, *On the Sources of Ovid's Heroides* I, III, VII, X, XII (Berlin, 1896).

62. Monti, *The Dido Episode*, p. 42. In addition, Pease notes that the term *infelix*, used frequently enough as an adjective for Dido that it might be considered her epithet, literally means "unfruitful" or "sterile." And he comments on the appropriateness of this term: "Underlying the tragedy of Dido is the fact . . . that she leaves no descendant to carry on her race." He adds: "Note that Ovid's Dido, possibly pregnant . . . is not called *infelix*" (*Publi Vergili: Maronis Aeneidos*, p. 145).

63. See Khan, "Dido and the Sword of Aeneas," pp. 283–85.

64. See Paul Allen Miller, "*Sive Deae Seu Sint Dirae Obscenaeque Volucres*," *Arethusa* 22 (1989), p. 65.

65. For texts, see Ethel Leigh Chubb, *An Anonymous Epistle of Dido to Aeneas* (Philadelphia, 1920); Gianniana Solimano, *Epistula Didonis ad Aeneam: Introduzione, Testo, traduzione et commento* (Genoa, 1988). The Chubb edition includes a translation.

66. See the discussion in the Introduction to Chubb's edition, pp. 9–10.

67. On the transmission of Ovid's *Heroides*, see R. J. Tarrant, "Ovid," in L. D. Reynolds, ed., *Texts and Transmission: A Survey of the Latin Classics* (Oxford, 1983), pp. 268–72. See also Ralph J. Hexter, *Ovid and Medieval Schooling: Studies in Medieval School Commentaries on Ovid's* Ars Amatoria, Epistulae ex Ponto, *and* Epistulae Heroidum (Munich, 1986), pp. 1–13. On printed editions of the *Heroides*, see Ann Moss, *Ovid in Renaissance France: A Survey of the Latin Editions of Ovid and Commentaries Printed in France Before 1600* (London, 1982), pp. 8–16.

68. For text of the commentary, see Ralph Hexter, *Ovid and Medieval Schooling*; for the *accessus*, see R. B. C. Huygens, ed., *Accessus ad auctores; Bernard d'Utrecht; Conrad d'Hirsau, Dialogus super auctores* (Leiden, 1970). Hexter comments that "it is relatively rare . . . for medieval school commentaries on classical authors to explicate verses in light of passages from another work" (p. 216). He adds: "Medieval readers lacked a feel for the literary depth behind any of Ovid's works" (p. 217). *Heroides* 7 is perhaps the one exception, since the text's relationship to the *Aeneid* should have been recognizable.

69. *Heroides* 7 is specifically said to exemplify a love that is *furor*, a category that suggests the text of *Aeneid* 4 as much as *Heroides* 7, where much of Dido's madness and fury are softened.

70. Rita Copeland, *Rhetoric, Hermeneutics, and Translation in the Middle Ages: Academic Traditions and Vernacular Texts* (Cambridge, 1991), p. 116. "Translations" of the *Heroides* (often in the form of very loose vernacular paraphrases) are enfolded into larger narrative frameworks. Several manuscripts of the thirteenth-century *Histoire ancienne*

jusqu'à César, for instance, contain vernacular adaptations of the *Heroides* interspersed at the appropriate moments in the narrative and carefully noted by rubrics. Although several manuscripts of the *Histoire* are known to contain "translations" of selected *Heroides,* these manuscripts do not contain Dido's *Heroides* 7. See L. Constans, "Une traduction française des Héroïdes d'Ovide au XIIIᵉ siècle," *Romania* 43 (1914), pp. 177–98.

71. For the text of the *Ovid moralisé,* see *Ovid moralisé: Poème du commencement du quatorzième siècle,* ed. C. de Boer, 5 vols. (Amsterdam, 1915–38).

72. See William Caxton, *Ovyde: Hys Booke of Methamorphose Books X-XV* (Oxford, 1924).

73. On the circulation of Octovien de Saint-Gelais's translation of the *Heroides,* see Christine M. Scollen, *The Birth of the Elegy in France* 1500–1550 (Geneva, 1967): "Between the first printed edition of the *Epistres d'Ovide,* which dates from the turn of the century, until 1550, there were nearly twenty editions, by various printers in Paris, Lyons and Rouen" (p. 24). For an analysis of Saint-Gelais's translation, see pp. 21–24.

74. For an excellent study of the "Letter of Dido," see Julia Boffey, "Richard Pynson's *Book of Fame* and *The Letter of Dido,*" *Viator* 19 (1988), pp. 339–53; see also Götz Schmitz, *The Fall of Women in Early English Narrative Verse* (Cambridge, 1990), pp. 39–43. For a partial text of the "Letter of Dido," see Douglas Gray, *The Oxford Book of Late Medieval Verse and Prose* (Oxford, 1985), pp. 91–93. The complete text is not available in a modern edition.

75. A more appropriate visual image for illustrating the text of *Heroides* 7 would be the depiction of Dido as she describes herself—writing with a sword on her lap. See figure 1.

76. For a discussion of the exempla tradition and the historical Dido, see Lord, "Dido as an Example of Chastity." An interesting moment in Dido's itinerary is the survival of a rhetorical exercise *dictiones* produced by Ennodius, Bishop of Pavia, in the sixth century; this prose declamation is a speech from Dido's point of view upon the departure of Aeneas at *Aeneid* 4.365–87. See Marbury B. Ogle, "The Later Tradition of Vergil," *Classical Journal* 26 (1930), p. 70. For the text of this declamation, see F. Vogel, ed., *Magni Felicis Ennodi Operi* (Berlin, 1885), pp. 324–25.

77. For a discussion of the Dido *planctus* in the context of medieval Latin woman's song, see Anne Howland Schotter, "Woman's Song in Medieval Latin," in *Vox Feminae: Studies in Medieval Woman's Song,* ed. John F. Plummer (Kalamazoo, Mich., 1981), pp. 19–33.

78. Text from F. J. E. Raby, *The Oxford Book of Medieval Latin Verse* (Oxford, 1959), c. 235. Translations are my own.

79. Text from Jean de Meun, *Le Roman de la Rose,* ed. Félix Lecoy (Paris, 1966). Translations are my own.

80. John Gower, *Confessio Amantis,* ed. G. C. Macaulay (Oxford, 1900), 4.77–142; Machaut, *Le Judgement dou Roy de Navarre,* in Ernest Hoepffner, *Œuvres de Guillaume Machaut* (Paris, 1906; rpt. 1965), vv. 2089–2124. On Gower and Machaut, see chapter 4.

81. On the various voices in the *Roman de la Rose,* see Sylvia Huot, *From Song to Book: The poetics of Writing in Old French Lyric and Lyrical Narrative Poetry* (Ithaca, N.Y., 1987). See also Susan Stakel, *False Roses: Structures of Duality and Deceit in Jean de Meun's Roman de la Rose* (Stanford French and Italian Studies no. 69 (Stanford, Calif., 1991); on La Vieille, see pp. 71–75.

82. For a discussion of other traditional catalogs, see Glenda McLeod, *Virtue and Venom: Catalogs of Women From Antiquity to the Renaissance* (Ann Arbor, Mich., 1991), pp. 11–57.

83. Text from the *Riverside Chaucer,* ed. Larry Benson (Riverside, Calif., 1987).

84. For discussion of the illuminations of the *Roman de la Rose,* see Sylvia Huot, *The Romance of the Rose and Its Medieval Readers: Interpretation, Reception, Manuscript Transmission* (Cambridge, 1993), pp. 273–322; Michael Camille, *The Gothic Idol: Ideology and Image-Making in Medieval Art* (Cambridge, 1989), pp. 316–32; John V. Fleming, *The*

Roman de la Rose: A Study in Allegory and Iconography (Princeton, N.J., 1969), and *The Roman de la Rose and Its Manuscript Illustrations* (diss., Princeton, N.J., 1963).

85. The issues of perspective and sexuality developed here were suggested to me by Patricia Emison's discussion of Renaissance images of Lucretia; see "The Singularity of Raphael's *Lucretia,*" *Art History* 14 (1991), pp. 372–96.

86. Camille, *The Gothic Idol,* pp. 322–23.

87. See the Introduction, note 91.

88. Macrobius, *The Saturnalia,* trans. Percival Vaughan Davies (New York, 1969), p. 359; Macrobius, *Saturnalia,* ed. Jacob Willis (Leipzig, 1963).

89. For a discussion of this mosaic, see J. M. C. Toynbee, *Art in Roman Britain* (London, 1962), pp. 203–5.

90. Jerome, *Adversus Jovinianum, PL* 23.273.

91. Ibid., *PL* 23.335.

92. For a general discussion of Jerome's changing attitudes toward sexuality and women, see Peter Brown, *The Body and Society: Men, Women and Sexual Renunciation in Early Christianity* (New York, 1988), pp. 366–86.

93. For a thorough discussion of Tertullian's interest in the chaste Dido, see Lord, "Dido as an Example of Chastity." For a discussion of the popularity of the historical Dido as a sort of African Lucretia—among North African writers in late antiquity—see Carlo Pascal, "Didone nella Lettura Latina d'Africa," *Athenaeum* 5 (1917), pp. 285–93.

94. For an excellent discussion of the social context of misogynous and misogamous discourse—"the hatred of (opposition to) marriage"—in medieval cultures, see Katharina M. Wilson and Elizabeth M. Makowski, *Wykked Wyves and the Woes of Marriage* (Albany, N.Y., 1990). See also R. Howard Bloch, *Medieval Misogyny and the Invention of Western Romantic Love* (Chicago, 1991). This survey of misogyny fails to place the discourse of misogyny within the social order; see the discussion in the *Medieval Feminist Newsletter* 7 (1989), pp. 2–16. On the "tortuous patriarchal gender-bending at work in Bloch's analysis," see Tania Modleski, *Feminism Without Women: Culture and Criticism in a "Postfeminist" Age* (New York, 1991), p. 11.

95. See Birger Munk Olsen, *L'Étude des auteurs classiques latins aux XIe et XIIe siècles* (Paris, 1982), pp. 537–51. For a discussion of Justin's text in Spanish historiography, see Maria Rosa-Lida de Malkiel, *Dido en la Literatura Española: Su Retrato y Defensa* (London, 1974), pp. 57–62.

96. See Craig Kallendorf, "Boccaccio's Dido and the Rhetorical Criticism of Virgil's *Aeneid,*" *Studies in Philology* 82 (1985), pp. 401–15. See also Kallendorf, *In Praise of Aeneas: Virgil and Epideictic Rhetoric in the Early Italian Renaissance* (Hanover, 1989), pp. 58–76; Lord, "Dido as an Example of Chastity," pp. 221–24; Anna Cerbo, "Didone in Boccaccio," *Annali Istituto Universitario Orientale, Napoli, Sezione Romanza* 21 (1979), pp. 177–219; Leo Paoletti, "Virgilio e Boccaccio," in *Présence de Virgile,* pp. 249–63. For a study of Boccaccio's vernacular texts that emphasizes his interest in the Virgilian Dido, see James H. McGregor, *The Shades of Aeneas: The Imitation of Vergil and the History of Paganism in Boccaccio's Filostrato, Filocolo, and Teseida* (Athens, Ga., 1991).

97. Kallendorf, "Boccaccio's Dido," p. 413. On the relationship between Boccaccio and Petrarch, see Vittore Branca, *Boccaccio: The Man and His Works,* trans. Richard Monges (New York, 1976). Branca notes that Boccaccio began his three major Latin works, *Genealogia, De casibus virorum illustrium,* and *De claris mulieribus* in the 1350s: "They are works which Boccaccio would recast in successive editions, almost to the time of his death. He reworked them as he was prompted or inspired by new spiritual and literary attitudes, new learned and cultural acquisitions, or by discoveries of new manuscripts and new authors" (p. 109).

98. Janet Levarie Smarr, *Boccaccio and Fiammetta: The Narrator as Lover* (Urbana, Ill., 1986), p. 227.

99. Ibid., p. 226. See also Smarr's discussion of Boccaccio's implied women readers in relation to the fact that "the ambivalence of literature's powers of seduction seems to have become more problematic for Boccaccio" (p. 227).

100. See Concetta Carestia Greenfield, *Humanist and Scholastic Poetics, 1250–1500* (Lewisburg, Pa., 1981), p. 110.

101. The Latin text of the *Genealogia* is taken from Vincenzo Romano, ed., *Genealogie Deorum gentilium libri* (Bari, 1951); English translations from book 14 of the *Genealogia* are from Charles Osgood, *Boccaccio on Poetry* (Princeton, N.J., 1930); all other Boccaccio translations are my own.

102. Boccaccio cites Augustine as an authority on interpretation in Book 14. For a discussion of Boccaccio's concerns with reading, see Susan Noakes, *Timely Reading: Between Exegesis and Interpretation* (Ithaca, N.Y., 1988), pp. 69–97; Smarr, *Boccaccio and Fiammetta*, pp. 205–22.

103. As Christiane Klapisch-Zuber notes, "Even when old, a widow represented a threat to the reputation of good families. Since she had tasted the pleasures of the flesh, she was considered prone, like the hideous merry widow portrayed in Boccaccio's *Corbaccio*, . . . to fall into debauchery" (*Women, Family and Ritual in Renaissance Italy*, trans. Lydia Cochrane [Chicago, 1985]), pp. 122–23. Boccaccio's assumptions concerning the sexual nature of widows, such as Cressida in *Il Filostrato*, can be seen throughout his vernacular texts.

104. See Thomas Hyde, "Boccaccio: The Genealogies of Myth," *Publications of the Modern Language Association* 100 (1985), pp. 737–45.

105. Liliane Dulac, "Un mythe didactique chez Christine de Pizan: Sémiramis ou la veuve héroïque," *Mélanges de philologie romane offerts à Charles Camproux* 1 (Montpellier, 1978), p. 323.

106. The Latin text of *de claris mulieribus* is taken from Vittorio Zaccaria, ed., *De mulieribus claris*, in *Tutte le Opere di Giovanni Boccaccio*, 10 (Milan, 1967). The text of *De casibus* is taken from *De casibus virorum illustrium*, ed. Pier Giorgio Ricci and Vittorio Zaccaria," in *Tutte le Opere di Giovanni Boccaccio* 9 (Milan, 1983).

107. Susan Noakes sees Boccaccio's attitudes toward his women readers as paradigmatic of his "developing view of the author-reader relationship as one of struggle" (*Timely Reading*, p. 96).

108. Klapisch-Zuber, *Women, Family and Ritual*, p. 120.

109. Ibid., pp. 117–31; David Herlihy and Christiane Klapisch-Zuber, *Tuscans and Their Families: A Study of the Florentine Catasto of 1427* (New Haven, Conn., and London, 1985), pp. 202–31 ("Marriage"); Richard C. Trexler, *Public Life in Renaissance Florence* (New York, 1980), pp. 10–19.

110. Isabelle Chabot, "Widowhood and Poverty in Late Medieval Florence," *Continuity and Change* 3 (1988), pp. 291–311.

111. Only a very small portion of women in the elite class were taught to read Latin. On the education of women, see Paul F. Grendler, *Schooling in Renaissance Italy: Literacy and Learning 1300–1600* (Baltimore, Md., 1989); see chapter 4, "Girls and Working Class Boys at School," pp. 87–108. As Grendler summarizes the prevalent attitude: "A girl ought not acquire Latin learning, because she had no public role to play" (p. 89). On the few women humanists who are the exceptions to this rule, see Margaret L. King, "Book-lined Cells: Women and Humanism in the Early Italian Renaissance" (pp. 66–90), and Paul Oskar Kristeller, "Learned Women of Early Modern Italy: Humanists and University Scholars" (pp. 91–116), in *Beyond Their Sex: Learned Women of the European Past*, ed. Patricia H. Labalme (New York, 1980); and Margaret L. King and Albert Rabil, Jr., *Her Immaculate*

Hand: Selected Works By and About the Women Humanists of Quattrocento Italy (Binghamton, N.Y., 1983), pp. 16–30.

112. For a discussion of the philosophy of the humanists of the earlier fifteenth century (a generation later than Boccaccio) in relation to the exclusionary practices of mercantile handwriting and the castigation of texts, see Jed, *Chaste Thinking*, pp. 74–124.

113. See "Women Humanists: Education for What?" in Anthony Grafton and Lisa Jardine, *From Humanism to the Humanities: Education and the Liberal Arts in Fifteenth- and Sixteenth-Century Europe* (London, 1986), pp. 29–57. As Grafton and Jardine note, "When a woman becomes socially visible—visible within the power structure—Renaissance literary convention makes her a sexual predator" (p. 41).

114. Boccaccio's interest in the historical Dido and his anxieties about the response of the female reader to the exemplary text of Dido's life are profitably seen in relation to the politics of philology and the strategies of "chaste thinking" that Stephanie Jed has traced in the reading and writing practices of the humanists in the century after Boccaccio and Petrarch. Jed has shown how "textual encounters and philological conjectures provide the material for the construction of a political self-image for Florence," a description that aptly fits the construction of authorial identity in the production of Boccaccio's Latin texts; writing in the fourteenth century, Boccaccio was much less inclined than fifteenth-century Florentines such as Salutati to construct a civic or political identity in his text. The historical Dido, supported by the testimony of Justin, allows for a reading of history that centers on the chaste body of Dido, sacrificed before the sexual corruption of her involvement with Aeneas. As Jed has shown, the story of Lucretia, particularly her choice of suicide in the face of the corruption she faces as a rape victim, provided the humanist Salutati with a narrative through which the various discourses of chastity in relation to politics and philology might be expressed. The chaste body of the historical Dido, like the chaste texts of antiquity that result from humanistic philological activity, constructs the reader in terms of sexual vulnerability. See Jed, pp. 18–50.

115. See McLeod, *Virtue and Venom*, pp. 59–80. See also the analysis of *De claris mulieribus* by Constance Jordan, "Boccaccio's In-Famous Women: Gender and Civic Virtue in the *De mulieribus claris*," in *Ambiguous Realities: Women in the Middle Ages and Renaissance*, ed. Carole Levin and Jeanie Watson (Detroit, Mich., 1987), pp. 25–47. Jordan maintains that the poem initially presents what she calls a "humanistic feminism," which is eventually rendered ironic in the course of the text. See also Constance Jordan, "Feminism and the Humanists: The Case of Sir Thomas Elyot's *Defence of Good Women*," *Renaissance Quarterly* 36 (1983), pp. 181–201.

116. Constance Jordan attempts to use the details from *De casibus* to read the implications of *De claris mulieribus* when she asserts that Boccaccio—in *De casibus*—emphasizes that Dido takes the time before her suicide to strengthen the fortifications and foundation of her city so that it would survive her death (see "Boccaccio's In-Famous Women," pp. 35–56). However, as I have tried to show, *De claris mulieribus* is explicitly directed at a gender-specific audience, and the fact that Boccaccio does not include these details about Dido's civic responsibility in this text is a significant feature of his manipulation of women readers or the woman as reader. Jordan's article also explores the possibility that Boccaccio's texts, particularly *De casibus*, suggest "his perception that the threat of social chaos is posed not by a tyrant but by a figure representing the socially subordinate, typically represented . . . by a woman" (p. 43). It is certainly possible to find in Boccaccio's distrust of women/widows/ readers an expression of class divisions whereby *woman* becomes a figure for the subordinate classes. For a discussion of the role of learning in relation to the "deep social divisions" that were particularly acute in fourteenth- and fifteenth-century Italy, see Grendler, *Schooling in Renaissance Italy*, pp. 11–22. However, to see Boccaccio's deployment of gender as simply an allegorical model for his distrust of the *populus* in general removes the interpre-

tive issues away from the higly specific and carefully directed (and misogynist) discussion of *female* readers and *female* sexuality that exists throughout his work and appears especially urgent in *De claris mulieribus.*

117. For the text of the Dante commentary, see Gaetano Milanesi, *Il Comento di Giovanni Boccacci Sopra La Commedia* I (Florence, 1863), p. 452. Translations are my own.

118. Carla Bozzolo, "Manuscrits des traductions françaises d'œuvres de Boccace, XVᵉ siècle," *Medioevo e Umanesimo* 15 (Padua, 1973), p. 15. On Laurent de Premierfait, see pp. 3–15. See also R. C. Famiglietti, "Laurent de Premierfait: The Career of a Humanist in Early Fifteenth Century Paris," *Journal of Medieval History* 9 (1983), pp. 25–42; Patricia M. Gathercole, "Fifteenth Century Translation: The Development of Laurent de Premierfait," *Modern Language Quarterly* 21 (1960), pp. 365–70, and "Laurent de Premierfait: The Translator of Boccaccio's *de casibus,*" *French Review* 27 (1954), pp. 245–52; Florence A. Smith, "Laurent de Premierfait's French Version of the *De casibus virorum illustrium* with Some Notes on Its Influence in France," *Revue de Littérature Comparée* 14 (1934), pp. 512–26. For an edition of the first book of *De casibus* in Premierfait's version, see Patricia M. Gathercole, trans., *Des cas des nobles hommes et femmes Book 1* (Chapel Hill, N.C., 1968).

119. Bozzolo, "Manuscrits," pp. 23–24. *De claris mulieribus* was also translated into English in 1547 by Lord Morley. See Herbert G. Wright, *Forty-six Lives Translated from Boccaccio's de claris mulieribus by Henry Parker, Lord Morley* (Oxford, 1940).

120. Bozzolo, "Manuscrits," p. 39.

121. Lydgate appends a stanza that sets Boccaccio's Dido in the larger traditions:
Touchyng Dido lat ther be no striff:
Thouh that she be accusid off Ouide,
Afftir Bochas I wrot her chaste liff,
And the contrary I haue set a-side;
For me thouhte it was bet tabide
On hir goodnesse, than thyng reherse in deede,
Which myhte resowne ageyn hir womanheede. (2.2150–56)
John Lydgate, *Fall of Princes*, ed. Henry Bergen, EETS e.s. 121–24 (Oxford, 1927; rpt. 1967). See Edmund Reiss, "Boccaccio in English Culture of the Fourteenth and Fifteenth Centuries," *Il Boccaccio nella cultura Inglese e Anglo-Americana*, ed. Giuseppe Galigani (Florence, 1974), pp. 15–26, and Patricia M. Gathercole, "Lydgate's «Fall of Princes» and the French Version of Boccaccio's «*de casibus*»," in *Miscellanea di Studi e ricerche sul Quattrocentro Francese* (Turin, 1967), pp. 65–78.

122. Brigitte Buettner, "Les affinités sélectives. Image et texte dans les premiers manuscrits des «cleres femmes»," *Studi sul Boccaccio* 18 (1989), pp. 281–99; Millard Meiss, "The Boucicaut Master and Boccaccio," *Studi sul Boccaccio* 5 (1969), pp. 251–63.

123. For a discussion of the illustrations from this Lydgate manuscript, see A. S. G Edwards, "Lydgate Manuscripts: Some Directions for Future Research," in *Manuscripts and Readers in Fifteenth-Century England: The Literary Implications of Manuscript Study*, ed. Derek Pearsall (Cambridge, 1983), pp. 15–26. Edwards notes that "the degree and kind of its decoration is extremely unusual." For a description of the entire program of illustrations, see Bergen, ed., Lydgate's *Fall of Princes*, vol. 4, pp. 30–51.

124. In *De claris mulieribus*, Boccaccio describes Dido's suicide: "cultro, quem sub vestibus gesserat, exerto . . . in cultrum sese precipitem dedit" (p. 176) ("having pulled out a knife, which she had carried under her clothes, she threw herself forward into the knife"); The French reads: "elle print un coustel mout agu quelle avoir porte se artement desous sa robe . . . elle se laissa cheir sa force dessus la pointe du coutel" ("she took a very sharp knife, which she had carried so artfully under her dress . . . she threw herself on the point of the

knife"). In *De casibus*, Boccaccio first refers to the weapon as *cultro*, but adds: "et illico gladio superincubuit" (p. 142) ("And instantly she lay herself on the sword").

125. See Buettner, "Les affinités sélectives," p. 287; BL Royal 16 G v (figure 7) exemplifies this tradition; the same image is found in BL Royal 20 C v.

2. Dido as *Libido*

1. Text from J. B. Hall, ed., *Ioannis Saresberiensis, Metalogicon* Corpus Christianorum, continuatio Mediaeualis 98. (Toronto, 1991). Translations are my own.

2. Mary Carruthers takes *lectio* as a voiced reading and *meditatio* as closer to the activity of silent reading (*The Book of Memory: A Study of Memory in Medieval Culture* [Cambridge, 1990], pp. 170–71). For an overview of the various activities of reading, see Carruthers, "Memory and the Ethics of Reading," pp. 156–88. For the status and importance of *lectio* in monastic cultures, see Jean Leclercq, *The Love of Learning and the Desire for God: A Study of Monastic Culture* (New York, 1982). See also Brian Stock, *The Implications of Literacy: Written Language and Models of Interpretation in the Eleventh and Twelfth Centuries* (Princeton, N.J., 1983), pp. 236–454, and Daniel McGarry, "Educational Theory in the *Metalogicon* of John of Salisbury," *Speculum* 23 (1948), pp. 659–75.

3. For a thorough discussion of the relationship between education and the affairs of state, see Hans Liebeschutz, *Medieval Humanism in the Life and Writings of John of Salisbury* (London, 1950).

4. On the purposes of the *Policraticus*, see Cary Nederman and Catherine Campbell, "Priests, Kings and Tyrants: Spiritual and Temporal Power in John of Salisbury's *Policraticus*," *Speculum* 66 (1991), pp. 572–90.

5. *PL* 32.670. Translations from Augustine are my own.

6. For a discussion of the place of the *Confessions* in Augustine's biography, see Peter Brown, *Augustine of Hippo: A Biography* (Berkeley, Calif., 1967), pp. 158–81. See also Marcia L. Colish, *The Mirror of Language: A Study in the Medieval Theory of Knowledge* (Lincoln, Neb., 1968; rev. ed. 1983), pp. 7–49.

7. Brown, *Augustine of Hippo*, p. 162. For a discussion of classical rhetoric in the *Confessions*, see Sarah Spence, *Rhetorics of Reason and Desire: Vergil, Augustine and the Troubadours* (Ithaca, N.Y., 1988), pp. 55–102. See also Eugene Vance, *Mervelous Signals: Poetics and Sign Theory in the Middle Ages* (Lincoln, Neb., 1986), pp. 1–50, and "Augustine's *Confessions* and the Grammar of Selfhood," *Genre* 6 (1973), pp. 1–28.

8. Peter Brown, *The Body and Society: Men, Women and Sexual Renunciation in Early Christianity* (New York, 1988), p. 407. See also Brown, *Augustine of Hippo*, p. 37. For a discussion of reading in the *Confessions*, see Ralph Flores, "Reading and Speech in St. Augustine's Confessions," *Augustinian Studies* 6 (1975), pp. 1–13.

9. For a discussion of concubinage and Augustine's attitudes toward it, see James A. Brundage, *Law, Sex, and Christian Society in Medieval Europe* (Chicago, 1987), pp. 98–103. See also Brown, *The Body and Society*, pp. 392–93.

10. See Augustine, *Confessions* 2.2, 6.15.

11. Brundage, *Law, Sex, and Christian Society*, p. 100.

12. See Augustine, *Confessions* 4.8; Brown, *The Body and Society*, pp. 389–90. For a powerful discussion of Augustine's contribution to the construction of perversion through his conflation of sexuality, transgression, and his conception of the role of evil in human nature, see Jonathan Dollimore, *Sexual Dissidence: Augustine to Wilde, Freud to Foucault* (Oxford, 1991), pp. 131–47.

13. Brown, *Augustine of Hippo*, p. 37.

14. As Brown comments, "Carthage had first appeared to Augustine as his 'cauldron'

(3.i)—the Latin *sartago* deliberately echoes Karthago" (ibid., p. 72). On the politics of Dido and Carthage for the North African bishop, see p. 23.

15. For a discussion of the Virgilian presence in *De civitate Dei*, see Harald Hagendahl, *Augustine and the Latin Classics* (Göteborg, 1967), pp. 444–59. Hagendahl considers *De civitate Dei* to be one of the most Virgilian of Augustine's works. See also James J. O'Donnell, "Augustine's Classical Readings," *Recherches Augustiniennes* 15 (1980), pp. 144–75; John O'Meara, "Augustine the Artist and the *Aeneid*," in *Mélanges offerts à Mademoiselle Christine Mohrmann* (Utrecht, 1963), pp. 252–61. The fact that Augustine is clearly aware of the historical tradition of Dido's story and yet he avoids incorporating the historical Dido into his vision of history perhaps illustrates the ambiguous status of the *Aeneid* in *De civitate Dei*: although Augustine aggressively appropriates the *Aeneid* to suit his Christian design of history and dismisses much of the ideological vision of Virgil's text, he appears to respect the *Aeneid* too much to contradict it on the story of Dido.

16. The emphasis on Lucretia and the omission of Dido in this discussion of suicide are even more significant when one considers how frequently Dido and Lucretia were linked as rhetorical *exempla*. See Mary Louise Lord, "Dido as an Example of Chastity: The Influence of Example Literature," *Harvard Library Bulletin* 17 (1969), pp. 22–32.

17. See David S. Wiesen, trans., Saint Augustine, *City of God against the Pagans* (Cambridge, 1968), vol. 3: "Most modern commentators believe that Augustine has either misread this line or has simply forced it to bear a meaning not intended by Virgil. In the original, according to this view, the mind is Aeneas', but the tears Dido's" (p. 166 n. 1). See also Hagendahl, *Augustine and the Latin Classics*, p. 423.

18. Text of *De civitate Dei* from *PL* 41.13–804. See 8.19, 16.6, 21.6, 21.8.

19. See, for instance, the assumptions made by B. G. Koonce, *Chaucer and the Tradition of Fame: Symbolism in the House of Fame* (Princeton, N.J., 1966). Throughout his discussion of *House of Fame* Book 1, Koonce assumes that Bernard Silvestris represents the "conventional interpretations of the *Aeneid*." See also Joseph S. Wittig, "The Aeneas-Dido Allusion in Chrétien's *Erec et Enide*," *Comparative Literature* 22 (1970), pp. 237–53. Wittig assumes that the *Aeneid* could only be read the way the commentary tradition—namely Bernard Silvestris's commentary—interpreted the story. And Winthrop Wetherbee, *Platonism and Poetry in the Twelfth Century: The Literary Influence of the School of Chartres* (Princeton, N.J., 1972) asserts: "Not only were Bernardus' exercises in mythography a rich source of material for later poets, but his readings of Vergil and Martianus in terms of the intellectual pilgrimage from earthly to divine knowledge defined a basic element of later medieval allegory, Latin and vernacular" (p. 105).

20. On the rhetorical organization of commentaries, see Rita Copeland, *Rhetoric, Hermeneutics, and Translation in the Middle Ages: Academic Traditions and Vernacular Texts* (Cambridge, 1991), pp. 63–86.

21. Petrarch's Virgil, reprinted in facsimile, demonstrates quite visually the actual "marginal" position of the commentaries and glosses of the *Aeneid* in relation to the text of the *Aeneid* itself. In Petrarch's edition, for instance, the commentaries and glosses of Servius and Donatus are situated around the margins of the page; the Latin *Aeneid* is itself in the center. See Francisci Petrarcae, *Vergilianus codex* (Milan, 1930); Domenico Comparetti, *Vergil in the Middle Ages*, trans. E. F. M. Benecke (London, 1895; rpt. 1966), p. 55.

22. Copeland, *Rhetoric*, p. 76.

23. See Comparetti (*Vergil in the Middle Ages*, p. 153), who notes that the attribution to Ovid dates from this period. In my own acquaintance with the medieval manuscripts of Virgil's *Aeneid* in the British Library, I found that it was a rare text that did not contain these arguments, though they are attributed to Ovid in only a relatively small portion of manuscripts, all of which date from the fifteenth century. Manuscripts representative of this tradition include *BL* Harley 2503, 3963; *BL* Arundel 193. Incunubula and early printed

books often contain these arguments under the rubric *descriptio*; examples include the following editions of Virgil: Venice, 1475; Nuremberg, 1492; Venice, 1501; Venice, 1544.

24. Text from Vatican 3867 in Alexander Riese, *Anthologia Latina*, vol. 1 (Amsterdam, 1964), p. 10. Translations are my own.

25. Comparetti, *Vergil in the Middle Ages*, p. 35.

26. For the text of Servius, see H. Hagen, ed., *Serviani in Aeneidem III-IV Commentarii*, vol. 3 (Bildesheim, 1881–83; rept. 1961). Translations are my own.

27. See Comparetti, *Vergil in the Middle Ages*, pp. 57–58.

28. J. W. Jones, Jr., "The Allegorical Traditions of the *Aeneid*," in John D. Bernard, *Vergil at 2000* (New York, 1986), p. 108. See also the discussion of Servius's commentary in Jerome Singerman, *Under Clouds of Poesy: Poetry and Truth in French and English Reworkings of the Aeneid, 1160–1513* (New York, 1986), pp. 1–8; James E. G. Zetzel, *Latin Textual Criticism in Antiquity* (Salem, N.H., 1981), pp. 81–147. See also J. W. Jones, Jr., "Allegorical Interpretation in Servius," *Classical Journal* 56 (1961), pp. 217–26; Comparetti, *Vergil in the Middle Ages*, p. 59.

29. For a consideration of the appropriateness of these remarks, see William S. Anderson, "Servius and the 'Comic Style' of *Aeneid* 4," *Arethusa* 14 (1981), pp. 115–25.

30. For a brief discussion of the *flamen* and *flaminica*, see Jones "The Allegorical Traditions," pp. 115–17.

31. The passage on the historical Dido, "ut habet historia," can be found in the following medieval manuscripts of the *Aeneid*: Oxford Auct. F.22; British Library, Harley 2553, 4097; Arundel 82; and 32, 319.

32. Text from Rudolf Helm, ed., Fulgentius, *Opera* (Stuttgart, 1898; rpt. 1970). Translation from Leslie George Whitbread, *Fulgentius the Mythographer* (Columbus, Ohio, 1971).

33. The most thorough study of the "ages of man" as an organizing principle of medieval thought is found in J. A. Burrow, *The Ages of Man: A Study in Medieval Writing and Thought* (Oxford, 1986).

34. The attribution of this commentary to Bernard Silvestris is currently under debate. Julian Ward Jones and Elizabeth Frances Jones, editors of *The Commentary on the First Six Books of the Aeneid of Virgil Commonly Attributed to Bernardus Silvestris* (Lincoln, Neb., and London, 1977), state simply: "The authorship of Bernardus may no longer be assumed" (p. ix). Another Bernard—Bernard of Chartres—had been proposed as the author of this commentary (see Jones and Jones, p. xi; and E. R. Smits, "New Evidence For the Authorship of the Commentary on the First Books of Virgil's *Aeneid* Commonly Attributed to Bernardus Silvestris?" in *Non nova, sed nove: Mélanges de civilisation médiévale dédiés à Willem Noomen*, ed. Martin Gosman and Jaap Van Os, Mediaevalia Groningana 5 [Groningen, 1984], pp. 239–46). Yet another Bernard ("The Bernard who was sent by Gilbert Foliot to reform the Abbey of Cerne between 1145 and 1148") has been proposed as a possible author; see Christopher Baswell, "The Medieval Allegorization of the 'Aeneid': Ms Cambridge, Peterhouse 158," *Traditio* 41 (1985), pp. 181–237; see also Julian Ward Jones, Jr., "The So-Called Silvestris Commentary on the *Aeneid* and Two Other Interpretations," *Speculum* 64 (1989), pp. 835–48.

35. Text of the commentary from Jones and Jones. Translations are my own. See also Earl G. Schreiber and Thomas E. Maresca, trans., *Commentary on the First Six Books of Virgil's Aeneid by Bernardus Silvestris* (Lincoln, Neb., 1979).

36. Edouard Jeauneu, "L'usage de la notion d'*integumentum* a travers les gloses de Guillaume de Conches," *Archives d'hisoire doctrinale et littéraire du moyen âge* 22 (1957), p. 39. For a further discussion of *integument*, see Winthrop Wetherbee, *Platonism and Poetry*. Wetherbee discusses the Chartrain concept of *integumentum* in relation to the "Chartrain's reading of the Universe" (pp. 36–48). See also Simone Viarre, "L'Interprétation

de l'Enéide à propos d'un commentaire du douzième siècle," in *Présence de Virgile: Actes du colloque des 9, 11 et 12 décembre 1976*, ed. R. Chevallier (Paris, 1978), pp. 223–32.

37. For the concept of "embodied logic" on which this discussion relies, see John O'Neill, *Five Bodies: The Human Shape of Modern Society* (Ithaca, N.Y., and London, 1985). O'Neill describes the embodied logic of our experience: "We are continuously caught up and engaged in the *embodied look of things*. . . . It is through our senses that we first appreciate and evaluate others. . . . What we see, hear, and feel of other persons is the first basis of our interaction with them" (p. 22). O'Neill explicates five representations of the body that result from such "embodied logic": The World's Body, Social Bodies, The Body Politic, Consumer Bodies, and Medical Bodies. As we will see, the "embodied logic" of this commentary on the *Aeneid* depends on the representation of the world's body and the medical body.

38. For the Latin text and commentary of the medieval *Timaeus*, see J. H. Waszink, *Timaeus a Calcidio translatus commentarioque instructus* (London, 1962). The medieval version of the *Timaeus* ends before the elaborate medical description of the body, beginning on chapter 64 of the Greek. On the place of the *Timaeus* in Chartrain thought, see Wetherbee, *Platonism and Poetry*; Raymond Klibansky, "The School of Chartres," in *Twelfth-Century Europe and the Foundations of Modern Society*, ed. M. Clagett, G. Post, and R. Reynolds (Madison, Wis., 1961), pp. 3–14; Richard McKeon, "Poetry and Philosophy in the Twelfth Century: The Renaissance of Rhetoric," *Modern Philology* 43 (1946), pp. 217–34.

39. Bernard states Virgil's purpose: "Atque in hoc describendo naturali utitur ordine atque ita utrumque ordinem narrationism observat, artificialem poeta, naturalem philosophus" (p. 3) ("And so in describing this he employs the natural order; and so as a poet he complies with the artificial order of the narrative, as a philosopher, the natural"). On the physiological paradigm for the ages of man, see Burrow, *The Ages of Man*, pp. 12–54.

40. Fulgentius refers several times to medicine and physiology in relation to Virgil's poetry. He declares that Virgil was a "phisiognomicus et medicinalis" in the second book of the *Georgics* (139.10), and Fulgentius says that he himself has written a book of medical explanations ("de medicinalibus causis" [149.1]). For a discussion of Bernard's debt to Fulgentius, see Robert Edwards, "The Heritage of Fulgentius," in Aldo S. Bernardo and Saul Levin, eds., *The Classics in the Middle Ages: Papers of the Twentieth Annual Conference of the Center for Medieval and Renaissance Studies* (Binghamton, N.Y., 1990), pp. 141–51; and J. Reginald O'Donnell, "The Sources and Meaning of Bernard Silvester's Commentary on the Aeneid," *Mediaeval Studies* 24 (1962), pp. 233–49.

41. Burrow discusses Bernard's reading of the *Aeneid* as "an image of man's progress through the ages" (*The Ages of Man*, p. 118) without noticing or acknowledging the androcentric bias of the commentary.

42. On Constantine Afer, see Paul Oskar Kristeller, "The School of Salerno: Its Development and Its Contribution to the History of Learning," *Studies in Renaissance Thought and Letters* (Rome, 1969), pp. 508–10. For Constantine's influence on the medicine of the twelfth century, see Karl Sudhoff, *Archiv für Geschichte der Medizin* 9 (1916), pp. 348–56; H. Schipperges, *Sudhoffs Archiv für Geschichte der Medizin und der Naturwissenschaften* 39 (1955), pp. 62–67. A brief summary of Constantine's career can be found in Maurice Bassan, "Chaucer's 'Cursed Monk', Constantinus Africanus," *Mediaeval Studies* 24 (1962), pp. 127–40. See also G. Corner, *Anatomical Texts of the Earlier Middle Ages* (Washington, D.C., 1927), pp. 12–16. As Corner sums up Constantine's impact: "He gave the west . . . a great mass of important classical learning, in readable Latin, at a time when everything was ripe for growth. For a hundred years all western medical science grew out of these books" (p. 14). For a discussion of medical texts at Chartres, see Charles Burnett, "The Content and Affiliation of the Scientific Manuscripts Written at, or Brought to, Chartres in the Time of John of Salisbury," in *The World of John of Salisbury*, ed.

Michael Wilks (Oxford, 1984), pp. 127–60. See also Danielle Jacquart and Claude Thomasset, *Sexuality and Medicine in the Middle Ages* (Princeton, N.J., 1985).

43. On the study of human anatomy in the Middle Ages, see T. V. N. Persaud, *Early History of Human Anatomy: From Antiquity to the Beginning of the Modern Era* (Springfield, Ill., 1984), pp. 70–88. See also G. Corner, "Twelfth Century Texts: Demonstrations of Anatomy," *Anatomical Texts*, pp. 19–30. Corner describes the Salernitan anatomical texts intended to be used in dissections of animals: "The three little books taken together give us a lively picture indeed of these men engaged in actual dissection of the animal body, surrounded by questioning pupils for whose benefit they try to fit their newly recovered relics of Galenic description to the pig's organs before them" (p. 30).

44. See Brian Stock, *Myth and Science in the Twelfth Century: A Study of Bernard Silvester* (Princeton, N.J., 1972). Stock says of Bernard's intention in the *Cosmographia*: "He tried to bring together what he considered the two major sciences of his time, medicine and astronomy" (p. 26). On the development of medical study at Chartres, see Loren MacKinney, *Early Medieval Medicine With Special Reference to France and Chartres* (Baltimore, Md., 1937), pp. 115–51. MacKinney argues that the cathedral schools in France fostered an empirical approach to the study of medicine in the eleventh century.

45. On the connection between the theory of elements and medical discourse, see Richard McKeon, "Medicine and Philosophy in the Eleventh and Twelfth Centuries: The Problem of Elements," *The Thomist* 24 (1961), pp. 211–56. As McKeon states: "The theories of elements propounded in the medical works of the eleventh century and the cosmologies of the twelfth century likewise provide the principles of the relevant sciences" (p. 213); "The medical writings which were translated during the eleventh century used elements more systematically to explain the phenomena of nature and provided greater precision of statement and more diversified data of application in the use of elements as principles" (p. 227); "The medical conception of elements lent concreteness, specificity, and empirical detail to the consideration of the nature of things, but it also accentuated the tendency to use a variety of structures or organisms as models for the universe, or to use the structure of the universe as a model for other lesser wholes, and therefore to analogize man and universe (microcosm and macrocosm), human soul and world-soul, deliberate action and physical motion, in the treatment of cosmology, psychology, physiology, geography, and history. This merging of Platonism, the liberal arts and the new sciences was one of the distinguishing marks of the school of Chartres in the twelfth century" (p. 231). See also Theodore Silverstein, "Guillaume de Conches and Nemesius of Emessa: On the Sources of the 'New Science' of the Twelfth Century," *Harry Austryn Wolfson Jubilee Volume II* (Jerusalem, 1965), pp. 719–34; Theodore Silverstein, "*Elementatum*: Its Appearance Among the Twelfth Century Cosmogonists," *Mediaeval Studies* 16 (1954), pp. 156–62.

46. The dissection of animals was certainly practiced in Salerno, if not in the north. Kristeller summarizes the place of dissection and discussions of anatomy in medical texts in Salerno: "The extensive medical literature of the twelfth century obviously reflects a corresponding progress in medical teaching at Salerno. . . . The various treatises on anatomy clearly indicate the practice of anatomical demonstration in the classroom, based on the dissection of animal bodies" ("The School of Salerno," p. 512).

47. See chapter 13 of the *Cosmographia* (Bernardus Silvestris, *Cosmographia*, ed. Peter Dronke [Leiden, 1978], pp. 146–50). For a translation, see *The Cosmographia of Bernardus Silvestris*, trans. Winthrop Wetherbee (New York, 1973).

48. O'Neill, *Five Bodies*, p. 28.

49. Stock, *Myth and Science*, p. 259.

50. Ibid., p. 225.

51. On the nature of the texts translated by Constantine, see Marie-Thérèse d'Alverny, "Translations and Translators," in *Renaissance and Renewal in the Twelfth Century*, ed.

Robert L. Benson and Giles Constable, with Carol D. Lanham (Cambridge, Mass., 1982), pp. 422–26.

52. Seth Lerer, "John of Salisbury's Virgil," *Vivarium* 20 (1982), p. 35.

53. For a brief description of the political context in which the *Policraticus* was composed, see Nederman, "Priests"; Janet Martin, "Uses of Tradition: Gellius, Petronius and John of Salisbury," *Viator* 10 (1979), pp. 57–58. See also Liebeschutz, *Medieval Humanism*, pp. 8–22.

54. On the organic metaphor in the *Policraticus*, see Cary J. Nederman, "The Physiological Significance of the Organic Metaphor in John of Salisbury's *Policraticus*," *History of Political Thought* 8 (1987), pp. 211–24; Tilman Struve, "The Importance of the Organism in the Political Theory of John of Salisbury," in *The World of John of Salisbury*, pp. 303–17; Paul Edward Dutton, "*Illustre civitatis et populi exemplum*: Plato's *Timaeus* and the Transmission from Calcidius to the End of the Twelfth Century of a Tripartite Scheme of Society," *Mediaeval Studies* 45 (1983), pp. 79–119; Janet Martin, "John of Salisbury as Classical Scholar," in *The World of John of Salisbury*, pp. 57–76. See also Kate Langdon Forhon, "Polycracy, Obligation and Revolt: The Body Politic in John of Salisbury and Christine de Pizan," in *Politics, Gender and Genre: The Political Thought of Christine de Pizan*, ed. Margaret Brabant (Boulder, Colo., 1992), pp. 33–41.

55. See Lerer, "John of Salisbury's Virgil"; Martin, "John of Salisbury as Classical Scholar," pp. 179–206.

56. See Peter Von Moos, "The Use of *Exempla* in the *Policraticus* of John of Salisbury," in *The World of John of Salisbury*, pp. 207–61.

57. Text from Clemens C. I. Webb, ed. *Ioannis Saresberiensis Episcopi Carnotensis Policratici* (Oxford, 1909). Translations are my own.

58. Earlier in Book 6.22, the *Policraticus* includes an exemplum drawn from *Aeneid* 1 that presents a misogynist reading of Dido's role as hostess when she receives Aeneas in Carthage and entertains him at the banquet. She is denounced for her frivolity and curiosity, and for her hospitable treatment of an unknown guest; the banquet, the story telling, the hunting all resulted in lewdness and the downfall of the city; the exemplum draws the following conclusion: "Hic finis feminei et effeminati regni" ("This is the end of womanly and womanish kingship").

59. Erick Hicks, "A Mirror for Misogynists: John of Salisbury's *Policraticus* (8.11) in the Translation of Denis Foulechat (1372), in *Reinterpreting Christine de Pizan*, ed. Earl Jeffrey Richards et al. (Athens, Ga., 1992), pp. 77–107.

60. See Amnon Linder, "The Knowledge of John of Salisbury in the Late Middle Ages," *Studi Medievali*, 3d series 18 (1977), pp. 315–66.

61. On Dante and Bernard Silvestris, see David Thompson, "Dante and Bernard Silvestris," *Viator* 1 (1970), pp. 201–6; Giorgio Padoan, "Tradizione e Fortuna del Commento All' 'Eneide' di Bernardo Silvestre," *Italia Medioevale e Umanistica* 3 (1960), pp. 227–40; H. Theodore Silverstein, "Dante and Vergil the Mystic," *Harvard Studies and Notes in Philology and Literature* 14 (1932), pp. 76–82. On the ages of man paradigm in the *Convivio*, see Alan Robson, "Dante's Reading of the Latin Poets and the Structure of the *Commedia*," in *The World of Dante: Essays on Dante and His Times*, ed. Cecil Grayson (Oxford, 1980), pp. 90–91.

62. Text of *Il Convivio* from Dante Alighieri, *Il Convivio*, ed. Maria Simonelli (Bologna, 1966). Translation from Richard H. Lansing, *Dante's Il Convivio (The Banquet)* (New York, 1990). For a discussion of the *Convivio*, see Teodolinda Barolini, *Dante's Poets: Textuality and Truth in the Comedy* (Princeton, N.J., 1984), pp. 23–31.

63. See Robert Hollander, "Dante's Use of *Aeneid* I In *Inferno* I and II," *Comparative Literature* 20 (1968), pp. 142–56. For the suggestion that it was due to his reading of the *Aeneid* that Dante set aside the *Convivio* and undertook the *Commedia*, see Ulrich Leo,

"The Unfinished *Convivio* and Dante's Rereading of the *Aeneid*," *Mediaeval Studies* 13 (1951), pp. 41–64. See also John Freccero, "The Prologue Scene," and "Medusa: The Letter and the Spirit," in *Dante: The Poetics of Conversion*, ed. Rachel Jacoff (Cambridge, 1986), pp. 1–28, 119–35. A brief survey of Dido's presence in Dante's texts is available in Giorgio Padoan, "Didone," *Enciclopedia Dantesca*, ed. Giorgio Petrocchi (Rome, 1970), pp. 430–31.

64. I have used the Petrocchi text as it is printed in Dante Alighieri, *The Divine Comedy*, trans. Charles Singleton (Princeton, N.J., 1973). This passage in *Inferno* 5, which emphasizes Dido's betrayal of her oath to Sychaeus as a measurement of her transgressive desire, is glossed by the comment in *Paradiso* 9, where Cunizza characterizes Dido's desire for Aeneas as a wrong done to Sychaeus *and* Creusa (l. 98), a comment meant to characterize Dido's involvement with Aeneas as adultery. Dido is also alluded to in *Paradiso* 8.9, in a passage that refers to Cupid's activities at the end of *Aeneid* 1. In both passages drawn from the *Paradiso*, Dido as a character is essentially synonymous with sexual desire.

65. For a discussion of canto 5 in relation to *Aeneid* 6, see Rachel Jacoff, "Transgression and Transcendence: Figures of Female Desire in Dante's *Commedia*," in *The New Medievalism*, ed. Marina S. Brownlee, Kevin Brownlee, and Stephen G. Nichols (Baltimore, Md., 1991), pp. 183–200. See also Peter Dronke, "Francesca and Héloïse," *Comparative Literature* 27 (1975), pp. 113–35.

66. Susan Noakes, *Timely Reading: Between Exegesis and Interpretation* (Ithaca, N.Y., 1988), p. 44. See also Barolini, *Dante's Poets*, pp. 4–13.

67. See Giuseppe Mazzotta, *Dante, Poet of the Desert: History and Allegory in the Divine Comedy* (Princeton, N.J., 1979), pp. 147–91. Mazzotta notes that Dante takes over verbatim Augustine's description of Dido's suicide. Although his analysis of *Inferno* 5 emphasizes that Dante is at pains to distance himself from Augustine's vision of Roman history even as he cites it, Mazzotta nonetheless sees Dante's conversion as a process that depends on "a dismissal of Dido's love" (p. 187). For a view that emphasizes Dante's incorporation of Dido into his representation of Beatrice, see Peter S. Hawkins, "Dido, Beatrice, and the Signs of Ancient Love," in *The Poetry of Allusion: Virgil and Ovid in Dante's "Commedia*," ed. Rachel Jacoff and Jeffrey T. Schnapp (Palo Alto, Calif., 1991), pp. 113–30. On the status of reading in this canto in relation to Augustine's reading of Dido, see Stephen Popolizio, "Literary Reminiscences and the Act of Reading in *Inferno* V," *Dante Studies* 98 (1980), pp. 19–33.

68. For a discussion of Dante's theories of empire and the relationship between *De monarchia* and the *Commedia*, see Joan M. Ferrante, *The Political Vision of the Divine Comedy* (Princeton, N.J., 1984), pp. 3–9. See also Larry Peterman, "An Introduction to Dante's *De monarchia*," *Interpretation: A Journal of Political Philosophy* 3 (1973), pp. 169–90.

69. Dante states: "Secunda Dido fuit, regina et mater Cartaginensium in Africa" ("the second was Dido, queen and mother of the Carthaginians in Africa"). Text from *Monarchia*, ed. Federico Sanguineti (Milan, 1985). Translations are my own.

70. On the relationship between the historiography of Dante and Augustine, see Peter S. Hawkins, "Divide and Conquer: Augustine in the *Divine Comedy*," *Publications of the Modern Language Association* 106 (1991), pp. 471–82. See also Marjorie Reeves, "Dante and the Prophetic View of History," in *The World of Dante*, pp. 44–60.

71. Hawkins, "Dido, Beatrice, and the Signs of Ancient Love," p. 120.

72. Hawkins puts it thus: "When Dante-Dido feels the rekindled tokens of old passion, he does so in the presence of his *antico amor*. . . . The Virgilian line that announces Dido's self-division, her pull between two loves, is here transformed to signal the pilgrim's return to unity" (ibid., p. 121). See also Jeffrey T. Schnapp, "Dante's Sexual Solecisms: Gender and Genre in the *Commedia*," in *The New Medievalism*, pp. 201–25; Rachel Jacoff, "Models of

Literary Influence in the *Commedia*," in *Medieval Texts and Contemporary Readers*, ed. Laurie Finke and Martin B. Shichtman (Ithaca, N.Y., 1987), pp. 158–76.

3. Dido in Courtly Romance and the Structures of History

1. The concept of the "trafficking in women" comes from the pioneering article of Gayle Rubin, "The Traffic in Women: Notes on the Political Economy of Sex," in Rayna R. Reiter, ed., *Toward an Anthropology of Women* (New York, 1975), pp. 157–210. For a highly effective analysis of medieval literature through the lens of Rubin's thesis, see Carolyn Dinshaw, "Reading Like a Man: The Critics, the Narrator, Troilus and Pandarus," in *Chaucer's Sexual Poetics* (Madison, Wis., 1989), pp. 28–64. See also Simon Gaunt, "From Epic to Romance: Gender and Sexuality in the *Roman d'Eneas*," *Romanic Review* 83 (1992), pp. 1–27; this article became available to me as I was doing final revisions on this chapter; Gaunt uses Rubin, Duby, and Sedgwick in his analysis and he consequently traces some of the same territory that I approach in this chapter. Text of *Erec et Enide* from Mario Roques, ed., *Erec et Enide* (Paris, 1968); translations are my own. Text of *Roman d'Eneas* from J.-J. Salverda de Grave, ed., *Eneas: Roman du XIIᵉ Siècle*, 2 vols. (Paris, 1973, 1983); translations from John A. Yunck, trans., *Eneas: A Twelfth-Century Romance* (New York, 1974).

2. For a synthetic discussion of kinship in twelfth-century culture, see R. Howard Bloch, *Etymologies and Genealogies: A Literary Anthropology of the French Middle Ages* (Chicago, 1983), pp. 44–91; Georges Duby, *The Knight, the Lady and the Priest: The Making of Modern Marriage in Medieval France*, trans. Barbara Bray (New York, 1983); and Gabrielle M. Speigel, "Genealogy: Form and Function in Medieval Historical Narrative," *History and Theory* 22 (1983), pp. 43–53.

3. On women's rights in marriage, see Duby, *The Knight*, pp. 99–106; on divorce, see pp. 140–44. See also Georges Duby, "The Structure of Kinship and Nobility," in *The Chivalrous Society*, trans. Cynthia Postan (London, 1977), pp. 139–70.

4. Julia Kristeva, *Tales of Love*, trans. Leon S. Roudiez (New York, 1987), p. 287.

5. Eve Kosofsky Sedgwick, *Between Men: English Literature and Male Homosocial Desire* (New York, 1985), pp. 1–5.

6. Rubin, "The Traffic in Women," p. 177.

7. Ibid., p. 182.

8. For an excellent discussion of this aspect of romance, see Penny Schine Gold, *The Lady and the Virgin: Image, Attitude, and Experience in Twelfth-Century France* (Chicago, 1985), pp. 18–42.

9. Thomas M. Greene, *The Light in Troy: Imitation and Discovery in Renaissance Poetry* (New Haven, Conn., 1982), p. 17. For a discussion of the historical consciousness in the *Roman d'Eneas*, see Lee Patterson, "Virgil and the Historical Consciousness of the Twelfth Century: The *Roman d'Eneas* and *Erec et Enide*," in *Negotiating the Past: The Historical Understanding of Medieval Literature* (Madison, Wis., 1987), pp. 157–95. See also Jean-Charles Huchet, "L'Eneas: Un Roman spéculaire," in *Relire le Roman d'Eneas*, ed. Jean Dufournet (Paris, 1985), pp. 63–81, for a discussion of the textual awareness of the relationship between the *Aeneid* and the *Eneas*.

10. The anonymous nature of this text requires a careful negotiation of our critical assumptions regarding authorship. Although there is nothing in the poem that would argue for a female author, it is important to remember that Marie de France—probably a member of the same court as the *Eneas* poet—proves that female authorship of vernacular texts was not a cultural impossibility in this milieu. On the theoretical issues posed to modern readers by anonymous medieval texts, see my "Voice of Exile: Feminist Literary History and the Anonymous Anglo-Saxon Elegy," *Critical Inquiry* 16 (1990), pp. 572–90. Although the modern reader would be very likely to read the *Roman d'Eneas* differently if a female author

seemed probable, the *Eneas* poet appears to be a product of the clerical elite, a masculine textual community. An argument was once made that Marie was the author of the *Eneas*, an argument that has never gained any legitimacy; see E. Levi, "Marie de France e il roman-zo di *Eneas*," *Atti del Real Instituto Veneto di Scienze, Lettre ed Arti* 81 (1921–22), pp. 645–86.

11. Roland Barthes's definition of "ekphrasis" in ancient rhetoric may be applied to a narrative context such as this romance: "L'ekphrasis est un fragment anthologique, trans-férable d'un discours à un autre: c'est une description réglée de lieux, de personnages" ("L'ancienne Rhétorique, aide-mémoire," *Communications* 16 [1970], p. 183). The saddle-bow seems completely detachable from the context of the narrative. In addition, the ekphra-sis is used to "cite" an earlier text, a function analyzed by Page duBois, *History, Rhetorical Description and the Epic* (Cambridge, 1983), pp. 5–6.

12. Frappier makes an analogous appeal to sculptured depictions of the Arthurian matter in order to access the reception of Celtic material. He refers to a scene depicted on the north portal of the Moderna cathedral in Italy. The scene represents the abduction of Guenevere—proof of the reception of Celtic material in some form. See Jean Frappier, *Chrétien de Troyes* (Paris, 1968), pp. 47–48. The depiction of the saddlebow is the textual equivalent: it testifies to the reception of the *Aeneid* story.

13. It has been suggested that the saddlebow summarizes the entire *Aeneid* tradition, including Virgil, the *Eneas*, and the commentary and allegory tradition. See Joseph S. Wittig, "The Aeneas-Dido Allusion in Chrétien's *Erec et Enide*," *Comparative Literature* 22 (1970), pp. 237–53. Wittig's reading of this allusion to the Aeneas-Dido story relies on his assump-tions that the *Aeneid* could only be read the way the allegory tradition (Fulgentius and Bernard Silvestris) presents the story: "The allusions enrich the poem by bringing it into contact with a work whose moral implications have been more clearly drawn" (p. 244). See the similar comment by Michelle A. Freeman, *The Poetics of Translatio Studii and Conjointure in Chrétien de Troyes's Cligés* (Lexington, Ky., 1979), pp. 142–43. The most thorough discussion of the two poems is in Lee Patterson, "Virgil and the Historical Consciousness," pp. 157–95. For a broadly thematic discussion of Chrétien and the *Eneas*, see Raymond J. Cormier, "Remarques sur le *Roman d'Enéas* et l'*Erec et Enide* de Chrétien de Troyes," *Revue des Langues Romanes* 82 (1976), pp. 85–97.

14. Lavinia and Eneas are evoked as an ideal couple in the *Conte du Graal* (8785–87). In *Erec et Enide*, Enide's cousin, the maiden in the Joy of the Court episode, is compared to Lavinia (5841–43). For an attempt to read this Lavinia reference in light of the *Aeneid* story on the saddle, see Patterson, "Virgil and the Historical Consciousness," pp. 183–95.

15. For a discussion of Chrétien's view of marriage, see Eugene Vance, *From Topic to Tale: Logic and Narrativity in the Middle Ages* (Minneapolis, 1987), pp. 36–37. The model Vance proposes, however, ignores the material manifestations of gender and power in the fourteenth century. Vance unquestioningly accepts an ideal formulation: "The very notion of marriage became centered upon the exercise of free consent between legitimate partners" (p. 37). On the issue of "free consent," however, see John T. Noonan, Jr., "Power to Choose," *Viator* 4 (1973), pp. 419–34; Noonan discusses the tension between "legal norm and social practice" (p. 431). Bloch also discusses the ideal of "the consent theory of marriage" in rela-tion to *Erec et Enide*: here the emphasis clearly falls on Erec's (not Enide's) consent (*Etymologies and Genealogies*, p. 189).

16. Roberta L. Krueger, "Love, Honor, and the Exchange of Women in *Yvain*: Some Remarks on the Female Reader," *Romance Notes* 25 (1985), pp. 302–17; here, p. 304. Krueger's analysis of the "problem of gender in romance" and her discussion of the "sexual tensions which qualify the ideology of chivalry" provide an excellent reading strategy for all of Chrétien's romances. See also Joan M. Ferrante, "Male Fantasy and Female Reality in Courtly Literature," *Women's Studies* 11 (1984), pp. 67–97.

17. On the implications of rape in relation to Chrétien's narratives, see Kathryn Gravdal, "Chrétien de Troyes, Gratian, and the Medieval Romance of Sexual Violence," *Signs* 17 (1992), pp. 558–85.
18. On the significance of Enide's social standing, see Vance, *From Topic to Tale*, pp. 32–33.
19. See Sarah Stanbury, "Feminist Film Theory: Seeing Chrétien's Enide," *Literature and Psychology* 36 (1990), pp. 47–66. See also Sally Mussetter, "The Education of Chrétien's Enide," *Romanic Review* 73 (1982), pp. 147–66.
20. See Jean-Charles Huchet, *Le Roman médiéval* (Paris, 1984), p. 13.
21. See Daniel Poiron, "L'Écriture épique: du Sublime au symbole," in *Relire Le Roman d'Eneas*; "De l'«Énéide» à l'«Eneas»: mythologie et moralisation," *Cahiers de civilisation médiévale* 19 (1976), pp. 213–29; G. Angeli, *L'Eneas e i primi romanzi volgari* (Milan, 1971); Beate Schmolke-Hasselmann, "Henry II Plantagenêt, roi d'Angleterre, et la genèse d'*Erec et Enide*," *Cahiers de civilisation médiévale* 24 (1981), pp. 241–46. See also Charles H. Haskins, "Henry II as a Patron of Literature," in *Essays in Medieval History Presented to T. F. Tout*, ed. A. G. Little and F. M. Powicke (Manchester, 1925), pp. 71–77. Haskins comments that Henry II was "first and foremost an administrator," and the literature of his court is in some sense a literature of administration (p. 74).
22. The *Roman d'Eneas* was also translated (adapted) into German by Heinrich von Veldeke. The Dido story is also briefly alluded to in Gottfried von Strassburg, *Tristan* (17198–203). A similar brief reference to the story of Aeneas and Dido occurs in the thirteenth-century Provençal poem, *Le Roman de Flamenca* (627–32).
23. For a classic statement, see Domenico Comparetti, *Vergil in the Middle Ages*, trans. E. F. M. Benecke (London, 1895; rpt. 1966), p. 246. Indeed, the process by which the *Eneas* poet transformed the *Aeneid* is well documented. The most careful and sensitive account of the relationship between the *Aeneid* and the *Eneas* is Jerome Singerman, *Under Clouds of Poesy: Poetry and Truth in French and English Reworkings of the Aeneid, 1160–1513* (New York, 1986), pp. 26–98. See also Nadia Margolis, "*Flamma, Furor*, and *Fol'Amors*: Fire and Feminine Madness from the *Aeneid* to the *Roman d'Eneas*," *Romanic Review* 78 (1987), pp. 131–47. J.-J. Salverda de Grave has presented a careful comparison of the two poems; see Salverda de Grave, *Eneas*, vol. 1 (Paris, 1973), pp. xxi–xxxiv. Edmond Faral catalogs the rhetorical impulses behind the transformation; see Edmond Faral, *Recherches sur les sources latines des contes et romans courtois du moyen âge* (Paris, 1913), pp. 73–167. Cormier has outlined the characteristics of Eneas as the hero of a medieval romance; see Raymond J. Cormier, *One Heart One Mind: The Rebirth of Virgil's Hero in Medieval French Literature* (University, Miss., 1973). Cormier traces the transformation of Aeneas, an epic hero, into Eneas, the hero of a romance.
24. For a brief discussion of this concept in relation to Chrétien de Troyes, see Vance, *From Topic to Tale*, pp. 5–6.
25. "Scriptural temporality" is Julia Kristeva's term for a particular narrative voice she distinguishes in La Sale's *Jehan de Saintre* (1456): "The temporality of La Sale's text is less a discursive temporality . . . than what we might call a '*scriptural* temporality' (the narrative sequences are oriented towards and rekindled by the very activity of writing)" (Julia Kristeva, *Desire in Language* [New York, 1980], p. 54). In her discussion of the first-person speaker in the prologue of the *Eneas*, Michelle Freeman notes that "the accent appears to be placed on history recounted by a self-effaced narrator figure" ("The *Roman d'Eneas*: Implications of the 'Prologue,' " *Medioevo Romanzo* 8 [1983], p. 38). My own discussion of the narrator's awareness of scriptural temporality considers the implications of the narrator's voice throughout the poem. See also Michel Rousse, "Le Pouvoir, La prouesse et l'amour dans l'Énéas," in *Relire le Roman d'Eneas*, pp. 149–67.
26. The use of the terms *scriptor* and *compilator* in this discussion of the *Eneas* is based

on the discussion of authorial roles from A. J. Minnis, *Medieval Theory of Authorship: Scholastic Literary Attitudes in the Later Middle Ages* (Philadelphia, 1988), pp. 94–99. Minnis's discussion is drawn from thirteenth-century texts and is not intended to be directly applied to twelfth-century courtly romance. However, the status of the *Eneas* as a "translation" of a latin *auctor* appears to shape the authorial roles in the *Eneas* in ways that make it analogous to the textual gestures Minnis explores. See also Michel Zink, "L'Héritage rhétorique et nouveauté littéraire dans le 'Roman Antique' en France au Moyen Âge: Remarques sur l'expression de l'amour dans le *Roman d'Eneas,*" *Romania* 105 (1984), pp. 248–69.

27. Patterson, "Virgil and the Historical Consciousness," p. 179.

28. See Jean Markale, *Aliénor d'Aquitaine* (Paris, 1979). On the cultural context of Eleanor's court and her role in it, see Rita Lejeune, "Rôle littéraire d'Aliénor d'Aquitaine et sa famille," *Cultura Neolatina* 14 (1954), pp. 5–57.

29. For a synthetic account of the issues of audience and patronage in twelfth-century court culture, see Georges Duby, "The Culture of the Knightly Class: Audience and Patronage," in *Renaissance and Renewal in the Twelfth Century,* ed. Robert L. Benson and Giles Constable (Cambridge, Mass., 1982), pp. 248–62. Duby comments that "the form we call the romance (*roman antique*) clearly represents the most striking expression of the effort then being made to adapt to the lay audience the *auctores* whom the school grammarians explicated" (p. 259).

30. The two stories clearly compiled from the *Metamorphoses* are the story of Mars and Venus (4.171–89; *Eneas,* vv. 4353–74) and the story of Arachne (6.5–145; *Eneas,* vv. 4520–42). Faral provides a detailed survey of Ovidian material in the *Eneas.* See also Barbara Nolan, *Chaucer and the Tradition of the* Roman Antique (Cambridge, 1992), pp. 75–96.

31. See F. M. Warren, "On the Latin Sources of *Thèbes* and *Énéas,*" *Publications of the Modern Language Association* 3 (1901), p. 384. Warren summarizes the mythological material that comes from Hyginus.

32. Eleanor Searle, *Predatory Kinship and the Creation of Norman Power, 840–1066* (Berkeley, Calif., 1988).

33. Nolan, *Chaucer and the Tradition of the* Roman Antique, p. 87. See Nolan's discussion of the love affair between Eneas and Lavine as a "counterexample," a "celebratory study of Lavine's courtship and marriage." I am much indebted to Nolan's study, which emphasizes the *Eneas* poet's reception of Ovid's *Heroides* (both text and gloss); she argues that the poem, shaped by the commentary material on Ovid's *Heroides,* juxtaposes the foolish love of Dido to the legitimate marriage of Eneas and Lavine. See also the resonant discussion of these issues in Jean-Charles Huchet, *Le Roman médiéval,* "Mariage et errance," pp. 19–38.

34. Eleanor Searle, "Women and the Legitimization of Succession at the Norman Conquest," *Proceedings of the Battle Conference on Anglo-Norman Studies III,* ed. R. Allen Brown (Suffolk, 1981), pp. 159–70. Searle comments: "The pattern of marriage of the knightly level was necessarily to marry Englishwomen, to become the lords of their male in-laws, and to produce children who were legitimate heirs of English grandfathers and legitimate claimants to the fiefs of Norman fathers" (p. 169). See also Charlotte A. Newman, *The Anglo-Norman Nobility in the Reign of Henry I: The Second Generation* (Philadelphia, 1988), pp. 35–39. For a general discussion of Norman values in the *Roman d'Eneas,* see Patterson, "Virgil and the Historical Consciousness," pp. 179–80; Huchet, *Le Roman médiéval,* pp. 12–14.

35. For a discussion of the *Eneas* poet's use of Servius here, see Francine Mora, "Sources de L'*Énéas*: La Tradition exégétique et le modèle épique Latin," in *Relire Le Roman d'Eneas,* pp. 83–104.

36. On lovesickness as a medical category, see Mary Frances Wack, *Lovesickness in the Middle Ages: The Viaticum and Its Commentaries* (Philadelphia, 1990).
37. This aspect of the condition is evident in the *Viaticum* (33–35); see Wack, *Lovesickness in the Middle Ages*, p. 190. This symptom also receives a comment from Gerard of Berry in his gloss (p. 202).
38. See the *Viaticum* and the glosses of Gerard of Berry; Wack, *Lovesickness in the Middle Ages*, pp. 190–91, 202–3.
39. "Prodest etiam uenatio et species diuerse ludorum" (Hunting and various types of games also help). Text and translation from Wack, ibid., pp. 202–3.
40. For a discussion of this passage, see David J. Shirt, "The Dido Episode in *Enéas*: The Reshaping of Tragedy and Its Stylistic Consequences," *Medium Aeuum* 51 (1982), pp. 3–17.
41. See Christiane Marchello-Nizia, "De l'*Énéide* à l'*Eneas*: les attributs du fondateur," in *Lectures médiévales de Virgile: Actes du colloque organisé par l'École française de Rome*, ed. Jean-Yves Tilliette (Rome, 1985), pp. 251–66.
42. On the privatization of the story of Aeneas and Dido, see Patterson, "Virgil and the Historical Consciousness, pp. 181–83.
43. For a discussion of Dido's relationship to history in the *Aeneid* and the *Eneas*, see Singerman, *Under Clouds of Poesy*, pp. 113–15.
44. Almost every discussion of the *Eneas* explores the juxtaposition of the Dido and Lavinia episodes. See Huchet, *Le Roman médiéval*, pp. 11–50; Singerman, *Under Clouds of Poesy*, pp. 77–98; Nolan, *Chaucer and the Tradition of the* Roman Antique, pp. 75–96; Gaunt, "From Epic to Romance."
45. On the significance of the *Heroides* to the *Eneas*, see Nolan, *Chaucer and the Tradition of the* Roman Antique, pp. 75–96.
46. See the excellent discussion of homophobia in the *Roman d'Eneas* in Gaunt, "From Epic to Romance."
47. See Markale, *Aliénor d'Aquitaine*, pp. 34–37.
48. Roberta L. Krueger, "Double Jeopardy: The Appropriation of Woman in Four Old French Romances of the 'Cycle de la Gageure,' " in *Seeking the Woman in Late Medieval and Renaissance Writings: Essays in Feminist Contextual Criticism*, ed. Sheila Fisher and Janet E. Halley (Knoxville, Tenn., 1989), p. 23.
49. Although no complete modern edition of the *Histoire* has been produced, the relevant sections from the *Aeneid* story have recently been excerpted and summarized by Jacques Monfrin; see Appendix I, "Les *translations* vernaculaires de Virgile au Moyen Âge," in *Lectures médiévales de Virgile*, pp. 221–41. For a discussion of this text, see P. Meyer, "Les premières compilations françaises d'histoire ancienne," *Romania* 14 (1885), pp. 1–81; and G. Raynaud de Lage, "L'Histoire ancienne jusqu'à César," *Le Moyen Age* 40 (1949), pp. 5–16. For the purposes of this study, I have consulted the *Histoire* in the following manuscripts: British Library, London, Royal 16 G vii; Morgan Library, New York, M 212–13.
50. The epitome of the *Aeneid* that occurs at the start of Geoffrey of Monmouth's *Historia regum Britanniae* describes Aeneas's journey from Troy to Italy; the passage names Ascanius and Lavinia. See Edmond Faral, *La légende arthurienne*, vol. 3 (Paris, 1929), pp. 73–74; for Wace, see *Roman de Brut*, ed. Ivor Arnold (Paris, 1938), lines 10–72. The epitome of the *Aeneid* occurs toward the end of the *Roman de Troie*; see Benoît de Sainte-Maure, *Le Roman de Troie*, ed Léopold Constans (Paris, 1948), lines 28253–56. On the significance of the Trojan history to French identity, see Colette Beaune, "L'utilisation politique du mythe des origines troyennes en France à la fin du Moyen Âge," in *Lectures médiévales de Virgile*, pp. 331–55. See also chapter 6, n. 34.
51. One important exception is the *Excidium Troiae*, which includes a version of *Aeneid* 4 that is slightly embellished with material from the historical tradition. See E. Bagby Atwood and Virgil K. Whitaker, eds., *Excidium Troiae* (Cambridge, Mass., 1944), pp. 26–37.

52. See Doris Oltrogge, *Die Illustrationszyklen zur »Histoire ancienne jusqu'à César«
1250–1400* (Frankfurt, 1992). See also Brian Woledge, *Bibliographie des Romans et
Nouvelles en Prose Française Antérieurs à 1500* (Geneva, 1954; supplement: Geneva, 1975),
p. 55. Woledge lists thirty-three manuscripts before 1400. A detailed survey of the iconographic tradition is likewise available in Pierre Courcelle and Jeanne Courcelle, *Lecteurs
païens et lecteurs chrétiens de l'Énéide*, vol. 2: *Les manuscrits illustrés de l'Énéide du Xᵉ au
XVᵉ siècle* (Paris, 1984), pp. 89–107. David J. A. Ross comments that the majority of *Histoire*
manuscripts are highly decorated and illuminated: "This [text] must have been regarded in
the later Middle Ages as an essential in the library of the average French noble or gentleman
with a leaning to literary culture" ("The History of Macedon in the «Histoire ancienne
jusqu'à César»: Sources and Compositional Method," *Classica et Mediaevalia* 24 [1963], p.
181).

53. See Singerman, *Under Clouds of Poesy*, pp. 152–79; Monfrin, "Les *Translations*,"
200–211.

54. Singerman makes a strong case for the *Histoire* arrangement as a reflection of the
manuscript tradition for a historical ordering of the *romans antiques*; see *Under Clouds of
Poesy*, pp. 99–135. See also G. Raynaud de Lage, "Les «Romans antiques» dans l'Histoire
ancienne jusqu'à César," *Le Moyen Age* 63 (1957), pp. 267–309.

55. See F. Saxl, "The Troy Romance in French and Italian Art," *Lectures* (London, 1957),
pp. 132–33.

56. For another version, see Saxl, vol. 2, plate 77b (Bib. Vaticana Cod. Vat. 5895) and plate
77d (BL Royal 20 D i). See also Courcelle and Courcelle, *Lecteurs païens et lecteurs chré-
tiens*, fig. 198 (BN français 9682), fig. 200 (BN français 20125), fig. 245 (Paris, Arsenal 5077).
Other manuscripts that contain a version of this image include Dijon, Bibliothèque
Communale, MS. 562; Brussels, Bibliothèque Royale 10175 (see H. Buchthal, *Miniature
Painting in the Latin Kingdom of Jerusalem* [Oxford, 1957], pp. 150, 115b); BL Stowe 54.

57. Courcelle and Courcelle, *Lecteurs païens et lecteurs chrétiens*, p. 90.

58. Ibid., p. 90.

59. Jeanne Courcelle, "Les illustrations de l'Énéide dans les manucrits du Xᵉ siècle au
XVᵉ siècle," in *Lectures médiévales de Virgile*, p. 397.

60. See Singerman, *Under Clouds of Poesy*, p. 161.

4. *Sely* Dido and the Chaucerian Gaze

1. Virginia Woolf, "The Pastons and Chaucer," *The Common Reader* (New York, 1953),
p. 11.

2. In his notes to the *House of Fame* in *The Riverside Chaucer* (ed. Larry D. Benson
[Boston, 1987]), John Fyler asserts that "there is no doubt that [Chaucer] knew Virgil and
Ovid at first hand, and thoroughly" (p. 977). In their notes to the "Legend of Dido," M. C. E.
Shaner and A. S. G. Edwards note that "the primary source is Virgil's *Aeneid*, with inciden-
tal use of Ovid's *Heroides* 7." Shaner and Edwards go on to summarize a commonplace that
"the character and motivation of Dido is particularly influenced by Ovid" (p. 1067). See also
Götz Schmitz, *The Fall of Woman in Early English Verse* (Cambridge, 1990), p. 21. I am in
general agreement that both the *House of Fame* and the "Legend of Dido" show a close
acquaintance with the *Aeneid* and the *Heroides*; both texts contain insistent citations of
Virgil's *Aeneid* and Ovid's *Heroides* as texts to be named by the narrators and recognized by
the audience, and both contain passages of translation that are specifically presented as
translations and meant to be recognized as such. These features of Chaucerian textuality
argue for a recognition of Virgil and Ovid as *auctores* whose texts have a recognizable cultural status. However, Chaucer would have known both texts in highly mediated forms:
both the *Aeneid* and the *Heroides* would have shown the effects of medieval textual tradi-

tions, particularly in the form of commentaries, such as Servius for the *Aeneid* and the sort of *accessus* and glosses for the *Heroides* discussed and edited by Ralph Hexter (see chapter 1 note 68). In addition, a large number of possible vernacular intermediaries in French and Italian have been proposed: Filippo Ceffi's translation of the *Heroides* (see Sanford Brown Meech, "Chaucer and an Italian Translation of the *Heroides*," *Publications of the Modern Language Association* 45 [1930], pp. 110–28); and Andrea Lancia's translation of the *Aeneid* as well as the *Roman d'Eneas*, (Louis Brewer Hall, "Chaucer and the Dido-and-Aeneas Story," *Medieval Studies* 25 [1963], pp. 148–59). Nonetheless, the cases made for these particular vernacular texts as "sources" have not received much consensus. As Shaner and Edwards note regarding Ceffi's Italian version of the *Heroides*: "It is possible, however, that Chaucer was unacquainted with this translation, and that both he and Filippo used manuscripts of the *Heroides* having the same tradition of glosses" (p. 1059). However, if we start from the working assumption of Virgil and Ovid as *auctores*, any number of vernacular texts could have been intermediaries without usurping the *auctoritas* of Virgil and Ovid. It is notable, for instance, that the *Ovide moralisé* contains a translation of *Heroides* 7 that might have worked as an intermediary text; several of the *Heroides* are often included as prose translations in the texts of the *Histoire ancienne jusqu'à César* as well. Indeed, texts of the *Histoire*—which circulated very widely—also provide an as yet overlooked intertext for Chaucer's engagement with Virgil and Ovid. Lee Patterson, for instance, suggests Chaucer's acquaintance with the *Histoire* (*Chaucer and the Subject of History* [Madison, Wis., 1991], p. 82), but the critical tradition has otherwise bypassed the possibility that the textual arrangements of history, narrative, and image in the texts of the *Histoire* could account for the experience in *House of Fame* 1, as I shall attempt to show. For a discussion of the popularity of historical texts in late medieval court and culture, see Richard Firth Green, *Poets and Princepleasers: Literature and the English Court in the Late Middle Ages* (Toronto, 1980), pp. 135–38.

3. See Fyler, *Chaucer and Ovid* (New Haven, Conn., 1979).

4. The narrator in the *Book of the Duchess* names Dido as an exemplum of excessive grief in a briefly glossed catalog of classical women (731–34) cited in chapter 1. In *Parliament of Fowls* 289, Dido is named as one of many literary figures portrayed on the walls of the temple (see note 46). For a discussion of Dido's placement in the "Man of Law's Tale" and other such catalogs, see chapter 1. On Dido as the "female figure who is not named, the femininity that is repressed in Scipio's dream at the beginning of the *Parliament*," see Elaine Tuttle Hansen, *Chaucer and the Fictions of Gender* (Berkeley, Calif., 1992), p. 87. For the invocation of Dido suggested by a quotation of *Heroides* 7 in *Anelida and Arcite*, see Patterson, *Chaucer and the Subject of History*, pp. 67–71. For a discussion of the bedroom scene in the *Troilus* in relation to the cave scene in the *Aeneid* and the possibility that Chaucer might wish to make a connection between Criseyde and Dido, see John V. Fleming, "Smoky Reyn: From Jean de Meun to Geoffrey Chaucer," in *Chaucer and the Craft of Fiction*, ed. Leigh A. Arrathoon (Rochester, Mich., 1986), pp. 14–21.

In addition, Dido appears in two ballades edited by James Wimsatt, *Chaucer and the Poems of "Ch"* (Cambridge, 1982). In an allusion to Dido's speech act in the *Heroides*, the spurned woman of Ballade V refers to herself as Dido: "Je vail Dido parlant a Eneas, / Lasse et deserte" (4–5) (I am like Dido speaking to Aeneas, / Dejected and deserted). In Ballade VIII, the lover refers to "Noble Dido" (7) in a catalog of biblical and classical figures. For the issues of authorship in these poems, see pp. 1–8. Text and translation from Wimsatt.

5. See note 2.

6. See Peter Godman, "Chaucer and Boccaccio's Latin Works," in *Chaucer and the Italian Trecento*, ed. Piero Boitani (Cambridge, 1983), pp. 269–95; Edmund Reiss, "Boccaccio in English Culture of the Fourteenth and Fifteenth Centuries," in *Il Boccaccio nella cultura Inglese e Anglo-Americana*, ed. Giuseppe Galigani (Florence, 1974), pp. 15–26.

7. Female characters like Criseyde are certainly literate, which allows her to read and write letters in private; however, she listens to literary texts read aloud to a group rather than reading them alone. There is no evidence that the Wife of Bath, for all her engagement in textual traditions, can actually read herself; she has certainly had enough material presented to her from the pulpit and from Jankin's reading aloud to her to account for her "textual" knowledge. In Chaucer's poetry, the male characters of a certain social class, such as the dream narrators and the Clerk, engage in solitary reading.

8. For an excellent survey of medieval dream theory, see Steven F. Kruger, *Dreaming in the Middle Ages* (Cambridge, 1992). V. A. Kolve notes that in medieval dream theory, the *visio* and the *somnium* were highly visual; see *Chaucer and the Imagery of Narrative: The First Five Canterbury Tales* (Stanford, Calif., 1984), p. 31.

9. Chaucer refers to this text as "the book also of Fame," in the "Retraction," after calling it the "House of Fame" in the *Prologue to the Legend of Good Women*. Richard Pynson's edition in 1526 titles it the "Book of Fame" (see chapter 1 note 74).

10. According to the *Middle English Dictionary* (Ann Arbor, Mich., 1985), *reden* (*rǣddan*) denotes: (1a.) "to read; to engage in reading; to know how to read"; (1b.) "to read for particular information"; (1c.) "to read with understanding"; (2) "to read aloud"; (3) "to learn by reading"; (4) "to teach; instruct"; (5) "to relate (a narrative), tell (a story), recount"; (6) "to interpret (a dream, parable, etc.)"; (7) "to perceive something, discern"; (8) "to counsel, give advice, advise." The frequency of the term *rede* in the *House of Fame*, and its range of meanings from "as men read," to "as men speak," emphasizes, at the linguistic level, the perceptual basis of this poem. See John Finlayson, "Seeing, Hearing and Knowing in the *House of Fame*," *Studia Neophilologica* 58 (1986), pp. 47–57.

11. See the discussion of "Vernacular Literacy and Lay Education" in Janet Coleman, *Medieval Readers and Writers 1350–1400* (New York, 1981), pp. 18–57.

12. See the discussion in Coleman. On the connections between literacy and social class in relation to the Peasants' Revolt, see Susan Crane, "The Writing Lesson of 1381," in *Chaucer's England: Literature in Historical Context*, ed. Barbara Hanawalt (Minneapolis, 1992), pp. 201–21. See also Graham D. Caie, "Nationalism, Language and Cultural Identity in Fourteenth-Century England," *Culture and History* 6 (1987), pp. 79–89; Stephen Knight, *Geoffrey Chaucer* (Oxford, 1986), pp. 15–23.

13. See Coleman, *Medieval Readers and Writers*, pp. 202–4; "English Culture in the Fourteenth Century," in *Chaucer and the Italian Trecento*, pp. 33–63. See also J. J. G. Alexander, "Painting and Manuscript Illumination for Royal Patrons in the Later Middle Ages," in *English Court Culture in the Later Middle Ages*, ed. V. J. Scattergood and J. W. Sherborne (London, 1983), pp. 141–62.

14. Paul Saenger, "Silent Reading: Its Impact on Late Medieval Script and Society," *Viator* (1982), p. 399. Saenger notes: "Vernacular authors of the late fourteenth century began to assume that their audience was composed of readers rather than listeners" (p. 411).

15. Ibid., p. 401. In addition to Saenger, see Coleman, *Medieval Readers and Writers*, p. 51; see also Mary Carruthers, *The Book of Memory: A Study of Memory in Medieval Culture* (Cambridge, 1990), pp. 170–72, and Kolve, *Chaucer and the Imagery of Narrative*, pp. 11–18. I do not mean to imply here that silent reading was only coming into use in the fourteenth century; rather, the issue of silent reading in fourteenth-century vernacular, lay culture is dependent on the increase in the literacy rate and the wider circulation of texts.

16. For a linguistic analysis of the construction of the subject in the *House of Fame*, see Terry Threadgold, "Changing the Subject," in *Language Topics: Essays in Honour of Michael Halliday*, vol. 2 (Philadelphia, 1987), pp. 549–97. Threadgold uses Chaucer's text to illustrate that subjects are semiotically constructed in historically contingent ways. Among Threadgold's conclusions are his assertion that "The dream world and the 'I' who is 'other'—the dreamer—is a projection of the narrator's mind and voice. *There is no separa-*

tion between subject and object. The subject tells, tries to know this world from a position within it" (p. 576). Threadgold's argument is based largely on language theory; my intention in this discussion of the *House of Fame* is to explore the construction of the subject in this text specifically in relation to gender and reading.

17. See Norman Bryson, *Vision and Painting: The Logic of the Gaze* (London: 1983).

18. As Michael Camille distinguishes between the perceptual demands of text and image for the reader: "An awareness of the conflict between the discursive (the text) and the figural (the image) or at least their tension, meant that more than in any other type of medieval art, the form of manuscript illustrations retained a heavily encoded linguistic component" ("The Book of Signs: Writing and Visual Difference in Gothic Manuscript Illumination," *Word and Image* 1 [1985], p. 139). See also Michael Camille, "Seeing and Reading: Some Visual Implications of Medieval Literacy and Illiteracy," *Art History* 8 (1985), pp. 26-49; "The Language of Images in Medieval England, 1200-1400," in *The Age of Chivalry: The Art of Plantagenet England*, ed. J. J. G. Alexander and Paul Binski (Cambridge, 1992), pp. 33-40; and "Making the Margins," *Image on the Edge: The Margins of Medieval Art* (Cambridge, 1992), pp. 11-55. On the visual and page layout of medieval manuscripts, see M. T. Clanchy, *From Memory to Written Record: England 1066-1307*, 2d ed. (London, 1993), p. 278-93; Richard H. Rouse and Mary A. Rouse, "*Statim invenire*: Schools, Preachers, and New Attitudes to the Page," in *Renaissance and Renewal in the Twelfth Century*, ed. Robert L. Benson and Giles Constable (Cambridge, Mass., 1982), pp. 201-25; A. I. Doyle and M. B. Parkes, "The Production of Copies of the *Canterbury Tales* and the *Confessio Amantis* in the Early Fifteenth Century," in *Medieval Scribes, Manuscripts and Libraries: Essays Presented to N. R. Ker*, ed. M. B. Parkes and Andrew G. Watson (London, 1978), pp. 163-210; Sylvia Huot, *From Song to Book: The Poetics of Writing in Old French Lyric and Lyrical Narrative Poetry* (Ithaca, N.Y., 1987), pp. 11-80. On memory and page layout, see Carruthers, *The Book of Memory*, pp. 221-29. A technical description of manuscript layout is provided by Christopher F. R. De Hamel, *Glossed Books of the Bible and the Origins of the Paris Book Trade* (Cambridge, 1984). The best synthetic discussion of the issues of text and image in Chaucer is V. A. Kolve, "Audience and Image: Some Medieval Hypotheses," *Chaucer and the Imagery*, pp. 9-58.

19. For a discussion of the *House of Fame* that emphasizes the importance of voice in this equation, see Martin Irvine, "Grammatical Theory and the *House of Fame*," *Speculum* 60 (1985), pp. 850-76. Irvine's study focuses on the relationship between written language and voice: "Writing was seen as essentially phonetic, inscribing articulate spoken sound, or utterances capable of being resolved into minimal constituents, in a pattern of graphic images which are reconstituted as articulate sounds when read" (p. 857). My reading suggests, however, that the awareness about the visuality of written language in *House of Fame* 1 becomes insistently verbalized in *House of Fame* 2.

20. Teresa de Lauretis, *Technologies of Gender* (Bloomington, Ind., 1987), p. 20. See also, de Lauretis, *Alice Doesn't: Feminism, Semiotics, Cinema* (Bloomington, Ind., 1984); Kaja Silverman, *The Subject of Semiotics* (New York, 1983). It appears to me that film theory offers a valuable interpretive tool to build on the concept of the construction of the subject in the *House of Fame*, and the existing exploration of the text in terms semiotics (Eugene Vance, "Chaucer's *House of Fame* and the Poetics of Inflation," *boundary 2* 7 [1979], pp. 17-37) and postmodern writing (Robert Jordan, *Chaucer's Poetics and the Modern Reader* [Berkeley, Calif., 1987], pp. 22-50). Feminist film theory specifically offers valuable models for incorporating gender into an explorations of semiotic systems. A model for understanding gender as part of the construction of knowledge might make a critic such as Vance aware of his own gendered bias, evident in the following passage: "In Virgil's poem at no point are we allowed to perceive Aeneas' obligations to found a new Troy as unworthy, but in the Temple of Venus, 188 lines are devoted to his scandalous liaison with Dido and to her seem-

ingly righteous anger, while only six lines are devoted to excusing him" (p. 29). For a discussion of the misogynist bias of Chaucer criticism, see Hansen, *Chaucer and the Fictions of Gender*.

21. As Sylvia Huot observes: "The narrator's first act of reading is focused on the wall surrounding the garden, quite literally a text of words and images, since the allegorical representations are equipped with labels. This visual text is reproduced in nearly all manuscripts of the *Rose* by a series of miniatures representing each personified vice in turn and often accompanied by explanatory rubrics" (*From Song to Book*, p. 87). See Stephen G. Nichols, "Ekphrasis, Iconoclasm, and Desire," in *Rethinking the Romance of the Rose*, ed. Kevin Brownlee and Sylvia Huot (Philadelphia, 1992), pp. 133–66. As Caroline D. Eckhardt has demonstrated, the English translation of the *Rose* highlights the narrator's presence in the poem and emphasizes the images as things seen by a spectator; see Caroline D. Eckhardt, "The Art of Translation in the *Romaunt of the Rose*," *Studies in the Age of Chaucer* 6 (1984), pp. 41–63.

22. For a discussion of the manuscript context of the *Roman de la Rose*, see Huot, *From Song to Book*, pp. 83–105; John V. Fleming, "The *Romance de la Rose* and Its Manuscript Illustrations" (Diss., Princeton, N.J., 1963); and John V. Fleming, *The Roman de la Rose: A Study in Allegory and Iconography* (Princeton, N.J., 1969). See chapter 1 note 84.

23. As John Fleming puts it, "Chaucer's actual translation of the *Roman* we do not have, yet we see him 'translating' Jean de Meun on virtually every page he wrote" (*Reason and the Lover* [Princeton, N.J., 1984], p. 70). John Norton-Smith, *Geoffrey Chaucer* (London, 1974), suggests that the ekphrasis of the *House of Fame* connects it to the *Roman de la Rose* (p. 35).

24. Huot notes that the "proliferation of *Rose* manuscripts does indicate that this poem was experienced as a book by a relatively large number of people" (*From Song to Book*, p. 102).

25. See Lisa Kiser, *Truth and Textuality in Chaucer's Poetry* (Hanover, N.H., 1991), pp. 25–41.

26. Hansen notes that "the dreamer's characterization brings out the paradoxical double bind of proper masculinity as it is often normatively defined in Western culture and the deep and complex feminization that is involved in the very reliance on authority that authoritative discourse recommends" (*Chaucer and the Fictions of Gender*, p. 103). Hansen's analysis effectively places the *House of Fame* narrator in the context of the Chaucerian narrator's "anxious misogyny." For a general discussion of the "gendered models of literary activity" as they are enacted in other Chaucerian texts, see Carolyn Dinshaw, *Chaucer's Sexual Poetics* (Madison, Wis., 1989).

27. The most thorough consideration of the concept of Fame and Chaucer's *House of Fame* itself within the intellectual traditions of medieval culture remains Sheila Delany, *Chaucer's House of Fame: The Poetics of Skeptical Fideism* (Chicago, 1972). See also Piero Boitani, *Chaucer and the Imaginary World of Fame* (Totowa, N.J., 1984).

28. See Mary Carruthers, chapter 4, "The Arts of Memory," in *The Book of Memory*, pp. 122–55.

29. For a discussion of the art of memory in relation to the *House of Fame*, see Mary Carruthers, "Italy, *Ars memorativa*, and Fame's House," *Studies in the Age of Chaucer*, Proceedings series 2 (1987), pp. 179–87. Carruthers's discussion focuses attention largely on Book 3 of the *House of Fame*. See also Beryl Rowland, "Bishop Bradwardine, the Artificial Memory, and the House of Fame," *Chaucer at Albany*, ed. Rossell Hope Robbins (New York, 1976), pp. 41–62. Rowland suggestively links the structures of the *House of Fame* with the artificial memory: "The *House of Fame* may be seen as an externalization of this memory process" (p. 48). In a later article, "The Art of Memory and the Art of Poetry in the *House of Fame*" (*University of Ottawa Quarterly* 52 [1981]), Rowland goes a little further in

her connections between memory and the production of poetry: "In effect, memory is the power that makes the poem" (p. 162). For a discussion of the text of the *House of Fame* and the architectural practices of the late Middle Ages, see Mary Flowers Braswell, "Architectural Portraiture in Chaucer's *House of Fame*," *Journal of Medieval and Renaissance Studies* 11 (1981), pp. 101–12. For a specific architectural reference, see Laura Kendrick, "Chaucer's *House of Fame* and the French Palais de Justice," *Studies in the Age of Chaucer* 6 (1984), pp. 121–33.

30. See Carruthers, chapter 7, "Memory and the Book," in *The Book of Memory*, pp. 221–60.

31. Carruthers's study focuses on theorists such as Hugh St. Victor, Albertus Magnus, and Thomas Bradwardine; she traces the role of memory training in gender-specific communities such as educational institutions, monasteries, and universities.

32. See Fyler, *Chaucer and Ovid*, pp. 23–64. Many readings of *House of Fame* 1 see the Virgilian and Ovidian discourse as oppositional; see, for instance, Jesse Gellrich, *The Idea of the Book in the Middle Ages* (Ithaca, N.Y., 1985), pp. 167–201.

33. For a discussion of the issues of history versus fable here, see Alistair J. Minnis, *Chaucer and Pagan Antiquity* (Cambridge, 1982), pp. 22–24.

34. See chapter 1 note 70.

35. On the status of medieval historiography in relation to *House of Fame* 3, see Patterson, *Chaucer and the Subject of History*, pp. 86–104.

36. On the construction of authorship at work here, see Alistair J. Minnis, *Medieval Theory of Authorship* (Philadelphia, 1988), pp. 160–210.

37. Michael Riffaterre, "The Mind's Eye: Memory and Textuality," in *The New Medievalism*, ed. Marina S. Brownlee, Kevin Brownlee, and Stephen G. Nichols (Baltimore, Md., 1991), p. 33.

38. See especially Meg Twycross, *Medieval Anadyomene* (Oxford, 1972). On the various connotations of Venus, see Robert Hollander, *Boccaccio's Two Venuses* (New York, 1977).

39. See E. Ann Kaplan, "Is the Gaze Male?" in *Powers of Desire: The Politics of Sexuality*, ed. Ann Snitow, Christine Stansell, and Sharon Thompson (New York, 1983), pp. 309–27. See also Elisabeth Bronfen, "Violence of Representation—Representation of Violence," *Literature Interpretation Theory* 1 (1990), pp. 303–21; Kaja Silverman, *Male Subjectivity at the Margins* (New York, 1992), pp. 125–81.

40. Jane Gallop, *The Daughter's Seduction* (Ithaca, N.Y., 1982) p. 27.

41. For the implications of the visual importance of female castration as a comforting spectacle that the male viewer depends upon to shore up his own sexual identity, see the classic article by Laura Mulvey, "Visual Pleasure and Narrative Cinema," in *Feminism and Film Theory*, ed. Constance Penley (London, 1988), pp. 57–68. See also Kaja Silverman, *The Acoustic Mirror: Female Voice in Psychoanalysis and Cinema* (Bloomington, Ind., 1988), and *Male Subjectivity*.

42. On the construction of the phallic gaze in relation to the female image in medieval art, see Michael Camille, *The Gothic Idol: Ideology and Image-Making in Medieval Art* (Cambridge, 1989), pp. 298–316.

43. On ekphrasis, see chapter 3 note 11. Chaucer's use of ekphrasis itself is a form of citation of Dante; for a discussion of *House of Fame* 1 and Dante's *visibile parler*, see Karla Taylor, *Chaucer Reads "The Divine Comedy"* (Stanford, Calif., 1989), pp. 23–24.

44. Interpretations of the significance of the Dido-Eneas story in *House of Fame* 1 have usually followed the scholar's approach to the overall poem. B. G. Koonce, who reads the *House of Fame* allegorically, takes the commentary of Bernard Silvestris on the *Aeneid* as the standard, fixed interpretation, which he then uses to explain the *Aeneid* story in *House of Fame* 1 (*Chaucer and the Tradition of Fame* [Princeton, N.J., 1966]). In Koonce's view, Eneas represents "what the human spirit does and suffers in the body" (p. 108), and Dido

represents carnal love that must be abandoned (pp. 111–12). J. A. W. Bennett, *Chaucer's Book of Fame* (Oxford, 1968), takes a thematic view of the poem and suggests that Chaucer uses the plight of Dido to introduce the twin themes of the poem: the nature of fame and the search for Love's folk (p. 60). For Delany, *House of Fame* 1 acknowledges a dual tradition of the *Aeneid* story: the irreconcilable tradition of Aeneas as a traitor with the Virgilian tradition of "Pius Eneas"—a conflict that fits her skeptical interpretation of the *House of Fame* (*Chaucer's House of Fame*, pp. 48–57). For Fyler, the literary tension between Ovid and Virgil in *House of Fame* 1 exemplifies all the problems of "poetic truth versus falsehood" (*Chaucer and Ovid*, p. 39).

45. See Kolve, *Chaucer and the Imagery*, pp. 41–42, and Carruthers, *The Book of Memory*, pp. 221–22.

46. The ekphrasis on the temple of Diana in the *Parliament of Fowls*, brief as it is, suggests the same schematic citation of tradition:
    and peynted overal
Ful many a story, of which I touche shal
A fewe, as of Calyxte and Athalante,
And many a mayde of which the name I wante.

Semyramis, Candace, and Hercules,
Biblis, Dido, Thisbe, and Piramus,
Tristram, Isaude, Paris, and Achilles,
Eleyne, Cleopatre, and Troylus,
Silla, and ek the moder of Romulus:
Alle these were peynted on that other syde,
And al here love, and in what plyt they dyde. (1.288–94)
Another important ekphrasis, which does not develop the potential of the depiction of the work itself, is the brief imitation of the ekphrasis from Virgil's *Aeneid* 1, alluded to in the *Legend of Dido*:
And when this Eneas and Achates
Hadden in this temple ben overal,
Thanne founde they, depeynted on a wal,
How Troye and al the lond destroyed was. (1024–26)
In the *Knight's Tale*, a similarly brief, provocative, intertextual ekphrasis occurs:
And by his baner born is his penoun
Of gold ful riche, in which ther was ybete
The Mynotaur, which that he wan in Crete. (978–80)
In addition, like most narrative poets, Chaucer uses ekphrasis to incidentally dispose of matters of plots such as in the Legend of Philomela, where Philomela weaves a written account of her imprisonment and abuse at the hands of her brother-in-law, which simultaneously acts as a citation of Ovid:
She hadde ywoven in a stamyn large
How she was brought from Athenes in a barge,
And in a cave how that she was brought;
And al the thyng that Tereus hath wrought,
She waf it wel, and wrot the storye above,
How she was served for hire systers love. (2360–65)
This ekphrasis employs both pictures and text, suggestive of the problems posed by the "text and glose" in the *Book of the Duchess*.

47. I agree with Karla Taylor's comment that this "yif I kan" insertion is "distinctly un-Virgilian; indeed, it is characteristically Chaucerian" (*Chaucer Reads the Divine Comedy*, p. 28). I take this "yif I kan" as a phrase indirectly attributed to Virgil by Chaucer, but ultimately impossible to assign to anyone but Geffrey. In linguistic terms, this "yif I kan"

would be considered a "discourse parenthetical," assigned to the speaker's (here, Geffrey's) point of view. See Ann Banfield, *Unspeakable Sentences: Narration and Representation in the Language of Fiction* (Boston, 1982), pp. 81–100. See also Joseph Dane, "Yif I 'arma virumque' kan: Note on Chaucer's *House of Fame* line 143" (*American Notes and Queries* 19 [1981], pp. 134–36).

48. Carruthers, "Italy," pp. 182–84.

49. One interpretive judgment—"Al this seye I be Eneas / And Dido, and hir nyce lest, / That loved al to sone a gest" (287–88)—may well be an echo of John of Salisbury's condemnation of Dido as a leader who carelessly receives Aeneas into her city; see the *Policraticus* 6.22; see chapter 2, n.57.

50. The reception of the *House of Fame* recorded in Richard Pynson's 1526 edition seems to explicitly gloss this passage by juxtaposing Ovid's *Heroides* 7 in an English translation entitled *The Letter of Dido* to Chaucer's *Book of Fame*. For an excellent discussion of the *Letter of Dido* in relation to Richard Pynson's edition and the *House of Fame*, see Julia Boffey, "Richard Pynson's *Book of Fame* and the *Letter of Dido*, *Viator* 19 (1988), pp. 339–53.

51. For a discussion of Chaucer's interests in reading in relation to gendered subject positions in texts other than the *House of Fame*, see Dinshaw, *Chaucer's Sexual Politics*.

52. See the discussion by Fyler in the notes to the *House of Fame* in Benson, *The Riverside Chaucer*.

53. Wolfgang Iser describes this process: "The reader is absorbed into what he himself has been made to produce through the image; he cannot help being affected by his own production. . . . But if we are absorbed into an image, we are no longer present in a reality—instead we are experiencing what can only be described as an irrealization, in the sense that we are preoccupied with something that takes us out of our own given reality. . . . And it is only logical that, when the process of irrealization is over— i.e., when we put the book down—we should experience a kind of 'awakening' " (*The Act of Reading* [Baltimore, Md., 1978], p. 140).

54. Silverman describes historical trauma in Lacanian terms as "any historical event, whether socially engineered or of natural occurrence, which brings a large group of male subjects into such an intimate relation with lack that they are at least for the moment unable to sustain an imaginary relation with the phallus, and so withdraw their belief from the dominant fiction" (*Male Subjectivity*, p. 55). Patterson's approach to Chaucer designates a "sense of marginality" in Chaucerian texts (*Chaucer and the Subject of History*, p. 39); Silverman's analysis of the structure of male subjectivity at the margins allows us to consider the implications of such "marginality."

55. See Christopher Allmand, *The Hundred Years War* (Cambridge, 1988), pp. 20–26. For further bibliography on the Hundred Years War, see chapter 6 note 35.

56. Hansen, *Chaucer and the Fictions of Gender*, p. 106.

57. For a recent survey of the Chaucer-Dante relationship in terms of their attitudes toward Dido, see Steve Ellis, "Chaucer, Dante and Damnation," *Chaucer Review* 22 (1988), pp. 282–94. Ellis's points are hampered by a relatively simplistic approach to Dido's status in *Inferno* 5; as we saw in chapter 2, Dido is carefully distinguished from the other condemned lovers.

58. Rita Copeland, *Rhetoric, Hermeneutics, and Translation in the Middle Ages: Academic Traditions and Vernacular Texts* (Cambridge, 1991), pp. 186–202. On the nature of the narrator's authority, see Kiser, *Truth and Textuality*, pp. 95–110. See also Peter L. Allen, "Reading Chaucer's Good Women," *Chaucer Review* 21 (1987), pp. 419–34.

59. On the status of the *Prologue* as a dream vision, see Michael D. Cherniss, "Chaucer's Last Dream Vision: The *Prologue* to the *Legend of Good Women*," *Chaucer Review* 20 (1986), pp. 183–99.

60. For a discussion of Queen Anne's literary tastes and the possibility that she shaped the literary productions of her court through her patronage of a particular kind of literary activity that favored classical themes, see Coleman, "English Culture," pp. 59–60.

61. See Richard Firth Green, "Chaucer's Victimized Women," *Studies in the Age of Chaucer* 10 (1988), pp. 3–21.

62. See Eleanor Winsor Leach, "A Study in the Sources and Rhetoric of Chaucer's *Legend of Good Women* and Ovid's *Heroides*" (Diss., Yale, 1963), pp. 97–211; Robert Worth Frank, *Chaucer and the Legend of Good Women* (Cambridge, Mass., 1972), pp. 14–15; Fyler, *Chaucer and Ovid*, pp. 96–123; Lisa Kiser, *Telling Classical Tales* (Ithaca, N.Y., 1983), pp. 95–131; Janet M. Cowen, "Chaucer's *Legend of Good Women*: Structure and Tone," *Studies in Philology* 82 (1985), pp. 416–36.

63. The relationship of the *Legend of Dido* to its sources has been variously discussed in E. F. Shannon, *Chaucer and the Roman Poets* (Cambridge, Mass., 1929), pp. 196–208; Bagby Atwood, "Two Alterations of Virgil in Chaucer's Dido," *Speculum* 13 (1938), pp. 454–57; Albert C. Friend, "Chaucer's Version of the *Aeneid*," *Speculum* 28 (1953), pp. 317–23; Kevin Doherty, "Dido in Virgil and Chaucer," *Classical Bulletin* 31 (1955), pp. 29–35; D. R. Bradley, "Fals Eneas and Sely Dido," *Philological Quarterly* 39 (1960), pp. 122–25; Louis B. Hall, "Chaucer and the Dido-and-Aeneas Story," *Medieval Studies* 25 (1963), pp. 148–49; Frank, *Chaucer and the Legend*, pp. 57–78; Alan T. Gaylord, "Dido at Hunt, Chaucer at Work," *Chaucer Review* 17 (1983), pp. 300–315; Marilynn Desmond, "Chaucer's *Aeneid*: 'The Naked Text in English,' " *Pacific Coast Philology* 19 (1984), pp. 62–67; Nancy Ruff, "Sely Dido: A Good Woman's Fame," *Classical and Modern Literature* 12 (1991), pp. 59–68.

64. Only three of the legends do not refer to their source in the text: the *Legend of Cleopatra*, the *Legend of Philomela*, and the *Legend of Hypermnestra*. These three legends nevertheless stress their nature as "received material"; see lines 608–9, 2239, and 2675. The *Legend of Dido* contains by far the largest number of narrative intrusions. In additon, see W. Nelson Francis, "Chaucer Shortens a Tale," *Publications of the Modern Language Association* 68 (1953), pp. 1126–41. Nelson counted the frequency of *abbreviatio* in the corpus. He shows that the *Legend of Dido* is second only to the *Legend of Phyllis* in terms of the density of occurrences of *abbreviatio*. The *Legend of Dido* averages one *abbreviatio* for every thirty-seven lines; the *Legend of Phyllis*, one for every thirty-three lines.

65. See chapter 1.

66. The Harvard edition of Servius contains the following comment as an alternate reading: "multi vituperant comparationen hanc nescientes exempla vel parabolas vel comparationes adsumptas non semper usquequaque congruere" ("Many fault this comparison not knowing that examples and proverbs and comparisons applied do not always altogether suit").

67. Silverman, *Male Subjectivity*, p. 47. On the role of the female subject in the dominant fiction, see pp. 42–51.

68. See Guillaume de Machaut, *Le Judgement dou Roy de Navarre*, whose brief exemplum of Dido's story includes the following detail:

Mais elle ne morut pas seule,
Einsois a deus copa la gueule,
Car d'Eneas estoit enceinte,
Dont moult fu regretée et plainte. (2119–22)

But she did not die alone, thus she cut the throat of two, because she was pregnant by Eneas, for which she was greatly regretted and lamented.
Text from Ernest Hoepffner, *Œuvres de Guillaume de Machaut* (Paris, 1906; rpt. 1965).

69. Kiser, *Telling Classical Tales*, p. 145.

70. Mulvey, "Visual Pleasure and Narrative Cinema," p. 64.

71. Silverman, *Male Subjectivity*, p. 48.

72. As Lord puts it: "In the *Franklin's Tale* (1367–1456) Chaucer uses a long list of examples drawn specifically from *Adversus Iovinianum* I. 41–46. They include in somewhat mixed order almost all of Jerome's *exempla*, both virgins and chaste wives, each with her accompanying story. From Chapter 43 the wife of Hasdrubal and her leap into the fire are mentioned. One must suppose that Chaucer was acquainted with her companion example and predecessor in Jerome, the chaste Dido, but that he omitted her from the list in the *Franklin's Tale* because of his preference for the Vergilian and Ovidian forms of the story" (Mary Louise Lord, "Dido as an Example of Chastity: The Influence of Example Literature," *Harvard Library Bulletin* 17 [1969], p. 225).

73. See Dinshaw for an assessment of Chaucer's poetics as an interpretive model that depends on sexual difference in a binary, heterosexist paradigm, in terms of its allegorical representation of a "text as a woman read and interpreted by men" (*Chaucer's Sexual Politics*, p. 12).

74. Text from G. C. Macaulay, *The English Works of John Gower* (Oxford, 1900).

75. For a discussion of Gower's use of Ovid, see Götz Schmitz, "Gower, Chaucer, and the Classics: Back to the Textual Evidence," in *John Gower: Recent Readings*, ed. R. F. Yeager (Kalamazoo, Mich., 1989), pp. 95–111.

76. Text from George Kane and E. Talbot Donaldon, *Piers Plowman: The B Version* (London, 1988); Passus 13.172. I am grateful to Jeanne Krochalis, chair of the Modern Language Association session on Middle English translation, December 1987, for pointing out to me Langland's use of this term.

5. Dido's Double Wound in Caxton's *Eneydos* and Gavin Douglas's *Eneados*

1. For the text of the *Eneados*, see David F. C. Coldwell, ed., *Virgil's Aeneid Translated into Scottish Verse by Gavin Douglas* (Edinburgh, The Scottish Text Society, 1957–64), 4 vols. For the text of the *Palice of Honour*, see Priscilla J. Bawcutt, ed., *The Shorter Poems of Gavin Douglas* (Edinburgh, The Scottish Text Society, 1967). For the text of Caxton's *Eneydos*, see W. T. Culley and F. J. Furnivall, eds., *Eneydos* (Oxford, Early English Text Society, 1890; rpt. 1962). The text of Guillaume Le Roy's 1483 edition of *Le Livre des Eneydes* has not been made available in a modern edition.

2. Indeed, Douglas's translation has historically been judged by direct reference to the *Aeneid*. See C. S. Lewis, *English Literature in the Sixteenth Century Excluding Drama* (Oxford, 1944), pp. 81–82; John Speirs, *Scots Literary Tradition* (London, 1940), p. 56; Lauchlan Maclean Watt, *Douglas's Aeneid* (Cambridge, 1920), pp. 77–103. Priscilla Bawcutt presents the most useful study of the two texts; see *Gavin Douglas: A Critical Study* (Edinburgh, 1976). See also the careful discussion of Douglas's diction and choices as a translator in Coldwell, *Virgil's Aeneid*, vol. 1, pp. 39–78.

3. See Stephanie Jed, *Chaste Thinking: The Rape of Lucretia and the Birth of Humanism* (Bloomington, Ind., 1987).

4. See Timothy Hampton, *Writing from History: The Rhetoric of Exemplarity in Renaissance Literature* (Ithaca, N.Y., 1990), p. 19. See especially pp. 8–30.

5. See Craig Kallendorf, *In Praise of Aeneas: Virgil and Epideictic Rhetoric in the Early Italian Renaissance* (Hanover, N.H., 1989).

6. Jenny Wormald notes that Douglas's use of "Scottis" to refer to the lowland dialect marks a shift from fifteenth-century usage, in which "Scottis" refers to the Celtic, highland language; see *Court, Kirk and Community: Scotland 1470–1625* (London, 1981), pp. 59–62. On the distinctions between the two languages, see Alex Agutter, "Middle Scots as a Literary Language," in *History of Scottish Literature 1: Origins to 1600*, ed. R. D. S. Jack (Aberdeen, 1988), pp. 13–25.

7. On vernacular translation as a source of linguistic enrichment, see Rita Copeland, "Rhetoric and Vernacular Translation in the Middle Ages," *Studies in the Age of Chaucer 9* (1987), pp. 41–75.

8. On Douglas's relationship to Scottish court culture, see Denton Fox, "Middle Scots Poets and Patrons," in *English Court Culture in the Later Middle Ages*, ed. V. J. Scattergood and J. W. Sherborne (London, 1983), pp. 109–27; see also Ruth Morse, "Gavin Douglas: 'Off Eloquence the Flowand Balmy Strand,' " in *Chaucer Traditions: Studies in Honour of Derek Brewer*, ed. Ruth Morse, Barry Windeatt, and Toshiyuki Takamiya (Cambridge, 1990), pp. 107–21. For a wider discussion of Scottish courtly culture, see Louise Olga Fradenburg, *City, Marriage, Tournament: Arts of Rule in Late Medieval Scotland* (Madison, Wis., 1991).

9. Fox, "Middle Class Poets and Patrons," p. 119.

10. See Priscilla Bawcutt, "William Dunbar and Gavin Douglas," in *History of Scottish Literature* 1, pp. 73–89.

11. See Christine M. Scollen, "Octovien de Saint-Gelais' Translation of the *Aeneid*: Poetry or Propaganda?" *Bibliothèque d'Humanisme et Renaissance* 39 (1977), pp. 253–61. For a brief excerpt, see Jacques Monfrin, "Les *Translations* vernaculaires de Virgile au Moyen Age," in *Lectures médiévales de Virgile: Actes du colloque organisé par l'École française de Rome* (Rome, 1985), pp. 246–49. See also H. J. Molinier, *Essai biographique et littéraire sur Octovien de Saint-Gelays, Evêque d'Angoulême* (Rodez, 1910), pp. 232–39.

12. For a discussion of the complex ambiguity that the issue of the myth of Trojan origins posed for Douglas as a Scot, see Jerome Singerman, *Under Clouds of Poesy: Poetry and Truth in French and English Reworkings of the Aeneid, 1160–1513* (New York, 1986), pp. 271–76.

13. R. James Goldstein, *The Matter of Scotland: Historical Narrative in Medieval Scotland* (Lincoln, Neb., 1993); Fradenburg, *City, Marriage, Tournament*. See also John MacQueen, "The Literature of Fifteenth-Century Scotland," in Jennifer Brown, *Scottish Society in the Fifteenth Century* (New York, 1977), pp. 184–208; in particular, MacQueen notes that James III possessed a luxury edition of Virgil, MS. Edinburgh 195.

14. See Ranald Nicholson, *Scotland: The Later Middle Ages* (New York, 1974), p. 590.

15. As Nicholson notes, the aims of the Education Act were that "all barons and substantial freeholders . . . were to send their eldest sons and heirs to grammar school from age 8 or 9; after they had mastered Latin, they were to spend three years studying arts or law in the universities" (ibid.).

16. Jerome Singerman notes that the *Eneydos* may more likely be a translation from "a manuscript of the unidentified prose romance that Le Roy put into print" (*Under Clouds of Poesy*, p. 198). Rudolf Hirsch comments that "in contrast to Paris, Lyons was then not a center of learning but rather a predominantly commercial city in which wealthy businessmen and the clergy were the most likely customers for books" ("Printing in France and Humanism, 1470–80," *The Library Quarterly* 30 [1960], p. 116). Hirsch discusses the fact that Guillaume Le Roy was the first printer to publish "a book entirely in French," and to employ woodcut illustrations. According to Hirsch, none of the activities of the Lyons printers are to be associated with "Humanism."

17. See Singerman, *Under Clouds of Poesy*, pp. 211–16. From chapter 30 on, the *Eneydes* represents a close paraphrase of the *Histoire*. See also Eberhard Leube, *Fortuna in Karthago: Die Aeneas-Dido-Mythe Vergils in den romanischen Literaturen vom 14. bis zum 16. Jahrhundert* (Heidelberg, 1969), pp. 65–76.

18. For a biographical treatment of Caxton's life and work, see George D. Painter, *William Caxton: A Biography* (New York, 1977), and Frieda Elaine Penninger, *William Caxton* (Boston, 1979).

19. Natalie Zemon Davis, "Printing and the People," *Society and Culture in Early Modern France* (Palo Alto, Calif., 1965; rpt. London, 1987), p. 192.

20. For a general discussion of Caxton's "utilitarian theory of literature," see R. F. Yeager, "Literary Theory at the Close of the Middle Ages: William Caxton and William Thynne," *Studies in the Age of Chaucer* 6 (1984), pp. 135–64; and Russell Rutler, "William Caxton and Literary Patronage," *Studies in Philology* 84 (1987), pp. 440–70. On Caxton's interest, which he shared with Lydgate, of "using the past as a guide to the present," see N. F. Blake, "John Lydgate and William Caxton," *Leeds Studies in English* 16 (1985), pp. 272–89.

21. For a discussion of the woodcuts in the 1483 *Eneydes*, see Ruth Mortimer, "Vergil in the Rosenwald Collection," in *The Early Illustrated Book: Essays in Honor of Lessing J. Rosenwald*, ed. Sandra Hindman (Washington, D.C., 1982), pp. 211–30.

22. Michael Camille, "Reading the Printed Image: Illuminations and Woodcuts of the *Pèlerinage de la vie humaine* in the Fifteenth Century," in *Printing the Written Word: The Social History of Books, circa 1450–1520*, ed. Sandra L. Hindman (Ithaca, N.Y., 1991), pp. 259–91; here, p. 283.

23. For an excellent discussion of the purpose of repetition in printed books, see Camille, ibid., pp. 268–69; in a discussion of the reuse of the same image in the *Pèlerinage*, Camille notes that it works to "signal continuity in sameness" (p. 269).

24. For a discussion of Caxton and his cultural context, see N. F. Blake, *William Caxton and English Literary Culture* (London, 1991).

25. Some of the issues implicit in the discussion of audience, dialect, and class in Caxton's prologue are parallel to Natalie Zemon Davis's survey of printing in the lives of French peasants in the fifteenth and sixteenth centuries: "And yet there were a few ways that printing did enter rural life in the sixteenth century to offer some new options to the peasants. The important social institution for this was the *veillée*, an evening gathering within the village community held especially during the winter months. . . . If one of the men were literate and owned books, he might read aloud. In principle, printing increased significantly the range of books available for the *veillée*. . . . Did such reading aloud change things much in the village? *Reading* aloud? We might better say 'translating,' since the reader was inevitably turning the French of his printed text into a dialect his listeners could understand. And we might well add 'editing' ("Printing and the People," pp. 201–2). See also Camille, "Reading the Printed Image." On Caxton's choice to publish in English, see Norman Blake, "William Caxton," in *Middle English Prose: A Critical Guide to Major Authors and Genres*, ed. A. S. G. Edwards (New Brunswick, N.J., 1984), pp. 389–412.

26. For a discussion of the relationship between the two texts, see Singerman, *Under Clouds of Poesy*, p. 198–216.

27. For a text of the *Polychronicon*, see Churchill Babington, ed., *Polychronicon Ranulphi Higden, Monachi Cestrensis: Together with the English Translations of John Trevisa and of an Unknown Writer of the Fifteenth Century* (London, 1865).

28. H. Oskar Sommer, *The Recuyell of the Historyes of Troye* (London, 1894).

29. See Caxton, *Ovyde: His Booke of Methamorphose Books I-XV*, ed. Stephen Gaselee. (Oxford, 1924), pp. 138–40.

30. For texts of Caxton's prologues and epilogues, see N. F. Blake, *Caxton's Own Prose* (London, 1973); see also W. J. B. Crotch, *The Prologues and Epilogues of William Caxton*, EETS, o.s. 176 (London, 1956). I have used Blake's edition for the material cited.

31. For instance, in the epilogue to *The Dictes or Sayinges of the Philosophers* (1477), Caxton expresses his surprise that the Earl of Rivers had omitted the misogynist comments of Socrates from his English edition. Having noticed this omission in "overseeing" the translation and comparing it to the French original, Caxton considers the possible reasons the Earl of Rivers might have had for such deletions and takes it upon himself to provide his own translation of the missing segments, thereby assuring that "Socrates' " antifeminist comments on women are available to English readers. A similar impulse is evident in

Caxton's addition to Chaucer's *Book of Fame* (1483). In response to the fragmentary shape of Chaucer's text, Caxton composed a verse ending of twelve lines to close off the narrative of the dream vision; he comments in the epilogue that he found it incomplete ("I fynde no more of this werke tofore-sayde" [p. 103]). Likewise, in the second edition of the *Canterbury Tales*, he describes how it came to his attention that his first edition might be considered faulty if compared to the manuscript version owned by the father of one of his clients. Caxton notes that he acquired "the said book . . . by whiche I have corrected my book" (p. 62). The same editorial sensibility is evident in the prologue to the *Polychronicon* (1482), where Caxton comments that the text is "now at this tyme symply empyrynted and sette in forme by me, William Caxton, and a lytel embelysshed fro th'olde makyng. And also have added suche storyes as I coude fynde" (p. 131). See Lotte Hellinga, "Manuscripts in the Hands of Printers," in *Manuscripts in the Fifty Years after the Invention of Printing*, ed. J. B. Trapp (London, 1983), pp. 3–11.

32. For a comparison of the *Eneydos* and the *Eneydes* to Boccaccio's text, see Singerman, *Under Clouds of Poesy*, pp. 231–33.

33. For a theoretical discussion of the relationship between the violence of death and the violence of representation, see Elisabeth Bronfen, "Violence of Representation—Representation of Violence," *Literature, Interpretation, Theory* 1 (1989), pp. 303–21.

34. On the history of printing, see Lucien Febvre and Henri-Jean Martin, *The Coming of the Book: The Impact of Printing 1450–1800* (London, 1976); Elizabeth Eisenstein, *The Printing Press as Agent of Change: Communications and Cultural Transformations in Early Modern Europe*, 2 vols. (Cambridge, 1979). On the relationship between books and manuscripts in the fifteenth century, see Curt F. Bühler, *The Fifteenth-Century Book: The Scribes, the Printers, the Decorators* (Philadelphia, 1960); M. D. Reeve, "Manuscripts Copied from Printed Books," in Trapp, ed., *Manuscripts*, pp. 12–20. Sandra Hindman's Introduction to *Printing the Written Word* provides an excellent overview of the theoretical issues that arise from the study of manuscripts and printed texts in the fifteenth and sixteenth centuries. See also N. F. Blake, "Manuscript to Print," in *William Caxton and English Literary Culture*, pp. 275–304.

35. See Lotte Hellinga, "Importation of Books Printed on the Continent into England and Scotland before c. 1520," in *Printing the Written Word*, pp. 205–24. See also R. J. Lyall, "Books and Book Owners in Fifteenth-Century Scotland," in *Book Production and Publishing in Britain 1375–1475*, ed. Jeremy Griffiths and Derek Pearsall (Cambridge, 1989), pp. 239–56.

36. See Bawcutt, *Gavin Douglas*, pp. 98–102.

37. As Bawcutt notes, "Nevertheless a keen desire for books existed among many Scots at this time. . . . It was satisfied partly by the traditional method of copying books by hand, partly by importing printed books from the main northern European centres . . . Vernacular poems still circulated chiefly in manuscript . . . and Douglas clearly envisaged that the *Eneados* would be copied by 'writaris' rather than printed" (ibid., p. 25).

38. As Bawcutt notes, five complete manuscripts survive, as well as a sixth fragmentary one (ibid., p. 192).

39. See Eleanor Winsor Leach, "Illustration as Interpretation in Brant's and Dryden's Editions of Vergil," in Hindman, ed., *The Early Illustrated Book*, p. 176. See also Theodore K. Rabb, "Sebastian Brant and the First Illustrated Edition of Vergil," *The Princeton University Library Chronicle* 21 (1960), pp. 187–99.

40. See the discussion in Bawcutt, *Gavin Douglas*, pp. 31–36.

41. Ibid., p. 108.

42. Fradenburg, *City*, p. 185.

43. For the text of Ascensius, I consulted the Badius 1501 text.

44. The *Palice* was produced the same year as the Badius 1501 text; my sense that the

Palice depends on a reading of Virgil in the context of Ascensius assumes that Douglas either had access to earlier editions that included Ascensius or that he acquired the Badius edition just as he was composing the *Palice*.

45. John M. Fyler, "Man, Men, and Women in Chaucer's Poetry," in *The Olde Daunce: Love, Friendship, Sex and Marriage in the Medieval World*, ed. Robert Edwards and Stephen Spector (Albany, N.Y., 1991), pp. 154–76.

46. On the prologues, see A. E. C. Canitz, "The Prologue to the *Eneados*: Gavin Douglas's Directions for Reading," *Studies in Scottish Literature* 25 (1990), pp. 1–22; Ian S. Ross, "'Prolong' and 'Buke' in the *Eneados* of Gavin Douglas," *Scottish Studies* 4 (1984), pp. 393–407; Lois Ebin, "The Role of the Narrator in the Prologues to Gavin Douglas's *Eneados*," *Chaucer Review* 14 (1980), pp. 353–65.

47. For the Servius commentary, see chapter 2; Ascensius does not draw particular attention to this detail.

48. For an outline of the medieval tradition of Virgil's being hoisted up in a basket, see Domenico Comparetti, *Vergil in the Middle Ages*, trans. E. F. M. Benecke (London, 1895; rpt. 1966), pp. 325–39.

49. See Bawcutt, *Gavin Douglas*, p. 107.

50. For a discussion of this preamble that articulates Douglas's potential sympathy for Dido, see Singerman's discussion of the prologue to the fourth book (*Under Clouds of Poesy*, pp. 255–68).

51. For a discussion of the stylistic implications of Douglas's translation practices, see Florence Ridley, "The Distinctive Character of Douglas's *Eneados*," *Studies in Scottish Literature* 18 (1983), pp. 110–22. A. E. C. Canitz, in his discussion of Douglas's choices as a translator, notes that Douglas creates a more hysterical Dido; see Canitz, "From *Aeneid* to *Eneados*: Theory and Practice of Gavin Douglas's Translation," *Medievalia et Humanistica* 17 [1991], pp. 81–99).

52. See Bawcutt, *Gavin Douglas*, p. 115.

53. Kallendorf, *In Praise of Aeneas*, p. 9.

54. Ibid., p. 148.

55. Singerman, *Under Clouds of Poesy*, p. 239.

56. Likewise, at 1.6.69, Douglas translates "miserae" (1.344) as "silly Dido."

6. Christine de Pizan's Feminist Self-Fashioning and the Invention of Dido

1. See Sister Mary Louis Towner, *Lavision-Christine* (Washington, D.C., 1932), p. 181. On Christine's change of gender, see Nadia Margolis, "Christine de Pizan: The Poetess as Historian," *Journal of the History of Ideas* (1986), pp. 361–75; Jacqueline Cerquiglini, "L'étrangère," *Revue des Langues Romanes* 92 (1988), pp. 239–51. All quotations from the *Mutacion* are taken from Suzanne Solente, *Le Livre de la Mutacion de Fortune*, 4 vols. (Paris, l959); quotations from the *Cité des dames* come from Maureen Cheney Curnow, *The Livre de La Cité des Dames of Christine de Pisan: A Critical Edition* (Diss., Vanderbilt, 1975). Translations from the *Cité des dames* are taken from Earl Jeffrey Richards, trans., Christine de Pizan, *The Book of the City of Ladies* (London, 1983); all other translations are my own.

2. Christine de Pizan has been the subject of several biographies. See Charity Cannon Willard, *Christine de Pizan: Her Life and Works* (New York, 1984); Enid McLeod, *The Order of the Rose: The Life and Ideas of Christine de Pizan* (London, 1976); Régine Pernoud, *Christine de Pisan* (Paris, 1982). See also Marie-Josèphe Pinet, *Christine de Pisan 1364–1430: Étude biographique et littéraire* (Paris, 1927).

3. Stephen Greenblatt, *Renaissance Self-Fashioning: From More to Shakespeare* (Chicago, 1980), p. 9.

4. Greenblatt opens his discussion of self-fashioning with the observation that "there may well have been less *autonomy* in self-fashioning in the sixteenth century than before" (ibid., p. 1). My purpose in this discussion of Christine's self-fashioning is to explore the relations between gender and authorial self-fashioning. This focus on the early fifteenth century also implicitly engages some of the issues about the historically contingent aspect of Greenblatt's model.

5. See Karen Sullivan, "At the Limit of Feminist Theory: An Architectonics of the Querelle de la Rose," *Exemplaria: A Journal of Theory in Medieval and Renaissance Studies* 3 (1990), pp. 435–66; Susan Schibanoff, "Taking the Gold out of Egypt: The Art of Reading as a Woman," in *Gender and Reading: Essays on Readers, Texts, and Contexts,* ed. Elizabeth A. Flynn and Patrocinio P. Schweickart (Baltimore, Md., 1986), pp. 83–106.

6. Kevin Brownlee, "Discourses of the Self: Christine de Pizan and the *Rose,*" *Romanic Review* 79 (1988), p. 200.

7. For a general critique of the tendency of feminist literary history to focus on women novelists, especially of the nineteenth and twentieth centuries, see Janet Todd, *Feminist Literary History* (New York, 1988). On the construction of literary history and the status of early women writers, see Susan Schibanoff, "Early Women Writers: In-scribing, or Reading the Fine Print," *Women's Studies International Forum* 6 (1983), pp. 475–89.

8. Christine's early lyric poems represent her apprenticeship as a court poet in the 1390s. This apprenticeship was followed by several works in both verse and prose, which she developed in response to Jean de Meun's *Roman de la Rose.* By the start of the next decade, her work shows a shift in focus and form. The *Livre du chemin de long estude* (1403) and the *Livre de La Mutacion de Fortune* (1403) illustrate her production of poetic narratives, especially in an allegorical framework. But this decade particularly saw the presentation of her prose texts, such as the *Livre de la Cité des dames* (1405) and the *Livre des Trois vertus* (1405), along with her biography of Charles V (1404) and her autobiographical *Avision* (1405). Finally, the end of her career as a professional writer is remarkable for her prose treatises on a variety of topics, particularly the *Livre des fais d'armes et de chevalerie* (1410) on warfare, and the *Livre de la paix* (1412–14). A brief description of the corpus of Christine de Pizan can be found in Richards, trans., *The Book of the City of Ladies,* pp. xxii–xxci. For a full bibliography of manuscripts and modern editions, see Edith Yenal, *Christine de Pizan: A Bibliography,* 2d ed. (Metuchen, N.J., 1988).

9. The most outspoken critic of Christine's "feminism" is Sheila Delany, " 'Mothers to Think Back Through': Who are They? The Ambiguous Example of Christine de Pizan," in *Medieval Texts and Contemporary Readers,* ed. Laurie A. Finke and Martin B. Schichtman (Ithaca, N.Y., 1987), pp. 177–97, and "History, Politics, and Christine Studies: A Polemical Reply," in *Politics, Gender and Genre: The Political Thought of Christine de Pizan,* ed. Margaret Brabant (Boulder, Colo., 1992), pp. 193–206. See also Joël Blanchard, "Compilation et légitimation au XVᵉ siècle," *Poétique* 74 (1988), pp. 139–57; Beatrice Gottlieb, "The Problem of Feminism in the Fifteenth Century," in *Women of the Medieval World: Essays in Honor of John H. Mundy,* ed. Julius Kirshner (New York, 1985), pp. 337–64; Sylvia Huot, "Seduction and Sublimation: Christine de Pizan, Jean de Meun, and Dante," *Romance Notes* 25 (1985), pp. 361–73. See also F. Douglas Kelly, "Reflections on the Role of Christine de Pisan As a Feminist Writer," *Substance* 2 (1972), pp. 63–71; Susan Groag Bell, "Christine de Pizan (1364–1430): Humanism and the Problem of a Studious Woman," *Feminist Studies* 3 (1976), pp. 173–84; Charity Cannon Willard, "The Manuscript Tradition of the *Livre des Trois Vertus* and Christine de Pizan's Audience," *Journal of the History of Ideas* 27 (1966), pp. 433–44.

10. See Sullivan, "At the Limit of Feminist Theory." See also the discussion by Earl

Jeffrey Richards, "Christine de Pizan, the Conventions of Courtly Diction, and Italian Humanism," in *Reinterpreting Christine de Pizan*, ed. Earl Jeffrey Richards et al. (Athens, Ga., 1992), pp. 250–71; Richards, "Sexual Metamorphosis, Gender Difference and the Republic of Letters, or Androgyny as a Feminist Plea for Universalism in Christine de Pizan and Virginia Woolf," *Romance Languages Annual* 2 (1991), pp. 146–52; Richards, "Christine de Pizan and the Question of Feminist Rhetoric," *Teaching Language Through Literature* 22 (1983), pp. 15–24; Sandra L. Hindman, *Christine de Pizan's "Epistre Othéa": Painting and Politics at the Court of Charles VI* (Toronto: 1986), pp. xiii-xxii; Christine Reno, "Feminist Aspects of Christine de Pizan's *Epistre d'Othea a Hector*," *Studi Francesi*, 24 (1980), pp. 271–76. The topic of Christine's "feminism" has a long history; see Lulu McDowell Richardson, *Forerunners of Feminism in French Literature of the Renaissance: From Christine de Pisan to Marie de Gournay* (Baltimore, Md., 1929); Rose Rigard, *Les Idées féministes de Christine de Pisan* (Neuchâtel, 1911).

11. See the discussion in Maureen Quilligan, *The Allegory of Female Authority: Christine de Pizan's Cité des Dames* (Ithaca, N.Y., 1991), pp. 1–10; see also Renate Blumenfeld-Kosinski, "Christine de Pizan and the Misogynist Tradition," *Romanic Review* 81 (1990), pp. 279–92.

12. For examples of Christine's authorial portraits, see Quilligan, *Allegory*.

13. Christine's comments about her own education as a child specifically note that she was an exception: her mother—in conformity with the general practices of her time—opposed Christine's education, but her father encouraged her learning. See *The Book of the City of Ladies* (Richards, trans.), pp. 154–55. Although Christine managed to acquire some learning contrary to the customs of the day, she comments that this was a sort of pilfered acquisition, and that as a daughter she could not inherit her father's wealth of learning as a son would have. See the *Mutacion*, (379–468).

14. On Christine's relationship to late medieval humanism, see Richards, "Christine de Pizan, the Conventions of Courtly Diction." For a description of the textual materiality of late medieval humanism, see Millard Meiss, *French Painting in the Time of Jean de Berry. The Limbourgs and their Contemporaries*, 2 vols. (London, 1974), and "Humanisme et traduction au Moyen Age," *Journal des Savants* (1963), pp. 161–90.

15. For a discussion of medieval theories of gender, see Kathleen Biddick, "Genders, Bodies, Borders: Technologies of the Visible," *Speculum* 68 (1993), pp. 389–418; Caroline Walker Bynum, *Holy Feast and Holy Fast: The Religious Significance of Food to Medieval Women* (Berkeley, Calif., 1987), p. 257; Bynum, "The Complexity of Symbols, in *Gender and Religion: On the Complexity of Symbols*, ed. Caroline Walker Bynum, Steven Harrell, and Paula Richman (Boston, 1986), pp. 1–20. For a discussion of medical theories of gender in medieval culture, see Danielle Jacquart and Claude Thomasset, *Sexuality and Medicine in the Middle Ages*, trans. Matthew Adamson, (Princeton, N.J., 1988), pp. 7–47.

16. See A. C. Spearing, *Medieval Dream Poetry* (Cambridge, 1976).

17. See Glenda McLeod, "Poetics and Antimisogynist Polemics in Christine de Pizan's *Le Livre de la Cité des Dames*," in *Reinterpreting Christine*, pp. 37–47.

18. For a discussion of Christine's interpretive negotiations of classical texts, see Judith L. Kellogg, "Christine de Pizan as Chivalric Mythographer: *L'Epistre Othea*," in *The Mythographic Art: Classical Fable and the Rise of the Vernacular in Early France and England*, ed. Jane Chance (Gainsville, Fla., 1990), pp. 100–124. Dido does not appear in the *Othea*. For the social context of the *Othea*, see Hindman, *Christine de Pizan's "Epistre Othéa."*

19. James J. Murphy, *Rhetoric in the Middle Ages: A History of Rhetorical Theory from St. Augustine to the Renaissance* (Berkeley, Calif., 1974), pp. 135–93. Nicholas Orme notes the pervasive presences of the treaties by Alexander de Villedieu and Evrard Bethune in the late Middle Ages; see *English Schools in the Middle Ages* (London, 1973), pp. 89–90.

20. "Ironia est tropus per contrarium quod conatur ostendens . . . antiphrasis est unius verbi ironia, ut [bellum lucus et parcae] bellum, hoc est minime bellum, et lucus eo quod non luceat, et Parcae eo quod nulli parcant" (Donatus, *Ars Grammatica* iii 6, in Henry Keil, ed., *Grammatici latini*, vol. 4 [Leipzig, 1864], pp. 401–2) ("Irony is a trope that attempts to signify through opposition . . . antiphrasis is irony of a single word, for example, *bellum*, *lucus*, and *Parcae*; war is not at all pleasant [*bellum*] adj., and a grove, because it does not shine [*lucere*]; and the Parcae, because they spare none"; my translation).

21. See the description of "antiphrasis" in the *Etymologia* 1.63 "Antiphrasis est sermo e contrario intelligendus, ut *lucus*, quia caret luce per nimiam nemorum umbram. . . . Inter ironiam autem, et antiphrasim hoc distat, quod ironia pronuntiatione sola indicat quod intelligi vult, sicut cum dicimus homini agenti male: *Bonum est quod facis*. Antiphrasis vero non voce pronuntiantis significat contrarium, sed suis tantum verbis, quorum origo contraria est" (*PL* 82. 115–16) ("Antiphrasis is discourse to be understood from its opposite, as for example *lucus* [grove] because it is devoid of light by reason of the excessive shade of woods. But this separates antiphrasis from irony—that irony signifies what it wishes to be understood through delivery alone, as when we say to someone acting badly 'what you do is good.' Antiphrasis signifies the opposite not indeed by the tone of delivery but only by its words, the origin [derivation] of which is its opposite"; my translation). For a discussion of Christine's use of this text in the composition of the *Mutacion*, see Solente, *Le Livre de la Mutacion de Fortune*, pp. l–lxiii. In medieval rhetorical and allegorial texts, it became almost a commonplace to speak *per antiphrasim*; see, for instance, Augustine, *De doctrina Christiana* III.29.40. Quilligan notes that Alain de Lille uses the phrase ("Allegory and the Textual Body: Female Authority in Christine de Pizan's *Livre de la Cité des Dames*," in *The New Medievalism*, ed. Marina S. Brownlee, Kevin Brownlee, and Stephen G. Nichols [Baltimore, Md., 1991], p. 295 n. 17. See also Schibanoff, "Taking the Gold."

22. Richards, *The Book of the City of Ladies*, p. xlii.

23. See Quilligan, *Allegory*, pp. 18–31; Yvonne Batard, "Dante et Christine de Pisan (1364–1430)," in *Missions et démarches de La critique: Mélanges offerts au Professeur J. A. Vier* (Paris, 1973), pp. 345–51. On Christine's reception of Dante, see Earl Jeffrey Richards, "Christine de Pizan and Dante: A Reexamination," *Archiv für das Studium der Neueren Sprachen und Literaturen* 222 (1985), 100–111.

24. See Pinet, *Christine de Pizan*, pp. 377–408.

25. See the discussion in Curnow, *The* Livre de La Cité des Dames *of Christine de Pisan*, p. 1037.

26. For a discussion of the library of Charles V, see Geneva Drinkwater, "French Libraries in the Fourteenth and Fifteenth Centuries," *The Medieval Library*, ed. James Westfall Thompson (Chicago, 1939), pp. 414–52. See also Muriel J. Hughes, "The Library of Philip the Bold and Margaret of Flanders, First Valois Duke and Duchess of Burgundy," *Journal of Medieval History* 4 (1978), pp. 145–88; F. Avril, "Trois Manuscrits napolitains des collections de Charles V et de Jean de Berry," *Bibliothèque de L'École des Chartes* 27 (1969), pp. 291–328.

27. For a discussion of the manuscript traditions and patrons of the *Cité de Dieu*, see Alexandre de Laborde, *Les manuscrits à peinture de la "Cité de Dieu" de Saint Augustin* (Paris, 1909). See also Meiss, *French Painting*, and Sharon Dunlap Smith, "New Themes for the *City of God* Around 1400," *Scriptorium* 36 (1982), pp. 68–82.

28. For an excerpt from the Prologue to Raoul de Presles's translation of the *Cité de dieu*, see de Laborde, *Les manuscrits à peinture*, p. 65.

29. See the discussion of Augustine in chapter 2.

30. For a discussion of the *Mutacion de Fortune*, see Kevin Brownlee, "The Image of History in Christine de Pizan's *Livre de la Mutacion de Fortune*," *Yale French Studies:*

Contexts: Style and Values in Medieval Art and Literature (New Haven, Conn., 1991), pp. 44–56. On Christine as historian, see Margolis, "Christine de Pizan."

31. See Solente, *Le Livre de la Mutacion de Fortune*, vol. 3, p. 282, for the citations from the *Histoire ancienne jusqu'à César*. See also Eberhard Leube, *Fortuna in Karthago: Die Aeneas-Dido-Mythe Vergils in den romanischen Literaturen vom 14. bis zum 16. Jahrhundert* (Heidelberg, 1969), pp. 54–65.

32. See, for instance, London, BL Royal 16 G vii, fol. 180b; London, BL Royal 20 D i, fol. 304b.

33. Boccaccio comments specifically on the relationship between Dido's anger at Aeneas and the Carthaginian wars in book 14 of the *Genealogia*. See Charles G. Osgood, *Boccaccio on Poetry* (New York, 1930), p. 69.

34. See A. Bossuat, "Les Origines Troyennes: Leur rôle dans la littérature historique au XVᵉ siècle," *Annales de Normandie* 8 (1958), pp. 187–97; P. S. Lewis, "War Propaganda and Historiography in Fifteenth-Century France and England," *Transactions of the Royal Historical Society* 15 (1965), pp. 193–213; Collette Beaune, "L'utilisation politique du mythe des origines troyennes en France à la fin du Moyen Âge," in *Lectures médiévales de Virgile: Actes du colloque organisé par l'École française de Rome* (Rome, 1985), pp. 333–55.

35. For a brief introductory commentary on the Hundred Years War, see Kenneth Fowler, "Introduction: War and Change in Late Medieval France and England," in the *Hundred Years War*, ed. Kenneth Fowler (London, 1971), pp. 1–27. Standard historical accounts include Edouard Perroy, *The Hundred Years War*, trans. David C. Douglas (London, 1951); Christopher Allmand, *The Hundred Years War: England and France at War c. 1300-c. 1450* (Cambridge, 1988); Philip Contamine, *La Guerre de cent ans* (Paris, 1968).

36. See Allmand, *The Hundred Years War*, pp. 78–79. See also John Barnie, *War in Medieval Society: Social Values and the Hundred Years War 1337–99* (Ithaca, N.Y., 1974), pp. 28–29; Perroy, *The Hundred Years War*, p. 163. In her biography of Charles V, Christine praises the wisdom and artistry of his building campaign and specifically notes that he had walls built around Paris. See Suzanne Solente, ed., *Le Livre des fais et bonnes meurs du sage Roy Charles V*, vol. 2 (Paris, 1936–40), p. 39.

37. Christine's texts on warfare include *Le Livre des fais d'armes et de chevalerie* (1410); *Le Livre de la paix* (1412–14); *L'Epistre de la prison de vie humaine* (1418); and *Le Ditié de Jehanne d'Arc* (1429). See Charity C. Willard, "Christine de Pizan's Treatise on the Art of Medieval Warfare," in *Essays in Honor of Louis Francis Solano*, ed. Raymond S. Cormier and Urban T. Holmes (Chapel Hill, N.C., 1970), pp. 179–91.

38. Allmand, *The Hundred Years War*, p. 10.

39. On the Salic law, see Perroy, *The Hundred Years War*, p. 71; Contamine, *La Guerre de cent ans*, p. 11; M. Paul Viollet, "Comment les femmes on été exclues, en France, de la succession à la couronne," *Mémoires de l'institut National de France. Académie des inscriptions et belles-lettres* 34 (1893), pp. 125–78.

40. John Milton Potter, "The Development and Significance of the Salic Law of the French," *Speculum* 28 (1937), pp. 235–53.

41. See Christopher Allmand, "The War and the Non-Combatant," in Fowler, ed., *The Hundred Years War*, pp. 163–83. Allmand's discussion, however, makes no specific allusion to women, and no comment at all on their particular vulnerability. See also Robert Boutruche, "The Devastation of Rural Areas during the Hundred Years War and the Agricultural Recovery of France," in *The Recovery of France in the Fifteenth Century*, ed. P. S. Lewis, trans. G. F. Martin (London, 1971), pp. 23–59.

42. Froissart's account of sieges frequently includes the rape of women. See also Maurice Keen, *The Laws of War in the Late Middle Ages* (London, 1965). Keen comments: "In a city taken by storm almost any license was condoned by the law. . . . Women could be raped, and men killed out of hand. . . . If lives were spared, it was only through the clemency of the vic-

torious captain; and spoliation was systematic. The prospect of this free run of his lusts for blood, spoil and women was a major incentive to a soldier to persevere in the rigors which were likely to attend a protracted siege" (pp. 121–22).

43. Ibid., p. 243. See Christine's comments in *The Book Fayttes of Armes and of Chyvalrye*, ed. A. T. P. Byles, EETS, o.s. 189 (London, 1932), p. 233.

44. For instance, see the comment concerning the "Sicambrians" who attended their husbands on a siege of Rome, but when their husbands began to lose the battle, "they [the women] knew well that, following martial custom ("selonc l'usaige de guerre"), they would be raped" (*The Book of the City of Ladies*, p. 163).

45. Hindman, *Christine de Pizan's "Epistre d'Othéa,"* p. 81. On Christine as a publisher, see J. C. Laidlaw, "Christine de Pizan: A Publisher's Progress," *Modern Language Review* 82 (1987), pp. 35–75.

46. Sandra L. Hindman, "With Ink and Mortar: Christine de Pizan's *Cité des Dames* (An Art Essay)," *Feminist Studies* 10 (1984), p. 469. My comments on the manuscript context of the *Cité des dames* follow Hindman's discussion fairly closely, though I wish to suggest a slight revision of Hindman's analysis, particularly on the relationship between the *Cité des dames* and Augustine's *Cité de Dieu*.

47. Ibid., p. 465.

48. Ibid., p. 465. See also Blanchard, "Compilation et Légitimation."

49. See Meiss, *French Painting*, p. 377.

50. Both copies of the *Cité de Dieu* illuminated in the *Cité des dames* workshop are roughly contemporary with the illumination of the *Cité des dames*; Meiss dates the first manuscript (Paris Bib. Nat. fr. 174) to 1403–5, the second (Paris Bib. Nat. fr. 23–24), to 1404–7—exactly the same period during which the workshop would have been employed in illuminating the first copies of the *Cité des dames*. I have provided a reproduction of the celestial city from the later manuscript of the *Cité de Dieu* (Bib. Nat. fr. 23–24), since the earlier manuscript (Bib. Nat. fr. 174), according to de Laborde, has not survived in a complete copy (*Les manuscrits à peinture*, p. 260). De Laborde's study of the "families" of manuscript illuminations (see table, pp. 174–76) shows that both these manuscripts belonged to the same family—the existing illuminations in Bib. Nat. fr. 174 correspond to Bib. Nat. fr. 23–24 in the case of all but one miniature, a predictable correspondence given that these two manuscripts were produced by the same workshop. Thus, though I cannot provide an example of the "celestial city" from the clearly anterior manuscript, the representation from the contemporary manuscript provides enough evidence to suggest the intertextuality that appears to be at work in Christine's choice of illuminations for the *Cité des dames*. The representation of the celestial city is a standard feature of Family II—occurring in all but one of the manuscripts that survive in complete form. See de Laborde, pp. 194–95.

51. For both Latin and French texts, see A. G. van Hamel, *Les Lamentations de Mathéolus et Le livre de Leesce de Jehan Le Fèvre des Ressons* (Paris, 1905), p. 87. For a discussion of the relationship between the French and Latin texts, see pp. liv-cvii.

52. On the texts of the *Histoire ancienne jusqu'à César*, see chapter 3. On the *Mutacion*, see note 31.

53. For Dante, see chapter 2; for Jean de Meun, chapter 1.

54. Quilligan provides a general outline of the revision of Boccaccio in the *Cité des dames* (see *Allegory*). See also Patricia A. Phillippy, "Establishing Authority: Boccaccio's *De claris mulieribus* and Christine de Pizan's *Le Livre de la Cité des Dames*," *Romanic Review* 77 (1986), pp. 167–94; Curnow, *The* Livre de la Cité des Dames *of Christine de Pisan*, pp. 138–67; Liliane Dulac, "Un mythe didactique chez Christine de Pizan: Sémiramis ou la veuve héroïque," in *Mélanges de philologie romane offerts à Charles Camproux I* (Montpellier, 1978), pp. 315–43; A. Jeanroy, "Boccace et Christine de Pisan: Le *De Claris*

Mulieribus, Principale source du *Livre de la Cité des dames*," *Romania* 48 (1922), pp. 93–105.

55. See "Le debat de deux amans" (1481–92), "Lay de dame," in "Cent balades d'Amant et de Dame" (85–95), and "L'epistre au dieu d'amours" (445–60). Maurice Roy, *Œuvres poétiques de Christine de Pisan* (Paris, 1896; rpt. 1965). "L'epistre au dieu d'amours" was translated by Hoccleve as the *Letter of Cupid*; in the process, Hoccleve transformed it into an antifeminist text; see Diane Bornstein, "Anti-Feminism in Thomas Hoccleve's Translation of Christine de Pizan's *Epistre au Dieu d'Amours*," *English Language Notes* 19 (1991), pp. 7–14.

56. For the general relationship between the *Cité des dames* and *Des cleres femmes*, see the discussion by Curnow, *The* Livre de la Cité des Dames *of Christine de Pisan*, pp. 138–67. For the text of *Des cleres femmes*, I have used London, BL Royal MS. 20 C v, entitled *Des cleres et nobles femmes*, a lavishly executed manuscript. The "hystoire de Dido" appears on fol. 65r-71r. All quotes from this text are taken from Royal 20 C v. The French translation of the Dido story in *Des cleres femmes* follows Boccaccio's Latin in outline, though a few of the episodes are slightly amplified. Overall, the moral and thematic emphasis remains the same. Another French version of *De claris mulieribus*, sometimes mistakenly confused with this translation, appears in early printed books, such as the 1493 edition by Antoine Vérard. See chapter 1, note 118. See also Henri Hauvette, "Les Plus Anciennes Traductions Françaises de Boccace," *Bulletin Italien* 9 (1909), pp. 193–96.

57. For a full analysis of the concept of chastity within the *Cité des dames*, see Christine Reno, "Virginity as an Ideal in Christine de Pizan's *Cité des dames*," in Diane Bornstein, *Ideals for Women in the Works of Christine de Pizan* (Detroit, Mich., 1981), pp. 69–90.

58. The most significant recent discussion of chastity for medieval women is found in Bynum, *Holy Feast and Holy Fast*. See also Jo Ann McNamara, "Sexual Equality and the Cult of Virginity in Early Christian Thought," *Feminist Studies* 3 (1976), pp. 145–58.

59. The only pictorial of Dido that exists in all of Christine's manuscripts, as far as I have been able to determine, is an unfinished image of Dido looking out at Aeneas's departing ship in the Flemish translation of the *Cité des dames*, *De Stede Der Vrouwen* (1475), BL Add. 20,698; this image results from the tendency in late fifteenth-century versions of the *Cité des dames* toward a proliferation of images in contrast to the three images Christine herself intended (see Curnow, *The* Livre de la Cité des Dames *of Christine de Pisan*, p. 576).

60. See Eric Hicks, *Le Débat sur le Roman de la Rose: Édition critique, introduction, traductions, notes* (Paris, 1977), p. 168.

Epilogue

1. See Michel Foucault, *Discipline and Punish: The Birth of the Prison* (New York, 1977), pp. 195–228.

2. Gertrude Atherton, *Dido, Queen of Hearts* (New York, 1929).

3. Hélène Cixous and Catherine Clément, *The Newly Born Woman* (Minneapolis, 1986), p. 97.

Select Bibliography

❖

Manuscripts

Des cleres femmes. British Library, London Royal 20 C v.

L'Histoire ancienne jusqu'à César. British Library, London Royal 16 G vii.

———. Morgan Library, New York, M 212–3.

Primary Sources

Augustine. *Confessions,* PL 32.659–868.

———. *De civitate Dei,* PL 41.13–804.

Benoît de Sainte-Maure. *Le Roman de Troie,* ed. Léopold Constans. Paris, 1948.

Boccaccio, Giovanni. *De casibus virorum illustrium,* ed. Pier Giorgio Ricci and Vittorio Zaccaria, in *Tutte le Opere di Giovanni Boccaccio,* 9. Milan, 1983.

———. *De mulieribus claris,* ed. Vittorio Zaccaria, in *Tutte le Opere di Giovanni Boccaccio,* 10. Milan, 1967.

———. *Il Comento di Giovanni Boccacci Sopra La Commedia.* Florence, 1863.

———. *Genealogie Deorum gentilium libri,* ed. Vincenzo Romano. Bari, 1951.

Caxton, William. *Caxton's Own Prose,* ed. N. F. Blake. London, 1973.

———. *Eneydos,* ed. M. T. Culley and F. J. Furnivall. EETS ex. ser. 57. Oxford, 1962.

Chaucer. *The Riverside Chaucer,* ed. Larry Benson. Boston, 1987.

Chrétien de Troyes. *Erec et Enide,* ed. Mario Roques. Paris, 1968.

Dante Alighieri. *Il Convivio,* ed. Maria Simonelli. Bologna, 1966.

———. *Divine Comedy,* ed. Petrocchi, trans. Charles Singleton. Princeton, N.J., 1973.

———. *De monarchia,* ed. Federico Sanguineti. Milan, 1985.

Douglas, Gavin. *Shorter Poems of Gavin Douglas*, ed. Priscilla J. Bawcutt. Edinburgh, 1967.

———. *Virgil's Aeneid Translated into Scottish Verse by Gavin Douglas*, 4 vols., ed. David F. C. Coldwell. Edinburgh, 1957–64.

Excidium Troiae, ed. E. Bagby Atwood and Virgil K. Whitaker. Cambridge, Mass., 1944.

Fulgentius. *Opera*, ed. Rudolf Helm. Stuttgart, 1898; rpt. 1970.

Geoffrey of Monmouth. *Historia regum Britanniae*, ed. Edmond Faral, *La légende arthurienne*, vol. 3 Paris, 1929.

Gower, John. *Confessio Amantis*, ed. G. C. Macaulay. EETS ex. ser. 82. Oxford, 1900.

Jerome. *Adversus Jovinianum. PL* 23.221–352.

Justin. *Epitoma historiarum Philippicarum Pompei Trogi*, ed. O. Seel. Leipzig, 1972.

Le Roy, Guillaume. *Le Livre des Eneydes*. Lyons, 1483.

Lydgate, John. *Fall of Princes*, ed. Henry Bergen. EETS ex. ser. 121–24.

Machaut, Guillaume de. *Le Judgement dou Roy de Navarre*, ed. Ernest Hoepffner. Paris, 1906; rpt. 1965.

Macrobius. *Saturnalia*, ed. Jacob Willis. Leipzig, 1963.

de Meun, Jean. *Le Roman de la Rose*, ed. Félix Lecoy. Paris, 1966.

Ovid. *Epistulae Heroidum*, ed. H. Dörrie. Berlin, 1971.

———. Hexter, Ralph J. *Ovid and Medieval Schooling: Studies in Medieval School Commentaries on Ovid's* Ars Amatoria, Epistulae ex Ponto, *and* Epistulae Heroidum. Munich, 1986.

———. Huygens, R. B. C., ed. *Accessus ad auctores; Bernard d'Utrecht; Conrad d'Hirsau, Dialogus super auctores*. Leiden, 1970.

———. *Metamorphoses*, ed. W. S. Anderson. Leipzig, 1982.

———. *Ovide moralisé: Poème du commencement du quatorzième siècle*, ed. C. de Boer. 5 vols. Amsterdam, 1915–38.

———. *Tristium Libri Quinque*, ed. S. G. Owen. Oxford, 1978.

Petrarch, F. *Opera*. Venice, 1501.

de Pizan, Christine. See Maureen Cheney Curnow.

———. *Le Débat sur le Roman de la Rose: Édition critique, introduction, traductions, notes*, ed. Eric Hicks. Paris, 1977.

———. *Le Livre de la Mutacion de Fortune*, ed. Suzanne Solente. Paris, 1959.

Roman d'Eneas, ed. J.-J. Salverda de Grave. 2 vols. Paris, 1983.

Salisbury, John of. *Metalogicon*, ed. J. B. Hall. Toronto, 1991.

———. *Policraticus*, ed. Clemens C. I. Webb. Oxford, 1909.

Servius. *Serviana in Aeneidem III-IV Commentarii*, ed. H. Hagen. Bildesheim, 1881–83; rpt. 1961.

Silvestris, Bernard. *The Commentary on the First Six Books of the Aeneid of Vergil Commonly Attributed to Bernardus Silvestris*, ed.

Julian Ward Jones and Elizabeth Frances Jones. Lincoln, Neb., and London, 1977.

Solimano, Gianniana. *Epistula Didonis ad Aeneam: Introduzione, Texto, traduzione et commento.* Genoa, 1988.

Timaeus. Felix Jacoby, ed. *Die Fragmente der griechischen Historiker.* 3 vols. Leiden, 1950.

Virgil. *P. Vergili Maronis Opera,* ed. A. B. Mynors. Oxford, 1969.

Wace. *Roman de Brut,* ed. Ivor Arnold. Paris, 1938.

Secondary Sources

Allen, Don Cameron. "Marlowe's *Dido* and the Tradition," in *Essays on Shakespeare and Elizabethan Drama in Honor of Hardin Craig.* Columbia, Mo., 1962, 55–68.

Austin, R. G. *P. Vergili Maronis Aeneidos Liber Quartus.* Oxford, 1955.

Bawcutt, Priscilla. *Gavin Douglas.* Edinburgh, 1975.

Bernal, Martin. *Black Athena: The Afroasiatic Roots of Classical Civilization,* vol. 1: *The Fabrication of Ancient Greece 1785–1985.* New Brunswick, N.J., 1987.

Biddick, Kathleen. "Genders, Bodies, Borders: Technologies of the Visible," *Speculum* 68 (1993), 389–418.

Boffey, Julia. "Richard Pynson's *Book of Fame* and the *Letter of Dido,*" *Viator* 19 (1988), 339–53.

Bono, Barbara. *Literary Transvaluation: From Vergilian Epic to Shakespearean Tragicomedy.* Berkeley, Calif., 1984.

Boswell, John. *Christianity, Social Tolerance, and Homosexuality: Gay People in Western Europe from the Beginning of the Christian Era to the Fourteenth Century.* Chicago, 1980.

———. "Concepts, Experience and Sexuality," *Differences* 2 (1990), 67–87.

Brown, Peter. *The Body and Society: Men, Women and Sexual Renunciation in Early Christianity.* New York, 1988.

Brownlee, Kevin. "Discourses of the Self: Christine de Pizan and the *Rose,*" *Romanic Review* 79 (1988), 44–56.

Brundage, James A. *Law, Sex, and Christian Society in Medieval Europe.* Chicago, 1987.

Bynum, Caroline Walker. *Holy Feast and Holy Fast: The Religious Significance of Food to Medieval Women.* Berkeley, Calif., 1987.

Cairns, Francis. *Virgil's Augustan Epic.* Cambridge, 1989.

Camille, Michael. "The Book of Signs: Writing and Visual Difference in Gothic Manuscript Illumination," *Word and Image* 1 (1985), 133–48.

———. *The Gothic Idol: Ideology and Image-Making in Medieval Art.* Cambridge, 1989.

———. "Reading the Printed Image: Illuminations and Woodcuts of the *Pèlerinage de la vie humaine* in the Fifteenth Century," in *Printing the Written Word: The Social History of Books, circa 1450–1520*, ed. Sandra L. Hindman. Ithaca, N.Y., 1991, 259–91.

———. "Seeing and Reading: Some Visual Implications of Medieval Literacy and Illiteracy," *Art History* 8 (1985), 26–49.

Carruthers, Mary. *The Book of Memory: A Study of Memory in Medieval Culture.* Cambridge, 1990.

———. "Italy, Ars memorativa, and Fame's House. Studies in the Age of Chaucer.* Proceedings series 2 (1987), 179–87.

Cerbo, Anna. "Didone in Boccaccio," *Annali Istituto Universitario Orientale, Napoli, Sezione Romanza* 21 (1979), 177–219.

Clanchy, M. T. *From Memory to Written Record: England 1066–1307.* Oxford, 1993.

Comparetti, Domenico. *Vergil in the Middle Ages*, trans. E. F. M. Benecke. London, 1895; rpt. 1966.

Conte, Gian Biagio. *The Rhetoric of Imitation: Genre and Poetic Memory in Virgil and Other Latin Poets*, trans. Charles Segal. Ithaca, N.Y., 1986.

Copeland, Rita. *Rhetoric, Hermeneutics, and Translation in the Middle Ages: Academic Traditions and Vernacular Texts.* Cambridge, 1991.

Courcelle, Jeanne. "Les illustrations de l'Énéide dans les manuscrits du Xe siècle au XVe siècle," in *Lectures médiévales de Virgile: Actes du colloque organisé par l'Ecole française de Rome.* Rome, 1985, 395–409.

Courcelle, Pierre, and Jeanne Courcelle, *Lecteurs païens et lecteurs chrétiens de l'Énéide.* 2 vols. Paris, 1984–85.

Curnow, Maureen Cheney. *The* Livre de la Cité des Dames *of Christine de Pisan: A Critical Edition.* Diss., Vanderbilt, 1975.

Desmond, Marilynn. "Chaucer's *Aeneid*: The Naked Text in English," *Pacific Coast Philology* 19 (1984), 62–67.

———. "The Voice of Exile: Feminist Literary History and the Anglo-Saxon Elegy," *Critical Inquiry* 16 (1990), 572–90.

Dinshaw, Carolyn. *Chaucer's Sexual Poetics.* Madison, Wis., 1989.

Farron, Steven. "The Aeneas-Dido Episode as an Attack on Aeneas' Mission and Rome," *Greece and Rome* 27 (1980), 34–47.

Fowler, R. " 'On Not Knowing Greek': The Classics and the Woman of Letters," *Classical Journal* 78 (1983), 337–49.

Fradenburg, Louise Olga. *City, Marriage, Tournament: Arts of Rule in Late Medieval Scotland.* Madison, Wis., 1991.

Fyler, John. *Chaucer and Ovid.* New Haven, Conn., 1979.

Gaunt, Simon. "From Epic to Romance: Gender and Sexuality in the *Roman d'Eneas*," 83 (1992), 1–27.

Ginsburg, Warren. "Ovid and the Problem of Gender," *Mediaevalia* 13 (1989), 9–28.

Gold, Penny Shine. *The Lady and the Virgin: Image, Attitude and Experience in Twelfth-Century France.* Chicago, 1985.

Green, Richard Firth. "Chaucer's Victimized Women," *Studies in the Age of Chaucer* 10 (1988), 3–21.

Grendler, Paul. F. *Schooling in Renaissance Italy: Literacy and Learning, 1300–1600.* Baltimore, Md., 1989.

Hallett, Judith P. *Fathers and Daughters in Roman Society: Women and the Elite Family.* Princeton, N.J., 1984.

———. "Women as *Same* and *Other* in Classical Roman Elite," *Helios* 16 (1989), 59–78.

Hansen, Elaine Tuttle. *Chaucer and the Fictions of Gender.* Berkeley, Calif., 1992.

Hardie, Philip. *Virgil's* Aeneid: *Cosmos and Imperium.* Oxford, 1986.

Hawkins, Peter. "Dido, Beatrice, and the Signs of Ancient Love," in *The Poetry of Allusion: Virgil and Ovid in Dante's "Commedia,"* ed. Rachel Jacoff and Jeffrey Schapp. Palo Alto, Calif., 1991, 113–30.

———. "Divide and Conquer: Augustine in the Divine Comedy," *Publications of the Modern Language Association* 106 (1991), 471–82.

Holtz, M. Louis. "La survie de Virgile dans le haut Moyen Age," in *Présence de Virgile: Actes du colloque des 9, 11 et 12 décembre 1976.* Paris, 1978, 209–22.

Huchet, Jean-Charles. *Le roman médiéval.* Paris, 1984.

Huot, Sylvia. *From Song to Book: The Poetics of Writing in Old French Lyric and Lyrical Narrative Poetry.* Ithaca, N.Y., 1987.

———. *The Romance of the Rose and Its Medieval Readers: Interpretation, Reception, Manuscript Transmission.* Cambridge, 1993.

Jacquart, Danielle, and Claude Thomasset. *Sexuality and Medicine in the Middle Ages.* Princeton, N.J., 1985.

Jed, Stephanie. *Chaste Thinking: The Rape of Lucretia and the Birth of Humanism.* Bloomington, Ind., 1987.

Johnson, W. R. "The Broken World: Virgil and His Augustus," *Arethusa* 14 (1981), 49–56.

———. *Darkness Visible: A Study of Vergil's Aeneid.* Berkeley, Calif., 1976.

Jordan, Constance. "Boccaccio's In-Famous Women: Gender and Civic Virtue in the *De mulieribus claris*," in *Ambiguous Realities: Women in the Middle Ages and Renaissance,* ed. Carole Levin and J. Watson. Detroit, Mich., 1987, 25–47.

Kallendorf, Craig. *In Praise of Aeneas: Virgil and Epideictic Rhetoric in the Early Italian Renaissance.* Hanover, 1989.

Kiser, Lisa. *Truth and Textuality in Chaucer's Poetry*. Hanover, N.H., 1991.

Kolve, V. A. *Chaucer and the Imagery of Narrative: The First Five Canterbury Tales*. Stanford, Calif., 1984.

Kowalski, Jerzy. *De Didone Graeca et Latina*. Cracow, 1929.

Krueger, Roberta L. "Double Jeopardy: The Appropriation of Woman in Four Old French Romances of the 'Cycle de la Gageure,' " in *Seeking the Woman in Late Medieval and Renaissance Writings: Essays in Feminist Contextual Criticism*, ed. Sheila Fisher and Janet E. Halley. Knoxville, Tenn., 1989, 21–50.

———. "Love, Honor, and the Exchange of Women in *Yvain*: Some Remarks on the Female Reader," *Romance Notes* 25 (1985), 302–17.

Leach, Eleanor Winsor. "Illustration as Interpretation in Brant's and Dryden's Editions of Vergil," in *The Early Illustrated Book: Essays in Honor of Lessing J. Rosenwald*, ed. Sandra Hindman. Washington, D.C., 1982, 175–210.

———. "A Study in the Sources and Rhetoric of Chaucer's *Legend of Good Women* and Ovid's *Heroides*." Diss., Yale, 1963.

Lerer Seth. "John of Salisbury's Virgil," *Vivarium* 20 (1982), 24–39.

Leube, Eberhard. *Fortuna in Karthago: Die Aeneas-Dido-Mythe Vergils in den romanischen Literaturen vom 14. bis zum 16. Jahrhundert*. Heidelberg, 1969.

Lilja, Saara. *The Roman Elegist's Attitude to Women*. New York, 1978.

Lord, Mary Louise. "Dido as an Example of Chastity: The Influence of Example Literature," *Harvard Library Bulletin* 17 (1969), 22–44, 216–32.

de Malkiel, Maria Rosa-Lida. *Dido en la Literatura Española: Su Retrato y Defensa*. London, 1974.

McLeod, Glenda. *Virtue and Venom: Catalogs of Women From Antiquity to the Renaissance*. Ann Arbor, Mich., 1991.

Miles, Gary B., and Archibald W. Allen. "Vergil and the Augustan Experience," in *Vergil at 2000*, ed. John D. Bernard. New York, 1986, 13–41.

Miller, Paul Allen. "*Sive Deae Seu Sint Dirae Obscenaeque Volucres*," *Arethusa* 22 (1989), 47–79.

Minnis, Alistair J. *Medieval Theory of Authorship*. Philadelphia, 1988.

Monfrin, Jacques. "Les *translations* vernaculaires de Virgile au Moyen Âge," in *Lectures médiévales de Virgile: Actes du colloque organisé par l'École française de Rome*. Rome, 1985, 189–249.

Monti, Richard C. *The Dido Episode and the* Aeneid: *Roman Social and Political Values in the Epic*. Leiden, 1981.

Moore, R. I. *The Formation of a Persecuting Society: Power and Deviance in Western Europe 950–1250*. Oxford, 1987.

Noakes, Susan. *Timely Reading: Between Exegesis and Interpretation.* Ithaca, N.Y., 1988.

Nolan, Barbara. *Chaucer and the Tradition of the* Roman antique. Cambridge, 1992.

Ogle, Marbury B. "The Later Tradition of Vergil," *Classical Journal* 26 (1930), 63–73.

Olsen, Birger Munk. *L'Étude des auteurs classiques latins aux XIᵉ et XIIᵉ siècles.* Paris, 1982.

―――. "Virgile et la renaissance du XIIᵉ siècle," in *Lectures médiévales de Virgile: Actes du colloque organisé par l'École française de Rome.* Rome, 1985, p. 31–48.

Pascal, Carlo. "Didone nella letteratura Latina d'Africa," *Athenaeum* 5 (1917), 285–93.

Patterson, Lee. "Virgil and the Historical Consciousness of the Twelfth Century," in *Negotiating the Past: The Historical Understanding of Medieval Literature.* Madison, Wis., 1987, 157–95.

Pease, Arthur Stanley. *Publi Vergili Maronis Aeneidos: Liber Quartus.* Cambridge, 1935.

Perkell, Christine G. "On Creusa, Dido, and the Quality of Victory in Virgil's *Aeneid*," in *Reflections of Women in Antiquity*, ed. Helene P. Foley. New York, 1981, 355–77.

Pomeroy, Sarah B. *Goddesses, Whores, Wives, and Slaves: Women in Classical Antiquity.* New York, 1975.

Quilligan, Maureen. *The Allegory of Female Authority: Christine de Pizan's Cité des Dames.* Ithaca, N.Y., 1992.

Quint, David. *Epic and Empire: Politics and Generic Form from Virgil to Milton.* Princeton, N.J., 1993.

Richards, Earl Jeffrey. "Christine de Pizan, the Conventions of Courtly Diction and Italian Humanism," in *Reinterpreting Christine de Pizan*, ed. Earl Jeffrey Richards et al. Athens, Ga., 1992, 250–71.

Richardson, J. S. "*Imperium Romanum*: Empire and the Language of Power," *The Journal of Roman Studies* 81 (1991), 1–9.

Roberts-Baytop, Adrianne. *Dido Queen of Infinite Variety: English Renaissance Borrowings and Influences.* Salzburg, 1974.

Rudd, Niall. "Dido's *culpa*," in *Lines of Enquiry: Studies in Latin Poetry.* Cambridge, 1976, 32–53.

―――. "The Idea of Empire in the *Aeneid*," in *Virgil in a Cultural Tradition: Essays to Celebrate the Bimillennium*, ed. Richard A. Cardwell and Janet Hamilton. Nottingham, 1986, 25–42.

Ruggini, Lellia Cracco. "Intolerance: Equal and Less Equal in the Roman World," *Classical Philology* 82 (1987), 187–205.

Saenger, Paul. "Silent Reading: Its Impact on Late Medieval Script and Society," *Viator* 13 (1982), 367–414.

Sanford, Eva Matthews, "The Use of Classical Latin Authors in the *Libri Manuales*," *TAPA* 55 (1924), 190–248.

Scaglione, Aldo. "The Classics in Medieval Education," in *The Classics in the Middle Ages: Papers of the Twentieth Annual Conference of the Center for Medieval and Renaissance Studies*, ed. Aldo S. Bernardo and Saul Levin. Binghamton, N.Y., 1990, 343–62.

Scollen, Christine M. "Octovien de Saint-Gelais' Translation of the *Aeneid*: Poetry or Propaganda?" *Bibliothèque d'Humanisme et Renaissance* 39 (1977), 253–61.

Searle, Eleanor. *Predatory Kinship and the Creation of Norman Power, 840–1066*. Berkeley, Calif., 1988.

Singerman, Jerome. *Under Clouds of Poesy: Poetry and Truth in French and English Reworkings of the Aeneid, 1160–1513*. New York, 1986.

Skinner, Marilyn. "Classical Studies vs. Women's Studies: *Duo moi ta noemmata*," *Helios* 12 (1985), 3–17.

Smarr, Janet Levarie. *Boccaccio and Fiammetta: The Narrator as Lover*. Urbana, Ill., 1986.

Spence, Sarah. *Rhetorics of Reason and Desire*. Ithaca, N.Y., 1988.

Stock, Brian. *The Implications of Literacy: Written Language and Models of Interpretation in the Eleventh and Twelfth Centuries*. Princeton, N.J., 1983.

Suzuki, Mihoko. *Metamorphoses of Helen: Authority, Difference, and the Epic*. Ithaca, N.Y., 1989.

Toll, Katharine. "The *Aeneid* as an Epic of National Identity: *Italiam Laeto Socii Clamore Salutant*," *Helios* 18 (1991), 3–14.

Verducci, Florence. *Ovid's Toyshop of the Heart: Epistulae Heroidum*. Princeton, N.J., 1985.

Wack, Mary. *Lovesickness in the Middle Ages: The Viaticum and Its Commentaries*. Philadelphia, 1990.

Wilson, Katharina M., and Elizabeth M. Makowski. *Wykked Wyves and the Woes of Marriage: Misogamous Literature from Juvenal to Chaucer*. Albany, N.Y., 1990.

Zetzel, James E. G. "Re-creating the Canon: Augustan Poetry and the Alexandrian Past," *Critical Inquiry* 10 (1983), 83–105.

Index

❖

Index

Index

Galen, 90
Gallop, Jane, 139
Gaunt, Simon, 256 n.1
gaze, 66; gendered dynamics of, 139; male, 14, 16, 104, 150–51, 266 n.39; reader's, 51–52, 140, 175
gender: and colonization, 32; and reading, 7–13; as a grammatical feature of language, 34; medieval theories of, 276 n.15; Roman constructions of, 31; technology of, 15–16, 132, 150
Genesis, 119
Geoffrey of Monmouth, 119, 137
Gerson, Jean, 223
Ginsberg, Warren, 34
glosses, 80, 83, 86, 91, 121, 131, 145, 176–77, 191, 215; on the *Viaticum*, 112; Servian, 109–10, 123
Goldstein, R. James, 165
Gottfried von Strassburg, 258 n.22
Gower, 50, 179; *Confessio Amantis*, 162, 173
grammar: in Servius, 83; instruction in, 74–76
Gravdal, Kathryn, 258 n.17
Graves, Robert, 10
Greenblatt, Stephen, 195–96
Greene, Thomas, 1, 6, 9, 101
Guido delle Colonne, 137
Guillaume de Lorris, 134. *See also Roman de la Rose*
Guillaume Le Roy. *See Eneydes*

Hallett, Judith, 31, 226, 232 n.19, 233 n.30, 239 n.20
Hampton, Timothy, 164
Hannibal, 31, 33, 115, 182
Hansen, Elaine Tuttle, 135, 262 n.4, 265 n.20
Hawkins, Peter, 97
Heinrich von Veldeke, 258 n.22
Helen, 180
Hemker, Julie, 239 n.10
Henry II, 105
Henry IV, 207
Hercules, 137
heterosexuality, 14, 77, 135, 140, 162; and female desire, 154; and physical consequences for women, 160; compulsory, 14, 16, 108, 116, 161, 236 n.81
Hindman, Sandra, 210

Histoire ancienne jusqu'à César, 58, 70, 119–27, 129, 137, 140, 143, 161, 167, 174, 202–5, 215, 222–23, 243–44 n.70, 262 n.2
history: and Eurocentric structures, 119; as lineage, 119, 203; excluding constructions, 137–38; framework developed by Augustine, 79; imperial ideal in, 97; Norman vision of, 107; patrilinear structures, 119; removal of Dido from, 114–15, 124; Roman, 119; structures of, 119, 137; Theban, 119, 137; Trojan, 119, 137
Holcot, Robert, 239 n.14
Homer, 26, 137
homoerotic desire, 16–17
homophobia, 10, 117
homosexuality, 9–10, 14; attributed to Virgil, 9–10; in the *Eneas*, 116. *See also* queer theory
homosocial desire, 9, 85, 234 n.45; and feudalism, 100, 104; and medieval academic cultures, 75, 88, 93–94; and the *Aeneid*, 98. *See also* male bonding
humanism, 166; Italian, 58–59, 68, 164, 177, 189, 194; medieval, 197, 223–24; vernacular, 166, 177
humanist portrait, 197, 210
Hundred Years War: English effort, 151, 209; French effort, 207–9
Huot, Sylvia, 244 n.81, 244 n.84, 265 n.21, 275 n.9
Hypsipyle, 149, 180

Iarbas, 2, 25–27, 56, 62, 101, 123, 174, 222
illustrations, 20, 70–73, 119, 124–27, 141, 177; in the *Cité de dieu*, 212; in the *Cité des Dames*, 210–12; in the *Eneydes*, 169
imperialism: and epic, 13; ideologies of, 2, 21. *See also* Normans
integument, 85
intertextuality, 19, 237 n.88; visual, 212
inventio, 215, 218, 223
Irigaray, Luce, 236 n.79
Iser, Wolfgang, 268 n.53
Isidore of Seville, 200, 277 n.2

James IV, 165, 194
Jean de Meun, 151, 153, 198, 203, 216, 222, 275 n.8. *See also Roman de la Rose*
Jean Le Fevre, 197–98, 215

Index

Mellah, Fawzi, 3, 227
memory: countermemory, 73; in textual cultures, 136, 140; "poetic," 27, 33, 73, 239 n.19; reader's, 147–48, 150; relation to textuality, 138; rhetorical properties, 136. *See also* architectural mnemonic
Miller, Paul Allen, 45
Minerva, 218
Minh-ha, Trinh, 3, 13
Minnis, Alistair J., 258–59 n.26, 266 n.33, 266 n.36
misogamy, 57–58
misogyny, 57–58, 68, 93, 192, 197, 199, 220, 245 n.94, 265 n.26, 272 n.31; in *Palice of Honour*, 180
Modleski, Tania, 245 n.94
Monti, Richard, 29–30, 42, 238 n.98
Moore, I. R., 3
More, Thomas, 195
Mulvey, Laura, 160, 266 n.41
Myrrha, 215

Naevius. *See Bellum Poenicum*
New Testament, 181
Nisus, 11
Noakes, Susan, 96, 237 n.84
Nolan, Barbara, 108
Normans: appropriation of Trojan identity, 119; dynastic vision, 117–18; expansion in eleventh century, 107; imperial power, 118; marriage practices, 108; vision of history, 107. *See also* predatory kinship

occupatio, 144
Octovien de Saint-Gelais *Aeneid*, 165; *Heroides*, 48, 244 n.73
Oenone, 50, 149
Old Testament, 181, 203
Ong, Walter J., 1, 8
ordo naturalis, 84, 86, 143
orientalism, 21, 33
Otis, Brooks, 10–11, 35, 241 n.51
Ovid, 80, 117, 128–29, 137, 156, 159, 179, 250 n.23; commentary on, 46–47, 128; *Amores*, 242 n.54; *Ars Amatoria*, 242 n.54; *Fasti*, 242 n.54; *Heroides*, 116, 137, 148, 153–54, 241 n.47; *Heroides 7*, 33–45, 128, 148–50, 152, 160, 162, 174, 181, 186, 215, 242 n.54, 262 n.2;

Metamorphoses, 34–35, 38, 46, 107, 173; *Tristia*, 36. *See also Ovide moralisé*
Ovide moralisé, 47–48, 216, 262 n.2
ox hide, trick of, 25, 47, 64, 70, 109–10, 121, 169, 219

page layout, 131, 176–77, 264 n.18
Palinurus, 150
Pallas, 9, 11
Papias, 239 n.14
Passman, Tina, 234 n.53
Paston Letters, 129
Patterson, Lee, 107
Pavlock, Barbara, 241 n.34
Peasants' Revolt, 151, 263 n.12
Penates, 39
Penelope, 46, 180, 221
Penthesilea, 121, 218
Perkell, Christine, 12–13, 39, 226, 238 n.98, 243 n.60
Petrarch, 23, 27, 55, 58, 189; *Africa*, 238 n.1; *Trionfo Della Castita*, 238 n.1
Phaedra, 180, 215
Phasiphaë, 215
Philip IV, 208
Philip V, 208
Philip VI, 208
Phillippy, Patricia A., 279 n.54
Philomela, 180, 267 n.46
Phyllis, 50–51, 146, 148, 180, 215
pietas, 11, 14, 25, 41
plague, 67
Plantagenet court, 105, 118. *See also* Normans
Plato, 87; cosmology of, 85; *Timaeus*, 85, 88, 92
Polychronicon. *See* Ranulf Higden
Pomeroy, Sarah B., 236 n.72
Pompeius Trogus, 24–25. *See also* Justin
predatory kinship, 107, 115. *See also* kinship; marriage
pregnancy. *See* Dido
Priam, 143
print technology, 167, 170, 176, 194
Priscian, 80
Proba, 218
Propertius, 59
Provence, 100
Punic Wars, 31, 114, 182

Marilynn Desmond is associate professor of English and comparative literature at the State University of New York-Binghamton. She has published articles on Ovid, Chaucer, *Beowulf*, Anglo-Saxon Elegy, and feminist theory.